THE COLOSSAL ELEPHANT
AND HIS SPIRITUAL FEATS

THE COLOSSAL ELEPHANT AND HIS SPIRITUAL FEATS:

Shaykh Ahmad-e Jâm

THE LIFE AND LEGEND OF A POPULAR

SUFI SAINT

OF 12TH CENTURY IRAN

Translated from the Persian and Annotated by
Heshmat Moayyad and Franklin Lewis

MAZDA PUBLISHERS, Inc. ◆ Costa Mesa, California ◆ 2004

The publication of this volume
was made possible by contributions from
A. K. Jabbari Family Trust Fund
and

The Iranica Institute at *www.iranicainstitute.org*

Mazda Publishers, Inc.
Academic Publishers since 1980
P.O. Box 2603
Costa Mesa, California 92628 U.S.A.
www.mazdapub.com

Library of Congress Cataloging-in-Publication Data

The Colossal Elephant and His Spiritual Feats: Shaykh Ahmad-e Jâm: The Life and
Legend of a Popular Sufi Saint of 12th Century Iran/ Translated from the Persian and
annotated by Heshmat Moayyad and Franklin Lewis.
p.cm.
Includes bibliographical references.

ISBN: 1-56859-119-5
(Softcover, alk. paper)

1. Ahmad Jam, 1049 or 50-1141 or 2. 2. Sufis—Iran—Biography.
3. Muslim saints—Iran—Biography.
I. Title: Shaykh Ahmad-e Jâm. II. Title: Life and Legend of a Popular Sufi Saint of 12th
Century Iran. III. Moayyad, Heshmat. IV. Lewis, Franklin, 1961-
BP80.A479C65 2004
297.4'092—dc22
[B]
2004042694

122104-5500 T8

TABLE OF CONTENTS

PART TWO

PART THREE

PART FOUR

APPENDICES

Translators' Preface

This is a collection of stories, many of a miraculous nature, about Shaykh Ahmad-e Jâm, nicknamed "the Colossal Elephant," who lived from 1049-1141. These stories of his spiritual feats constitute the life and legend of a popular Sufi saint of the period. The book also contains excerpts from Shaykh Ahmad's own writings, where we meet with an individual who seems quite different in character from the legendary image given by his followers.

The manuscripts of this unique collection were first edited and published by Heshmat Moayyad, one of the translators of the present book. The work was begun together at the University of Chicago, where Heshmat Moayyad was Professor of Persian Literature and Franklin Lewis was, at the time, Mellon Lecturer in Persian.

The anecdotes related here, while providing entertaining reading, are also of interest to specialists in Middle Eastern history, religion and cultural anthropology. The translation therefore aims for precision, and includes a scholarly scaffolding, for those wishing to make professional use of the text. However, we do hope that the anecdotes about the Colossal Elephant in this curious work will prove an engaging contribution to our understanding of saint formation and the hagiographical literature of Sufism.

INTRODUCTION

Hagiology and the Construction of Sainthood in Islam

Until recently, Islamicists interested in Sufism primarily concerned themselves with understanding the theosophical systems of the various mystical thinkers and the sources of their ideas. Popular Sufism and saint veneration has only recently become a more widely recognized field of study, probably inspired in part by a corresponding trend in Christian hagiology.[1]

Goldziher proposed the cult of saints in Islam as a topic of academic inquiry as early as 1911,[2] but the first in-depth treatment of the legendary vita and the reception history of a particular Sufi saint appeared in 1922, in Louis Massignon's magisterial volumes on Hallâj.[3] More recently, a study of the tradition of popular

---

[1] Of course, the locus classicus for modern hagiology is the work of the Bollandist Hippolyte Delehaye from 1895-1940, though the modern critical approaches derive more directly from Peter Brown's *The Cult of the Saints: Its Rise and Function in Latin Christianity* (Chicago: University of Chicago Press, 1981). Other studies include M. Goodich, *Vita Perfecta: The Ideal of Sainthood in the Thirteenth Century* (Stuttgart: A. Hiersemann, 1982); Alison Goddar Elliott, *Roads to Paradise: Reading the Lives of the Early Saints* (Hanover, NH: Brown University and University Press of New England, 1987); Thomas Heffernan's *Sacred Biography: Saints and Their Biographers in the Middle Ages* (New York: Oxford University Press, 1988), and T. Head, *Hagiography and the Cult of Saints: the Diocese of Orléans, 800-1200* (Cambridge: Cambridge University Press, 1990).

[2] Ignaz Goldziher, "The Cult of the Saints in Islam," *Muslim World* 1 (1911): 302-12.

[3] Massignon, *La Passion d'al-Hosayn-ibn-Mansour al-Hallaj, martyr mystique de l'Islam* (Paris: P. Geuthner, 1922); an English translation was published in four volumes by H. Mason as *The Passion of al-Hallâj, Mystic and Martyr of Islam* (Princeton, 1982).

veneration of the Prophet Muhammad,[4] along with a handful of detailed studies treating particular saints, have provided a broader basis for understanding the archetype of the Sufi saint.[5]

Scholars who have lately grappled with the construction of sainthood and the sociology of saint veneration in the Islamic world devote their attention mostly to North Africa,[6] primarily Egypt,[7] and especially Morocco;[8] though there have also been important studies of saints in the Indian subcontinent,[9] in

---

[4] Annemarie Schimmel, *And Muhammad is His Messenger: The Veneration of the Prophet in Islamic Piety* (Chapel Hill: University of North Carolina, 1985).

[5] Notable examples include Fritz Meier, *Abu Said-i Abu l-Hayr, 357-440/967-1049: Wirklichkeit und Legende* (Tehran and Liège: Bibliothèque Pahlavi, 1976); Richard Gramlich, *Die Wunder der Freunde Gottes: Theologien und Erscheinungsformen des islamischen Heiligenwunders* (Stuttgart: Steiner Verlag Wiesbaden, 1987); Bernd Radtke and John O'Kane, *The Concept of Sainthood in Early Islamic Mysticism: Two Works by Al-Hakim Al-Tirmidhi* (Richmond, Curzon Press, 1996). Carl Ernst presents an "inner structure of sainthood" based upon the various lives of a 12th-century Persian Sufi as depicted by autobiographical comments and hagiographies in his *Ruzbihan Baqli: Mysticism and the Rhetoric of Sainthood in Persian Sufism* (Surrey: Curzon Press, 1996).

[6] Jonathan Katz, *Dreams, Sufism, and Sainthood: The Visionary Career of Muhammad al-Zawawi* (Leiden: E.J. Brill, 1996); see also the conference proceedings edited by Moohamed Kably, *al-Târîkh wa adab al-manâqib* (Rabat: Manshûrât Ukâz, 1989).

[7] Michael Gilsenan, *Saint and Sufi in Modern Egypt: An Essay in the Sociology of Religion* (Oxford: Clarendon, 1973); Valerie Hoffman, *Sufism, Mystics, and Saints in Modern Egypt* (Columbia, SC: University of South Carolina, 1995); Thomas Emil Homerin, *From Arab Poet to Muslim Saint: Ibn al-Farid* (Columbia, SC: University of South Carolina, 1994); Christopher Taylor, *In the Vicinity of the Righteous: Ziyâra and the Veneration of Muslim Saints in Late Medieval Egypt* (Leiden: E.J. Brill, 1999).

[8] See Emile Dermenghem, *Le culte des saints dans l'Islam maghrébin* (Paris: Gallimard, 1954); Ernest Gellner, *Saints of the Atlas* (London: Weidenfeld and Nicholson, 1969); and Vincent Cornell, *Realm of the Saint: Power and Authority in Moroccan Sufism* (Austin: University of Texas, 1998).

[9] See Richard Eaton, *The Sufis of Bijapur, 1300-1700: Social Roles*

Anatolia[10] and in Syria.[11] Many studies have taken saints and sainthood of the 19th and 20th century as their focus,[12] or are primarily concerned with the theory of Sufi practice and ritual,[13] or the theory of sainthood reflected in the teachings of the classical manuals and thinkers of Sufism.[14]

The construction of sainthood and the topology of saintly miracles in a specifically Iranian context has also recently been addressed,[15] including the development of the bio-hagiographical genre of writing.[16] Despite these efforts, our understanding of popular Sufism in the medieval period remains rather hazy on such questions as how legendary vitae began to form, how they were developed and preserved; how literary topoi shaped the

---

of Sufis in Medieval India (Princeton: Princeton University, 1978) and Carl Ernst, The Eternal Garden: Mysticism, History and Politics at a South Asian Sufi Center (Albany: State University of New York, 1992).

[10] Ahmet Karamustafa, God's Unruly Friends (Salt Lake City: University of Utah, 1994) and especially Irene Mèlikoff, Hadji Bektach: un mythe et ses avatars (Leiden: E.J. Brill, 1998).

[11] Josef Meri, The Cult of the Saints among Muslims and Jews in Medieval Syria (Oxford: Oxford University Press, 2002).

[12] E.g., Katherine Ewing's, Arguing Sainthood: Modernity, Psychoanalysis, and Islam (Durham, NC: Duke University, 1997).

[13] See the recent studies by Ian Richard Netton, Sufi Ritual: The Parallel Universe (Richmond, Surrey: Curzon, 2000), on the Nimatullahi and Naqshbandi orders, and by Arthur Buehler, Sufi Heirs of the Prophet: the Indian Naqshbandiyya and the Rise of the Mediating Sufi Shaykh (Columbia: University of South Carolina Press, 1998).

[14] Studies of this nature are legion; important among them are the work of Henri Corbin; Leonard Lewisohn on Shabistari; William Chittick on Rumi; Chittick and Claude Addas on Ibn 'Arabi, etc. As just one example, we might mention Michel Chodkiewicz, Seal of the Saints: Prophethood and Sainthood in the Doctrine of Ibn 'Arabi, trans. Liadain Sherrard (Cambridge: Islamic Texts Society, 1993).

[15] Carl Ernst and Grace Martin, eds., Manifestations of Sainthood in Islam (Istanbul: Éditions Isis, 1994); Smith Pnina Werner and Helene Basu, eds., Embodying Charisma: Modernity, Locality and the Performance of Emotion in Sufi Cults (London: Routledge, 1998).

[16] Jawid Mojaddedi, The Biographical Tradition in Sufism (Richmond, Surrey: Curzon, 2001).

contours of saints' lives; and what role folklore played in the perception and explanation of saintly marvels or miracles (*karâmât*).[17] The present work on Shaykh Ahmad is offered as a contribution to the larger project of bringing the Islamic hagiographical tradition into sharper focus, in this case by contrasting the Shaykh's own words and those of his son with the legendary portrait of the Shaykh presented by his disciples.

The Subject of the Present Book
With the exception of brief articles in the *Encyclopedia of Islam* and the *Encyclopaedia Iranica*, only a few relatively inaccessible studies of Shaykh Ahmad-e Jâm have appeared in European languages: an article in English by Wladimir Ivanow in 1917,[18] an article in German by Fritz Meier in 1943,[19] followed by a 1959 dissertation by Heshmat Moayyad.[20] Indeed, until the first Persian edition of the present text was published in 1961,[21] works by or about Ahmad-e Jâm were virtually non-existent in Iran, itself.[22]

The Colossal Elephant and His Spiritual Feats consists of four separate texts by or relating to Shaykh Ahmad-e Jâm, a popular

---

[17]   Taylor's *In the Vicinity of the Righteous*, op. cit., is a very recent and very important step in this direction, as is also Mèlikoff's *Hadji Bektach*, op cit., and Meri's *Cult of the Saints*, op. cit. Brief studies of the subject have also been essayed in a number of articles, including Frederick Denny, "'God's Friends': The Sanctity of Persons in Islam," in *Sainthood: Its Manifestation in World Religions*, ed. R. Kieckhefer and G. Bond (Berkeley: University of California, 1988), 69-97.
[18]   W. Ivanow, "A Biography of Shaykh Ahmad-i-Jam," *Journal of the Royal Asiatic Society* 1917, pp. 291-307, and text of the Kholâsat al-Maqâmât, pp. 291-365.
[19]   F. Meier, "Zur Biographie Ahmad-e Ğām's und zur Quellenkunde von Ğāmi's Nafahātu'l-uns" *ZDMG*, Band 97, Heft 1 (1943): 47-67.
[20]   Heschmat'ullah Moayyad, *Die Maqâmât des Ġaznawi: Eine legendäre Vita Ahmad-i Ğām's gennant Žandapil* (Frankfurt, 1959).
[21]   *Maqâmât-e Zhandeh Pil*, ed. Heshmat Moayyad (Tehran: Bongâh-e Tarjomeh va Nashr-e Ketâb, 1340).
[22]   Since then 'Ali Fâzel has published several of Shaykh Ahmad's own works (see below), from which he has culled a selection of Shaykh Ahmad's writings, *Az jâm-e Shaykh-e Jâm* (Tehran: Sokhan, 1997), and a study of the life of Shaykh Ahmad, *Sharh-e ahvâl va naqd va tahlil-e âsâr-e Ahmad-e Jâm* (Tehran: Tus, 1994).

Sufi saint of eastern Iran known as "The Colossal Elephant" (Zhandeh-Pil), who lived from 1049 to 1141 of the common era. These four texts were written in Persian, mostly in the 12th century. Heshmat Moayyad published the editio princeps, with introduction, as *Maqâmât-e Zhandeh Pil (Ahmad-e Jâm)* in 1961 (1340 Sh.), on the basis of two shorter manuscripts of the text. A second, substantially revised edition, based upon all three surviving manuscripts of the work, was published under the same title by Moayyad as number seven in the Persian Texts Series (Tehran: Bongâh-e Nashr va Tarjomeh-ye Ketâb, 1345/1967). This translation, the first in English, follows the second edition of *Maqâmât-e Zhandeh Pil*.

Part One consists of *The Spiritual Feats* (or *Maqâmât*) of Shaykh Ahmad of Jâm, a collection of 369 miraculous anecdotes about Shaykh Ahmad, authored by a learned man from Ghazna, Khvâjeh Sadid al-Din Mohammad-e Ghaznavi, who became a disciple of Shaykh Ahmad and remained with him in Jâm for some time. Some of these anecdotes are related firsthand by Mohammad-e Ghaznavi; the others are ostensibly compiled from the texts or reports of various other witnesses, including Shaykh Ahmad, himself.

Part Two adds to Ghaznavi's collection of miracle tales a number of reports about miracles performed by Shaykh Ahmad from the next realm, after his death, nicely illustrating the type of hopes and expectations that led Muslims in the medieval period, and still today, to visit the tombs of saints. The author of this shorter treatise on the "Posthumous Miracles of the Shaykh," though not specified, is likely a certain Ahmad-e Tarkhestâni.

Following upon these miracle stories, which vividly portray the popular legend of Shaykh Ahmad, the reader will find two treatises which afford a far more sober view of Shaykh Ahmad and his teachings in Parts Three and Four. The first of these, a "Treatise on the Greatness of His Father" (*Resâleh dar esbât-e bozorgi-ye Ahmad-e Jâm*) was written by one of Shaykh Ahmad's sons, Shehâb al-Din Esma 'il. Shehâb al-Din Esma 'il downplays the significance of all the miraculous tales reported about Shaykh Ahmad and tries instead to establish the greatness of his father with rational proofs.

The second is a treatise by Shaykh Ahmad himself, *The Epistle to the Samarqandians (Resâleh-ye Samarqandiyeh)*. In his *Epistle to the Samarqandians*, Shaykh Ahmad replies to a number of questions sent to him from various quarters, principally from Samarqand, though the Epistle also includes one question posed by the Seljuk Sultan Sanjar. The Shaykh's epistle discusses some of the traditional questions that occupied piety-minded religious scholars and Sufi-minded theologians. It is noteworthy that throughout the epistle, the Shaykh stakes no claim, explicit or implicit, to performing miracles. Although the power to transmute elements is widely and repeatedly attributed to Shaykh Ahmad in the miracle stories, when Shaykh Ahmad replies to a question about alchemy, he interprets this science metaphorically, as the transformation of the mettle of men's hearts.

Apart from its primary interest as an illustration of the legendary beliefs about Sufi saints, and its depiction of an austere and atypical holy man, *Shaykh Ahmad-e Jâm: The Colossal Elephant and His Spiritual Feats* provides many details about the topography and demographics of the towns and villages of Khorasan and Qohestan; daily life in the villages of eastern Iran in the medieval period; modes of travel; the foods eaten and how they were stored; the drinking of wine; the relations between the sexes; sundry agricultural and husbandry practices (such as irrigation); the use of amulets; medieval diseases and their treatment; local political organization; the development of the Karrâmi sect; and so forth. Composed some 800 to 865 years ago, the text of the present work, written in a more or less colloquial style, also constitutes an important philological resource on the development of the Persian language. It should therefore prove of interest to historians, sociologists and linguists, as well as students of Sufism and popular religion.

Shaykh Ahmad and Popular Saint Worship
The Shaykh al-Islam Abu Nasr Ahmad ebn Abu al-Hasan ebn Ahmad ebn Mohammad of Nâmaq and latterly of Jâm, known in historical sources as Zhandeh Pil, "The Colossal Elephant," Ahmad-e Jâm, is a relatively early figure in the history of Iranian Sufism. Shaykh Ahmad's followers for the most part lacked formal schooling in the religious sciences and the miracle stories told about him therefore reflect popular religion and folk beliefs.

Ghaznavi's *The Spiritual Feats* (Part One, below) provides insight into how the beliefs and practices of Islam, especially the resolve to adhere to Islamic law and to repent (*towbeh*) from wine drinking and other illicit activities, spread among villagers through the efforts of charismatic preachers and holy men. In contrast to the more theoretical and theologically oriented speculation with which Sufism is normally identified in the West, the career and legend of Shaykh Ahmad of Jâm, and even his writings, reflect a mixture of stern admonitions, cajoling, miraculous powers and saint worship. It is this type of religiosity that must have characterized popular Sufism for the most part and appealed to the non-urban and uneducated populace, rather than a belief in transcendental esoteric doctrines of a gnostic character. Shaykh Ahmad is associated, at least in the popular imagination, with religious fervor among the common people in the environs, with stern imposition of conformity to Islamic law, and with the power to confound his enemies by seemingly miraculous means.

Aside from the information it provides about the life and the legend of Shaykh Ahmad-e Jâm, one of the most unusual saints in the Sufi pantheon, *The Spiritual Feats* therefore affords us a great deal of insight into the generic conventions and types of miracle stories that have circulated about the famous figures of Islamic and specifically Persian mysticism, and the hagiographical traditions that have grown up around them. In this respect *The Colossal Elephant and His Spiritual Feats* will deepen our understanding of the similar and better-known hagiographies, such as Mohammad ebn Monavvar's *Asrâr al-towhid* (*Secrets of God's Mystical Oneness*) about Abu Sa'id-e Abu al-Khayr (967-1049), and Shams al-Din Aflâki's *Manâqeb al-'ârefin* (*Acts of the Gnostics*), written about Jalâl al-Din Rumi (1207-1273) and his successors.

Story 172 in the present work reports that Shaykh Ahmad specifically attempted to perform all of the feats of asceticism practiced by prior saints, and even to surpass them. A number of the stories told here appear to have been expressly modeled upon stories told of Abu Sa'id-e Abu al-Khayr.[23] Comparison with the

---

[23] For a comparative study of the miracle stories about Shaykh Ahmad, see H. Moayyad, "Tâvus-e 'elliyyin: Dar bâreh-ye Zhandeh Pil Ahmad-e Jâm va Shaykh Abu Sa'id-e Abu al-Khayr," *Irân Shenâsi* 11,

legendary vitas of other Sufis from the medieval period, and with the miracle stories related in biographical dictionaries like 'Abd al-Rahmân Jâmi's *Nafahât al-ons*, would allow us to construct a typology of saintly miracles in Iran and the greater Islamic world. Such a catalogue would certainly help us to understand how biographical incidents are shaped (or created *ab ovo*) into the genre expectations of miracle narratives, as well as affording us a more historically nuanced profile of the saintly archetype or the component attributes and powers expected of a saint. Toward that end, a Motif Index of the miracles performed by Shaykh Ahmad, along with a table of sources for the reported anecdotes, is provided in the appendices.

SHAYKH AHMAD-E JÂM, THE COLOSSAL ELEPHANT

Ahmad-e Jâm was born in the year 1049 (441 A.H.) in the village of Nâmaq near Torshiz in Khorasan to a family of Arab stock. He claimed descent from the famous Jarîr bin 'Abd Allâh Bajalî, a companion of the Prophet Mohammad, who was reputed to have no rival in archery among the Arabs.[24] Ahmad's tall stature, physical strength and courage distinguished him amongst his peers. According to medieval accounts, Ahmad had red hair, a wine-colored beard and dark-blue eyes, but his features were not identifiably Arab.

The title *Zhandeh Pil*, "the Colossal Elephant," evidently refers to the Shaykh's physical strength and stature, as well as his gruff and irascible manner. Perhaps it was applied to Ahmad during his lifetime by those who knew him; Buzjâni writing in 1523 (929 A.H.) claims that Shaykh Ahmad himself received this nickname in prayer.[25] However, the title does not appear in our earliest

---

3 (Autumn 1999): 549-57, and 11, 4 (Winter 2000): 742-49. Stories which seem particularly designed to one-up specific anecdotes told of Abu Sa'id are singled out in the footnotes of the present text.

[24] See Ibn-i Sa'd, *al-Tabaqât al-kubrâ*, 9 vols. (Beirut: Dâr Sâdir, n.d.), 1:347-8; and Sam'âni's *Kitâb al-ansâb* (s.v. "Bajîla"). See also Qâzî Nûr Allâh Shushtari's *Majâlis al-mu'minîn* (Tehran Lithograph, 1268 A.H./1852), 102, who has collected the various traditions about Jarîr from the works of Hillî, Ibn Hajar 'Asqalânî and Ibn Athîr, etc.

[25] Darvish 'Ali Buzjâni, *Rowzat al-rayâhin*, ed. Heshmat Moayyad

source about Shaykh Ahmad, *The Spiritual Feats* of Mohammad-e Ghaznavi (see Part One, below). Ahmad was first referred to in writing as "the Colossal Elephant" about two centuries after his death, in the *Târikh-e gozideh*[26] and *Nozhat al-qolub*[27] of Hamd Allâh Mostowfi. This title appears again in the poems of Shâh Qâsem-e Anvâr (d. 1432 / 835 A.H.), nearly a century after that.

"Shaykh al-Islam" does appear ubiquitously as the title of Ahmad in our earliest source, *The Spiritual Feats* of Ghaznavi. In fact, it almost seems to serve as a proper name. The title "Shaykh al-Islam" came into general usage in Khorasan toward the end of the 10th century, sometimes used as a simple honorific. However, because it appears consistently in some of the cities of Khorasan, and because no two people in a given town appear to share this title at the same time, we may surmise that Shaykh al-Islam sometimes designated an appointed position of some sort. Some of the individuals bearing this title were Sufis or Hadith scholars, but not trained legal scholars. It would appear that the title was awarded to the most respected member of the ulama in a given area.[28]

Some information about Ahmad's childhood or his family life has survived. His parents and other relatives were simple people and made their living from farming; Shaykh Ahmad states that he was not even taught to read and write by his parents. During his lifetime, Ahmad's father did not believe in the spiritual station of his son, but repented on his deathbed, affirming his belief in his son's powers.[29]

(Tehran: Bongâh-e Tarjomeh va Nashr-e Ketâb, 1345/1966), 26.

[26] See the facsimile edition prepared by E.G. Browne (Leiden: E.J. Brill, 1910), 792.

[27] ed. Guy Le Strange (Leiden: E.J. Brill, 1915), 154. Le Strange also prepared an English translation (Leiden: E.J. Brill, 1919), 152.

[28] See *EI₂*, s.v. "Shaykh al-Islām."

[29] See Story 161. According to that story, Ahmad had completed his discipleship and a period of ascetic exercises and had already begun to perform miracles at the time of his father's death. However, it would appear from Story 5 (in which Shaykh Ahmad tells Bu Tâher the Kord that he has inherited a vineyard from his father), that the father died while Ahmad was still a novice. Since this statement in Story 5 is attributed directly to the Shaykh, it is perhaps more credible than the information given in Story 161.

According to the *Kholâsat al-maqâmât*, Ahmad conceived a fancy for raising partridges (*kabk*)[30] at the age of fifteen and used to trap them. A few years later, he fancied he would become a soldier and participate in the wars against infidel territory (*ghazâ*), to which idea his family objected. His family's pleading and weeping could not dissuade him, but when he realized it would mean leaving the coop of partridges he had so diligently tended to decline and perish without his attention, he gave up the idea of any foreign campaigning.

Shortly thereafter, he fell in love with a girl, to whom he demurely refers as "a veiled one" (*sar-pushideh-i, mastureh*). This infatuation kept him from attending to any of his business. For three years he managed to keep the fact of his having fallen in love to himself, but eventually he could no longer contain the secret. For five years all told, he could think of nothing but his beloved; he washed his face and clothes in hopes that someone would speak favorably of him to her, and thoughts of her disturbed his prayers. Later on, he would compare this all-consuming love to the love that saints have for God.[31]

According to Story 1 in Ghaznavi's *Spiritual Feats*, up to the age of twenty-two, that is circa 1070 (463 A.H.), Ahmad was given to the drinking of wine and would attend drinking parties with a circle of profligate friends. This same group of friends would chide Ahmad after he repented of his sins, complaining that he had spoiled their fun (see Story 74). The turning-point in Ahmad's religious life came one night when he witnessed the miraculous transformation of wine into grape juice (Story 1).

After this (according to Ghaznavi, at any rate), Shaykh Ahmad withdrew from his circle of friends to live the life of a pious ascetic and occupy himself with acts of worship. He took up the life of a hermit in the mountains and set to the task of purifying his soul. He lived in seclusion on the mountains for eighteen years, the first twelve of them on the mountain of Nâmaq, bringing us to circa 1082 (475 A.H.), and the latter six—until circa 1088 (481 A.H.)—on the mountain of Bizd near Jâm (see Stories 9, 10 and

---

[30] The raising of pigeons (*kabutar*) remains a common hobby among working-class urban dwellers in modern Iran.

[31] *Maqâmât*, 2nd ed., 350-51, citing the *Kholâsat al-maqâmât* (Lahore, 1335 A.H.), 139.

13). He then returned to society at the age of forty, in order to guide the people and make wine-drinkers and sinners to repent.

Shaykh Ahmad's Career in Jâm and Khorasan

According to Ghaznavi's *Spiritual Feats*, Ahmad-e Jâm was not at first appreciated by the people, but after several miraculous healings, his reputation spread and he attracted some followers (see Stories 13-15). At the beginning of his career, Shaykh Ahmad went to Sarakhs, where disease was evidently widespread. Located 70 farsangs (about 200 kilometers) east of Nayshabur and 30 farsangs west of Marv, Sarakhs is about 170 kilometers north of Jâm, and is now split by the Iran-Turkmenistan border.[32] Sarakhs had been one of the centers of Iranian Sufism, along with Balkh, Herat, Meihaneh, Nayshabur, Tus, Marv, and a number of other towns and cities in Khorasan.

From Sarakhs, Shaykh Ahmad proceeded to Estâd and Zur-âbâd, and from there to the village of Ma'd-âbâd, apparently now a neighborhood within the town Torbat-e Jâm. Ma'd-âbâd was a village just north of Jâm in the days of Ahmad, but is not mentioned in early medieval sources.[33] However, because Ahmad's grave, visited by many pilgrims and well-wishers, was located there, Ma'd-âbâd gradually replaced Jâm as the important town in the area and eventually appropriated the name of Jâm to itself.[34] The descendants of Ahmad would later become very influential throughout the region.

---

[32] See Mohammad-Rezâ Shafi'i-Kadkani's notes to his edition of *Asrâr al-towhid fi maqâmât al-Shaykh Abi Sa'id*, 2 vols. (Tehran: Enteshârât-e Âgâh, 1366/1987), 2:749, 756.

[33] Though this neighborhood was commonly pronounced as Mahd-âbâd by the 89 families living there in about 1960, it may originally have been a contraction of *Ma'âdh-âbâd*, a name attested for a village near Bayhaq, as mentioned in the *Târikh-e Bayhaq*. For further details, see the Persian text of the *Maqâmât*, 55n2 and 352.

[34] That is to say that Ma'd-âbâd is now virtually a neighborhood within Torbat-e Jâm. See also *Maqâmât-e Zhandeh Pil*, 2nd ed., 352, citing an article by Mo'ayyad-e Sâbeti. For details on the structure of Ahmad's grave and the adjacent mosque and *khâneqâh*, see Ernst Diez, *Churasanische Baudenkmäler* (Berlin, 1918), Band 1, 80.

Ahmad settled down in Ma'd-âbâd and began training disciples and composing books and propagating his ideas. He also built a Friday mosque and a *khâneqâh*, or Sufi lodge. From his home in Ma'd-âbâd, he made many trips throughout Khorasan, including visits to the major cities of Herât, Nayshabur, and Marv, and to Bâkharz and Bastâm. He evidently won many converts from the villages outlying Jâm. Shaykh Ahmad's activity therefore stretched across a territory that triangulates the modern borders of eastern Iran, northern Afghanistan and southern Turkmenistan.

Jâm was an intermediate sized town, according to Ibn Battûta, who visited in 1346 (747 A.H.), with many gardens and berry trees. It had a number of springs carried through underground water channels (*qanavât*) to irrigate the land and provide water to the city. A good deal of silk was also produced in Jâm in the 14th century,[35] though we cannot be certain that these conditions prevailed two centuries earlier when Shaykh Ahmad lived there.

Among the villages or small towns mentioned in the *Spiritual Feats* are:

Asfarghâbad, which has been identified with the modern Samarqâveh, a village 20 or 30 kilometers distant from Jâm, with a population of about 300.[36]

Barinân, mentioned in four stories, may be the same village now known as Farimân, though this is merely speculation based upon the similarity of the names. It is also possible that this locale has disappeared completely.

Bizd, a mountain and village referred to as Bizd-e Jâm by Ghaznavi. Because of the variant spellings given in the Persian, Bezd (or Bezad) and Bizd, we can deduce that it was pronounced in Shaykh Ahmad's time as Bêzd. The mountain of Bizd is located to the south of Torbat-e Jâm. The village of Bizd, now known as Bezg, 18 kilometers from Ma'd-âbâd, is a well-watered location on the slope of the hills south of Torbat-e Jâm, with gardens and many trees. Shaykh Ahmad evidently spent his summers here, staying in a spot on which a mosque called the Mosque of Light

---

[35] According to Hamd Allâh Mostowfi in *Nozhat al-qolub* and Ibn Battûta.

[36] *Maqâmât*, 352-3, citing Mo'ayyad Sâbeti's article in *Sokhan* and the *Farhang-e joghrâfiâ'i*, which give 20 and 30 kilometers, respectively, as the distance from Samarqâveh to Jâm.

(Masjed-e Nur) stands, a place of pilgrimage for the inhabitants of the area.[37] According to the *Kholâsat al-maqâmât*, this was the site of some of the miracles of the Shaykh.[38]

Buzjân, a town near Jâm which was one of the Shaykh Ahmad's major theaters of operation. Classical geographies, including the *Hodud al-'âlam*, mention a location by this name (Buzhgân) near Nayshabur, but since Jâm itself was considered among the cities near Nayshabur by the early Arab geographers (along with Bâkharz, Jovayn and Bayhaq), we may assume that the Buzjân in question is the same Buzjân mentioned in the present work, which is clearly in the vicinity of Jâm.

Estâd, mentioned first in Story 16, is a mountain in the Zur-âbâd region outside of Sarakhs. There is also a village by the name of Estâd in the same area, as specified in Story 62. Etymologically, Estâd is related to the Latin word "station."

Kâriz-e Sâ'ed, which is now called Kâriz-e Tâybâd. It is located near Bâkharz, about sixty kilometers from Torbat-e Jâm, and had a population of 276 families in about 1950.

Ma'd-âbâd, see above.

Oshtu, mentioned in Story 52 as being near Bâkharz, must be the modern-day Oshtivân, 72 kilometers from Torbat-e Jâm, with mid-twentieth century population estimates ranging from 70 families to 97 persons.[39]

Sâghu(n) is apparently the village now called Samâkhun. Sâbeti locates it 66 kilometers from Torbat-e Jâm, with a population of

---

[37] 'Ali Fâzel reproduces a photograph of this mosque in *Sharh-e ahvâl va naqd va tahlil-e âsâr-e Ahmad-e Jâm* (Tehran: Enteshârât-e Tus, 1373/1994), 514.

[38] This information comes mostly from Mo'ayyad-e Sâbeti's article in *Sokhan*, as the *Farhang-e joghrâfiâ'i* makes no mention of Bizd or Bezd or Bezg. However, Sâbeti's information is somewhat inconsistent, insofar as Sâbeti reports that Ma'd-âbâd is adjacent to Torbat-e Jâm, that Bezd is 18 kilometers from Ma'd-âbâd, and that Bezd is 30 kilometers from Torbat-e Jâm. He reports the population of Bezd as 1293 persons. See *Maqâmât*, 2nd ed., 352-3.

[39] Estimates by Sâbeti and the *Farhang-e joghrâfiâ'i*, respectively. Shafi'i-Kadkani, in the notes to his edition of *Asrâr al-towhid*, 2:729, discusses a similar sounding toponym under "Âstu" (also Ostu, Ostovâ) outside Nayshapur.

35 families at mid-century. The *Farhang-e Joghrâfiâ'i*, however, calculates Samâkhun's distance from modern Torbat-e Jâm at only 46 kilometers, and counts a population of 269.

Zur-âbâd, mentioned first in Story 15, was an area outlying Sarakhs comprising several villages. Sanâ'i, writing at the beginning of the twelfth century, mentions it, as does Yâqût in the *Mu'jam al-buldân* and Sam'âni in his *Ansâb*. There are several villages named Zur-âbâd on current maps of Khorasan.

With the exception of a pilgrimage to Mecca, Shaykh Ahmad evidently spent his entire life in Khorasan. All the sources agree that he lived to the age of 96 years according to the Islamic lunar calendar, and died in August 1141 (Muharram 536 A.H.).[40] Later sources all locate his grave in Jâm, but the oldest source, namely the present text of Ghaznavi, explicitly states that he was buried outside the gates of Ma'd-âbâd. According to Story 370, one of Shaykh Ahmad's disciples saw the location of Ahmad's grave in a dream and Ahmad, asking the disciple to point out the site to him, chose it for his resting-place.

The area of Jâm, frequently subject to invasions by Turks and Mongols, has productive soil and an agreeable climate. By the beginning of the 20th century, it had become so depopulated that many of the outlying villages no longer had chiefs and the underground water channels (*qanât*) had fallen into disrepair. Nâser al-Din Shah's government attempted to repopulate the area by giving the villages in the region, which belonged to the government, to army commanders as a source of income, so that they might station troops there and protect them from marauding bands of Turkoman and other plunderers. Since that time the area around Jâm and Bâkharz has flourished and by the 1960s, all the water channels were in good repair.

In the regions of Jâm, Bâkharz and Herat about 700 of the descendants of Shaykh Ahmad are still living, mostly in Torbat-e Jâm and Bizd. The Jâmi al-Ahmadi families—comprising the clans of Khvâjeh Fakhr al-Din, Khvâjeh Sayf al-Din, Khvâjeh Mohammad-e Yusof and Khvâjeh Najm al-Din—all trace their

---

[40] Note that Ahmad would actually have been in his 95th lunar year at the time of death if he was born in 441 A.H. and died in 536 A.H. In solar years this would correspond to a lifespan of 91 or 92 years, from 1049 to 1141 A.D.

lineage back to Shaykh Ahmad, whereas very few Iranian families can trace their lineage back uninterrupted for 900 years. Hâjji Qâzi of the Jâmi al-Ahmadi family was the head of the Hanafi school and the caretaker of Shaykh Ahmad's shrine in Jâm.[41]

Shaykh Ahmad and his Contemporaries

Despite the importance of the *Spiritual Feats* of Mohammad-e Ghaznavi as a source about Shaykh Ahmad, the impression it gives of Shaykh Ahmad's character and the details it provides of his methods of propagating his religious teachings cannot be considered a reliable depiction of Shaykh Ahmad's actual beliefs, insofar as it is filled with legendary tales and material. Mohammad-e Ghaznavi views Shaykh Ahmad with the eyes of a disciple gazing upon his spiritual master, one whom he believes capable of performing miracles; furthermore Ghaznavi would appear to have been a credulous person, unable or unwilling to subject the prevailing folk beliefs and miraculous tales he relates to closer scrutiny, despite the fact that he is described as a legal scholar (*faqih*) in Story 122. The tales we read here, therefore, while affording an insight into the popularity of Shaykh Ahmad and the mental image which the Shaykh's disciples held of him, do not necessarily tell us a great deal about Ahmad's actual beliefs or his relations with the various mystical schools and doctrines of his day. Indeed, in some cases, such as in Shaykh Ahmad's treatise on Alchemy in his Epistle to the Samarqandians (see Part Four), Shaykh Ahmad invests the transmutation of elements with a metaphysical and spiritual meaning, and seems to subtly undermine thereby the claims of his followers on his behalf of having changed various base elements into gold.

Bu Tâher-e Kord

Many scholars and mystics traveled to the various centers of Islamic civilization to study with famous teachers and theosophers, but Shaykh Ahmad does not appear to have traveled far beyond the area of Jâm for this purpose and, indeed, never pursued a formal education in the legal colleges or seminaries.

---

[41] The information about the history of Jâm and the Shaykh's descendants comes from Moayyad Sâbeti's article (cited in *Maqâmât*, 354-5).

Shaykh Ahmad evidently began his spiritual trek as a disciple of Shaykh Bu Tâher-e Kord. Evidently a local holy man and a Kurd, Bu Tâher is an otherwise unknown figure in the history of Persian mysticism. Mohammad-e Ghaznavi describes him as a direct disciple of Abu Sa'id-e Abu al-Khayr (Story 166). Jâmi gives a notice of Shaykh Bu Tâher-e Kord, but simply quotes Story 5 below directly from Ghaznavi's *Spiritual Feats*, and has no supplementary information about him.

Abu Sa'id-e Abu al-Khayr

Mohammad-e Ghaznavi portrays Shaykh Ahmad as the successor of Abu Sa'id-e Abu al-Khayr (967-1049), the famous Sufi saint memorialized by the hagiography of Mohammad ebn al-Monavvar, *Asrâr al-towhid*.[42] Ghaznavi says that Abu Sa'id foretold the coming of Shaykh Ahmad to Bu Tâher and his other disciples and left his mantle (*kherqeh*, a cloak or robe of honor symbolic of saintly authority among the Sufis) to be given to a person whose description he gives. When Shaykh Ahmad entered the khâneqâh of Bu Tâher, Bu Tâher saw in him the signs foretold by Abu Sa'id (See Story 166).

As charming as this story is, neither the *Asrâr al-towhid* provides no basis for it or anything that can be remotely interpreted as an allusion to Shaykh Ahmad. Mohammad-e Ghaznavi, or some other follower of Shaykh Ahmad, undoubtedly made up this story, which conforms to the typology of many other such stories about Sufi saints appointing subsequently famous successors. Perhaps the best-known example of such tales is the supposed meeting between an aged Farid al-Din 'Attâr and the

---

[42]   For the Persian text, see *Asrâr al-towhid fi maqâmât al-Shaykh Abi Sa'id*, ed. Mohammad-Rezâ Shafi'i-Kadkani, 2 vols. (Tehran: Enteshârât-e Âgâh, 1366/1987). An excellent English translation was done by John O'Kane as *The Secrets of God's Mystical Oneness, or the Spiritual Stations of Shaikh Abu Sa'id* (Costa Mesa, CA: Mazda Publishers and Bibliotheca Persica, 1992); an earlier one in French by Mohammad Achena also exists, *Les Étapes mystiques du Shaykh Abu' Sa'id* (Paris, 1974). For a study of the life and legend of Abu Sa'id, see Fritz Meier, *Abu Sa'id-i Abu al-Hayr...: Wirklichkeit und Legende*, op. cit.

young boy Jalâl al-Din Rumi in Nayshabur.[43] The tale told by Ghaznavi simply represents an attempt to invest Shaykh Ahmad with the spiritual authority and reputation of Abu Sa'id.

Mowdud-e Cheshti

According to *The Spiritual Feats*, Shaykh Ahmad visited Herat and was the object of immeasurable praise and honor from the descendants of 'Abd Allâh Ansâri (1006-1088/396-481 A.H.) and the people of that city. Mohammad-e San'ân (d. 1066 / 459 A.H.), who is believed to have been in contact with 'Abd Allâh-e Ansâri, appointed his son, Khvâjeh Qotb al-Din Mowdud-e Cheshti (d. 1133/527 A.H.), as the leader of the Cheshti order.[44] This Mowdud-e Cheshti, who would have been quite young at the time, was initially opposed to Shaykh Ahmad and made an effort to drive him from the city. Eventually, however, Cheshti recognized the greatness of Ahmad and dropped all schemes against him (See Stories 24 and 27).

Imam Mohammad-e Mansur of Sarakhs

Mohammad-e Ghaznavi's text also provides evidence of a meeting between Shaykh Ahmad and the Imam Mohammad-e Mansur of Sarakhs, a famous judge, preacher and religious scholar in Khorasan. Yâr Ahmad-e Rashidi in his *Tarab-khâneh* asserts that Mohammad-e Mansur was a teacher of 'Omar Khayyâm.[45] Sanâ'i (d. 525/1131) frequently mentions this Mohammad-e Mansur in his works, praising him at length in the *Sayr al-'ebâd elâ al-ma'âd* and in a number of poems from his *Divân*.[46] One

---

[43] For the argument establishing the mythical nature of this meeting of Rumi and 'Attâr, see Franklin Lewis, *Rumi: Past and Present, East and West* (Oxford: Oneworld, 2000), Chapter One.

[44] See the article "Čestiya" by Gerhard Böwering in the *Encyclopaedia Iranica*.

[45] *Tarab-khâneh*, ed. Jalâl al-Din Homâ'i (Tehran: Tâbân, 1342/1963), 148-150.

[46] *Masnavi-hâ-ye Hakim Sanâ'i*, ed. Modarres-e Razavi (Tehran: Enteshârât-e Dâneshgâh-e Tehran, 1348/1969), 218ff; *Divân-e Sanâ'i*, ed. Modarres-e Razavi, 2nd ed. (Tehran: Ketâbkhâneh-ye Sanâ'i, 1354/1975), e.g., 34, 164, 262, 635, 717, 731 and 1074; and *Hadiqat al-haqiqat*, ed. Modarres-e Razavi, 2nd ed. (Tehran: Enteshârât-e

qasideh in the *Divân* of Sanâ'i commemorates the amicable
conclusion of a dispute between this Imam Mohammad-e Mansur
and a certain "Shaykh." Quite possibly, this alludes to the Shaykh
al-Islam Ahmad, who, according to Mohammad-e Ghaznavi's text,
met and quarreled with Mohammad-e Mansur in Sarakhs.[47] For
the most part, however, Ahmad did not have contact with
distinguished members of the ulama, spreading his teachings
among the local population and minor dignitaries, except in the
case of Sultan Sanjar.

Sultan Sanjar
The Seljuk Sultan Sanjar was one of the historical figures who had
some dealings with Ahmad-e Jâm. According to the present text,
Ahmad was entrusted with the responsibility of protecting Sanjar
and saved him on several occasions from death.

Sanjar and Qarâjeh the Sâqi
    In Story 6 Qarâjeh the Sâqi, who is one of Sanjar's military
commanders, at the instigation of his wife, pours poison in
Sanjar's drink and sets it at his bedside. The situation is revealed
to Ahmad by a heavenly source and he travels to the Sultan's
bedchamber and pours out the poison and turns the cup upside
down. The following day Qarâjeh the Sâqi, fearing his treachery
will be discovered, flees from Sanjar and takes up the command of
a rebel army, which he leads against Sanjar only to suffer defeat.
    Qarâjeh the Sâqi is a historical figure, though no historical
source corroborates the incident described in Story 6. Ibn Athîr
mentions Qarâjeh the Sâqi in connection with two separate battles,
both of which resulted in victories for Sanjar: a conflict in the
year 1119 (513 A.H.) between Sanjar and his nephew, Mahmud,
in which Qarâjeh is listed as one of Mahmud's commanders; and

---

Dâneshgâh-e Tehran, 1359/1980), 486. For a translation of Sanâ'i's
poem dedicating the khâneqâh of Mohammad-e Mansur, see the
introduction to Lewis, *Rumi: Past and Present*, op. cit. For a translation
of a poem praising one of the gatherings of Mohammad-e Mansur, see
Franklin Lewis, "Reading, Writing and Recitation: Sanâ'i and the
Origins of the Persian Ghazal," Ph.D. Dissertation (University of
Chicago, 1995; UMI# 9609952), Poem 6.5, pp. 351, 412, 529-32.
[47] See *Divân-e Sanâ'i*, 262ff and Story 15 in the present text.

Sanjar's battle outside Hamadan in 1132 (526 A.H.). According to Ibn Athîr, Qarâjeh the Sâqi was captured in the latter battle and summoned by Sultan Sanjar. Ibn Athîr relates as follows:

> And when Qarâjeh appeared before him, Sanjar cursed him and said: "You traitor! What did you hope to gain by killing me?" Qarâjeh said, "I hoped to kill you and install a Sultan whom I could command."[48]

The report of Ibn Athîr is not unlike what Ghaznavi has Qarâjeh say at the end of Story 6:

> He summoned Qarâjeh and said, "Why have you rebelled?" He said, "I cannot lie in your presence. I desire to be a Sanjar and my wife to be a Torkân Khâtun. I gave her a potion to pour in the sherbet. I don't know who warned you not to drink the sherbet."

In a letter written by Sanjar to Sharaf al-Din Zaynabi, the minister of al-Mustarshid bi-Allâh, the Abbasid Caliph (r. 1118-1135/512-29 A.H.), dating to the year 1133 (527 A.H.), we read the following statement:

> Qarâjeh was one of our servants. Before he joined the service of our brother, Ghiâs al-Donyâ va al-Din [Muhammad, r. 1105-1118/498-511 A.H.], he was among the ranks of our attendants for many years. When he reached the rank of Atabek and Governor, he spent his days in the shadow of our blessings. In accordance with our recommendation, the son of Mahmud [a prince in the western Seljuk dominions], God have mercy upon him, afforded him patronage. Qarâjeh would send his trusted confidants and relatives before me to profess his servitude and allegiance. So it was that we kept him in that office. We have no idea how this conceit took hold in his mind.[49]

---

[48] Ibn Athîr, *al-Kâmil fî al-târîkh* (Cairo, 1303 A.H./1886) 10:477, and 387 and 475.

[49] 'Abbâs Eqbâl, *Vezârat dar 'ahd-e salâtin-e bozorg-e Saljuqi* (Tehran: Enteshârât-e Dâneshgâh-e Tehrân), 318. Eqbâl's text mistakenly identifies the Caliph of that year as al-Mustazhir bi-Allâh.

Sanjar and the Knife under his Pillow
Another of the stories narrated by Ghaznavi concerns the Ismaili (Ismâ'îlî) threat to the Seljuks. Sultan Sanjar had allowed the Ismailis in Khorasan to propagate their doctrines without any restrictions. In Story 22, Ghaznavi relates that a knife was placed under Sanjar's pillow, frightening him greatly. This fact is attested by important historical sources, such as Jovayni's *Târikh-e jahângoshâ*[50] and Khvândmir's *Habib al-seyar*,[51] but Ghaznavi, who wrote during the lifetime of Sanjar, claims to provide many further details about the incident, including how the knife was placed under Sanjar's pillow and who was involved. Ghaznavi adds that Shaykh Ahmad learned of this conspiracy. When the Ismaili propaganda assumed significant proportions in Khorasan, Ahmad could no longer remain neutral. He set out for Marv and supposedly revealed to Sanjar the truth about the Ismaili's scheme and the treachery of the Keeper of the Royal Wardbrobe. According to Ghaznavi, Ahmad asked Sanjar to suppress the Ismaili activities and Sanjar had the Ismailis in Marv arrested, executing eighteen of them who were unwilling to repent.

Sanjar and Toghrol Tegin
Story 17 concerns a certain Toghrol Tegin, identified as the fief holder of Jâm, who wanted to build himself a building in the town of Sâghu near Jâm. Because he did not find the proper lumber for the building to progress, he sent several horsemen to extract lumber from Ahmad, which the latter was using to build his own *khâneqâh*. Ahmad, according to Ghaznavi, was outraged and threatened this man with death. Toghrol's building had not yet been completed when several horsemen arrived from the desert, tied him by the neck, dragged him from his tent and galloped away with him. Toghrol's horsemen followed in search of him, but found only his decapitated body in the desert. When news of this incident reached Sultan Sanjar, he grew angry and threatened to kill the people of Jâm. The people of Jâm sought the help of Shaykh Ahmad, who wrote a letter to Sanjar upholding their innocence and detailing the crime of Toghrol Tegin. Ahmad in

---

[50]   ed. Mohammad-e Qazvini (Leiden, 1911-37), 2:214.
[51]   (Tehran, 1333/1954), 2:486.

this letter describes the event as a divine punishment. When Sanjar learned of the true situation, he rescinded his previous directive and showed favor to the people of Jâm. The letter from Shaykh Ahmad to Sanjar, harsh in tone and unflattering, is included in the present book. Yusof-e Ahl, who compiled a collection of 653 letters under the title *Farâ'ed-e ghiâsi* between 1433 and 1456 (837-861 A.H.), includes this letter of Shaykh Ahmad as the first and oldest example in his collection.[52]

Shaykh Ahmad's Meeting with Sanjar

Ghaznavi claims that Sanjar came to see Shaykh Ahmad once in the village of Ma'd-âbâd (see Story 16). This is not implausible since Sanjar appears to have been favorably disposed to Ahmad and to have treated him with respect; we need not take Ghaznavi's narrative at face value on this point, but we can see evidence of Sanjar's respect for Ahmad in another letter which Ahmad wrote to Sultan Sanjar (see "Sultan Sanjar's Question About the Characteristics of the Friends of God and the Answer of the Shaykh," in the *Epistle to the Samarqandians* in Part Four).

The Character and Beliefs of Shaykh Ahmad (as Portrayed by Mohammad-e Ghaznavi)

Unfortunately, *The Spiritual Feats of Ahmad-e Jâm* does not provide us with a picture of the daily routine of Shaykh Ahmad, even though one would assume that, since Mohammad-e Ghaznavi spent many years with Shaykh Ahmad, he would certainly have been aware of such matters. Ghaznavi portrays Shaykh Ahmad in the anecdotes included in his book as an influential and powerful man. As his nickname *Zhandeh-Pil* (the Colossal Elephant) suggests, Shaykh Ahmad appears as a man plowing forwards to achieve his aims through weighty spiritual powers, not infrequently trampling on those who stand in his way. Of course, even in those pre-Enlightenment days, there was tension between the educated and popular view of Sufi saints, a fact clearly reflected in Ghaznavi's introduction, where he is at pains to assert that, though some of the tales seem unbelievable, Ghaznavi had

---

[52] See Heshmat Moayyad's introduction to Jalâl al-Din Yusof-e Ahl, *Farâ'ed-e ghiâsi*, ed. H. Moayyad, 2 vols. (Tehran: Bonyâd-e Farhang-e Iran, 2536/1977), 1:xxix-xxxi.

seen and confirmed them with his own eyes. Furthermore, in Story 249 we find a group of scholars telling one of the followers of the Shaykh:

> You make extremely exaggerated claims on behalf of this Shaykh Ahmad. You have made him look foolish. What do you mean by this? You will lose [respect] on his account and the religious scholars will have none left either. Mind what you are doing!

Ahmad was not a retiring hermit who renounced all worldly pleasures to occupy himself with suffering and spiritual constriction (*qabz*), a state which is so typical of an earlier popular saint, Shaykh Abu Sa'id-e Abu al-Khayr. In Ghaznavi's anecdotes about Shaykh Ahmad we often find him attending feasts and enjoying the worldly blessings of God. He also married eight times, once at the advanced age of eighty (see Story 179).

Nevertheless, Ahmad was an inveterate opponent of wine and wine-drinking, ceaselessly striving to lead wine-drinkers to repentance and to smash jars of wine. Ghaznavi claims that Ahmad caused 180,000 individuals to repent of drinking and personally smashed 10,000 jars of wine. Likewise, he had a predilection for destroying musical instruments, of which he is said to have smashed 1200 (see Chapter One). Hâfez was aware of Shaykh Ahmad's legendary reputation in this respect and tauntingly alludes to it in the following line:

> *Hâfez gholâm-e jâm-e may ast ay sabâ be-row*
> *va-z bandeh bandegi be-resân Shaykh-e Jâm râ[53]*

Hâfez is enslaved by a cup of wine; go, zephyr
and pay the respects of this slave to the Shaykh of Jâm.

Likewise, Bâbâ Faghâni of Shiraz says:

---

[53] There is some dispute about the reading of this line, but this would appear, especially in light of the following line by Bâbâ Faghâni, to be the correct interpretation. See the Persian edition of the *(Maqâmât)*, introduction, 44n2. Khânlari's edition of the *Divân-e Hâfez* (Poem 7, p. 30) gives the line with the variant *Hâfez morid-e jâm-e may ast....*

mastân agar konand Faghâni be-towbeh mayl
pir-i be e'teqâd beh az Shaykh-e Jâm nist

O Faghâni, if the drunkards wish to repent
no mentor deserves more trust than the Shaykh of Jâm

Shaykh Ahmad's Severity

Another salient characteristic of Shaykh Ahmad which the reader will soon remark is his ruthlessness and severity. In order to achieve his goal, which is the propagation of religious law (*Shari'a*) and the repentance of sinners, he does not hesitate to use any means in his power. The Shaykh very rarely displays any fatherly connivance at or forgiveness toward the excesses of youth, when young men are prone to sow their oats. According to the *Spiritual Feats*, he sometimes visited illness, confinement or even death on youth whose only sin had been contemplating the temptations of backsliding and pleasure-seeking in their heart of hearts.

Shaykh Ahmad's Forbearance with his own Sons

In the case of his own sons, however, Shaykh Ahmad proves a generous and forgiving father, one who patiently waits for them to turn away from sin and return to their father's path, as demonstrated by his writing the book *Meftâh al-najât* (*The Key to Salvation*) in commemoration of the repentance of one of his son's, Najm al-Din Abu Bakr, who spent many long years in the pursuit of pleasure and wine-drinking.[54] When another one of his sons, Borhân al-Din, went into heavy debt and needed his father's assistance, Shaykh Ahmad extracted a thousand dinârs from his friends to pay back the loans, and a further 2000 dinârs for Borhân's living expenses, all of which he obtained in an imperious and manipulative manner (See Story 28).

Shaykh Ahmad's Severity with his Women Folk

As portrayed in *The Spiritual Feats*, Shaykh Ahmad was very cruel and unforgiving with his wives. When one of them went without Shaykh Ahmad's permission to the vineyard with one of

---

[54] See Meier, "Zur Biographie Ahmad-i Ğãm's," op. cit., 64-5.

her relatives, he paralyzed her. Two other women in his household who spied upon the Shaykh through the crack in the door when he was alone with another one of his wives were rendered blind (See Stories 60-62).

Ahmad's Intolerance

The legendary Shaykh Ahmad acted discourteously and unkindly towards members of other religions and other sects. Ghaznavi portrays the Shaykh as one who considered everyone bound for hell except the saints and miracle-workers of his own creed who had lived life in devout worship of God. Instead of treating backsliders with kindness and respect, he demonstrated intolerance and coercion, attempting to convert them to the true Islam (see Stories 8 and 65).

Shaykh Ahmad's Conceit

Another remarkable characteristic of the Shaykh, as the stories of the *Spiritual Feats* reflect, was his pride and overbearing self-conceit. He considers himself the cynosure (*qotb*) of all the saints, possessed of all the miracles and signs which each of the shaykhs of the past possessed only in part. One of his disciples even dreamed that the Prophet Mohammad prayed standing behind the Shaykh. Another dreamt that Shaykh Ahmad was conversing with the Prophet, but all at once, he realized that Shaykh Ahmad was sitting where the Prophet had been. Taken aback by this, a call arrived, "Why so surprised?! He is Us and We are him" (See Stories 50, 64, 69 [toward the end], 142, 143 and 170).

Of course, we must emphasize that this is the impression of Shaykh Ahmad as given by the anecdotes told in the *Spiritual Feats*. The picture that Mohammad-e Ghaznavi paints cannot be totally accurate; a Sufi with the fame and influence that Ahmad-e Jâm enjoyed (and still enjoys in his own town), could not have earned it by such barbaric and short-sighted methods. Furthermore, the spirit reflected in these stories often conflicts with the words of Shaykh Ahmad in his own writings.

Rather, these anecdotes prove the naiveté and small-mindedness of Mohammad-e Ghaznavi and the common folk of the day. Ghaznavi expresses his beliefs and suppositions as memories of the days of his teacher, shaping those memories to impress a popular audience. It is therefore not possible to extract a realistic biography from them. Only through the writings of the Shaykh himself can we approach the historical personality of the Shaykh.

His Attitude toward the Sufi Lodge

Shaykh Ahmad-e Jâm headed a Sufi lodge (*khâneqâh*), the ruins of which can still be seen. Of the practices and activities of the Shaykh and his disciples, his teaching methodology and the historical figures of Sufism who may have visited the lodge, however, we have little precise information. In one chapter of the *Lamp for Travelers (Serâj al-sâ'erin)*, Shaykh Ahmad talks about the difference between administering a khâneqâh or Sufi lodge (*khâneqâh-dâri*) and running a business (*dokkân-dâri*). A Sufi lodge admits people of good intention, for the most part, whereas a caravanserai admits soldiers, thieves and many others of ill intent. A khâneqâh must be dedicated to the purposes of knowledge and worship (*'elm va 'ebâdat*) and as soon as the profit motive or personal desire (*tama'*) enters the equation, the special benefits of a consecrated house are lost. However, the Shaykh felt that many of those who claimed to run khâneqâhs in his own day were neither administering Sufi lodges nor running a business, and that it would have been better if these had been made into churches, rather than khâneqâhs.

For the most part, however, Shaykh Ahmad is very positive about the people who frequent the khâneqâhs. He divides them into three groups: scholars, dervishes and Sufis, the origins of all three of which he sees among the companions of the Prophet Mohammad. He comments that the best people among each of these groups are among the best of all people, whereas even the bad amongst them are no worse than the common folk. He does, however, admit that sins sometimes occur, though mostly of an unpremeditated nature.[55]

Shaykh Ahmad's views about *samâ'* (the practice of meditation enhanced by listening to music and dancing, common to many Sufi orders) was complex. In the *Ons al-tâ'ebin*, Shaykh Ahmad distinguishes between various kinds of *samâ'* and the intentions of those who perform them. The listening to music and poetry for various kinds of passion and pleasure is forbidden or frowned upon, but listening to music out of spiritual fear, hope or ecstasy is

---

[55] *Montakhab-e serâj al-sâ'erin*, 17-22.

permissible.[56] However, only those who are in an advanced state of spiritual progress should perform these kinds of *samâ'*, and it would appear the Shaykh's lodge had a primarily orthodox and pious function as a center of sermons and religious studies, rather than a center of ecstatic, pentecostal-like worship.

Repentance

In the view of Ahmad of Jâm, repentance was the single most important condition for the spiritual quest, because all people are sinful and unless they repent in their hearts and wash their hands of sin, they cannot enter the paradise of divine good-pleasure. One of the great miracles attributed to Shaykh Ahmad was the number of people he caused to repent; in a history of Herat written in the early 1490s, it is related that 600,000 people repented through the efforts of Shaykh Ahmad.[57]

Not everyone attains to sincere repentance, which is not, in reality, a station acquired through human effort, but one bestowed by the grace of God. Shaykh Ahmad devotes a chapter to the difference between those who have truly repented (*tâ'ebân*) and those who have merely renounced sin (*târek-e gonâh*) in the *Serâj al-sâ'erin*.[58]

Grace

The honeybee, despite its smallness, has been blessed with grace and gift of God. It is the bee, as Shaykh Ahmad explains in his *Epistle to the Samarqandians*, which God has made the special recipient of His intuition (Qur'ân 16:68), and not the sweet-throated and beautiful birds, which, like the nightingale, the hawk and the peacock, are full of pride. The bee is unable to explain or understand this divine bounty, but its honey—which alleviates pain and sweetens palates—is the best and most convincing evidence of this grace.

---

[56] *Ons al-tâ'ebin*, ed. Fâzel, 2nd ed. (1368/1989), 221-32. On the other hand, Fritz Meier's personal notes to *Meftâh al-najât*, made available to Heshmat Moayyad, indicated that the Shaykh was quite opposed to *samâ'*.

[57] Zamchi Esfazâri, *Rowzât al-jannât*, 231.

[58] *Montakhab-e serâj al-sâ'erin*, 32-5.

Religious Law (*Shari'a*)

Shaykh Ahmad adhered to Islamic law (*Shari'a*) and did not hold it permissible, as some Sufis did, for anyone to consider himself above the law or to regard the law as the discardable husk of religion. Contrary to what some authors, such as Qâzi Nur Allâh Shushtari, have written, Shaykh Ahmad was no Shiite, but a Sunni. An anecdote related by Diez[59] suggests that the Safavid Shâh 'Abbâs passed through Jâm on his way to Qandahâr. Thinking that Shaykh Ahmad had been a Sunni, he ordered his tomb destroyed. As the workers began to tear it down, they discovered some writing, which suggested the Shaykh, had been a Shiite. Shâh 'Abbâs ordered a halt to the razing of the tomb and vowed that should he prove victorious in battle, he would have the Shaykh's tomb restored, which he did. According to other sources, however, the Shaykh was a Sunni, a fact born out by his own writings.[60]

Devotion to the Prophet

Shaykh Ahmad had a zealous belief in and devotion to the Prophet Mohammad. At one point he says that the collective attributes of all the prophets numbered 117, but that the Prophet Mohammad displayed in himself alone each and every one of these attributes. Mohammad, the Messenger of God, reached this station by renouncing egoism and practicing servitude to God through absolute poverty and denial of his own self.

Negligence in Loving God

Divine love is like physical love in the view of Shaykh Ahmad. Just as the attentions of a lover may be gradually diverted by daily preoccupations until he eventually forgets the beloved, so, too, forgetfulness and preoccupation with worldly affairs may make the mystic lover forget the Lord and busy himself with the pleasures of this world.

---

[59] Ernst Diez, *Churâsânische Baudenkmäler*, erster Band (Berlin, 1918), 81. Diez' source for this anecdote is obscure; it is not related in *Nâsekh al-tavârikh* or *Rowzat al-safâ* or *Târikh-e 'âlam-ârâ-ye 'Abbâsi*.

[60] See also Story 64 in the present collection, as well as the article by Fritz Meier in the 2nd edition of the *Encyclopaedia of Islam*.

The Signs of the True Friend

According to Shaykh Ahmad, the true Friend possesses five distinctive qualities. First, he takes pleasure in obedience and servitude to the Lord, not in selfish desires. Second, he rejoices in praise and glorification of the name of God, not in flattering or fawning over others. Third, his wealth and riches consist in contemplating God's beauty, not in the luxuries of this world. Fourth, he spends his life in solitude, not in society. Fifth, although eating, drinking and wearing clothes are physical necessities, he considers them a trial and tribulation.

True Poverty

Shaykh Ahmad explains that the sign of true poverty is desiring and longing search. If not for the spiritual practice of poverty, the Prophet would never have achieved his ascent into heaven (*me'râj*). True poverty obliterates all ugly attributes and vulgar thoughts. True poverty releases a person from all pride and vain imagination. A man of poverty is like a ball that does not roll at its own will. It absorbs every blow of the polo stick and rolls wherever it is directed, never knowing or asking why or how much or how long or by who it is being hit. A man must also be like this, avoiding all passions and selfish desires, to become truly poor, to become longing and search from head to toe.

THE WRITINGS OF SHAYKH AHMAD

In Mohammad-e Ghaznavi's *Maqâmât*, the *Kholâsat al-maqâmât*, and the treatise by Shehâb al-Din Esmâ'il, *On the Greatness of Shaykh Ahmad-e Jâm*, thirteen separate works are attributed to Shaykh Ahmad, as follows:

1) *Anis al-tâ'ebin* (Companion to the Repentant), a volume of 45 chapters in some 300 pages, also called *Ons al-tâ'ebin* ("Companionship of the Repentant") in the *Spiritual Feats*.[61]

---

[61] *Anis al-tâ'ebin* is the form of the title given in *Haft eqlim*, *Tarâ'eq al-haqâ'eq* and in *Kashf al-zunûn*, as well as other sources. This form of the title, *Anis*, makes more sense, as it describes the book as a "companion for the penitent." However, 'Ali Fâzel, who edited the text

Manuscripts of this work survive in the Library of the Asiatic Society of Bengal,[62] the Malek Library in Tehran (dated Rajab 928/May-June 1522), and 19th century copies held in the University Library of Tashkent, the Central Library of the University of Tehran,[63] and by the family of Hâjj Mohammad A'zam Jâmi al-Ahmadi. A manuscript dated 15 Muharram 847 A.H. (15 May 1443) was also in the possession of Jalâl al-Din Homâ'i, but is apparently inaccessible at present.[64] The work has been published by 'Ali Fâzel as *Ons al-tâ'ebin, serât Allâh al-mobin* (Tehran: Tus, 1368/1989).[65]

Shaykh Ahmad explains in the introduction as follows:

> Know that we have not begun this book for the sake of contention or prejudice, nor to speak ill of any Muslim, or that we might be hailed and praised among the people. It is not for all these things, but rather for the good pleasure of God, the Almighty and Exalted.[66]

The verdict of Hâji Ma'sum-'Ali Shâh, the Nâyeb al-Sadr (b. 1853), who read the work, was that "The *Companion* in particular is a good friend."[67]

---

in two volumes, chose *Ons al-tâ'ebin*, meaning "companionship of the penitent," for reasons he explains in the introduction.

[62] Wladimir Ivanow, *Concise Descriptive Catalogue of the Persian Mss. in the Collection of the Asiatic Society of Bengal* (Calcutta, 1924), vol. 1, #1169 (cited by Meier, "Zur Biographie, op. cit., 64) and the two articles of Ivanow in *JRAS* (1922, p. 398n1 and 1923, p. 6). Ivanow remarks that although the Shaykh tried to write in elegant Persian, he occasionally slips into expressions in his local dialect, in which respect the *Anis al-tâ'ebin* resembles the *Tabaqât* of Ansâri. (See "Tabaqât of Ansâri in the Old Language of Herat," *JRAS* 1923, p. 6).

[63] *Ons al-tâ'ebin*, introduction, 1:25-7.

[64] 'Ali Fâzel (ed.), *Ons al-tâ'ebin*, lxviii-lxix, lxxiii.

[65] He had published an incomplete version eighteen years earlier, containing only the first volume (Tehran: Bonyâd-e Farhang-e Irân, 1350/1971).

[66] *Ons al-tâ'ebin*, 11.

[67] *Tarâ'eq al-haqâ'eq* (printed 1318 A.H. / 1900 A.D.), 2:261. In the Mahjub edition, 2:586.

2) *Serâj al-sâ'erin* (A Lamp for Travelers), a three-volume work of 75 chapters written in 1119 (513 A.H.), apparently the largest and most important of Shaykh Ahmad's compositions, though one of the volumes was apparently lost in the Mongol invasions.[68] This book was widely popular with Sufis and perhaps still is. Hâji Mirzâ Ma'sum (b. 1853), a Nimatullahi Sufi, had a copy of this work. The full text of this work has yet to appear, but an annotated selection of some 130 pages of 24 chapters of the work, derived from a manuscript in the Hâjj Hosayn Âqâ Malek library, the date of which has been effaced and is now illegible, was published by 'Ali Fâzel as *Montakhab-e serâj al-sâ'erin* (Mashhad: Âstân-e Qods-e Razavi, 1368/1989). The introduction to this manuscript of the work mentions the *Meftâh al-najât*, which was not written until nine years after the *Serâj al-sâ'erin*,[69] so the introductory material to this copy must have been added at a later date, either by Shaykh Ahmad himself, or more likely, by a copyist.

The *Kholâsat al-maqâmât*[70] quotes the following passage from the *Serâj al-sâ'erin*:

> I knew nothing of the various religious sciences and when I reached the age of twenty-two, I could not even recite the opening Sura of the Qur'ân [*al-Hamd*][71] correctly. God on High bestowed so much knowledge on this transgressor [*jâfi*] from His grace, bounty and generosity that no Imam of my day could say anything against me. They never asked me any question that posed a problem for me. If anyone ever opposed me over any matter, the truth of it turned out to be what I

---

[68] *Kholâsat al-maqâmât* (Lahore, 1353), 20-21.

[69] 'Ali Fâzel, *Sharh-e ahvâl va naqd va tahlil-e âsâr-e Shaykh Ahmad-e Jâm* (Tehran: Enteshârât-e Tus, 1373/1994), 388.

[70] *Kholâsat al-maqâmât*, ed. Ivanow, *JRAS* (1917), 351.

[71] Normally referred to as (Surat) al-Fâtiha, Iranian authors in the medieval period often referred to this sura as "al-Hamd" because it began with the phrase, *al-hamdu li'llâh* (see, e.g., *Divân-e Sanâ'i*, ed. Modarres-e Razavi, 2nd ed., p. 1022, line 4). Al-Hamd/al-Fâtiha is one of the shortest suras in the Qur'ân and was recited ritually on many occasions, including funerals. It would have been the first sura anyone studying the Qur'ân learned; inability to recite or read it would therefore indicate complete illiteracy in Arabic.

had said. I have filled up three hundred sheets of paper on the conventional and esoteric religious sciences, on points which have I seen in the pages of no other authority. On the contrary, it was all inspired by God. Whoever writes a book takes it from other books, whereas what I have put down on paper came from the heart, without any deceit, hypocrisy, envy or prejudice. I have not taken things on paper to heart. Books like this are of a different hue and cry, a quality lacking in common books.

Shaykh Ahmad explains in the course of the book that:

One group of readers will look into this book to see what they can get out of it, that is, to see if they can find fault with it. Another group will read it to see what is in it. Another group will look over it and then look at one another; if the people say it is good, then it will be good, and if they say it is bad, it will be bad. But we do this for the group of people who are in pain, who have something like this weighing upon their hearts. If those people find benefit in the book, our intention is fulfilled.[72]

3) *Meftâh al-najât* (The Key to Salvation), a volume of seven chapters[73] written beginning in August 1128 (Sha'bân 522 A.H.) on the occasion of the repentance of Shaykh Ahmad's son, Najm al-Din Abu Bakr. Najm al-Din in this year forswore immoral activity and entered "the circle and society of the dear ones at the threshold," asking his father to compose a book that would explain what someone at his stage of the path of God would need to know. Shaykh Ahmad obliged with a relatively short treatise, so as not to tire the reader.[74] Shaykh Ahmad explains in his introduction that:

And so it is incumbent upon anyone who knows something to tell it, especially the kind of knowledge

---

[72] *Montakhab-e Serâj*, 58.
[73] Some cosmological significance is attributed to the number seven by the Shaykh; see *Meftâh*, 64-9.
[74] *Meftâh*, 62-3.

that holds the way to salvation today, the kind of knowledge that is destruction itself if you do not know it. [I had] a dream in which this belief and this path was presented three times to the Messenger, God's praise upon him. If I did not hear the Messenger, God's praise upon him, say in his own precious words (*lafz-e dorar-bâr*) in this dream, "This is my religion," then by God, I am no Muslim.[75]

The process by which the stories read or remembered about saints were gradually reformulated as legends can be seen in the following quotation of this passage as given in the *Kholâsat al-maqâmât* (ed. Ivanow, op. cit., 350), which transforms it subtly:

> I wrote this book as an explanation of belief. In a dream I presented this path and this belief to his holiness, the Messenger (God's praise and blessing upon him and his family). I heard him say three times in his own precious words, "This is my religion," or else I am no Muslim.

Manuscripts of this work survive in the Royal Library of Vienna,[76] the Süleymâniye (As'ad Efendi) Library in Istanbul,[77] the Mevlânâ Museum in Konya, the University Library in Tübingen, and the library of the former Ministry of Information and Culture in Kabul, Afghanistan.[78] 'Ali Fâzel edited and published the text as *Meftâh al-najât* in 1968 (Tehran: Bonyâd-e Farhang-e Irân, 1347).

4) *Rowzat al-moznebin* (The Sinners' Garden), a volume of 31 chapters which Shaykh Ahmad wrote in 1132 (526 A.H.) and dedicated to Sultan Sanjar. Shâh Qâsem Anvâr praised this book in the following lines:

---

[75] *Meftâh*, 61.

[76] Gustav Flügel, *Die...persischen Handschriften der Kaiserlich-Königlichen Hofbibliothek zu Wien* (Vienna, 1867), 3:121, #1679.

[77] Manuscript #1728, in 119 folios, cited by F. Meier, "Zur Biographie," *ZDMG* 97 (1943), 64.

[78] *Meftâh*, 32-7.

Rowzat al-moznebin-e Ahmad-e Jâm
ân nahang-e mohit-e bahr-âshâm
âsemâni-st por mah o parvin
busetâni-st por gol o nasrin

The *Rowzat al-moznebin* of Ahmad-e Jâm
–that leviathan who swallows whole seas–
It's a sky shining with the moon and Pleiades
It's a garden full of roses and jonquils[79]

The work has been edited by 'Ali Fâzel in 1976 as *Rowzat al-moznebin va jannat al-moshtaqin* (Tehran: Bonyâd-e Farhang-e Iran, 1355).

5) *Behâr al-haqiqah* (Seas of Truth), a volume of eighteen chapters written in 1133 (527 A.H.). The work has never been published, but at least one manuscript of it exists in the possession of Hâji Qâzi Jâmi al-Ahmadi, dated 1963. Another manuscript was acquired from him by Hâjj Mohammad A'zam Jâmi al-Ahmadi.

It begins with the following open-minded pronouncements:

> There is no teaching which is not worth hearing or reading; but you read and hearken to this teaching and look to it with the eye of truth, that you may achieve your aim through this book. We have not composed this book for the sake of self-love or hypocrisy, and to express prejudice.
>
> I am eighty years old and I've spent my life in this work....
>
> I have heard that a certain group have criticized our books for errors of diction and grammar and they say that the Arabic is not properly vowelled. We make no claim to philology or Arabic grammar, on the principle that all of these are just the husk; if a person does not know the vowelling of Arabic and its grammar, it does not harm his faith in any way. Our claim is to know the principles of religion and gnostic truth....These words

---

[79] *Kolliyât-e Qâsem Anvâr*, ed. Sa'id Nafisi (Tehran: 1337/1958), 351. Dowlatshâh also records these lines in his *Tazkerat al-sho'arâ*, Leiden edition, 348.

are not the kind of thing just anyone can write or talk about; it all comes from divinely inspired knowledge.[80]

The following passage, which the *Kholâsat al-maqâmât* and the *Kashf al-zunûn* attribute to *Behâr al-haqiqa*, makes the same kind of claims with somewhat more bravado, illustrating the Shaykh's milieu as a non-academic religious teacher and popular preacher:[81]

> See how this tells of learning and [not] of lack of knowledge [*nâ-shenâkhtegi*]. Look into these writings, your own beliefs and those of others will be blown away. Many the gentleman and leader of religion will reflect upon these writings and know nothing of them. Then they say, "This is nothing, for we have not seen such teachings in any book or heard them anywhere." How could they have heard them?! Their hearts are not open to these teachings, that they should take root in them. What can they do? There are matters in these books which have never been mentioned by or occurred to any pretender to knowledge [*modda'i*].
>
> Just read whatever you can and get what you can from it. What you are not able to understand, just skip—do not trouble yourself or become mired in debate. If someone finds a matter in this book unclear at first reading, he should learn it better, until it becomes clear....
>
> In my books there are many innovative, meaningful ideas that you will not find elsewhere even if you search the world over. Wherever you talk about them, you will astound everyone. But they should be read carefully and then these teachings will have a practical effect on the reader. He should make them the collyrium of the eyes of true understanding (*ma'refat*) and they will lift him from the ocean floor to the dome of heaven.

---

[80] H. Moayyad's introduction to *Rowzat al-rayâhin*, 11, also "Eine wiedergefundene Schrift," *AIUO di Napoli* 1964: 264.

[81] *Kholâsat*, ed. Ivanow, op. cit., 349-50 and *Kashf al-zonun* of Hâjji Khalifeh (Egypt, 1311/1893), 1:182.

6) *Konuz al-hekmah* (Treasures of Wisdom), a volume of 20 chapters.[82] One manuscript of the *Konuz al-hekmah* surviving in the possession of the descendants of Shaykh Ahmad in Jâm and copied out by Mohammad Ebrâhim Jâmi al-Ahmadi dated 17 February 1962[83] begins with a brief exordium and the following explanation:

> This book was begun in the middle of Jomâdi al-âkhar in the year 533 A.H. [mid-February 1133] towards the end of the life of the Shaykh al-Islam, the exemplar of the saints...Abi Nasr Ahmad b. Abi al-Hasan al-Nâmaqi al-Jâmi...with the aid, confirmation, assistance and inspiration of God the Almighty and Praiseworthy concerning the knowledge of the secret mysteries of Lordship and divinely-bestowed knowledge, and good and evil and everything else that God, the Almighty and Praiseworthy has inspired in our heart. Everything that we say and have said here, we say through divine inspiration, and not on the basis of the sayings bruited about by every liar and braggart....We have named the book *Konuz al-hekmah*, and within it are plentiful pearls and gems for all to take....but in the first place, anyone wanting to look into this book must confess to five things...in order to derive benefit from this book: First, he must recognize God as divinity and know Him to be all-powerful, all-knowing, all-wise and perfect, and in no need of the deeds of His servants....[84]

At least two other manuscripts of the work survive, one in Herat, copied out in 1940 (1359 A.H.), and one in Tübingen, the date of which is effaced and illegible.[85]

---

[82] See *Kholâsat al-maqâmât*, ed. Ivanow, op. cit., 352.

[83] The lunar and solar dates on the manuscript do not match. The scribe gives 28 Bahman 1340 [= 17 February 1962], which he considers equivalent to 10 Ramadan 1382 [= 4 February 1963].

[84] Related in H. Moayyad's introduction to Darvish 'Ali Buzjâni, *Rowzat al-rayâhin* (Tehran: Bongâh-e Nashr va Tarjomeh-ye Ketâb, 1345/1966), 9; also in "Eine wiedergefundene Schrift," *AIUO di Napoli* 1964: 262-3.

[85] Fâzel, *Sharh-e ahvâl*, 468.

Copies of the preceding six books, and the poetry of Shaykh Ahmad, were widespread among Iranians in the fifteenth century (9th century A.H.),[86] but the following works were all lost in the Mongol invasions, according to the author of the *Kholâsat al-maqâmât*:

7) *Fotuh al-ruh* (Revelations to the Spirit).

8) *E'teqâd nâmeh* (Book of Creeds), one volume. This title does not appear in the catalog prepared by Shehâb al-Din Esma'il, the son of Shaykh Ahmad.

9) *Tazkirât* (Admonitions), a volume of sermons and admonitions.

10) *Fotuh al-qolub* (Revelations to the Heart), one volume.

11) *Zohdiyât*, a volume about asceticism.

The latter two books (10-11) are not mentioned in the *Kholâsat al-maqâmât*, but the *Spiritual Feats* (see Chapter Four, in Part One below) and Shehâb al-Din's *Epistle on the Greatness of his Father* (see Part Three, below) do name them.

12) *Resâleh-ye Samarqandiyeh* (The Epistle to the Samarqandians), containing the Shaykh's answers to various questions. The Persian text of this epistle is preserved in various manuscripts of the *Maqâmât* (see the section on "Manuscripts of the Spiritual Feats," below).

13) *Divân-e ash'âr*, the collected poems of the Shaykh, the authenticity of which is disputed. All of the sources speak of a *divân* of Shaykh Ahmad's poetry and manuscripts of a *divân* attributed to him are held in various collections. The so-called *Divân-e Hazrat-e Ahmad-e Jâm (Zhandeh Pil)* has been lithographed in Cawnpore, India (Nawal Kishore, 1326/1908) and frequently reprinted (5th printing, 1923). Wladimir Ivanow first

---

[86] See Mohammad-Taqi Dânesh-pazhuh for the chapter headings of each of the above-mentioned works in *Farhang-e Irânzamin* 16 (1348/1969): 240-325.

expressed doubt about the attribution of this *Divân* to Shaykh Ahmad in 1917,[87] and both Hellmut Ritter and Fritz Meier also suspected it to be a forgery.[88]

The likelihood that another poet took the pen name "Ahmad-e Jâm" or "Ahmadi" has to be seriously considered, for this would have been an effective way for descendants or disciples of Shaykh Ahmad to express their devotion to him and receive his blessings from the next world (linking the poem to the name or memory of a famous saint also increased the likelihood of its literary success). Many lines in the *Divân-e Hazrat-e Ahmad* published in Cawnpore, India, contain praise of Shaykh Ahmad-e Jâm in terms and with titles that the Shaykh never applied to himself. The poems with the pen name "Ahmad" or "Ahmadi" therefore seem to be the work of a later poet.[89] The Nawal Kishore edition of the *Divân-e Hazrat-e Ahmad* also contains a *qasideh* (60-62) with lines in praise of the poet Nezâmi and his *Khamseh*, a clear indication that at least this particular poem was composed after the death of Shaykh Ahmad, which occurred only the year after Nezâmi was born.

A conclusive judgement on this matter would first require a critical edition of the *divân* attributed to Ahmad-e Jâm on the basis of the existing manuscript exemplars. Ahmad Karami produced a commercial edition of the *Divân* of Shaykh Ahmad-e Jâm, using the text printed in Cawnpore along with another equally corrupt manuscript, but as this work was accomplished without any attention to editorial standards or the textual problems involved, it does nothing to resolve any of the above-mentioned difficulties.[90] Once a text-critical edition of the *divân* is made available, it would

---

[87] "A Biography of Shaykh Ahmad-i-Jam," *Journal of the Royal Asiatic Society* 1917, p. 305.

[88] Ritter, *Das Meer der Seele*, 482 and 489; Meier, "Ahmad-i Djām," in *Encyclopaedia of Islam*, 2nd edition.

[89] See Heshmat Moayyad's introduction to the Persian text of the *Maqâmât* (2nd ed.), 65, for an example of such poems.

[90] *Divân-e Shaykh Ahmad-e Jâm*, ed. Ahmad Karami ([Tehran]: Nashriyât-e Mâ, [1365/1986]. See the review by Heshmat Moayyad in *Irân Shenâsi* 2 (1990): 642-8. The editor has not contributed to the establishment of a critical text, but does at least acknowledge the need for a future, more suitable edition of Shaykh Ahmad's *Divân* (13).

have to be carefully compared with the works of other poets to determine if there are any quotations or cross-influences. For example, if lines or poems from Hâfez, Sa'di or 'Attâr are quoted or imitated in the *divân* ascribed to Ahmad, this would probably indicate that the poems in question are based upon a knowledge of these authors, and must therefore be the work of a later author. Indeed, many of the poems contained in the so-called *divân* of "Shaykh Ahmad" do resemble ghazals by later poets to such an extent that we are almost compelled to conclude that the author, whoever he was, was familiar with and quoted or imitated thirteen separate poems of 'Attâr and ten of Shâh Ne'mat Allâh Vali. One of the poems of "Ahmad" bears a close resemblance to a ghazal of Hâfez and at least four poems in the *divân* attributed to Ahmad are also to be found in the *Divân-e Kabir* of Rumi.[91]

Of course, it is not impossible that later poets have quoted from Shaykh Ahmad-e Jâm, but if he had been so famed and accomplished as a poet that 'Attâr, Hâfez and Rumi quoted from him, we would expect to find Shaykh Ahmad included prominently in the various histories and biographies of the poets. However, neither the fourteenth century works of Hamd Allâh Mostowfi nor the fifteenth century work of Dowlatshâh of Samarqand number him among the great poets, nor do his poems appear in dictionaries or literary anthologies. Ahmad's fame rests upon his reputation as a Sufi and none of the medieval authorities praise him as a poet.

Most of the lines of verse quoted by Shaykh Ahmad in the *Serâj al-sâ'erin* seem to be popular poems composed by others, which he has merely repeated without attribution to a specific author. Furthermore, not a single one of the lines of poetry which the medieval biographers and historians from the 16th century (10th century A.H.) onwards do attribute to Shaykh Ahmad occurs in the published *Divân* which goes under his name.[92] We cannot simply assume that one medieval authority quoted some of the poems of Shaykh Ahmad and subsequent writers all copied from

---

[91] For the details of the poems compared here, see Moayyad's introduction to the Persian text of the *Maqâmât-e Zhandeh Pil*, 56-64.

[92] Nor do any of these lines occur in a manuscript of the *Divân* of "Shaykh Ahmad" kept in the Library of the India Office, a microfilm of which was consulted by H. Moayyad.

this, since the later books include poems which the earlier authors do not mention. For example, the *Majma' al-fosahâ* (Gathering of the Eloquent) and the *Riâz al-'ârefin* (Gardens of the Gnostics) by Rezâ-Qoli Khân Hedâyat (1800-1871) quote two quatrains (*robâ'i*), one line and a two-line fragment (*qet'eh*) which do not occur in earlier sources, like the 16th century *Majâles al-'oshshâq* of Kamâl al-Din Hosayn Gâzorgâhi, the *Majâles al-mo'menin* of Sayyed Nur Allâh Shushtari (w. c1585-1602 / 993-1010 A.H.), *Haft Eqlim* of Amin Râzi (w. 1594 / 1002 A.H.) or the *Âtashkadeh* of Lotf-'Ali Beg Âzar (d. 1781 / 1195 A.H.). We may safely conclude, therefore, that these authors all had access to a *Divân* other than the printed one which now goes under Ahmad's name.

Another textual reason to doubt the authenticity of the published *divân* involves poems which reflect either ecstatic expressions (*shathiyât*) of the poetic persona's identification with the Godhead, or the school of thought of Ibn 'Arabi and his followers—*vahdat al-vojud*, or unity of being. These seem inconsistent with the views and beliefs of Shaykh Ahmad as portrayed in the *Maqâmât* and in other sources. Likewise, though Sufi poets commonly transformed the symbols of profane poetry, the praise of love (*'eshq*), wine and spring in many of the poems of the published *divân* attributed to Shaykh Ahmad seems incompatible with his strict pietistic outlook and his vehement prohibition of anything to do with wine.

This is not to suggest that Shaykh Ahmad never had a *divân* or never composed any poetry. Lines of verse are attributed to him in the *Maqâmât*, at least eight to nine lines of which are definitely his. Other sources have attributed two ghazals, several quatrains, a few fragments (*qet'eh*) and one independent line, fifty-two lines of verse all told, to Shaykh Ahmad. The eight-line ghazal related in the *Majâles al-mo'menin* and the *Rowzât al-jannât*, as well as the *robâ'i* in the latter book are not by Shaykh Ahmad, but were created by the authors of those two books to "prove" that Shaykh Ahmad was a Shiite. The nine-line ghazal in the *Majâles al-'oshshâq* with the pen name (*takhallos*) "Ahmad," along with everything else in that book, should be regarded with a skeptical eye.

One hopes that an authentic, relatively unadulterated manuscript of the Shaykh's *Divân* will one day turn up. In the meantime, a sample of one poem perhaps composed by Shaykh Ahmad will have to suffice:

chon tisheh ma-bâsh jomleh bar khvod ma-tarâsh
chon randeh ze kâr-e khvish bi-bahreh ma-bâsh
ta'lim ze arreh gir dar 'aql-e ma'âsh
chizi su-ye khvod mikesh o chizi mipâsh

Don't be an axe, chipping away at yourself
Don't be a plane, stripped of all your labor
Learn from the saw a reasonable life:
Keep some shavings and scatter the rest around[93]

THE FAMILY OF SHAYKH AHMAD

Few Sufis were fortunate to have such a large and influential family to preserve their memory and promote their teachings. The efforts of the Shaykh's family played no small role in bruiting about the fame of the "Colossal Elephant" of Jâm, Shaykh Ahmad-e Zhandeh Pil. The author of the *Kholâsat al-maqâmât* writes that by about 1435 (840 A.H.), that is three centuries after the death of Shaykh Ahmad, the descendants of just one of the Shaykh's fourteen sons numbered a thousand individuals all told, scattered throughout Jâm, Nayshabur, Bâkharz, Herat and two or three other locales.[94] Khanikoff repeats this and adds that even as late as the mid-19th century, the descendants of Shaykh Ahmad were still the most influential family in the region of Jâm.[95] The many surviving letters exchanged between descendants of Shaykh Ahmad and various rulers of Herat and other parts of Khorasan, testify to the influence and importance of the family over the course of a number of dynasties, especially during the Kart and Timurid era.[96] Shaykh Ahmad's descendants have maintained a

[93] From *Haft eqlim*, ed. Javâd Fâzel, 3 vols. (Tehran: Ketâbforushi-ye 'Ali-Akbar 'Elmi, n.d.), 2:178.

[94] See the text of the *Kholâsat al-maqâmât*, 11, as published in the *JRAS* 1918; or in the edition published at Qandahar (Mohammad Qâsem-e Kotobforush, 1956/1335), 18.

[95] Nicolas de Khanikoff, *Mémoire sur la partie méridionale de l'Asie Centrale* (Paris, 1861), 116.

[96] See Yusof-e Ahl, *Farâ'ed-e ghiâsi*, ed. H. Moayyad, op. cit.

constant sense of family identity going back all the way to the 12th century, one of the few Iranian families that can credibly trace their lineage in this manner.[97]

Ahmad married eight times and fathered thirty-nine sons and three daughters. Fourteen sons survived him at the time of his death, whose names are enumerated in Shehâb al-Din Esma'il's *Epistle on the Greatness of his Father* and in the *Kholâsat al-maqâmât*. One of those sons, Zahir al-Din 'Isâ, composed a book called *Serr al-badâye'* (The Mystery of Marvels) in 1181 (577 A.H.), which he dedicated to the Ghurid Sultan Ghiâs al-Din Mohammad (r. 1163-1203/558-599 A.H.). According to an account preserved in the *Kholâsat al-maqâmât* (ed. Ivanow, 354), Zahir al-Din 'Isâ was an acquaintance of Fakhr al-Din Râzi (d. 1209 / 606 A.H.), who held the former in great esteem. The youngest of these fourteen sons was Shehâb al-Din Esma'il who wrote the brief treatise on the greatness of Shaykh Ahmad, which appears in Part Three of this book.

Several of the descendants of Shaykh Ahmad achieved some fame and importance on their own, as described in various histories. Some accompanied the retinue of kings into battle, some acted as mediators to reconcile hostile parties and sometimes saved a town from plunder and its people from the sword. One of these, named Shehâb al-Din, lived in Delhi in the fourteenth century. Ibn Battûta refers to him as the son of the Shaykh of Jâm in Khorasan, though he must be several generations removed from Shaykh Ahmad.[98]

---

[97] Other Iranian families with a traceable history stretching back to pre-Mongol times would include Jalâl al-Din Rumi's descendants; however, by virtue of moving to Asia Minor and intermixing with local Turks from an early period, this family (the Chelebis) belongs more properly to the history of Turkish than Iranian genealogy. Among Iranians, the ability to trace a family history back to a historical figure of the Safavid-era (e.g., Majlesi, Fayz-e Kâshâni, etc.), is somewhat more common than a lineage which extends to the Mongol or pre-Mongol period.

[98] Ibn Battûta confuses the matter by calling Shaykh Ahmad "Shehâb al-Din Ahmad" and his grandson "Shaykh Ahmad" known as "Zâdeh" (probably a manuscript corruption of "Zhandeh"). That the "Shaykh Shehâb al-Din" mentioned by Ibn Battûta is, indeed, Shaykh Ahmad cannot be doubted, because the story told of the circumstances of his

In any case, by 1436 (840 A.H.) the Shaykh Ahmad's descendants numbered about 1000 souls in Jâm, Nayshabur, Herat and surrounding areas.[99] Ibn Battûta mentions that the city of Jâm was in the hands of the descendants of Shaykh Ahmad, who were quite wealthy and had an exemption from paying taxes to the Sultan.[100] The Shaykh Shehâb al-Din of Jâm, as described by Ibn Battûta, was a pious and retiring man, banished by the Delhi Sultan Mohammad b. Toghloq (r. 1320-1351 / 720-752 A.H.) for refusing to accept office and then executed several years later for calling the Sultan a tyrant.[101] Ibn Battûta himself fell under suspicion in 1341 for having visited the cave where Shehâb al-Din's retreat was.[102]

Mention should also be made of Shaykh Qotb al-Din al-Nâmaqi al-Jâmi, who apparently died in the middle of the fourteenth century. Jonayd-e Shirazi's *Shadd al-ezâr* mentions him as one of the teachers of Mowlânâ Mo'in al-Din Ahmad b. Abi al-Khayr, who wrote the *Shirâz nâmeh*. Though Mohammad Qazvini, the editor of *Shadd al-ezâr* (14th century), mentions in a note that he had not found information about Shaykh Qotb al-Din in any other source,[103] the *Târikh nâmeh-ye Herât* describes a certain Khvâjeh Qotb al-Din Jâmi who interceded with Malek Ghiâs al-Din Toghloq Shâh in 1320 (720 A.H.) for a prince who had fallen out of favor.[104] Sa'id Nafisi also mentions a contemporary of Shâh

---

repentance from wine-drinking resembles in its gist the story told in the *Maqâmât* (Story 1). It is not possible that the Shehâb al-Din of Jâm whom Ibn Battûta met in Delhi in 1334 was the grandson of the Shaykh Ahmad (d. 1141) or even his great grandson. It is possible that the "Shaykh al-Jâm al-Khorâsâni" refers as a title to the head of the shrine in Jâm, and Shehâb al-Din in Delhi was therefore the son of the caretaker of the shrine, and a descendant of Shaykh Ahmad. See *Rihlat Ibn Battûta* (Beirut: Dâr Bayrût, 1985), 387-8 and 472.

[99] H. Moayyad, "Ahmad Jâm," *Encyclopaedia Iranica*.

[100] *Rihla*, 387. See the translation by H.A.R. Gibb, *The Travels of Ibn Battûta*, vol. 3 (London: Hakluyt Society, 1971), 580-81.

[101] *Rihlat*, 472-3; Gibb's translation, 697-700.

[102] *Rihla*, 528; Gibb's translation, 765-6.

[103] Mo'in al-Din Abu al-Qâsem Jonayd-e Shirâzi, *Shadd al-ezâr fî hatt al-owzâr 'an zavvâr al-mazâr*, ed. Mohammad Qazvini and 'Abbâs Eqbâl (Tehran, 1328/1949), 317 and 317n3.

[104] Sayf b. Mohammad b. Ya'qub-e Heravi, *Târikh nâmeh-ye Herât*

Qâsem Anvâr by the name of Khvâjeh Qotb al-Din Abu al-Fazl
Yahyâ Jâmi, born in Nayshabur to a family from Jâm, who died in
Herat in the year 1339 or 1340 (740 A.H.).[105] Quite likely, the
Qotb al-Din Jâmis mentioned in these three sources refer to a
single individual, obviously a scholar and mystic, who enjoyed
influence and respect at the royal court.[106]

Little is known about the contemporary practices of the
followers and descendants of Ahmad-e Jâm. Though the Shaykh's
tomb is in Torbat-e Jâm, the family's spiritual center is now in
Howz-e Karyâs near Herat, where the head (khalifeh) of the
family was residing in 1968.[107] As recently as 1974, local singers
in the area of Herat were recording verse prayers beseeching
Shaykh Ahmad for intercession and assistance.[108] Despite the fact
that his descendants kept his name alive and maintained his tomb
as a place of worship, the family and followers of Shaykh Ahmad
do not seem to have ever formed an order along the lines of the
Soharvardi Order, the Mevlevi Order, the Cheshti Order, and so
on. Perhaps the fact that no formal order or ritual praxis, other
than the visitation of Shaykh Ahmad's tomb, ever developed
around Shaykh Ahmad can account for the emphasis on saintly
miracles and marvels and the relative unimportance of speculative
theosophy.

The Influence of Shaykh Ahmad in India

Thanks to his descendants, Shaykh Ahmad also enjoyed great
repute in India for centuries after his death, though it is not clear
how or precisely when his family connections with the Moghul
court were established. As mentioned above, a descendant of the

---

(Calcutta: Khan Bahadur K.M. Asadullah, 1944), 772-3. Reprinted
Tehran: Golshan, 1974.

[105] See the introduction to Kolliyât-e Qâsem Anvâr, ed. Nafisi, op.
cit., 99. Jâmi also gives an account of this individual in Nafahât al-ons
ed. Mehdi Towhidipur (Tehran: Mahmud, 1336/1958), 577-78.

[106] For Qotb al-Din, see Rowzat al-rayâhin, 149-50.

[107] Moayyad, "Ahmad Jâm," Encyclopaedia Iranica.

[108] A compact disc The Traditional Music of Herat in the UNESCO
Collection (Gentilly, France: Auvidis/Unesco, 1996) includes a song
from Torbat-e Jâm called "Shaykh Ahmad-e Jâm," sung by Abdu'l-
Sha'er in Herat in 1974, accompanying himself on dotar.

Shaykh by the name of Shehâb al-Din lived in Delhi in the first half of the fourteenth century and was pressed into service at the court of Shah Toghloq, but was later executed. A few centuries later, however, the descendants of Shaykh Ahmad were on more intimate terms with royalty. Supposedly Timur (r. 1370-1405) and his son Shâhrokh (r. 1405-46), as well as the Safavid Shâh 'Abbâs (r. 1581-1629) visited his grave and helped construct the shrine complex. But it is among the Moghuls that Shaykh Ahmad's descendants became closest to royalty, according to the *Homâyun nâmeh* of Golbadan Begom, the sister of Shah Nâser al-Din Homâyun. Not only this work, but also the *Akbar nâmeh* of Abu al-Fazl and the *Târikh-e Send* of Mir Ma'sum Bhakari (d. 1610), indicate that both Mâham Begom, the wife of Bâbor (r. 1526-30) and the mother of Homâyun, and Hamideh Bânu, nicknamed Maryam Makâni, the wife of Homâyun and the mother of Akbar, were descendants of Shaykh Ahmad.

This makes the two great rulers of Moghul India, Homâyun (r. 1531-1540 and 1555-56) and Akbar (r. 1556-1605), descendants of Shaykh Ahmad on their mother's side.[109] When Homâyun was defeated in 1543 (950 A.H.) in a battle with Shêr-Shâh-e Afghâni, he fled to Iran, wandering for a while from city to city. In Khorasan, he made a pilgrimage to the shrine of Shaykh Ahmad in Jâm, where he composed the following poem and had it inscribed in marble around the perimeter of the shrine on 29 December 1544:[110]

> *ay rahmat-e to 'ozr-pazir-e hameh kas*
> *zâher be jenâb-e to zamir-e hameh kas*
> *dargâh-e to qebleh-gâh-e hameh khalq*
> *lotf-at be kereshmeh dastgir-e hameh kas*

---

[109] *Homâyun nâmeh*, Persian text with English translation by Annette S. Beveridge (London, 1902). Cf. the article "Humāyūn" in the first edition of the *Encyclopaedia of Islam*, which describes Hamideh Bânu as a descendant of Shaykh Ahmad, though the article on "Akbar" in the second edition simply indicates she was Iranian. Although there was some doubt at the beginning of the 20th century about the lineage of the mothers of Homâyun and Akbar, the matter is really no longer in question.

[110] Ney Elias, "Notice of an Inscription at Turbat-i-Jām in Khorasan about Half-way between Meshed and Herat," *JRAS* 1897, p. 47.

You whose mercy accepts penitence from all
who manifests the hidden thoughts of all
whose threshold is the point of prayer for all
with a wink your kindness lends a hand to all

– A wanderer in the never-ending wilderness,
Mohammad Homâyun, 14 Shavvâl in the year 951

Other famous figures in the history of Muslim India who came from the line of Shaykh Ahmad were the Prince Mohammad Dârâ Shokuh (b. 1615), the eldest son of Shâh Jahân and brother of Aurangzebe, who wrote the book *Safinat al-owliâ*,[111] and a number of short treatises, the *Majma' al-bahrayn*,[112] the *Hasanât al-'ârefin*[113] as well as the *Serr-e akbar*, a Persian translation of parts of the Upanishads,[114] all before being executed in the year 1659 (1069 A.H.) at a relatively young age. At least parts of Dârâ Shokuh's *Divân*, known as "The Greatest Elixir," *Eksir-e a'zam*, have been published.[115]

There is also the poet Hejri. Badâ'uni describes him as a poet who composed a *divân* of about 5000 lines during the reign of

---

[111] *Safinat al-owliâ* (Lucknow: Nawal Kishore, 1872; reprinted Lahore 1884 and Cawnpore, 1900).

[112] *Majma' al-bahrayn*, ed. Mohammad Rezâ Jalâli-ye Nâ'ini (Tehran: Noqreh, 1366/1987), a short treatise on the relations between Hinduism and Islam. An English translation was done by M. Mahfuz-ul-Haq as *Majma-ul-bahrain, or, The Mingling of the Two Oceans* (Calcutta: Asiatic Society, 1929; reprint 1982), and a French translation by Dâryush Shâyegân as *Les Relations de l'Hindouisme et du Sufisme* (Paris: Editions de la Différence, 1979).

[113] *Hasanât al-'ârefin*, ed. Makhdum Rahbun (Tehran: Vismân, 1352/1973). An English translation was done by Pandit Sheo Narain in the *Journal of Panjab Historical Society* 2 (1913-14): 28ff.

[114] ed. Mohammad-Rezâ Jalâli-Nâ'ini (Tehran: Tabân, 1340/1961).

[115] Zafar Hasan, "Manuscript Copy of the Divân of Dârâ Shikûh," *Journal of the Asiatic Society of Bengal* 3/5 (1939): 155-73; also *Divân-e Dârâ Shekuh*, ed. Ahmad Nabi Khân (Lahore: Research Society of Pakistan, University of the Panjab, 1969).

Akbar.[116] A manuscript of his *Divân* is owned by the India Office Library.[117]

GHAZNAVI'S *MAQÂMÂT*: *THE SPIRITUAL FEATS OF AHMAD-E JÂM*

The present work contains the earliest surviving sources about Shaykh Ahmad of Jâm. Sadid al-Din Mohammad ebn Musâ ebn Ya'qub-e Ghaznavi, an Imam, or religious leader, in Ghazna, with students and a following of his own authored/compiled the first work presented here, *The Spiritual Feats of Ahmad-e Jâm*. Mohammad-e Ghaznavi must have been born in the beginning of the 12th century. He first met Shaykh Ahmad, as he describes in the Exordium (and in Chapter Five), on his way from Ghazna to a pilgrimage in Mecca, accompanied by some of his own disciples. When they arrived in Jâm, Ghaznavi thought to himself that it would be interesting to see Shaykh Ahmad, whose fame had been bruited far and wide. As Mohammad-e Ghaznavi entered the *khâneqâh* of Shaykh Ahmad, one of his sons was preaching a sermon. Ghaznavi witnessed a number of miracles and fell under the spell of Shaykh Ahmad, to the extent that he forgot about his (obligatory) pilgrimage to Mecca, instead taking up residence at the *khâneqâh* in Jâm as a disciple of the Shaykh. He did return seven times to his native Ghazna, but each time he came back to be with the Shaykh, as he could not find peace anywhere else.

Other than this, we have little information about the life of Mohammad-e Ghaznavi. He once fell very ill and was cured by the prayers of the Shaykh (Story 32). Once he wanted to go to Ghazna, but the Shaykh did not consent. Mohammad was afflicted by an eye ailment which lasted for two years until the prayers of the Shaykh healed him (Story 35). Mohammad had a brother, who was held captive for a time by Afghans (Story 123). We know neither his date of birth nor date of death, but the *Spiritual Feats* implies that he lived a long life, as much as a hundred years.

---

[116] 'Abd al-Qâder Badâ'uni, *Montakhab al-tavârikh* (Calcutta, 1896), 3:386. English translation by George S. A. Ranking (Calcutta: Asiatic Society of Bengal, 1898-1925; reprinted Karachi: Karimsons, 1976-78).

[117] Ethé, *Catalogue of the Persian Manuscripts in the Library of the India Office*, 793.

Date of Composition of *The Spiritual Feats*

Mohammad-e Ghaznavi began composing the *Spiritual Feats* shortly after meeting the Shaykh Ahmad, while the latter was still alive. The fact that most people did not believe in the miracles of Shaykh Ahmad occasionally led Ghaznavi to despair of writing the book. But Shaykh Ahmad encouraged Ghaznavi to continue and gave a first-hand account of his initial repentance from wine-drinking and his period of hermitage and the early events of his career. Ghaznavi's notes apparently remained scattered and incomplete for a couple decades after the death of the Shaykh in 1141 (536 A.H.). At one point in the narrative, Ghaznavi writes:

> The Shaykh al-Islam then spoke these words, "You will be graciously blessed in both worlds."
> It is now nearly twenty years that I am enjoying the blessing and riches of God, and I have never needed to take provisions on any journey. The first half has been fulfilled, hopefully the second half will also be taken care of –God, the Almighty, willing.

If we assume that Mohammad-e Ghaznavi first met the Shaykh five or six years before the latter's death—that is, in about 1135 or 1136 (530 A.H.), and that Shaykh Ahmad made this remark in the beginning of their association, the sentence above would have been written around the year 1155 (550 A.H.), or about fourteen years after the death of the Shaykh. The phrase "may his dominion last forever," applied to Sultan Sanjar in Story 117, tends to confirm this judgement; Sanjar died in 1157 (552 A.H.) and since this phrase indicates Sanjar was still alive at the time of writing, the passage must have been recorded before 1157.

Though these two passages, along with several stories from the wives and companions of the Shaykh, point toward a date of composition prior to the year 1157 (552 A.H.), there are two other passages indicative of a much later date of composition. In Story 134 we read the following:

> Khvâjeh Imam Zahir-e Bayhaqi, may God have mercy on him, was one of the famous scholars of Islam and a prominent philosopher in his day, and the author of a

Koran commentary. Some thirty-odd years after the
death of the Shaykh al-Islam, he became a believer.

This passage must obviously have been recorded some thirty years
after the death of Shaykh Ahmad. In the introduction to *The
Spiritual Feats*, we meet with the names of several famous
scholars and books, including the *Khâlesat al-haqâ'eq* of 'Emâd
al-Din Fâryâbi (d. 1210 / 607 A.H.), which was completed in 1201
(597 A.H.). On this basis, Fritz Meier concluded that *The Spiritual
Feats* must have been written circa 1205 (that is, about 600 A.H.).

The *Spiritual Feats* of Shaykh Ahmad, being primarily a
collection of miracle stories, does not compare with earlier
hagiographies, such as the *Asrâr al-towhid*, the *Ferdows al-
morshediyeh* or the *Sirat* of Ibn Khafif in terms of the information
it provides on the philosophy and theory of Sufism. It is not
unlikely that the introductory chapters (Chapters One through
Five) were added to *The Spiritual Feats* at a later date in order to
buttress the miracle stories by distinguishing between the types of
miracles with verses of the Qur'ân and hadith, as was common in
earlier works on Sufism. If we accept that Mohammad-e Ghaznavi
added these chapters, he must have lived to be at least a hundred
years of age. Since he already had students or followers in about
the year 1136 (530 A.H.) when he first met Shaykh Ahmad,
Ghaznavi could not have been a youth, but must have been thirty
years old or more. It is, of course, not impossible that he lived this
long, but it does seem difficult to accept that a committed disciple
would wait for more than sixty years—until he was over the age of
one hundred—to complete a work about his master which he
began when that master was still alive and at that master's
direction.

It is perhaps easier to explain the matter with a different
hypothesis, namely that parts of the introductory chapters, at least
the passage concerning the *Khâlesat al-haqâ'eq* were added by a
later hand, probably another disciple of Shaykh Ahmad, or one of
his descendants. A similar phenomenon can be observed in the
case of the Treatise (*Resâleh*) of Faridun ebn Sepahsâlâr, written
about Jalâl al-Din Rumi; evidently the initial recension of that
book was composed as early as 1295 and certainly no later than
1320, but several pages were added to it as much as eighteen years
later, probably by Sepahsâlâr's son. In the case of the *Manâqeb al-*

'ârefîn of Shams al-Din Aflâki (d. 1360), perhaps the most famous medieval hagiography of a Sufi saint, we know Aflâki began collating the oral reports circulating about Rumi in 1318, but continued to expand and revise the work throughout his life, not completing the final recension until almost forty years later, in 1354.[118]

In any case, it is evident that Mohammad-e Ghaznavi began the composition of *The Spiritual Feats of Shaykh Ahmad* during the lifetime of the Shaykh, by collecting the stories which circulated orally among the disciples living near the Shaykh. Eventually, Ghaznavi added reports of others, some of them no doubt in the form of written notebooks. Perhaps the work was nearly in its final form by about the year 1175 (570 A.H.). If the introduction was indeed added at a later date, then we can presume a somewhat more typical lifespan for Ghaznavi.

Style of Ghaznavi's *The Spiritual Feats*
Mohammad-e Ghaznavi's narrative frequently preserves the colloquial elements of speech in the accounts it records, and generally conforms to the simpler style of Persian prose of the 11th and 12th centuries, before the vogue for intricate and even Gongorist wordplay along with an over-reliance on pedantry and Arabic derivations took over. *The Spiritual Feats* does not employ rhymed prose (*saj'*) nor does it delight in the juxtaposition of synonyms, both of these devices being common features of many works of Persian prose from the 13th and subsequent centuries. The sentences tend to be short and communicate directly, and move along in a fairly effective dramatic narrative, though the text is littered with pious phrases like most religious texts of the medieval period. Ghaznavi's work also preserves many rare or even unique words and expressions, a few of them in dialect form.

Manuscripts of *The Spiritual Feats*
In 1938 Hellmut Ritter discovered the first complete manuscript of this work in the Nâfiz Pâshâ Library in Istanbul (#399). Written in a medium-sized nasta'liq script[119] with 17 lines to the page, this

---

[118] See Lewis, *Rumi: Past and Present*, op. cit., Chapter Six.

[119] For the nasta'liq script, see William Hanaway and Brian Spooner, *Reading Nasta'liq: Persian and Urdu Hands from 1500 to the Present*

copy of the *Maqâmât* (*Spiritual Feats*) in 156 folios, is dated Rajab 825 (June/July 1422). The text actually begins with the *Resâleh-ye Samarqandiyeh* (*Epistle to the Samarqandians*) of Shaykh Ahmad (which appears in translation here in Part Four), with the text of the *Maqâmât* beginning on page 38b and concluding on page 132b. The final 24 pages of the manuscript contain two treatises, the first by the youngest son of the Shaykh, Shehâb al-Din Esma'il, and the second by one of his descendants, as well as more of the *Resâleh-ye Samarqandiyeh* (*Epistle to the Samarqandians*).

The script of this manuscript can be read without difficulty, though some words are obscured because of fading ink or holes in the paper. The occasional inattention of the scribe in copying or pointing the text sometimes make deciphering the text problematic. His spelling is inconsistent, particularly with respect to less well-known toponyms—Sâroqcheh sometimes appears as Sâroghcheh (Story 104); Amqân sometimes as Am'ân and sometimes as Amghân (Stories 19, 57, 71, 99); Sâghu sometimes as Sâghun (Stories 17 and 45). The scribe sometimes leaves out a few words or perhaps even whole sentences (e.g., Stories 84, 105, 143).

The orthography of the Persian text follows various conventions frequently seen in older manuscripts. Many words are written without dots throughout the text. The elongated initial *alef* (â) is consistently written without the *madda*, even on words like *âb* or *ân*. The *ezâfeh* following words ending in *alef* is written with *hamzeh* and the indefinite marker (i) is also written after final silent *he* as a *hamzeh*.

Another manuscript in the Preussische Staatsbibliothek of Berlin (Ms. Or. oct. 3784) provides a part of Ghaznavi's collection, from Story 148 through Story 180, plus an additional four stories that were not in the Nâfiz Pâshâ manuscript. This Berlin manuscript begins with several letters exchanged between the descendants of Shaykh Ahmad and the religious scholars and notables of their day, followed by the stories of the *Maqâmât*, the *Treatise* by Shehâb al-Din Esma'il and the two parts of the Shaykh Ahmad's *Epistle to the Samarqandians (Resâleh-ye Samarqandiyeh).*

(Costa Mesa, CA: Mazda, 1995); see also the article "Calligraphy" by Yusofi in the *Encyclopaedia Iranica.*

The first edition of the Persian text of *The Spiritual Feats* was based upon collation and comparison of the Nâfiz Pâshâ and Preussische Staatsbibliothek manuscripts.[120] Subsequently, the existence of a much larger manuscript by this name in the Chester Beatty Library in Dublin (Ms. 352) was made known,[121] a codex of 15 x 23.5 centimeters containing 153 folios with 15 lines to the page in nasta'liq script. On the first page of the text, two seals, probably placed on the title page as the manuscript came into the possession of various owners, provide the acquisition dates of 1650 (1060 A.H.) and 1664 (1074 A.H.). The name of the scribe and the date of the copy are not given, but on the basis of the script, the paper and the style of the opening rubric, it is estimated to have been written out in about 1570.

The Chester Beatty Library manuscript of the *Spiritual Feats* contains more than twice as many stories as the Nâfiz Pâshâ manuscript. Although the Chester Beatty manuscript identifies the work as the *Spiritual Feats* of Mohammad-e Ghaznavi, it is likely that many of these stories are taken from one of the other collections of Shaykh Ahmad's miracles mentioned in the *Kholâsat al-maqâmât* and now lost (see below, "Sources of Our Knowledge about Shaykh Ahmad"). We know this both because this manuscript contains so much more material than the Nâfiz Pâshâ manuscript of the work, and because certain stories reflect that they were written after the death of Ghaznavi. For example, Story 298 mentions Ghaznavi in the third person and cannot have been written by him. Even more telling, Story 244 is introduced with the phrase, "Mohammad-e Ghaznavi, God's mercy on him, related that..." In the Chester Beatty manuscript, this story follows Story 125, which along with Stories 122 through 124 name Mohammad-e Ghaznavi in the third person as their source. This strongly suggests that, even in the much shorter Nâfiz Pâshâ manuscript, some stories have been added after the death of Mohammad-e Ghaznavi.

---

[120] *Maqâmât-e Zhandeh Pil*, ed. H. Moayyad (Tehran: Bongâh-e Tarjomeh va Nashr-e Ketâb, 1340/1961).
[121] A.J. Arberry, B.W. Robinson, E. Blochet, J.V.S. Wilkinson, *The Chester Beatty Library: A Catalogue of Persian Manuscripts and Miniatures*, volume 3, Mss. 221-398 (Dublin, 1962).

Furthermore, Story 384 in Part Two (on the Posthumous Miracles of the Shaykh), which comes from the manuscript of the Chester Beatty Library, is also attributed by Darvish 'Ali-ye Buzjâni in *Rowzat al-rayâhin* to one of the other compilers of the miracles of Shaykh Ahmad. Buzjâni (59) introduces it with the phrase, "Imam Razi al-Din Jamâl al-Islam Tâybâdi has related...." This figure compiled his own collections of miracles of the Shaykh, to which Ghaznavi apparently had access (see "Sources of our Knowledge about Shaykh Ahmad," below). Buzjâni describes this Tâybâdi as one of the successors of the Shaykh and relates seven anecdotes on the authority of Tâybâdi.[122] Although these stories do not appear in the Nâfiz Pâshâ manuscript of Ghaznavi's *Spiritual Feats*, six of them do appear in the Chester Beatty Library manuscript. In addition to these six tales told on the authority of Tâybâdi, the Chester Beatty manuscript also relates seven other tales on the authority of Tâybâdi (Stories 197-99, 202-204 and 207 in Chapter Seven of the present collection). A further ten stories attributed to Ostâd Imam 'Ali (Stories 271-280) in the Chester Beatty manuscript, most probably also come from this same Imam Razi al-Din 'Ali-ye Tâybâdi. The Chester Beatty manuscript also attributes stories 168 and 169 to this Razi al-Din 'Ali ebn-e Ebrâhim ebn-e Elyâs-e Tâybâdi, whereas the Nâfiz Pâshâ manuscript does not specifically mention his name.

All together, then, the manuscript of the *Spiritual Feats* in the Chester Beatty Library relates twenty-seven anecdotes on the authority of Razi al-Din Jamâl al-Islam Tâybâdi, though the Nâfiz Pâshâ manuscript explicitly names him as the source of only one of these and relates two others without mentioning his name.

The Nâfiz Pâshâ manuscript also relates two stories (Story 138 and 139) on the authority of a certain Imam Shams al-Din, but the Chester Beatty manuscript relates a further eleven stories (Story 311 through 321) from this Shams al-Din. Another figure, 'Ali of Yahyâbâd, ha also written down his reminiscences of Shaykh Ahmad, for we read in the beginning of Story 301 that:

> Khvâjeh 'Ali of Yahyâbâd recounts in his own scrapbook [*safineh*] that....

---

[122] *Rowzat al-rayâhin*, 36.

Eight or nine stories by this 'Ali were incorporated either by Mohammad-e Ghaznavi or by later scribes.

Based on all of this, we may conclude that Mohammad-e Ghaznavi had access to a number of scrapbooks and collections of miracle stories compiled by the followers of Shaykh Ahmad. He included some stories from these along with other materials he had heard or witnessed himself in compiling his *Spiritual Feats of Shaykh Ahmad.*

The scribe of the Chester Beatty manuscript also had access to a number of the same sources used by Ghaznavi and quoted many more stories from them than Ghaznavi himself had. However, since the objective was to collect as many stories as possible about the miracles of Shaykh Ahmad in one volume, the scribe did not much care whether they had come from Ghaznavi's text or from other sources. This seems the only satisfactory explanation for how an exemplar of the work dated 1422 (825 A.H.) could have 180 stories, while another exemplar of the same work copied only about 150 years later, around 1570 A.D., could have 365 stories. Indeed, if we include the *Posthumous Miracles of the Shaykh*, the Chester Beatty manuscript relates all told 191 stories more than the Nâfiz Pâshâ manuscript.

Even the Chester Beatty Library manuscript does not contain all of the stories from all written sources about Shaykh Ahmad, as the Preussische Staatsbibliothek manuscript contains four stories (Stories 181 through 184) found neither in the Nâfiz Pâshâ nor the Chester Beatty manuscripts, and the *Rowzat al-rayâhin* has even more. The scribe of the Chester Beatty manuscript, wishing to make a compendium of the miracles of Shaykh Ahmad, perhaps included whatever stories he could find, without noting, or perhaps without knowing, that not all of them belonged to the work of Mohammad-e Ghaznavi.

The present translation is based upon the revised and expanded critical edition of the Persian text of the *Maqâmât-e Zhandeh Pil (Spiritual Feats)* edited by Heshmat Moayyad and published in Tehran by the Foundation for Translation and Publication of Books in 1967, which collates all three of the above-mentioned manuscripts and provides the only text-critical edition of the work.

SOURCES OF OUR KNOWLEDGE ABOUT SHAYKH AHMAD

As we have seen, *The Spiritual Feats of Shaykh Ahmad* was written and compiled some time between about 1135 and 1175, with an introduction probably added to it a quarter century later. A number of other works, some of them now lost, also deal directly with the life of Shaykh Ahmad. For example, it would appear that Ghaznavi consulted at least one written collection of miracles about the Shaykh, to which he alludes in Story 173:

> Khvâjeh Imam Razi al-Din Jamâl al-Eslâm 'Ali Ebn-e Ebrâhim-e Elyâs Tâybâdi, God have mercy upon him, has related the following miracles and divided them in three categories: those he has heard from the Shaykh al-Islam, those which he witnessed himself and third, those which he heard narrated by reliable followers of the Shaykh and by the pious leaders of religion.

This Elyâs-e Tâybâdi was evidently deceased when Ghaznavi wrote his own account, as the pious formula "God have mercy upon him" suggests. Unfortunately, Ghaznavi does not tell us what other stories, if any, he took directly from this source, and no copy of the work is known to exist.

Ahmad-e Tarkhestâni's *Posthumous Miracles of Shaykh Ahmad*

We know of two other early works about Shaykh Ahmad. The first of these is the *Maqâmât* of Ahmad-e Tarkhestâni, reputedly one of the leading saints of his age. According to the *Kholâsat al-maqâmât*, Tarkhestâni was from an area later known as the Slope of Jâm (*shib-e Jâm*), and had met the famous Abu Sa'id-e Abu al-Khayr,[123] though this seems extremely unlikely since Abu Sa'id died in 1049 whereas Tarkhestâni outlived Shaykh Ahmad, who died in 1141. Whatever Tarkhestâni's stature, he eventually devoted himself to Shaykh Ahmad of Jâm and composed a book of miracles that he had personally observed the Shaykh perform, both while alive on this earth and from the heavenly realm after

---

[123] *Kholâsat al-maqâmât*, ed. Ivanow, op. cit., 347.

his death. If this work had survived intact it would be an extremely important source to compare with Ghaznavi's *Spiritual Feats*, since both Ghaznavi and Tarkhestâni were apparently contemporaries and companions of Shaykh Ahmad, and it would be extremely interesting to know if their accounts corroborate one another as to various historical incidents described here.

Unfortunately Tarkhestâni's work has not been preserved in tact as an independent work, but survives only in excerpts as an appendix to Ghaznavi's work. Ghaznavi may well have drawn on and incorporated anecdotes from Tarkhestâni's collection into his *Spiritual Feats*, but if so, he did not indicate the source. However, some of the posthumous miracles of Shaykh Ahmad related here (Stories 370 through 386) would appear to be taken directly from the now lost text of Tarkhestâni. However, at least some of these seventeen stories also include later additions that cannot have been written by Tarkhestâni, such as Story 381 (see Part Two, below).

Other Works on Shaykh Ahmad
Tâj al-Din Mahmud-e Buzjâni wrote a second work on Shaykh Ahmad. The date of composition is not known, and the work is now presumably lost to posterity, but it survived as an independent work at least until the 15th century. Quite likely, both Buzjâni and Tarkhestâni's books were made obsolete by both Ghaznavi's *Spiritual Feats*, and a later collection of miracles entitled the *Kholâsat al-maqâmât*, and have disappeared forever. Of course, we cannot rule out the possibility that copies will yet turn up in the uncatalogued Persian manuscripts held in various public or private collections and repositories throughout the Middle East, Central Asia and South Asia; estimates are that several tens of thousand manuscripts survive in Iran, and as many as 50,000 to 100,000 Persian manuscripts in Turkey, the titles of which have never been noted in any union catalogues.

Among surviving sources on the life of Shaykh Ahmad, the *Kholâsat al-maqâmât*, or "Abridgement of the Spiritual Feats," is second in importance only to the *Spiritual Feats* of Mohammad-e Ghaznavi. The "Abridgement of the Spiritual Feats" was written in 1436 or 1437 (840 A.H.) by Abu al-Makârem ebn ʿAlâ al-Molk of Jâm, a descendant of Shaykh Ahmad whom Jâmi mentions in the notice on Shams al-Din Mohammad-e Kusavi in *Nafahât al-*

The Colossal Elephant and His Spiritual Feats

ons.[124] The Russian scholar Wladimir Ivanow discovered a defective and mistake-riddled copy of this manuscript in Bokhara and published it with an English introduction in 1917.[125] Ivanow subsequently discovered a better manuscript of the work[126] and published an article about it in 1922. A lithographed edition was published at Lahore in Rajab 1335 (April-May 1917) with the support of a certain Hâjji 'Abd al-Ghaffâr Khân and Shams al-Din, the son of Ziâ al-Din al-Jâmi al-Ahmadi, obviously followers and/or descendants of Shaykh Ahmad, and distributed through the bookseller Mohammad-e Qâsem in Qandahar, Afghanistan.[127]

Though the *Kholâsat al-maqâmât* is primarily, as its title suggests, an abridgement of Ghaznavi's *Spiritual Feats*, Abu al-Makârem also had access to a number of other sources, including works of the Shaykh, from which it quotes several passages. It also includes some stories and lines of verse not found in Ghaznavi's *Spiritual Feats*, such as the following quatrain:

Soon and suddenly will the drum sound our demise
all men will say (that regal Bestâmi, to boot):
As much as all of mankind dread the fires of hell,
so much is hell afraid of Shaykh Ahmad of Jâm![128]

---

[124] *Nafahât*, ed. Towhidipur, op. cit., 497. Ma'sum-'Ali Shâh, the Nâyeb al-Sadr, also gives a short notice on what must be the same figure, Khvâjeh Shehâb al-Din Abu al-Makârem, whose lineage goes back [*be shesh vâseteh*] to Ahmad-e Jâmi of Nâmaq. He indicates that the author of the *Habib al-seyar* claims that one side of his own family line traces back to this Abu al-Makârem (see *Tarâ'eq*, ed. Mahjub, 1:70).

[125] Wladimir Ivanow, "A Biography of Shaykh Ahmad-e Jâm," *JRAS* 1917: 308-65.

[126] See the *Catalogue of Persian Manuscripts in the Library of the Asiatic Society of Bengal*, vol. 1, no. 245.

[127] See the critical reviews of this work by Mo'ayyad-e Sâbeti in *Sokhan* #6, v10 (Shahrivar 1338/August 1959) and by Taqi Binesh in *Nâmeh-ye Âstâneh-ye Qods-e Razavi* 1 (Tir 1339/July 1960).

[128] Ghaznavi's *Maqâmât*, 2nd ed., 351, citing *Kholâsat al-maqâmât*, Lahore ed., 52. "That regal Bestâmi" is an allusion to the visionary Iranian mystic Bâyazid-e Bestâmi.

The fifty some pages of the *Kholâsat al-maqâmat* are divided into eight chapters, treating the genealogy of the Shaykh, the teachers of the Shaykh, the Shaykh's wives and sons, the dates and career of Shaykh Ahmad (19-22), the early miracles of the Shaykh (22-35, mostly following Ghaznavi), the miracles in Sarakhs (35-45), in Nayshabur and other places (45-51).

It is from the *Kholâsat al-maqâmât* that we know about the above-mentioned accounts of Tarkhestâni and Taj al-Din Mahmud-e Buzjâni, and from them the *Kholâsat al-maqâmât* sometimes provides details that are not found in Ghaznavi's *Spiritual Feats*. Another advantage of the "Abridgement" is its organization of disparate material into thematic categories and chapters, and the fact that it provides further detailed information about the family of the Shaykh and his sons.

In 1523 (929 A.H.) Darvish 'Ali Buzjâni wrote the last major medieval work on Shaykh Ahmad that has survived to us, the *Rowzat al-rayâhin*, some ninety years after Abu al-Makârem's "Abridgement" and over three centuries after Ghaznavi's *Spiritual Feats*. The *Rowzat al-rayâhin*, or "Garden of Sweet Herbs," is a family history, a kind of literary coat of arms for the Jâmi al-Ahmadi family. The second part of the work provides a genealogy of the family through biographies of 36 of the children and later descendants of Shaykh Ahmad. The first part provides a biography of Shaykh Ahmad, including several miracle stories about Shaykh Ahmad, most of them already found in Ghaznavi's *Spiritual Feats*, though the reports collected by Buzjâni not infrequently reflect differences of detail. For this reason, comparison of Buzjâni's "Garden of Sweet Herbs" with Ghaznavi's *Spiritual Feats*, provides instructive documentation on the interaction between oral and written accounts over time, and the growth of the legend of the Colossal Elephant, Shaykh Ahmad. The Persian text of Buzjâni's *Rowzat al-rayâhin* was published with an introduction and notes in 1966;[129] footnotes in the present translation refer the reader to similar miracle stories related in the *Rowzat al-rayâhin*.

---

[129] ed. Heshmat Moayyad (Tehran: Bongâh-e Tarjomeh va Nashr-e Ketâb, 1345/1966).

Shaykh Ahmad in the Medieval Dictionaries and Chronicles
Of course, in addition to these works devoted exclusively to
Shaykh Ahmad, a number of biographical dictionaries of poets,
Sufi saints or men of religion also mention Shaykh Ahmad and/or
his descendants, as do some local histories. Most of them take
their information directly from one of the above sources, but
sometimes appear to draw on other works, as well, not all of them
trustworthy. As such, the following list constitutes a kind of
reception history of Shaykh Ahmad, though it is not unlikely that
other works as yet unpublished or uncatalogued will also turn up.

It should be noted, however, that despite the tenacious promotion
of the legendary memory of Shaykh Ahmad by his descendants
and fellow townsmen in Jâm, and the fact that the name of Shaykh
Ahmad is mentioned in most of the biographical compendiums, he
appears as a relatively minor figure in the history of Iranian
Sufism and his own writings do not seem to have enjoyed much of
a vogue. For example, the great poet and Sufi thinker Farid al-Din
'Attâr does not mention Shaykh Ahmad in his lives of the saints
(*Tazkerat al-owliâ*) or in his poems. Since 'Attâr mentions other
figures of Sufism who were contemporaries of Shaykh Ahmad,
and since the name of Shaykh Ahmad was certainly known in
Nayshabur, where 'Attâr lived, we can only surmise that 'Attâr
deliberately neglected to mention Shaykh Ahmad. Most probably,
the image of Ahmad as a populist miracle worker who was
interested only in strict enforcement of religious law and not in
metaphysical speculation, did not appeal to 'Attâr.

Of course, this legendary Shaykh Ahmad is quite at variance
with the historical figure who emerges from a reading of Shaykh
Ahmad's own works, but it was evidently the powerful, vitriolic
and vindictive Shaykh Ahmad of legend rather than the gentler
and more sedate Shaykh Ahmad of his writings that was widely
known. It is therefore instructive to see how a relatively local
legend at first confined to the area around Jâm spread with the
descendants of Shaykh Ahmad as they moved to Herat, Nayshabur
and eventually to India. Besides their relevance to the history of
the historical and legendary Shaykh Ahmad, we felt it useful for
students and scholars of Sufism and Persian literature to have a
summary in chronological order of some of the major medieval
biographical sources:

1) The *Maqâmât-e Zhandeh Pil*, or *Spiritual Feats of Shaykh Ahmad*, by Mohammad-e Ghaznavi, translated in the present volume. Begun during the lifetime of the Shaykh and continued for several decades thereafter, it is the most extensive medieval work on Shaykh Ahmad. The work of Tarkhestâni also dates from the same period of 1140-1200, as, perhaps, does the work of Mahmud-e Buzjâni, though neither of these two latter works survive in independent form (see above).

2) Sayf b. Mohammad b. Ya'qub-e Haravi, who wrote his history of Herat, *Târikh nâmeh-ye Harât*, between the years 1318 and 1322 (718 and 722 A.H.), mentions the descendants of Ahmad on several occasions in connection with various historical events.[130]

3) Hamd Allâh Mostowfi of Qazvin first mentions the nickname Zhandeh Pil, "Colossal Elephant," in his discussion of the name, title and resting place of Shaykh Ahmad in both his *Târikh-e gozideh*[131] and his *Nozhat al-qolub*,[132] written in 1330 (730 A.H.) and 1340 (740 A.H.) respectively.

4) In his travelogue (*Rihla*), Ibn Battûta twice mentions Shaykh Ahmad, as we have seen above, once during his passage through Jâm, and once in connection with Shehâb al-Din Jâmi in Delhi. These passages pertain to the years 1330-1341, though Ibn Battûta's account was not actually written down until sometime between the years 1354 and 1357 with the help of an editor, Ibn Juzayy, after Ibn Battûta had returned from his travels.

5) The poet Shâh Qâsem-e Anvâr (d. 1432/835 A.H.) several times praises Shaykh Ahmad in his verse, but of course gives no substantive information about his life.[133]

6) The *Kholâsat al-maqâmât*, or "Abridgement of the Spiritual Feats," by Abu al-Makârem ebn 'Alâ al-Molk of Jâm, a descendant of Shaykh Ahmad. As described above (supra, 55-56), this was written in 1437 (840 A.H.).

---

[130] *Târikh nâmeh-ye Harât*, ed. Mohammad Zobayr al-Sadiqi (Calcutta, 1944), 397, 437-9, 691, 772-3, etc. (Reprinted in Tehran, 1352 / 1973).

[131] ed. Edward Browne (Leiden, 1910), 792.

[132] ed. Le Strange (Leiden, 1915), 154.

[133] *Kolliyât-e Qâsem-e Anvâr*, ed. Sa'id Nafisi (Tehran, 1337/1958), 84, 105, 303, 304, 351.

7) Fasihi-ye Khvâfi in his *Mojmal-e Fasihi* (w. 1441 / 845 A.H.) gives some information, mostly about the descendants of Shaykh Ahmad. What he does relate about Shaykh Ahmad adds nothing new to what had been written by this time.[134]

8) The *Nafahât al-ons* of 'Abd al-Rahmân Jâmi (1414-1492), a one volume compendium of the lives of the Sufi saints, is the first biographical dictionary to provide relatively extended information about Shaykh Ahmad. As his name suggests, Jâmi came from the hometown of Shaykh Ahmad and would therefore have had ample access to orally preserved local legends. However, Jâmi indicates that he has relied upon reputable sources for his work on the lives of about 600 mystics and Sufis, which he wrote between 1476 and 1478.[135] Jâmi would almost certainly have had access to rare manuscripts in Jâm of hagiographies of the Shaykh Ahmad about which few scholars in other locations would know, as well as manuscripts of the Shaykh's more obscure writings. However, Jâmi seems to have relied primarily upon the present work—the *Spiritual Feats* of Ghaznavi—and the *Kholâsat al-maqâmât* of Khvâjeh Abu al-Makârem ebn 'Alâ al-Molk of Jâm, for the information he provides in *Nafahât al-ons*.[136] Jâmi includes several of the stories of the miracles performed by the "Colossal Elephant," Shaykh Ahmad. Jâmi expressly states that he has quaffed from the pen of the Shaykh al-Islam of Jâm, for which (in addition to the fact that Jâmi was also born in Jâm), he chose this as his pen name.[137]

---

[134] ed. Mahmud Farrokh, 2 volumes (Mashhad, 1339-40/1960-61).

[135] *Nafahât al-ons*, ed. Mehdi Towhidipur (Tehran: Mahmud, 1336/1958), 3-4.

[136] Fritz Meier has created a table of Jâmi's borrowings from the *Maqâmât* and the *Kholâsat al-maqâmât* in his article, "Zur Biographie Ahmad-i Ğām's und zur Quellenkunde von Ğāmī's Nafahātu'l-uns," *ZDMG* 97 (1943): 47-67. He used the 1859 Calcutta edition of the *Nafahât* for this purpose, which, in addition to the notice devoted specifically to Shaykh Ahmad (pp. 322-29), also mentions the Shaykh in passing in several other places (pp. 379, 405, 417, 574 and 576). In the Towhidipur edition of the *Nafahât* (Tehran, 1336/1957), the notice on Shaykh Ahmad appears on pages 357 to 366.

[137] 'Ali Asghar Hekmat, *Jâmi* (Tehran: Bânk-e Melli, 1320/1941), 59.

9) Dowlatshâh of Samarqand, author of the famous biographical dictionary of poets, *Tazkerat al-sho'arâ*, which he completed in 1487, mentions Shâh Qâsem Anvâr's devotion to Shaykh Ahmad, and includes several lines of the latter's poetry in this connection.[138]

10) *Rowzât al-jannât fi owsâf-e madinat-e Harât*, a history of Sufism in Herat written by Mo'in al-Din Mohammad-e Zamchi Esfazâri between the years 1491 and 1494 (897-99 A.H.) gives a relatively detailed notice of Shaykh Ahmad, relating several stories from the lifetime of the Shaykh. Esfazâri has obviously relied upon the text of the *Maqâmât* of Ghaznavi which follows this introduction, as well as the *Nafahât al-ons* of Jâmi (see above).[139] In addition to the notice devoted to Shaykh Ahmad, further mention of Shaykh Ahmad is made in the description of Zayn al-Din Abu Bakr-e Tâybâdi (226) and in explaining the family tree of Qâzi al-qozât Shams al-Din Mohammad (216). In another place, Esfazâri attributes the following two lines to Shaykh Ahmad (323), though they do not particularly sound like something the Shaykh would have believed:

khwosh bâsh ke dar azal be-pardâkhteh-and
kâr-e man o to bi man o to sâkhteh-and
shatranj-e qazâ va ka'batayn-e taqdir
nard-e man o to bi man o to bâkhteh-and

Relax! All was fixed in pre-eternity
the deeds of you and I were done without us
the dice of destiny and fate's checkmate:
Long back we lost our gammon, you and I.

11) The *Habib al-seyar* of Khvândmir (d. 1498 / 903 A.H.),[140] gives a brief description of the life of Shaykh Ahmad,

---

[138] *Tazkerat al-sho'arâ* (Leiden, 1901), 348.

[139] *Rowzât al-jannât fi owsâf-e madinat-e Harât*, ed. Sayyed Kâzem Emâmi, 2 vols. (Tehran: University of Tehran, 1338-39/1959-60), 1:230-35.

[140] The work was continued up to the year 1523 (929 A.H.), probably by his grandson.

occasionally mentioning the names of various of his sons and successors in passing.[141]

12) Bâbâ Faghâni of Shirâz (d. 1518 / 925 A.H.) describes Shaykh Ahmad as the best of spiritual masters (pir) in one line.[142]

13) Kamâl al-Din Hosayn Gâzorgâhi (d. 1524 / 930 A.H.) in his *Majâles al-'oshshâq*[143] relates a completely made-up tale about Shaykh Ahmad falling in love with the son of Amir Onar, one of the commanders of Sanjar. Amir Onar's friendship with Shaykh Ahmad is discussed below in the *Spiritual Feats* (see Stories 115-119 and 285), and the information given about the relations between Sultan Sanjar, Shaykh Ahmad, and Amir Onar may actually have some value for historians.

14) The *Rowzat al-rayâhin* of Darvish 'Ali Buzjâni, written in 1523 (929 A.H.), and devoted entirely to the life and miracles of Shaykh Ahmad, as described above.[144]

15) In Mehrâbi Kermâni's *Ketâb-e mazârât-e Kermân*, a work of the first half of the 16th century, mention is made of the spiritual relationship between a pious ascetic by the name of Bâbâ Ebrâhim Garmsiri with Shaykh Ahmad.[145]

16) In his *Majâles al-mo'menin*, written between 1585 and 1602 (993 and 1010 A.H.), Qâzi Nur Allâh Shushtari gives separate notices for Shaykh Ahmad, and his grandfather, Jarir b. 'Abd Allâh Bajali, attempting to prove that both were Shiites.[146]

17) Amin Ahmad Râzi in his *Haft eqlim* (w. 1619 / 1028 A.H.) relates some general information about Shaykh Ahmad along with

---

[141] *Habib al-seyar* (Tehran, 1333/1954), 2:323.

[142] *Divân-e Bâbâ Faghâni-ye Shirâzi*, ed. Sohayli Khonsâri (Tehran, 1316/1939), 56.

[143] ed. Gholâm-Rezâ Tabâtabâ'i (Tehran: Zarrin, 1375/1996). The passage referred to here was found in the Aya Sophia Ms. # 4238.

[144] The existence of a manuscript of this work was uncovered by Moayyad in the summer of 1964 in Jâm in the possession of the Jâmi al-Ahmadi family, and first noted in his article, "Eine wiedergefundene Schrift über Ahmad-e Ğâm und seine Nachkommen," *Annali dell' Istituto Universitario Orientale di Napoli* 1964, 255-86. The text itself was published in 1966.

[145] ed. Hâshemi Kermâni (Tehran, 1330/1951), 70.

[146] *Majâles al-mo'menin* (Tehran lithograph, 1268/1852), 102 and 262.

a few lines of verse. Later sources possibly copied their samples of Shaykh Ahmad's poetry from the *Haft eqlim.*[147]

18) Dârâ Shokuh's *Safinat al-owliâ'*, written in 1639 (1049 A.H.), gives a notice of Shaykh Ahmad without adding anything new.[148]

19) The *Kashf al-zunûn* of Hâjji Khalifeh (Kâteb Chelebi, 1608-1657 / 1017-1067 A.H.) names five of the books of Shaykh Ahmad and mentions the date of his death after each one.[149]

20) Lotf-'Ali Beg Âzar's *Âtashkade*, written between 1760 and 1779 (1174-1193 A.H.) gives a brief description of the life of Shaykh Ahmad and provides three *robâ'i* not related in previous sources, which it attributes to Shaykh Ahmad[150]

21) 'Ali-Ebrâhim Khân Khalil's *Sohof-e Ebrâhim*, written in 1791 (1205 A.H.), a detailed biographical dictionary of Persian-language poets that more or less repeats what previous biographical compendiums relate.[151]

22) The Qajar ruler Mohammad Shâh is said to have inscribed a verse in Jâm praising Shaykh Ahmad during his trip to Herat in 1834 (1249 A.H.), though no trace of this remains today.[152]

23) Mirzâ Mohammad Bâqer Khwânsâri (1811-95), in his *Rawdât al-jannât fi ahwâl al-'ulamâ wa al-sâdât,*[153] simply reiterates the material found in *Majâles al-mo'menin.*

---

[147] *Haft eqlim*, ed. Javâd-e Fâzel (Tehran: 'Elmi va Adabiyeh, n.d.), 2:177-9.

[148] Ethé, 305. *Safinat al-owliâ* (Lucknow: Nawal Kishore, 1872; reprinted Lahore 1884 and Cawnpore, 1900).

[149] *Kashf al-zunûn 'an asâmî al-kutub wa al-funûn* (Dâr Sa'âdat, 1310-1311/1892-94) 1:168, 1:182, 1:503, 1:555, 2:486.

[150] *Âtashkade* in the edition of Hasan Sâdât-e Nâseri (Tehran: Amir Kabir, 1336/1957), 1:288-91. In the earlier edition (Bombay, 1299/1882), 78.

[151] Manuscript in the Königliche Staatbibliothek, Ms. # 663 in Pertsch's catalogue.

[152] H. Moayyad, "Eine wiedergefundene Schrift," *AIUO di Napoli* 1964: 261.

[153] In 8 vols. (Beirut: Dâr al-islâmiyyah, 1411 A.H./1991), 1:302-304.

24-5) Rezâ Qoli-Khân Hedâyat's two works, *Majma' al-fosahâ*[154] and *Riâz al-'ârefin*[155] both relate brief histories of the life of Shaykh Ahmad and some examples of his poetry.

26) Mohammad Hasan Khân Sani' al-Dowleh in the fourth volume of his *Mer'ât al-boldân*, lithographed in 1880,[156] gives a short notice of the life of the Shaykh, drawing upon the *Kholâsat al-maqâmât*. However, the novel thing about this work is its useful description of the sites in Jâm associated with Shaykh Ahmad: the dome over his mausoleum, the mosque and the khâneqâh. He gives the history of the numerous times the site fell into disrepair or was destroyed and the occasions it was rebuilt through the centuries.

27) Hâj Mirzâ Ma'sum Nâyeb al-Sadr (b. 1853), a Nimatullahi Sufi from Shiraz, provides our final pre-modern source with information about Shaykh Ahmad and his family. His *Tarâ'eq al-haqâ'eq*, published in 1900 (1318 A.H.),[157] does not add anything new, but collects information found in many of the above-mentioned sources. He mentions that he himself had viewed copies of the *Serâj al-sâ'erin* in three volumes and of the *Anis al-tâ'ebin*.[158]

Western Sources

In the 19th century, western travelers also began to acquaint European readers with the legend of Shaykh Ahmad. J.B. Fraser traveled to Jâm and speaks of the Shaykh in his *Reise nach und in Churasan in den Jahren 1821 bis 1822*.[159] Other Europeans who visited Jâm include Conolly in 1840, Nicolas de Khanikoff in

---

[154] (Tehran lithograph, 1295 A.H./ 1878), 1:67.
[155] (Tehran, 1316 sh./ 1937), 51.
[156] (Tehran, 1297/1880), 92. Recent editions include that of Partow Nuri-'Alâ and Mohammad-'Ali Sepânlu (Tehrân: Asfâr, 1364/1985) and another by 'Abd al-Hosayn Navâ'i and Mir Hâshem Mohaddes (Tehran: University of Tehran, 1367-1368/1989-1990).
[157] (Tehran, 1318-19/1900-1901), 2:261. In the edition of Mohammad-Ja'far Mahjub (Tehran: Ketâbkhâneh-ye Bârâni, 1339/1960), the notice on Shaykh Ahmad occurs at 2:585-8.
[158] *Tarâ'eq*, ed. Mahjub, 2:585-6.
[159] Übersetzt in Neue Bibliothek der wichtigsten Reisebeschreibungen. Band 52 (Weimar, 1829), 494.

1858 and C.E. Yate in 1894. They take their information from the
Persian sources enumerated above, and do not add anything new
of substance. In 1897 Ney Elias published the quatrain of Shâh
Nâser al-Din Homâyun mentioned earlier, along with English
translation in the *Journal of the Royal Asiatic Society*. Next, in his
"Neupersische Litteratur," in *Grundriss der Iranischen
Philologie*,[160] Hermann Ethé provided some information about the
life of Shaykh Ahmad and his writings, the first modern scholarly
notice of the Shaykh. In his 1918 work on historic buildings in
Khorasan, Ernst Diez mentions the life and works of Shaykh
Ahmad, but more important are his detailed explanations about the
mosque and khâneqâh structures next to the tomb of the Shaykh,
along with photographs.[161]

But the first real scholarly investigation into the life of Shaykh
Ahmad came by way of Wladimir Ivanow's introduction to the
Kholâsat al-maqâmât, a manuscript of which he discovered in
Bokhara in 1915 and published along with a translation in the
article, "A Biography of Shaykh Ahmad-i-Jam."[162] The late and
much lamented Fritz Meier critically evaluated the source material
about Shaykh Ahmad in his penetrating study, "Zur Biographie
Ahmad-i Ğâm's und zur Quellenkunde von Ğâmi's Nafahātu'l-
uns."[163] Meier's primary objective was to identify the sources
used by Jâmi in his *Nafahât al-ons*, but in the course of doing so,
Meier devotes a great deal of attention to the life of Shaykh
Ahmad as reflected in the *Kholâsat al-maqâmât*, and what was
then the newly discovered text of the present work—the *Maqâmât*
of Ahmad-e Jâm by Mohammad-e Ghaznavi.

Heshmat Moayyad completed a doctoral dissertation on Shaykh
Ahmad in 1958 and the publication of his edition of the *Maqâmât*
in 1961 has inspired the appearance of several other works by and
about Shaykh Ahmad. Meier provided the article about "Ahmad-i
Djām" in the *Encyclopaedia of Islam*, and Moayyad the article
"Ahmad-e Jâm" in the *Encyclopædia Iranica*. 'Ali Fâzel has
edited several of the works of Shaykh Ahmad himself, who
nevertheless remains largely unknown in the West. We hope that

---

[160] (Strassbourg, 1895-1904), Band 2, 284.
[161] *Churasanische Baudenkmäler* (Berlin, 1918), Band I, 80.
[162] *JRAS* (1917): 291-307.
[163] *ZDMG* 97 (1943): 47-67.

this book will go some way toward introducing Shaykh Ahmad and the folklore of popular Persian Sufism to a wider audience.

REMARKS ON THE TRANSLATION

As in many medieval texts, the dialogue is signaled by fairly repetitive occurrences of the words *goft* and *goftam*, "He said" and "I said." Rather than render these literally each time they appear, we have sometimes varied the English wording to read "he answered," "he replied," and so forth, both to save the modern reader from monotonous repetition, and to better signal the change of speakers. Likewise, the original Persian is littered with pious honorifics following references to God or the names of various prophets or holy figures; we have generally preserved these as representative of a kind of formulaic piety, though occasionally they have been dropped where they add nothing of emotional or theological significance to the narrative.

Sometimes the translation supplies a phrase or a word for the sake of clarity that was not in the original. These clarifications are given in brackets, and where the original diction was judged curious or needed a somewhat freer translation than usual, we include the Persian word or phrase in brackets. Occasionally there are lacunae or scribal omissions in the original Persian text; in such cases, we have reflected the ambiguity in the translation and noted the problem in a footnote. The page numbers of the second edition of the Persian text are supplied in brackets for those wishing to check the original.

In general, however, relatively few concessions have been necessary, as the anecdotes are already quite readable as they are. We hope that the flavor of the salt and pith of this unique Persian text style is still discernible in the English narrative.

A note on transliteration

Persian names and words are rendered according to one style, and the occasional Arabic titles according to another. The fonts available did not allow us to show all consonantal diacriticals, but we trust that specialists will find the transliterations self-evident. Words with an accepted English equivalent (e.g., Imam, Islam, ulama, etc.) are given as per their common English forms, except in the titles of books.

Quotations from the Qur'ân

Verses of the Qur'ân have been taken from A.J. Arberry's translation, *the Koran Interpreted* (London: George Allen and Unwin, 1955), except where noted. Verse numbers are given in the footnotes. Attention has also been paid in the footnotes to philological questions, as well as various textual questions about the forms of the stories as they appear in various manuscripts of the *Spiritual Feats* and in other works.

PART ONE

The Spiritual Feats of Ahmad-e Jâm

by
Sadid al-Din Mohammad-e Ghaznavi

How I Met the Shaykh

In the Name of God, the Merciful, the Compassionate

Praised be God, the Lord of the worlds (and to the pious belongs the next world!), and peace and blessings upon the best of His creatures, Mohammad, the Chosen one, and his family and his companions and his wives and his descendants, all of them, for as long as the celestial spheres rotate in the firmament and the angels shall hover in the heavens.

The learned scholar Sadid al-Din Mohammad, the son of Musâ, son of Ya'qub of Ghazna, may God have mercy upon him, relates as follows:[1]

I resolved to go on a pilgrimage to the Hijâz.[2] A group of friends and students accompanied me. We went as far as the town of Buzjân in the district of Jâm. All along the way I had heard talk of our most venerable master [*mowlânâ*] and leader [*sayyedonâ*], the Shaykh al-Islam, the exemplar to the saints, the caller of the masses to God, the friend of the people, the dispenser of justice on God's earth, and God's proof among His people, Abu Nasr Ahmad, the son of Abu al-Hasan, formerly of Nâmaq and now of Jâm, God sanctify his soul and beautify his resting place. I thought I should go and greet this Shaykh about whom everyone was talking, to find out what kind of a man he was.

I entered his *khâneqâh*[3] with a suspicious mind, only for the

---

[1] This phrase was certainly added to the manuscript by a scribe after the death of the author. The subsequent words are those written by the author.

[2] This is the coastal region in west-central Arabian peninsula where Mecca and Medina, the sites of Muslim pilgrimage, are situated.

[3] A lodge or hospice dedicated to the study of Islam, usually from a non-academic and more mystically-minded approach than was found in the mosque or the law college, *madrasa*. Travelers would often stay in a *khâneqâh* and in many cases disciples of the head of the lodge might also live there. As evident from this passage, curious individuals might also attend lectures or sermons at a given *khâneqâh*.

purpose of testing him. One of his sons was giving a sermon and a crowd was gathered around. I sat down [2] in a corner in the back row of people. A person entered when the sermon was finished, while a large group of people were still seated. He placed a common melon and a watermelon in front of the Shaykh al-Islam, who said to the servant, "Cut this up and give each person a slice."

When I heard this, I thought to myself, "This is really impossible. Even if there had been ten melons, there would still not be enough slices for everyone." The servant got up and cut the melon and went around the crowd, giving one slice to each person. There was one slice left over, which he took and set before the Shaykh al-Islam. When he repeated this statement, I thought, "This can only be a miracle."

An idea came to me which had not occurred to me before. "Let me try him. If he is a man of vision, let him give me the slice of melon which the servant put in front of him."

As this thought came to me, the Shaykh al-Islam called out, "Who among you is Mohammad-e Ghaznavi? Let him come forward and take this." I hid my face and the Shaykh al-Islam then said, "O Mohammad! You make a request and then hide your face? That's not right!"

Having pronounced these three miraculous statements in the span of an hour, I could no longer control myself and threw myself at his feet. As his spiritual power [*ahvâl*] radiated over me, I was overcome by a feeling which I had never before had. I told the friends who were with me and my fellow believers and students, "You go, for something unexpected has happened to me here and I must [stay] to see what will occur, for this is the goal of my pilgrimage."

I bid farewell to my friends and students and took up residence in the presence of the Shaykh al-Islam. So many were the benefits I obtained from the words, acts and deeds of the Shaykh al-Islam—I gained all kinds of knowledge and was witness to his miraculous acts and intuition—that even had I gone on the journey to the Hijâz ten times and traveled all throughout Damascus and the province of Syria, I would not have gained so much benefit. All the stories which I had heard throughout my life or read about in books concerning the leaders of the Dervishes, I saw him accomplish with my own eyes, though I had rarely heard of any of the Shaykhs of the path, or the wayfarers of the road of God, or the true searchers accomplishing such things. Everything about miraculous acts and intuition, and words of wisdom [3] about the laws and traditions of Islam [shari'at va sonnat], which I had read about in books, I heard from this very Shaykh al-Islam. I have not seen anyone loftier, more resplendent, than this great figure of religion and model for the people of certainty.

So many were the benefits I received that it is not possible to write them all down. I decided to recall and write about a small sample of the spiritual states [ahvâl] of that great figure of religion, that it might serve as a memento for the friends, and as a consolation for his disciples and the seekers on the path to God, as well as a memento for readers and observers. Any dervish who is a wayfarer on the path of God and has held fast to the hem of truth, upon hearing these words about the saintliness of this friend and the spiritual stations of this exalted leader, will have a good prayer for me.

And now let us return to our story. When I first attained the presence of this exalted leader, I sent off my companions on their way to the Hijâz and remained with him until they returned, at which point they said to me, "Come on, let us go, for if we return to our homes without you, your family and relatives will worry." I said, "You go on and tell my relatives that Mohammad is staying in the service of the Shaykh al-Islam." They left and I stayed there, reaping the benefits.

In the end, I went seven times back and forth to Ghazna, for I found no repose in my own city nor could I choose to reside anywhere other than [Jâm]. While I was in the presence of the Shaykh al-Islam I would write down what he said and would not omit any of his sayings, acts, or states. Everything I witnessed was purity, miracle and truth, itself. Wherever I went and whomever I came across, I would tell about the spiritual states of the Shaykh. It made everyone feel good and it was likewise beneficial for me and made me feel good. My hope is that the friends and disciples and those who are sincere will like it and remember me in their prayers – God, the Almighty, willing.

CHAPTER ONE

The Author's Intention in Writing this Book [5]

Let it be known that my intention in putting together this book and collecting these sayings and stories of miracles are two-fold. The first has already been mentioned and the second is this: there are some people who are at the root of the destruction of religion, while others there are among the Muslims who are the source of error and heresy, who anthropomorphosize God and deny the miracles [*karâmât*] of the saints. Yet other groups in the lands of Islam, such as the Jews, Zoroastrians and Christians deny all the miracles [*mo'jezeh*] of the Messenger [Mohammad], and all the heretics [*molhedân*], atheists [*zendiqân*] and those who would gainsay God's omnipotence [*mo'atteleh*]—and others as well—all of them deny the miracles of the Messenger, who was the pride of the prophets and messengers, superior in rank to them all, the foremost, the greatest and the most honored, and was the pride of the whole of mankind, he whose companions were the elect, God's most cherished ones, capable of performing miracles.

The groups mentioned above all deny these stories [of the Shaykh al-Islam's miracles]. My purpose in writing this book was to refute all of these groups. After five hundred-odd years only one of the servants and humble followers of Mohammad, the Chosen one, God's blessings upon him, performed such manifold miracles and good works and could see into the hearts of others. [Even so], he and the likes of him cannot match one in a thousand of the superior qualities of those companions of the Prophet. If in these times of the end [*âkher zamân*], in spite of all these upheavals and tribulations we are experiencing, there is one servant and humble follower who can produce manifold miracles, good works, read the hearts of others and perform deeds the nature of which we cannot comprehend, [6] it is an even more complete proof of the truth of the prophethood and mission of Mohammad, the Chosen one, God's blessings and peace be upon him.

Another kind of good work that the Shaykh al-Islam, God sanctify his precious soul, has performed is this: that one hundred and eighty thousand persons have repented through his blessed influence and seven [thousand][4] outsiders have converted to Islam because of him and more than ten thousand jugs of Magian wine have been spilt and he has smashed one thousand two-hundred harps, ringing castanets,[5] tambourines, lutes and all sorts of other instruments; and cut off enough locks and tresses of hair to fill more than ten saddle-bags.[6] All of these show just one sort of the good deeds that that great man of religion has performed. You can from this imagine his other virtues, for if I continue in this vein, there will be no end of it.

Any intelligent man who is not unmindful knows, and any man of insight who is not blind sees, while he who is doomed and at a loss will persevere in his ignorance, denial and stupidity. When the sincere friends read this book, they will rejoice and take pride, while the deniers and the deprived who hear these things will waste away. May both camps receive in abundance what they deserve, and it is through God that confirmation comes.

---

[4] The manuscript gives simply "seven," but it appears that the scribe has left out a numerator here, probably "thousand." The number seven is incongruously small in this catalog of the massive throngs of people influenced by Shaykh Ahmad.

[5] *Chaghâneh,* a medieval Persian percussion instrument, a kind of hand-held castanet that resembled two wooden spoons joined together at one end, the other end holding small bells enclosed in a kind of gourd, which would sound when knocked together. For a full description, see the article "Čaġāna" in *Encyclopædia Iranica.*

[6] This perhaps alludes to the custom of shearing off the hair of the head and face as a sign of ascetic commitment, and/or of discipleship to a particular Sufi saint.

CHAPTER TWO

Concerning the Difference Between the Miracles of the Prophets, the Miracles of the Saints, Divine Deception and Human Fraud [7]

May God grant you the good fortune you deserve and increase your happiness. Let it be known that anything that appears to defy the laws of nature falls into one of four categories: Either it is the miracle of a prophet [*mo'jezeh*], the miracles of saints [*karâmât*], divine deception [*estedrâj*][7] or an act of fraud [*mokhreqeh*].[8] Miracles of prophets, miracles of saints and divine deception are all three the work of God, accomplished without the interference of any other power or physical means. Although these may also occur through physical means, it is not the case that they are dependent on the physical instrument. There are degrees and ranks for each of these [kinds of miracles].

As for the miracles of the prophets and establishing the truth thereof, there is no need for explanations, argumentation, or proofs. They are frequently mentioned in the noble Book, the pre-eternal word of God [the Qur'ân]. As for the miracles of the saints, they are established by holy verses and traditions, by the reports of trustworthy believers and the consensus of those who have achieved salvation. As for the verses of the noble Book, as God, magnified be His glory, relates in the story of Solomon and his vizier Âsaf ebn-e Barkhiyâ from the Qur'ân:

Said one who had knowledge of the Book, "I will bring it to thee, in the twinkling of an eye."[9]

He, glorified be His mention, also says, in the story of Mary:

---

[7] See Qur'ân 7:127-8 for the origin of this concept.

[8] A detailed discussion of the Islamic/Sufi beliefs about saint's miracles (*karâmât*) and their subcategories, as well as *estedrâj*, can be found in Shaykh Yûsuf b. Isma'îl al-Nabahânî, *Jâmi' karâmât al-awliyâ*, vol. 1 (Egypt, 1352 A.H./1933).

[9] Qur'ân 27:40, following the translation of A. Yusuf Ali.

Whenever Zachariah went in to her in the Sanctuary, he found her provisioned. "Mary," he said, "how comes this to thee?" "From God," she said.[10]

And from another part of the story of Mary:

Shake also to thee the palm-trunk, and there shall come tumbling upon thee dates fresh and ripe.[11]

According to the general consensus, Âsaf and Mary were not prophets, especially because women, in the nature of things, [8] lack the capacity for the station of prophethood. From this, three things become evident to us: the existence of saintly miracles is absolutely established, as is the permissibility of manifesting miracles, and the propriety of informing others about them. Now, since it is established that the saints performed miracles in the presence of prophets; and that manifestation of miracles can both be a proof for disbelievers and a source of zeal for the pious— both of which objectives are the duty of the prophets, who, while they are alive, have no need of the saints—it is therefore established that manifesting of miracles by the saints is permissible, preferably in the absence of a prophet, after his life is over, so that these two important objectives may still be achieved.

Now, there are well-established traditions [*motawâter*][12] confirming the existence of saintly miracles, which in the view of the authorities on religious law, provide irrefutable certainty: A tradition which is established and has been unquestionably transmitted by people who cannot be imagined to have conspired together in a falsehood, provides incontrovertible fact.[13]

---

[10] Qur'ân 3:37.

[11] Qur'ân 19:25.

[12] This is a technical term in the science of transmission of the Hadith, meaning a tradition from or about the Prophet that is reported by so many different reliable sources, who could not have been in collusion with one another and had no reason to lie, that it is widely known and has never been challenged.

[13] This quote, in Arabic, is probably taken from a canonical authority on the principles of Islamic jurisprudence.

One report, which belongs in this category of well-established, well-known traditions, is a story about the Commander of the Faithful, [the third caliph], 'Umar ibn al-Khattâb, may God be pleased with him. He was in the pulpit in Medina while Sâriah was with the army in Nahâvand, a distance of one month's travel. The Commander of the Faithful, may God be pleased with him, called out to him: "Sâriah, the mountain! The mountain!" Sâriah heard this in Nahâvand.[14]

In another story about the Commander of the Faithful, may God be pleased with him, he was in Medina and gave his whip a shake. The Caesar of the day was sitting on his throne in Rome and his head fell from his body.[15]

There is also the story of Khâled,[16] God be pleased with him, drinking poison while in Hira.[17] There are many such [9] stories

---

[14] This story is quoted in many Sufi texts to establish the validity of saintly miracles. See, for example, Kalâbâdhî's *al-Ta'arruf li-madhhab ahl al-tasawwuf*, 44 and Arberry's English translation, 57-8 (see note 19, p. 79 for full citation); *Kholâseh-ye sharh-e ta'arrof*, ed. Ahmad 'Ali Rajâ'i (Tehran: Bonyâd-e Farhang-e Irân, 1349/1970), 193-4; Qushayrî's *Risâlat*, 159; Sarrâj's *al-Lum'a*, 135 and 321; *Rawz al-rayâhîn*, 17; *Jâmi' karâmât al-awliyâ*, 1:93; *Nafahât al-ons*, 24-5; *Tabaqât al-shâfi'iyyat al-kubrâ* by Abû Nasr 'Abd al-Wahhâb ibn Taqî al-Dîn al-Subkî, pt. 2, p. 65. Poets have also alluded to the story, as in Sanâ'i's *Hadiqat al-haqiqeh*, 236 (line 16) and 238.

[15] We have been unable to trace this story to any source.

[16] Khâlid ibn al-Walîd (d. 641 / 21 A.H.), a great general under the Caliph 'Umar, he led the Muslim forces in many of the important battles of conquest against the Persians and Byzantines.

[17] Hira was a city outside of Kufa, in present-day Iraq. For this story, see *Kashf al-mahjub*, Persian text 297, and the English translation by Nicholson, the footnote on p. 232; *Tabaqât al-shâfi'iyyat al-kubrâ*, pt. 2, p. 71; *al-Isâbah fî tamyîz al-sahâbah*, pt. 2, p. 99 (Egypt, 1323 A.H.). *Jâmi' karâmât al-awliyâ* of Shaykh Yûsuf ibn Isma'îl al-Nabahânî, pt. 1, p. 80. The gist of the story is that Khâlid ibn al-Walîd was sent by the Caliph Abu Bakr to capture Hira and was given poison by an enemy. Khâlid said, "In the name of God, the Lord of the earth and the heavens, in the name of God whose name prevents the action of poison," and took the poison. His enemy reported this and advised his people to make peace with Khâlid.

related by the Companions of the Prophet and the two generations which came after him [*tâbe'in va teba'-e tâbe'in*], about whom the Prophet says, "My companions are as the stars; any of them upon whom you rely will guide you."[18]

As for the consensus of the community, all of the books by the scholars of Islamic jurisprudence are filled with mention of [the miracles of saints], and the compositions of the religious authorities and the seekers on the path of certainty testify to them—such as the *Acquaintance [with the School of the People of Sufism]* by Shaykh Abu Bakr Eshâq-e Kalâbâdi of Bokhara,[19] the *Luster of Sufism* of Shaykh Bu Nasr-e Sarrâj of Tus,[20] the *Treatise [on Sufism]* of Abu al-Qâsem Qoshayri,[21] the *Abridgement of Mystic Truths* of 'Emâd al-Din Fâryâbi,[22] the *Vivication of the [Religious] Sciences* of the Pride of Islam (Fakhr al-Islam) Ghazzâli,[23] and other books as well of the ancient and recent

---

[18] For this tradition (hadith), see *Konuz al-haqâ'eq*, 13; Abu Nasr al-Sarrâj, *al-Luma'*, 120. See also B. Foruzânfar, *Ahâdis-e Masnavi*, 35.

[19] al-Kalâbâdhî (d. 385/995), *Kitâb al-ta'arruf li-madhhab ahl al-tasawwuf*, ed. A. J. Arberry (Cairo, 1934); an English translation by Arberry appeared as *The Doctrine of the Sufis* (Cambridge: Cambridge University Press, 1935).

[20] Abu Nasr al-Sarrâj (d. 378/988), *Kitâb al-luma' fî al-tasawwuf*, ed. R. A. Nicholson (Leiden: E.J. Brill, 1914). See also Richard Gramlich's German translation, *Schlaglichter über das Sufîtum: Abu Nasr as-Sarrag's Kitab al-luma'* (Stuttgart: F. Steiner, 1990).

[21] Abû al-Qâsim 'Abd al-Karîm al-Qushayrî (986-1074 / 376-465 A.H.), *al-Risâlah fî al-tasawwuf* (Cairo, 1330/1912). B.R. Von Schlegell has translated this to English as *Principles of Sufism* (Berkeley; Mizan Press, 1990); see also the German translation by R. Gramlich, *Das Sendschreiben al-Qušayrîs über das Sufîtum* (Wiesbaden: F. Steiner, 1989) and B. Foruzânfar's biography of Qushayrî in his edition of the Persian translation of Qushayrî's *Resâleh* (Tehran: Bongâh-e Tarjomeh va Nashr-e Ketâb, 1345/1966), 13-84.

[22] Author of the *Khâlesat al-haqâ'eq*, but one whose name we have not found in the standard biographical dictionaries.

[23] Abû Hâmid Muhammad al-Ghazzâlî of Tûs (1058-1111 / 450-505 A.H.), *Ihyâ' 'ulûm al-dîn* (Cairo, 1334/1916). For a list of partial English translations of the work, see Appendix II (225-31) of Al-Ghazâlî, *On Disciplining the Soul...and On Breaking the Two Desires*, trans. by T.J.

authorities on this class—to the extent that if you collect every single mention of them, you will meet the standards for authenticity [*hadd al-tavâtor*].

We come, then, to the various degrees of miracles. The miracles of the prophets differ with respect to their various stations. Some are constant, such as the staff of Moses, which, whenever he wanted, would turn now into a snake, now a genie, now a serpent, sometimes it would turn into a rope or a bucket, sometimes into a shady tree. Others occur only rarely, such as the parting of the sea and so forth. By analogy, the miracles of the saints differ with respect to the various stations they occupy on the mystical path. With some of them the power to perform miracles is second nature: whenever they want they can perform whatever they like. As it is [10] said: "The miracle of the saint consists in an answer to prayer, or the completion of a spiritual state, or the granting of power to perform an act, or the supplying of the means of subsistence requisite for deserving kin-folk, in a manner extraordinary."[24] And others of them are rare, but in such wise that [the power to perform them] comes upon and then leaves the saint, he being unaware of it: "The miracles accorded to the saints come to them they know not whence, whereas the prophets know the origin of their marvels, and speak in confirmation of them."[25]

As for divine deception, it is when the Almighty God causes a

---

Winter (Cambridge: Islamic Texts Society, 1995).

[24] The quotation as it appears in the text of the *Spiritual Feats* of Ghaznavi varies slightly from the published version of Kalâbâdhi's treatise (Arabic text, 46; e.g., *li-qawm* in place of *yaqûm* and *kharaqa al-'âdiyât* in place of *yakhruju 'an al-'âdât*). The English translation here is slightly modified from what Arberry provides in *Doctrine of the Sufis* (60) in order to conform to the variations in Kalâbâdhi's text as preserved in the Persian manuscript of the *Spiritual Feats*. For similar discussions of this topic, see also *Kholâseh-ye sharh-e ta'arrof*, ed. Ahmad 'Ali Rajâ'i (Tehran: Enteshârât-e Bonyâd-e Farhang-e Irân, 1349/1970), 192-199; *Nafahât al-ons* (ed. Towhidipur, 21ff) and *Kashf al-Mahjub*, 220ff in Nicholson's translation.

[25] The Arabic quotation which Ghaznavi gives here displays some minor variations from Kalâbâdhi's treatise (Arabic text, 46), e.g., *etyân* in place of *esbât*, and *karâmat* instead of the plural, *karâmât*). The English translation is taken from Arberry, *Doctrine of the Sufis*, 59-60.

wayward soul to perform an act that is contrary to nature with the intent of making the one who performs it, as well as others, to wax proud and go astray. This happens to a person who is, according to all logical evidence, destined for and revealed to be in a state of loss and futility, as in the stories of the realms of Nimrod[26] and those of 'Âd,[27] and the wonders related therein. There are also the stories of Pharaoh and how the waters of the Nile would flow with him when he ventured forth and flow back with him upon his return;[28] the story about the one who had a horse which, as it went up, its forelegs would grow shorter and its hind legs longer, whereas when it came to a downward slope, its forelegs would grow longer and its hind legs shorter;[29] and, as is related in the traditions about the Prophet, upon whom be peace, and the anti-Christ [Dajjâl]: "He kills a man and then brings him to life again, according to what he supposes."[30] These are all cases which any rational observer cannot help but notice, proving the falsehood of the claims of these people [11] who pretended to be God or some such thing. The literal meaning of "divine deception" [estedrâj] is God leading His servant step by step closer to his punishment. And this is how the decrees of God, glorified and exalted be He, under various guises, overtake his servants, as for example, when He makes some miracles the means of a nation's guidance and some divine deceptions the means of a nation's loss:

---

[26] Nimrod was a Babylonian king who, according to many of the Qur'ân commentaries and the Islamic stories about the prophets, opposed Abraham. The Quranic basis of the story, which does not mention Nimrod by name, occurs in 2:257ff.

[27] The story of the destruction of this people, who disobeyed the Prophet Hûd, sent to them by God, is mentioned numerous times in the Qur'ân, e.g., 7:65ff.

[28] See the version of this story given by Kalâbâdhi, (Arabic text, 46; and the English, Doctrine of the Sufis, 60). It also appears in Kashf al-Mahjub, 282 (see in Nicholson's English abridgement, 224).

[29] We have not found a source for this story.

[30] See Kalâbâdhi, Arabic text, 46 (for the English, Doctrine of the Sufis, 60), and a longer version of this same story, as related by Muhammad ibn Yazîd ibn Mâjah of Qazvin, in his Sunan (Egypt, 1313 A.H./1895), pt. 3, 266. Cf. Majlesi, Behâr al-anvâr (Iran, 1304-5 A.H./ 1887-88), 13:24.

He leads astray whom He will and guides whom He will.[31]

As for an act of fraud [*mokhreqeh*], it is falsehood and a patchwork of lies. Though it may appear to defy the normal course of events, in reality, it does not.

As for the difference between the miracles of the prophets and the miracles of the saints, just as there is an enormous difference in the relative rank and station of the prophets versus the saints, so, too, the distinction between the miracles of prophets and saints is great. One difference, in brief, is this: a prophetic miracle is accompanied by a claim to prophethood, whereas a saintly miracle is void of any claim. If a person were to perform a saintly miracle and lay claim to prophethood, he would instantly become an infidel and would no longer possess the power to perform the miracle in question. Rather, one who performs a saintly miracle lays claim to the truth of the prophet he follows. Thus, in reality, his miracle is derivative of the miracles performed by said prophet. Another difference is that a prophetic miracle must needs be manifested and accompanied by the claim [to prophethood], whereas a saintly miracle must be cryptic, with no claims attached. Yet another difference: Bringing something into physical existence ex nihilo is one of the categories of prophetic miracles, whereas saintly miracles have no access to such powers, which are restricted to the prophets. But nowadays, there is no need to distinguish between the two, for if, God forbid, anyone were to lay claim to a prophetic miracle, his death would immediately become obligatory.

There are various factors which can contribute to the miracles of the saints—the grace of God, divine reward [*mokâfât*], self-conceit, individual effort [*kasbi*].[32] Much could be said about each of these factors, but if we proceed to explain them in detail, it will lead only to boredom.

The essence of [12] all three of these [kinds of miracles] is a

---

[31] See Qur'ân 16:93, 35:8 and 74:31.

[32] These four categories are not mentioned in the other canonical Sufi texts, upon which the author frequently draws.

disruption in the normal course of events. The transmutation of matter which God, glorified and exalted be He, manifests unto a prophet is called a prophetic miracle [*mo'jezeh*]; if He manifests it unto a saint, it is called a saintly miracle [*karâmat*]; and if manifested to anyone else [*bigâneh*], it is called divine deception [*estedrâj*]. All three of them are disruptions in the normal course of events. As it has been said: "Those pertaining to prophets, peace be upon them, are prophetic miracles; those pertaining to saints are saintly miracles, and those pertaining to the enemies of God are deceptions."[33]

And what we have explained in this chapter is sufficient to convince the Sultan [sic]. And it is through God that assistance and confirmation come.

---

[33] Quoting once again from Kalâbâdhi, 46. We have departed from Arberry's rendering of this quote in *Doctrine of the Sufis*, 59.

CHAPTER THREE

The Reason for Writing Down the Miracles of the Shaykh [13]

The blessings which God, glorified and exalted be He, has bestowed upon the Shaykh al-Islam Ahmad, God sanctify his precious soul, cannot be compared with the works of others. In the beginning of the period when I was fortunate enough to attain his presence, I would record every miracle I saw him perform. When I went to Ghazna I would relate these, but no one would believe me. Even though I swore an oath about each of the miracles, they wouldn't accept it. I returned and left off writing down the miracles.

The Shaykh al-Islam asked me, "How is it that you no longer write down my words and deeds [*maqâmât*]?" I said, "Long live the Shaykh! What use were the things I wrote down? I wrongly thought that perhaps the people are right when they ask me, 'What are all these illusions that you have been made to witness?'"

The next time I returned from Ghazna, I thought to myself that I am more ignorant than they are: It would be illogical to find fault with myself on account of the things which people who have not and never will see them say, when I, and a couple of thousand other people along with me, do see them with our very own eyes. So, I again resumed writing them down and thought, "He who accepts it, good for him; and he who does not, forget him. It's your choice, you can listen or not."

I then asked the Shaykh al-Islam, "How is it that these people will not believe these miracles and sayings of yours?" [14].

"Because it is not in accordance with their nature," he said. "Had it not been the case that you, my followers, were in my company and constantly witnessed these things yourself, you, also, would have disbelieved. I, myself, at times wonder how it is I see these things or know how things are." Then he said, "Do not blame them."

Among those occurrences which not everyone would believe are the stories of what happened to Imam Shehâb al-Din, who was the

vizier of Sultan Sanjar ebn-e Malekshâh;[34] Imam Abu al-Ma'âli
Ashraf, God have mercy upon him, and the appointment of the
official preacher;[35] the story of how Amir Onar was killed;[36] the
story of Sultan Sanjar ebn-e Malekshâh, God have mercy upon
him, and his march on Iraq;[37] the story of the killing of Majd al-
Molk two hundred farsangs away;[38] the story of the heretics in
Zuzan and how it was captured;[39] and the story of Nâmaq and the
killing of the scholar Abu al-Mahâsen, God have mercy upon
him.[40] There are many such occurrences, though not every mind
can comprehend them nor every intellect accept them. For each of
them there are a thousand or two thousand witnesses; for some of
them there are even as many as ten thousand witnesses who, upon
hearing what I have written, would confirm that they have seen it
with their own eyes and heard it with their own ears.

Nevertheless, there are some people who consider these to be
fairy tales and do not believe them. It is small wonder, for they
behaved likewise when confronted with the miracles of the
Chosen one, Mohammad, the peace and blessings of God upon
him, saying, *"This is naught but the fairy-tales of the ancients"*[41]
and also, *"Our eyes have been dazzled; nay, we are a people
bewitched."*[42] But we have collected these stories and written
them down that it may fortify the conviction of the believers, the
[...],[43] the gnostics and the sincere ones, [15] and that they might
not despair of the mercy of Almighty God, but rather place greater
hope in His grace and bounty than what reliance they may have in
their own deeds. Our acts of worship and our deeds carry no great

---

[34] See Story 88.

[35] See Story 93.

[36] See Story 119 and the footnote to Story 116.

[37] See Story 6. By Iraq is meant the central western province of Iran.

[38] See Story 72.

[39] See Story 77.

[40] Apparently a reference to Story 83, though the name of the mayor is
given as Abu al-Hasan in the text of the story and he is not killed. It is
possible that this refers to a story not included in the manuscript.

[41] See Qur'ân 6:25, 8:31, 23:85, 27:70 and 46:16.

[42] Qur'ân 15:15.

[43] There is a lacuna here due to the deterioration of the manuscript.

weight at the threshold of Him Who lacks nothing.

CHAPTER FOUR

The Early Days of the Shaykh al-Islam Ahmad's Calling [16]

One extremely cold and snowy day, at the time of the afternoon prayer, in the early days after our master, the Shaykh al-Islam, discerned the proofs of God, praised and exalted be He, and came to his senses, he went to perform a major ritual ablution. There was a monastery there, on the outskirts of the village of Nâmaq—the village where the Shaykh al-Islam was born. He went in to that monastery, resolved to repent and stood in prayer. Prior to this, a couple feet of water or so—God knows best—had poured into the monastery and frozen solid. He remained in prayer until the following dawn and, in the fervor of his remorse, did not realize that he was standing on the ice. When he left, the ice below where his feet had stood was melted, all the way through to the ground.

> At daybreak he returned to his home. His mother and father asked him, "O Ahmad, what has made you so tearful and miserable?"
> I said:[44] Indeed, a feeling [*kâri*] has overtaken me which makes me wish I did not exist and had never been born, so that I would never have drawn a single breath contrary to God's good-pleasure. My evil companions, along with the Devil and his hosts, gathered together, surrounding me with their counsels: "You are still a child; it's not yet time for you to repent and practice self-renunciation." Every one of them offered such advice as the Devil whispered in his heart, while I stared at them in amazement, thinking, "You are all my enemies and ill-wishers." Since they would not leave, [17] I got up and left, telling them, "This feeling has overcome me and I must attend to it alone."
> I went from mountaintop to mountaintop, from town to town, from shrine to shrine. I would lay my head anywhere—on a hill, in a valley—and there were times

---

[44] At this point, the text apparently shifts from third- to first-person narrative, and Shaykh Ahmad himself relates the rest of this and the following paragraph.

when I did not eat for a full month. I would go for periods of at least ten or twenty days without eating, sometimes by choice and sometimes out of necessity. To cover my private parts, I had clothes and shoes and headgear of woolen rags.

He spent twenty years in such feats of asceticism, during which his blessed face was never seen, except that it was wet with tears. After twenty years everything changed, his grief was relieved and God opened to him a door of heavenly knowledge [*'elm-e men ladoni*). Eventually, without having studied anything or having been the pupil of any teacher, he composed several good books, of such quality that no one could find any fault with them. They were well received and approved by all of the religious scholars, who made many copies of them. These books are well-known and widely circulated among the people—*Anis al-tâ'ebin* [Companion to the Repentant],[45] *Meftâh al-najât* [The Key to Salvation],[46] *Fotuh al-ruh* [Revelations in the Spirit], and *Fotuh al-qolub* [Revelations in the Hearts]; *Rowzat al-moznebin* [The Sinners' Garden],[47] *Serâj al-sâ'erin* [A Lamp for Travelers], *Konuz al-hekmah* [Treasures of Wisdom], *Behâr al-haqiqeh* [Seas of Truth], and his book *Tazkirât* [Admonitions], and the *E'teqâd-nâmeh* [Book of Creeds], *Zohdiyât* [Asceticism] and a collection of poems [*Qasâ'ed*].[48] The book *Serâj al-sâ'erin* is in three thick volumes, totaling more than one hundred twenty quires of paper [*sad o bist tâ-ye kâghaz*].

These books are all adorned with and substantiated by quotations from Qur'ân commentaries and the Hadith of the

---

[45] Published as *Ons al-tâ'ebin*, ed. 'Ali Fâzel (n.p.: Haydari, 1368/1989); an incomplete edition by the same editor had appeared separately, almost two decades earlier, through Bonyâd-e Farhang-e Irân (1350/1971).

[46] *Meftâh al-najât*, ed. 'Ali Fâzel (Tehran: Bonyâd-e Farhang-e Irân, 1347/1968).

[47] *Rowzat al-moznebin va jannat al-moshtâqin*, ed. 'Ali Fâzel (Tehran: Bonyâd-e Farhang-e Irân, 1355/1976).

[48] See the introduction for a discussion of the extant works of Shaykh Ahmad.

Prophet, peace and blessings upon him, such that no author could raise any objection or find any weakness to attack. Praise God that it is so, for when the Almighty God chooses one of his servants and showers him with grace, none have the right to contend. There is no avoiding His decree. As it is said:

> *Say: "In the bounty of God, [18] and in His mercy, in these let them rejoice; it is better than what they amass."*[49]

> *Then they found one of Our servants unto whom We had given mercy from Us, and We had taught him knowledge proceeding from Us.*[50]

As the Messenger of God, blessings upon him, has said:

> Whoever worships God sincerely for forty days, the fountains of wisdom will appear in his heart and [flow] from his tongue.[51]

There are many holy verses and traditions which support and confirm this fact. A man who, in full sincerity and correct belief, treads the path of God will not be deprived of divine bounties; as the Almighty Creator has said:

> *Surely We leave not to waste the wage of him who does good works.*[52]

This Shaykh al-Islam Ahmad, God sanctify his precious soul,

---

[49] Qur'ân 10:58 (with slight modification from Arberry's rendering).

[50] Qur'ân 18:65.

[51] See Abû Nu'aym Ahmad ibn 'Abd Allâh al-Isbahânî, *Hilyat al-awlîyâ wa tabaqât al-asfiyâ* (Cairo, 1932-38), 5:189 and Jalâl al-Dîn 'Abd al-Rahmân al-Suyûtî, *al-Jâmi' al-saghîr* (Cairo: 1352 A.H./1933), 2:160. A slightly different version of the same hadith is also quoted in Qushayrî, *al-Risâlah*, 162, and in al-Sarrâj, *al-Luma'*, 315, as well as in *Kanz al-'ummâl*, v. 2, #1066.

[52] Qur'ân 18:30.

was a brave and courageous man, with whom none of the youth of the village of Nâmaq could compete. He was of Arab lineage, both from his father and from his mother's side, from the tribe of Jarir ebn 'Abd Allâh al-Bajali, who was a peerless archer among the Arabs. The epithet "the Arab" was added to the name of everyone on his father's side of the family—Abu Nasr the Arab and Ahmad the Arab and Abu al-Hasan the Arab, and so forth, as, indeed, the Arabs are gifted with special valor and courage. That valor, courage and sagacity was evident in the Shaykh al-Islam. So that all may know. Peace be upon them.

CHAPTER FIVE

Explanation of the Verses and Traditions Concerning the Saints [19]

Any act that is undertaken which is not based upon the word of God, the Almighty and Glorified, or the word of His Messenger, has no firm foundation. Let us, therefore, record them here, so that those who read this book will find it plausible and have no trouble accepting the words contained therein. For whatever one may say or write that is neither supported by the Hadith nor substantiated by the verses of God, the Almighty and Glorified, is unacceptable and is devoid of blessing and sincerity. Even so, there are those who say that on this plane of existence [moqâm] people of ecstatic bent cannot attain such spiritual stations [maqâmât] nor perform such miracles [karâmât]. We, however, will focus on the words of him who brought the religion of Islam [shari'at], rather than the talk of those who are not free of bias.

The Messenger of God, peace and blessings upon him, says that there are always forty men in my community whose certitude in their faith is equal to that of Abraham, upon whom be peace.[53]

Though he has said, "Even the best [deeds of mankind] are but evil [in the sight of God],"[54] he has also indicated that "Whoso holds fast to my example [Sunna] when corruption prevails in my community will receive the reward of seventy of those who fought [by my side] at Badr."[55] [20] It is related that the Messenger of God, blessings upon him, said:

---

[53] This is a Persian translation of an Arabic hadith that appears in Kashf al-mahjub, 202.

[54] This hadith also appears in 'Attâr, Tazkerat al-owliâ (Leiden, 1905-1907), 1:6.

[55] An Arabic version of these two traditions is quoted and then the author provides a translation in Persian. The second hadith refers to an early battle at which the Muslims were greatly outnumbered by their enemies; a tradition similar to it is quoted in Kanz al-'ummâl, pt. 1, nos. 885, 937 and 1072 [the text of these versions of the hadith is quoted in the Persian text of the Maqâmât (Spiritual Feats), 2nd ed., 19n4].

"There will come a time when nine out of every ten people deny the truth. None but the faithful man and the faithful woman will escape the evil of that age."[56]

"Verily, days of patience await you. The one who holds fast through them as you have held fast will receive the reward of fifty of the most observant among you." They asked three times: "O Messenger of God, of the most observant among *them*?" He said three times, "Nay, the most observant among *you*."[57]

So, he who brought the religion of Islam says that whoever clings to his example in those days will receive a reward equal to fifty of your people. To be stubborn and deny that which we see with our own eyes and that which the Messenger of God, blessings upon him, has stated, and the likes of which the former generations have experienced, would be stupidity itself and lack of faith in the word of God and His Messenger.

One day the greatest of the world, the pride of mankind [Mohammad, the Prophet], blessings and salutations upon him, was sitting among his companions like the moon among the stars. He had loosed his sugar-sweet tongue in discussion of various matters and was relating the story of his community and describing the lords of the Dervishes in the days of the end. He then opened his honeyed mouth and said: "O People, hearken and consider. Indeed, God has servants who are neither prophets nor martyrs, and yet they are the envy of prophets and martyrs on account of [21] their sermons and their nearness to God." A man among the Arabs interjected, "O Messenger of God, explain to us who they are." He said, "They are among the most selfless of

---

[56] We have not been able to find this hadith in any source, though there are many similar traditions in various books under the rubric "fitnah," or tribulations that befall the religious community.

[57] A version of this hadith, lacking the question and its response, appears in *Kanz al-'ummâl*, 6:607. The author at this point in the text now proceeds to translate these two Arabic quotations into Persian.

people, bound by close-knit ties, unaffected by the contentions of the tribes. They love and embrace one another in God and God will erect pulpits of light for them to sit upon on the day of Resurrection and will illumine their faces. The people will be frightened on the day of Resurrection, but they will not be frightened; the people will fear, but they will not fear, for they are the holy men of God, 'who will grieve not and upon whom will be no fear.'"[58]

Such were all the holy men of God, the Almighty, in the past. There is no graver matter than blasphemy and idolatry. Except the prophets and messengers of God, there is none better or more virtuous than the companions of the Prophet, blessings upon him, though all of them were, in the beginning, idolaters and sons of idolaters, blasphemers and sons of blasphemers. If, despite these faults, the companions were the best of Muslims, then why do you deny [the station of these holy men]? For if God sheds his bounty on a Muslim and the son of a Muslim, He is not bestowing that bounty out of my pocket or yours, nor does the store of His grace and generosity diminish in any way, nor is anything lost.[59] Wretchedness is entirely on our part; His Majesty is free of all such want. The earth will never be void of this people [the holy men of God]. The Messenger of God, peace and blessings upon him, said: O Hudhayfah! Countless people have made pilgrimage to this House who were not riding fine-bred camels and mounts, but were true to God and were carried upon a white horse[60] as He willed and in the manner He willed. They were the righteous. Then We said when they withdrew from the people there came to one of them a gardener from the garden and God directed his

---

[58] This last phrase occurs many times in the Qur'ân, for example 2:38. A variant version of the *hadith* quoted here can be found in Hojviri, *Kashf al-mahjub*, 268. Truncated versions of this *hadith* can also be seen in *Sharh-e bahr al-'olum*, v. 3, 310 (as cited by Foruzânfar, *Ahâdis-e Masnavi*), and in 'Afîf al-Dîn 'Abd Allâh Ibn Asad Yâfi'î, *Rawz al-rayâhîn* (Cairo, 1332/1914), 7.

[59] There seems to be a slight corruption or a grammatical lapse on the part of the Persian text at this point.

[60] *Sâ'if* is not a word in common use in Arabic, but would seem to be a white horse.

sustenance to him according to his needs. Then 'Abd Allâh bin al-Salâm [22] said, "Describe them to us, o Messenger of God." He said, "They are dead,[61] pliant, pious, righteous, generous. When they give, they give for the sake of God. When they withhold, they withhold for the sake of God. They are those upon whom rests God's affection and mercy."[62]

This, which you hear, is the story of the Messenger of God, blessings upon him. A beggar who frets day and night about how to get his hands on a morsel of food, whether licitly or otherwise, we call him a righteous man and a saint, though he may have no idea about God, whereas if a true righteous man or saint eats a single slice of bread, we consider him a worldly person [*jahân bar vay be-forushim*], though if he serves sacks full of grain without distinction between guests and strangers [*mosâferân*], that raises him in our opinion above the seven heavens. In fact, if we are honest about it, we are a people disagreeable and lost. May the Almighty God lead us into righteousness through His grace and attributes. The Prophet, blessings upon him, said:

> "Verily, the holy men of my community will not enter Paradise on account of constant fasting or prayers; rather they will enter it because of the mercy of the Almighty God and because of their mercy and generosity of spirit towards the entire community of Muslims."[63]

Prayer and fasting, upon which the peace of mind of Muslims hangs, are of no great account. As God decrees in his Mighty Book:

> *No good will come of their whispered conversations, unless they command people to charity and good deeds and goodwill amongst men.*[64]

---

[61] That is, dead to the promptings of their own desires.

[62] We were unable to find a source for this.

[63] We have not found this *hadith* in any source.

[64] Qur'ân 4:114 [our translation].

It is reported that one day the Commander of the Faithful, 'Umar ibn al-Khattâb, may God be pleased with him, asked "Who is the best of people?" The Messenger of God, blessings upon him, replied: "He who is most beneficent to the people."[65] Likewise, "The Prophet, peace be upon him, says: 'The holy men of the Almighty God are those people who, when others see them, they are reminded of God, the Mighty and Glorified.'"[66] However, I have mentioned the names of those holy men of the Almighty God who, when we see them, [23] feelings of envy, jealousy and enmity arise in our hearts which we cannot rid ourselves of for some time, so great is the ill will that fills our hearts because of them.[67]

The following hadith aptly illustrate such feelings. Avoid such evil behavior, for the day will come when all the swindlers will be punished on the gallows in a most public and humiliating manner [bar sar-e chahâr-su-ye fazi'at] and their arms and legs will be cut off. How unchivalrous! In view of what we are, who are we to concern ourselves with such matters? If we mind our own business, we will not become mired in such discussions.

> The Prophet, blessings upon him, said, "Verily, the holy men of God are those of his creatures who hunger and thirst. Therefore, God will take revenge upon any who humiliate or harm them by word or by deed in this world, and will tear away the veil that covers his sins and deprive him of livelihood and happiness."[68]

---

[65] This hadith is given as *khayr al-nâs anfa'uhum li al-nâs* in *al-Jâmi' al-saghîr*, 4044 and *Kanz al-'ummâl*, pt. 8, no. 2363.

[66] There is a slight difference between the Arabic *hadith* quoted here and the Persian translation given by the author. We have not located this *hadith* in any other source.

[67] Grammatically this sentence is somewhat ambiguous, as it changes subject midway. One might also understand from it that: Whosoever sees those holy men of God, their hearts are filled with envy, jealousy and enmity, which causes complications for us for some time, because it creates hostility in our hearts against them.

[68] This *hadith* appears, with minor variation, in *Kanz al-'ummâl*,

> The Prophet, blessings upon him, said: "There
> is nothing in the sight of God as virtuous as self-
> renunciation in this world."[69]

Indeed, this is the case.

> The Messenger of God, blessings upon him,
> said: "If God loves one of His servants, He
> afflicts him, and if He loves him utterly, He keeps
> him for Himself." The Messenger of God was
> asked, "What does it mean, 'He keeps him for
> Himself?'" He replied, "He leaves him neither
> wealth nor children."[70]

Many a person supposes that he is in tribulation when he is being
rewarded, for he will not be punished [in the next world] on
account of that tribulation, which is [in reality] a perfect bounty.
We inflict tribulations upon ourselves and suffer pain and troubles
day and night, believing that we must prepare a trousseau for our
daughters and furnish a home for our sons that is better and more
pleasing than what others have. This [we believe] to be best, as
others will praise us. [24] Such things are not the kind of
tribulations which the holy men of God suffer. The suffering and
afflictions they bear are on account of the community of Muslims,
not wishing to see them in misery and so forth.

Anyone who has a desire to achieve something, it should be
done for the good pleasure of God, not for the sake of the people;
love of this world is one of the cardinal sins [*kabâ'er*]. In short,
you should love above all that which the Almighty God loves, and
look upon as your enemy whomever God looks upon as an enemy.
As the *hadith* say:

3:4839.

[69] *Kanz al-'ummâl*, 2:1049.

[70] *Kanz al-'ummâl*, 6:422. A slight variation on this tradition is also
related by al-Ghazzâli, *Ihyâ 'ulûm al-dîn*, 4:329, under the rubric *Bayân
mahabbat Allâh li al-'abd wa ma'nâ-hâ*.

The Prophet, blessings upon him, said: "Knowledge is obligatory and fighting on behalf of religion is obligatory, but migration to a territory after it has been conquered is voluntary."[71]

The Prophet, peace upon him, has said: "A time will come upon the people when a religious man will not be safe unless he flees on account of his faith from village to village and region to region to perform his prayers." They said, "O Messenger of God, when will this time be?" He said, "When one cannot earn a living except through sin and the people are not content with what God has decreed. At that time, celibacy is permitted and it is safe to stay single." They said, "How can you permit celibacy when you have commanded us to marry, and you say: 'When a Muslim marries, he carries his religion with him and the devil flees from him?'" He answered, "In the case that a person chooses this world and prefers it to the next, the destruction of the man is in the hands of his wife and his son and his relatives and neighbors. They will make him do things which he cannot bear and will condemn him for his modest means to the extent that he will earn his living by illicit means and resort to activities which will bring about his destruction. But were he to be patient, it would be better for him." He then said, "O Ibn Mas'ûd, in the year one hundred and sixty-six, you must neither marry nor treat anyone as your brother."[72]

[25] When the Messenger of God, peace and blessings upon him, has given these signs to us and we, today, witness their fulfillment with our own eyes, it would not be wise to be deceived by any actions or gilted words, nor to rely upon anyone and feel

---

[71] We have not located this *hadith* in any other sources.

[72] The first part of this *hadith* is quoted in *Hilyat al-awliyâ*, 1:25 and also appears, with some significant differences and without the last two sentences, in *Kanz al-'ummâl*, 6:639.

ourselves safe from the evil of these days. In such a time as this, when God, the Mighty and Glorified, has kindled a lamp such that both the chosen ones and the common folk, the knowledgeable as well as the ignorant, are illumined by it and can see its brilliant rays with their own eyes, to ignore it would not be right, nor would it be reasonable, nor a sign of devotion and faith, to cast oneself like a moth into its burning flame. Anyone who denies such manifest miracles and obvious instances of mind-reading, which are proof of the truth of the Mohammadan religion, blessings upon him, and evidence of the truth of his claim, he is the same as those people who saw the miracles of the prophets and denied them, calling them sorcery. *"Praise be to God who guided us to this, for had God not led us, we would not have been guided."*[73]

Now this brings us to the miracles which I have witnessed and heard from trustworthy individuals. I will record some of them, only a few among the many, the Lord Almighty willing.

The first of those many is the story of what happened to me, the author of this book, when I first attained to the presence of this great shaykh, Ahmad, God sanctify his precious soul. I had not yet greeted him and he had not yet seen me. He was sitting among a large crowd with some slices of melon and watermelon in front of him. It crossed my mind that if what they say about this man is true and he can perform miracles, let him give that melon slice to me. The Shaykh al-Islam called out, "Where among us is Mohammad of Ghazna?" He couldn't see me because of the large crowd in the way. [26] I stood up and the Shaykh al-Islam said, "Take this slice of melon, since you cannot bear to see me have it." He gave it to me, I took it and my circumstances changed, as you now can clearly see, though God knows best.

---

[73] Qur'ân 7:43 [our translation].

CHAPTER SIX

The Miracles of the Shaykh

When the evidences of the grace, favor and attention of God (magnified and exalted be He!) concerning the special, chosen, servant of His Majesty, glorified be his station, The Shaykh al-Islam Ahmad, may God sanctify his precious soul, were observed and his strange and wondrous miracles became manifest to the eye, none of the great scholars and sages who heard of them would give credence to them. They vociferously denied the [miracles], discredited those who reported them, and attempted to prevent and stop them. Yet, when they would come and witness for themselves, they were unable to say a thing, [for as the saying goes] "the eye is honest and the ear a liar." I, Mohammad-e Ghaznavi, the compiler of this book, was one of those deniers, but having witnessed it for myself, I saw no alternative but acquiescence and submission.

Whenever one of the scholars would approach the Shaykh al-Islam about any subject, whether theoretical or practical, he would explain it in such a manner that no word could be said against it.

This being the state of affairs, I decided to write down some of the spiritual feats (just a few of the many – but one out of every thousand) of this man chosen by the divine grace and singled out by the Lordly favors (as the verse says: "Thy Lord creates whatsoever He wills and chooses"),[1] namely the Shaykh al-Islam Ahmad-e Jâmi, God sanctify his precious soul. I decided to collect them all in a book, that there might remain of me a memento, in the perusing of which [28] friends and disciples would feel proud, while those who deny and detest would be consumed [with envy]. May both objectives be increasingly attained, as the poem says:

> The burning of the foes, the pride of friends -
> Let both live thus until the trumpet's blast

And now to the point—when this poor, needy one resided for a

---

[1] Qur'ân 28:68; Arberry's translation has been altered to conform to the meaning of the verse as it pertains to this particular context.

time in the service of this great master and he had allowed me to grow somewhat bold in his presence, I stated to him, "It occurs to me that I should collect whatever I see and hear of your spiritual feats, stations, states and miracles."

He replied, "Fine. It should be done."

I said, "Since you permit me, you must inform me about the beginning of your repentance and the reasons for it, as well as the occurrences, states and miracles which you experienced in those few years, so that I may begin there, God willing."

The Shaykh then answered in this fashion:

1. The Story of the Shaykh's Repentance [as told by the Shaykh himself]

I was twenty-two when God, exalted and glorified be He, in His grace and generosity opened the door of forgiveness to me and favored me that I might repent. The reason for my repentance was this: when it was my turn to entertain the people of sin and debauchery, the village constable was away. The companions demanded their party. I said that the constable was away; when he returned I would give the party. The companions said, "We will not wait, he may not come until much later." I thought, no problem, when he returns, if they fail to host a party, I will give another one. When the constable returned, he asked that a party be held.

When they came together at my place for the second time [29] and consumed some food, someone went to the wine cellar to bring wine. He found all the jugs to be empty, although in this house there had been forty jugs full of wine. I was greatly astonished at this and hid it from my companions, obtaining some jars of wine from somewhere else, which I placed before them. With great haste I rode my donkey toward the vineyard and ordered wine. I found their wine jugs to be in tact. When I loaded them on the donkey, it proceeded only with great reluctance and I beat it quite hard in order to return more quickly, for my heart was with my companions.

All at once I heard a voice say in my ear, "O Ahmad, why do you harm that animal? We will not order it to go. You offer excuses for the constable, but he does not accept them; why do you not excuse yourself before Us, perchance We will accept?"

A great fear overtook me. I prostrated my face to the ground and said "O God, I repent. From now on I will never drink wine and no unseemly act will proceed from me. Command the donkey to go, so that I will not be shamed before those people."

The donkey set off. When I returned and set the jug in front of them, they filled a goblet and held it out to me. I did not take it, saying, "I have repented and will no longer drink wine."

My companions said, "Ahmad, are you trying to fool us, or yourself?" They kept insisting.

Suddenly I heard a voice calling in my ear, "O Ahmad, take it and taste it, and give all a taste of this goblet." I took and tasted it. By the power of God, the Exalted, it had turned to honey. When I had made every one of those present to drink from that goblet, they at once repented. Crying out, they scattered in different directions and every one of them took up doing good deeds.

As for me, enthused, I set off for the mountains and occupied myself with worship and acts of asceticism. What I have related here is the cause of my repentance, and through God comes success.

2. How God Provided the Shaykh's Family with Daily Sustenance [told by the Shaykh himself]

Some time after that a voice said to me, "O Ahmad, is this how you follow the path of God, [30] leaving those who are dependent upon you and for whose welfare you are responsible and abandoning them? Where will this path lead you?"

Then, after that, another thought occurred to me: "In your house, in addition to everything else, there are forty jugs, which had been full of wine. Let [those dependent on me] spend whatever they have on themselves. When you see that it has run out and nothing more is left, then you can worry about their needs."

After a while, the voice came to me again, saying, "O Ahmad, so you are righteously following the path of God, relying on jugs of wine?! You have strayed from the path. Why do you not rely upon the grace and generosity of God, the Exalted, that He may provide sustenance for your dependents from His treasure-house of grace and generosity, for He, in truth, is the Sustainer. Is it proper that you should rely upon wine jugs?"

A great choleric zeal overcame me and I came rushing down from the mountain, entered the house, began swinging at the jugs with my cane, breaking them to pieces. The constable was informed that Ahmad had come down from the mountain, had gone into his house and was smashing and pouring out everything he saw. "He has been seized with madness!"

The constable sent someone who brought me out of the house and held me in the horses' stable [*pâygâh*]. I went up to a feed-bag, began clapping and said: (verse)

The camel turns around the mill a hundred times;
in honor of the Friend, you whirl a turn or two

The horses lifted their muzzles from the hay, knocked their heads against the walls, and tears flowed from their eyes. The stablemaster heard and told the constable, "They have brought a lunatic and locked him in the stable. Now all the horses have gone mad, lifted their muzzles from the hay, and are knocking their heads against the walls and weeping."

The constable came, they set me free, apologized to me and went on their way. I returned to my place on the mountain and did not come down anymore from the mountain for some years. [31] God, glorified and exalted be He, granted my dependents one maund of grain each morning from His treasure-house of generosity and grace.[2] Each morning when they awoke, everyone in my household would find a maund of grain had appeared under their pillow by the power of God, glorified and exalted be He. My family members ate of this, and it also sufficed for any guest they might have.

---

[2] "granted my...each morning" is supplied from Jâmi's *Nafahât al-ons*, ed. Towhidipur, op. cit., 361. It is missing from the original manuscript, due certainly to a scribal error. Note that 'Abd al-Rahmân Jâmi, who lived about three hundred years later in the same area as Shaykh Ahmad, evidently had access to a complete manuscript of Ghaznavi's work.

3. The Self-mortifications of the Shaykh [told by the Shaykh himself]

The following year the winter was cold and I had no shelter. One day, I quarreled with my concupiscent soul, which said: "Ahmad, you cause me much pain and trouble. I feel cold, I need a warm house; I feel hunger, I need a warm cider.[3] What do you think you are doing? You're killing me!"

I replied to it, "Okay, I'll prepare a warm place for you right away and give you some warm cider." I went and gathered a bundle of thorns—the kind they call acacia thorns—and piled them on the ground. I took off my cloak and began rolling on the thorns, shouting out, "Here is your warm place and hot cider," until every member of my body was lacerated and the thorns were embedded in my skin and my wounds began to bleed.

Then I got up, took my cloak and went over to a spring where I would bathe and perform my ablutions. The spring was frozen over. My concupiscent soul said, "You do not listen to me, will you not obey the word of God, the Almighty? Does He not say, 'Cast not yourselves by your own hands into destruction'?"[4] There was nothing I could say to this. I sat at the edge of the spring for a while reflecting, as the blood continued to spill from my limbs.

I looked and suddenly noticed a dragonfly[5] under the ice, turning on the surface of the water. I said to myself, "Senseless fellow that you are, you are yet not weaker than that fly. If He who keeps it alive on the water's surface below the ice, should will to do so, [32] He can keep you alive as well."

I put down my cloak, picked up a rock, broke the ice and sat in the water. The surface of the water turned bloody. I waited a while until the water washed away the blood. Then I got up, washed myself and came out of the water. By the power of God, glorified and exalted be He, my wounds had healed such that not a trace of

---

[3] The word is Persian *pâludeh*. Modern-day *fâludeh*, consisting of angelhair noodles with sugar, rosewater and usually some lemon flavoring, is served chilled. In the time of Shaykh Ahmad, it evidently was also served warm, perhaps more as a beverage than a dessert.

[4] Qur'ân 2:195

[5] The text has *magas-e sabz*, or "a green fly."

them remained.

I then put on my cloak and went back. The mountain goats and other game rushed down the mountain and headed towards me. I got up and sat on the edge of a rock, and, astonished, offered repeated exaltations to the Lord. When they got close to me, they formed a circle around me, breathing over me, until I began to sweat.

Then, suddenly, they fled in terror. I looked and saw a huge dragon coming toward me. I remained sitting calmly in my place. The dragon came and circled around me, nudged me with its head and pointed towards the mountain. I set out in the direction it indicated. It took me to a cave which I had never seen before, led me inside, placed its head on my lap and displayed its regard for me. The time for prayer came and though my heart was fixed on saying the prayer, I could not move.

Finally, I got up intending to see how the dragon would react. It gestured toward the mouth of the cave and I realize it was telling me to go, so I came out. From then on, as long as I was on that mountain, I would often see the dragon in that cave, and if two or three days would go by when I did not show up, he would come looking for me in the place where I was.

4. The Poverty of Ahmad-e Jâme'

Then one day a man came whom they called Ahmad-e Jâme'. He said, "I am a family man and have no worldly possessions. I have always asked God, glorified and exalted be He, to make me independent of all other people. Last night in a dream I was told to go before [33] Shaykh al-Islam Ahmad that he might give me something to make me independent from others. Now I have come to you, the rest is up to you."

The Shaykh al-Islam said,[6] "If what you just said is true, how much would suffice your daily needs?"

He said, "One *dâng*."[7]

---

[6] Here and in the following paragraphs, scribal interference interrupts what is otherwise a direct quotation of Shaykh Ahmad.

[7] A *dâng*, or *dânq* was a unit of weight, as well as a coin, equal to one-sixth of a dinâr or of a dirham. According to Khwârazmi, it was equal to 4

The Shaykh said, "Go. Every day a *dâng* will be waiting for you at the nest of that bird. You come and take it."
And it was the nest of a partridge. As long as that man lived, he would come every day and take that gold coin.

5. The Story of the Shaykh, Bu Tâher the Kurd, the Apricot and the Forbidden Food [told by the Shaykh himself][8]

Then one day my concupiscent soul craved an apricot. I said, "If you fast for one whole year, I'll give you an apricot." When the year was over, my soul said, "I have done my part; now you keep your promise."
I went to the vineyard which I had inherited from my father. When I entered, I saw an apricot which had passed intact through the bowels of an animal that had eaten it. I picked it up and cleaned it off. My soul cried out, "Ahmad, you are cleaning it off, what do you intend to do with it?"
I said, "I will give it to you to eat. I have promised you an apricot and here it is. The only thing is that it has passed through the bowels of an animal."
My soul shouted out,[9] "Ahmad, I give in to you and promise never again to wish for anything; don't give this to me." I said, "Now, that's how it should be."
I picked several apricots from the tree, ate a few of them and kept a few up my sleeve. I went to Shaykh Bu Tâher the Kurd and set them before him. He asked, "Where did these apricots come from?"
"They're from a vineyard which I inherited from my father," I said.
"Well, well!," he said. "You bring apricots to me from an estate devoted to public charity and you represent it to me as your own! Do you think I am blind?"

Tasuj, or one-sixth of a *Mithqâl* (see Moʻin and Dehkhodâ for details).
[8] Jâmi retells this story nearly word-for-word in his *Nafahât al-ons*, ed. Towhidipur, op. cit., 366-7.
[9] The sentences from "cried out..." to "...shouted" are missing from the manuscript, certainly due to a lapsus calami of the scribe. However, the missing sentences are preserved in Jâmi's *Nafahât al-ons*, op. cit., 366-7.

I kept quiet, praying inwardly to God on High, saying [34], "O Lord, you know that I picked them with my own hands from a tree belonging to me. I have inherited that tree from my father. Reveal this to him."

A while later, the Shaykh Bu Tâher called for his son. The son came and the Shaykh told him, "Go and fetch a sheep from the flock, slaughter it, prepare a stew and bring it here, for hunger's bile has overcome Ahmad's brain. He does not know what he is doing or saying."

I kept quiet until the table was spread and the food was served. It was intimated to my heart that I should not eat from the meat of that stew as it was not from a lawful source. I ate bread, but did not reach for the stew. Shaykh Bu Tâher asked, "Ahmad, why don't you eat? This food was prepared specially for you."

"This is enough for me," I said.

He insisted, "Tell me the truth. Why won't you eat?"

I replied, "A voice has told me that this meat is not lawful, and I should not eat it."

Shaykh Bu Tâher said, "Well, well! You bring apricots to me from an estate devoted to public charity and you call it your own, but you call my food unlawful and will not eat it. Who taught you to behave like this?"

For a while I sat with lowered head, then looked up and said, "Call your son to come here".[10]   Shaykh Bu Tâher asked for his son. When the latter came, he asked him "Where does this meat come from? Tell me the truth."

The boy answered, "You told me to bring a sheep from the flock and slaughter it. The flock had wandered far away. The butcher had half a juicy sheep hanging in his shop. I took it and made the food."

Shaykh Bu Tâher said, "That's another matter altogether. Call for the butcher." They called him and Shaykh Bu Tâher said, "Tell me the truth. Where did this meat that you sent for us today come from?"

The butcher replied, "I cannot lie to you. The constable was angry with a certain person, and they had removed a sheep from

---

[10] The bracketed text is supplied from *Nafahât al-ons*.

his flock and brought it to me. [35] I slaughtered it. The constable took one half and I hung the other half in my shop. Your son came and got it. This is the story, as I have described."

Shaykh Bu Tâher bowed his head. I got up and left. There was a monastery. I entered that monastery and was choked with tears. I prayed to God, the Almighty, saying, "You have left me with not a single friend. There was a spiritual master with whom I could associate for a while. You have made it so that, out of shame, I cannot even go before him any longer."

After a while, Shaykh Bu Tâher came in and sat down. I was silently praying, "O Lord, just as you have disclosed the matter of the meat to him, so, too, disclose the matter of the apricots." A while passed. Suddenly, Khezr,[11] blessings upon him, appeared and said, "O Bu Tâher, you call Ahmad's property a public endowment and you call suspicious meat lawful? Who taught you to behave like this?" Khezr severely reproached him, "Don't interfere with [Ahmad], for his path is different from yours. He travels toward the highest of stations." Shaykh Bu Tâher apologized profusely, saying, "I didn't know. Be gracious and forgive me."

Peace be with you.

6. The Shaykh, Sultan Sanjar and Qarâjeh-ye Sâqi [as told by the Shaykh himself]

And then one day two travelers[12] came. "O Ahmad, know that

---

[11] Khezr (Khidr) is a mythical figure, sometimes associated with the Biblical Elijah, believed to have initiated Moses into the ways of esoteric knowledge and guided Alexander through the realms of darkness to the fount of life. The Qur'ân does not mention Khezr by name, but commentators identify him with the man described as "one of God's servants" in a parable from the Sura of the Cave (*Surat al-kahf*, K18:65-82).

[12] The Persian word *âyandeh* (active participle of the verb *âmadan*, "to come") sometimes means a guest or traveler, though the usual meaning of the word is "future." The author has used the word here, as also in Story 241, to designate a person who appears from a mysterious place to warn the Shaykh to watch out for Sultan Sanjar and protect him from the danger of death or defeat in battle.

the King of the age, Sanjar, the son of Malekshâh, has been entrusted to you. You must keep informed of his activities and his situation, and you must pray for him. We have given you notice."

I asked, "What must I do?"

They answered, "You must be mindful of his condition at all times."

I said, "Fine. I will do so to the extent that God, glorified and exalted be He, assists me."

They said, "May God assist you," and left.

Some time passed. Then one day at sunset those two people suddenly appeared and said, "O Ahmad, did we not ask you [36] to watch over Sanjar and be mindful of him?"

I said, "Yes. What has happened?"

They said, "Don't you know they have prepared poison to pour in his sherbet goblet."[13]

I said, "What should I do now?"

They said, "Let's go and we will tell you."

They brought me to Marv where we arrived before midnight and they told me: "Enter the palace of the Sultan. There is a domed chamber where Sultan Sanjar sleeps and his maidservant, who is called Nurse Foot-Masseuse [*dâyeh-ye pây-mâl*], stands at the foot of his bed. His goblet of sherbet has been placed next to the golden candelabra at his bedside and the poison has been mixed in it. Go in, take the goblet, pour it out down the sewer pit, place the goblet upside down at his bedside, move the golden candelabra to the foot of the bed and the silver one to the head of the bed. Stay a while to see if you see or hear anything and then turn around and come back to your own place."

I did as they commanded. I went in. Everything was just as they had described to me. I picked up the goblet, brought it out and poured it down the pit in the middle of the palace. Then I went back, replaced the goblet upside down and switched the places of the candelabras. The maidservant noticed the candelabras moving. She was frightened, covered her face with her hands and began to

---

[13] *Qadah-e sharbat.* The English word "sherbet" comes originally from an Arabo-Persian word (*sharbat*), and in Persian refers to a cool refreshing drink of plain or mixed fruit juice.

pray.

After a while Sultan Sanjar woke up. He wanted to drink but found the goblet overturned. He said to the maidservant, "Why did you drink my sherbet?"

She answered, "I did not drink the sherbet; how would I dare to do so?"

The Sultan said, "The goblet has not fallen and the sherbet is not spilled. I did not drink it and you did not drink it, so who did and where did he go?" He whipped the nurse twice and said, "Didn't I tell you to stay awake and not fall asleep?"

The maidservant said, "I did not sleep, I just saw the candelabras move. That's all I know." The Sultan looked and saw that the candelabras had been switched. He told her, "Girl, if you reveal this secret and inform anyone about it, I shall kill you." [37] When things got to this point, I left.

The reason for poisoning Sultan Sanjar was as follows: Qarâjeh-ye Sâqi, the royal wine-steward, was one of the elite servants of the Sultan, honored and esteemed by him, to whom the Sultan had given his special slave-girl in marriage, because he trusted him with his meals and wine. One day Qarâjeh said to that slave girl, "I desire to be a Sultan Sanjar myself. Don't you long to be a Torkân Khâtun?"[14]

She said, "Even if I did, what of it? What could I do about it?"

Qarâjeh replied, "I'll tell you if you obey me and do not say a word about it to anyone."

The woman said, "Tell me, I will obey and tell no one."

Qarâjeh said, "When I have become a Sanjar, you will be a Torkân Khâtun."

The woman replied, "By what stratagem can you become a Sanjar?"

Qarâjeh said, "I'll give you a potion to pour into the sherbet and place at the Sultan's bedside. He will die the moment he drinks it. I'll take the place of Sanjar and you, the place of Torkân Khâtun."

When he had prepared his wife, who was the maid-servant of the Sultan, one greatly trusted by him, who used to place the sherbet at the Sultan's bedside, to do all this, he ordered her to mix the

---

[14] The famous queen of Sultan Sanjar.

poison in the sherbet and put it at the Sultan's bedside. All night long he awaited the news of Sanjar's death. When the night was over and no news of the Sultan's death was heard, Qarâjeh was frightened—as the Arabic proverb says, "The traitor waits in trepidation." He supposed that the Sultan and been informed of the situation. "In the morning, they'll capture me and execute me."

Early in the morning he rose, took his wife and rode out of the city of Marv towards their own estate in Iraq.[15] From there he began to assemble an army. He remained there until the Sultan sent someone to summon them, but they would not come. The Sultan did not know what was wrong with Qarâjeh, whereas the latter was preparing for battle.

Some time passed and Qarâjeh [38] did not return. The Sultan marched the army towards Iraq and a battle took place between them. The Sultan was put to flight. I [Shaykh Ahmad] was in the mountains and those two travelers came again, saying, "The Sultan has been defeated in battle and has fled. Go help him!" Right away I grabbed the reins of Sanjar's horse and shouted at him, "Turn back."

Sultan Sanjar said, "O Shaykh, let go, my troops have gone."

I insisted, "Turn back." He wouldn't go back, as he was afraid. I said, "Do not be afraid, for Qarâjeh will be delivered into your hands."

The Sultan turned back and made a stand. The troops gathered around him and attacked the enemy. They immediately knocked down Qarâjeh and captured him. Right then the Sultan came to the spot where he had seen me. I was standing there. He dismounted and came before me, showing respect.

He asked, "Who are you and what do they call you?"

I said, "They call me Ahmad Abu al-Hasan-e Nâmaqi."

He asked, "How did you happen to come to this place, and what's this all about? Why are you here?"

I said, "You were entrusted to my care some years ago and I

---

[15] Medieval and pre-modern Persian and Arabic texts refer to the central provinces of greater Iran (including Isfahan, Tehran and Hamadan) as Iraq, or *'erâq-e 'ajam*. It does not intend the area of Mesopotamia, further to the west, situated in modern-day Iraq.

pray for you and watch over you."

He asked, "How can you prove that I have been entrusted to you?"

I said, "Qarâjeh desires to be a Sanjar and his wife a Torkân Khâtun. Qarâjeh's wife, at her husband's command, pours poison in the sherbet. Ahmad is informed about it and, according to orders, he pours out the poison and turns the goblet upside down at the bedside and switches the candelabras. What had Nurse Foot-masseuse done wrong that you should whip her twice?"

The Sultan answered, "You are right. It happened just as you say. When will I see you again and pay my respects?"

I said, "Whenever God the Almighty should will."

Sanjar paid his respects and withdrew. He summoned Qarâjeh and said, "Why have you rebelled?"

He said, "I cannot lie in your presence. I desire to be a Sanjar and my wife [39] to be a Torkân Khâtun. I gave her a potion to pour in the sherbet. I don't know who warned you not to drink it. I feared for my life, so I fled and rebelled against you. This is what happened. The rest is left to your sublime decision; whatever you command is the law, whether execution or amnesty."

7. The Poverty of Khvâjeh Abu al-Qâsem-e Kord[16]

Another story was that of Khvâjeh Abu al-Qâsem the Kurd, which goes as follows:

An unfortunate thing happened to me and I lost all my property, [animal] stock and whatever I owned in the world. I reached a point of such straightened circumstances that I was obliged to beg. I had a large household and no one was looking out for us. I had no trade or skill, and so I would go to see religious leaders and charitable individuals and frequent the important shrines, asking for help from them, because I could not stand to beg from the common folk.

Then one day I was sitting in the mosque, sad and depressed. A holy man came in and performed two ritual prayers. He then came

---

[16] The previous stories were narrated by Shaykh Ahmad in the first person. From here on, the stories are related by Mohammad-e Ghaznavi, or on the authority of various other individuals, as noted.

up and greeted me. I was struck by awe on account of his luminous and imposing appearance. I returned his greetings. I was at this time greatly distracted.

He asked me, "Why are you so sad?" I said, "It's a long story. Who are you and where are you from? I have not seen you before and do not know you." He said, "Tell me about yourself, why do you ask about me?"

I told him my story. He asked, "Would you like me to offer you some counsel?" "May God reward you well!," I said. "It would be wonderful, for I am at a complete loss."

He said, "Do you know Ahmad Abu al-Hasan, who lives on this mountain?" I said, "Yes, I am well acquainted with him. I know him very well—he is an old friend of mine." He asked, "Have you approached him recently and told him of your situation?" "No," I said. "Go and see him and tell him your situation," he said, "for he is a miracle-worker and he is greatly blessed by God. Perhaps you will find a solution to your troubles through him." [40] "Very well," I said, "I will do so."

The next day I got up and went to the mountain. I saw him, attained his presence and said hello. He returned my greetings and asked, "How are you and how is everything?" I said, "Don't ask how I am and how things are going. Help me or I will be lost."

I described my situation in detail for him. He told me, "For several days now I have been thinking of you. I knew there was a reason my thoughts were turning toward you. Do not worry or be distressed. I will in my prayers and meditations submit your situation to the attention of His Majesty, the Lord, and we will see how he responds. Stay here tonight."

I stayed. The next day I entered his blessed presence to see what he would say. When his gaze fell upon me he said, "Come closer. God, glorified and exalted be He, has righted your affairs and your needs have been met." Then he asked, "How much do you need per day?"

I said, "Sir, I need four dângs per day to meet my needs." The Shaykh said, "Your four dângs will be delivered at that rock over here. You come pick it up and spend it."

When Bu'l-Qâsem the Kurd was sore in need,
the feats of Ahmad opened doors to him.
His daily needs delivered at a rock -
"Come here each day and get yourself four dângs"

The moment I went up to the rock he had mentioned, I saw, by
the power of Almighty God, a piece of gold sticking out of the
rock. I picked it up and went before the Shaykh al-Islam, saying,
"O Shaykh al-Islam, I am old and have small children; when I am
no longer here, how will this [arrangement] continue?" He
answered, "So long as they do not betray it, any one of your
children may come and take it."

After that, when death overtook Bu al-Qâsem, his descendants
continued to receive it. Anyone else who would come near that
rock [41] would not see anything but the rock. When one of his
descendants divulged this secret, it came no more.

8. The Shaykh and the Christian Ascetic

Another time the Shaykh al-Islam Ahmad, God sanctify his
precious soul, said:

One day I was sitting on a mountain looking in every direction
all about me at the wide world. All of a sudden, my gaze fell upon
one of the mountains of Anatolia [Rum], and there I saw a
monastery and a hermit was sitting there looking at me, just as I
was looking at him. I approached him. He intimated that he knew
everything which had happened to me in these few years, telling
me what I had done or said at such-and-such a time.

I was amazed. "What is your religion?," I asked.[17]

"I am Christian," he said. A feeling of religious zeal took hold of
me [ghayrati garibân-e man gereft]. Wherever I looked
throughout the expanse of land and sea, he named it.[18] I thought,
"How amazing! What difference, then, is there between my Islam
and his infidelity?!" My zeal waxed so strong, I was afraid I might
lose my spiritual footing.

---

[17] The Shaykh addresses and converses with the hermit in Arabic.

[18] That is, the Christian could read the Shaykh's mind and tell him
what objects he was thinking of.

All at once divine grace and blessings came to my aid and inspired this zealous needy one with the words: "Just as you have tested him in this world, so too test him in the sphere of the planets, and see what happens." I had found his observations in this world to be so precise that I fixed my gaze on the planet Saturn. He said nothing. I realized that he could not see it and I gradually lowered my gaze until I reached the birds. As God says: "Have they not regarded the birds that are subjected in the air of heaven?"[19]

Even at the lower elevations he said nothing, and I realized he could not see them. I was inspired with the following words, "Ahmad, do you see the difference between your Islam and his infidelity? We do not act unjustly with anyone, nor do we permit anyone else to act unjustly. He has undergone countless ascetic exercises and exertions in Our path and has submitted himself to so many tribulations, of which you know nothing. You do not realize what sufferings he has endured and continues to endure. If in this world he is not rewarded for his deeds and in the next world [42] he is taken to hell because he is an infidel, it would be unjust. These are the rewards for his deeds, which we have granted abundantly in this world. If we grant him Islam as well, he shall win both worlds. If not, he has no outstanding claim on Our majesty, so they will lead him to hell."

I waited for a while. His servant came in and held a tray out before him. On it were several white shelled almonds. He ate seven of those almonds and offered the tray to me. I ate none. The servant removed the tray. I followed the servant out of the room and asked him, "What does he eat each day and night?" He answered, "Just what you saw." "How long has this been the case," I asked. The servant replied, "I have served him for twelve years and this is how I have found him to be. I don't know anything about the matter prior to that."

Know, however, my children, companions and followers, that if, God forbid, anyone like him should arise among the masses, possessing those qualities which I observed in and heard from him, he would mislead many people and cause them to stray from

---

[19] Qur'ân 16:79, though in Arberry's translation, it occurs as verse 81.

the path of Islamic law and tradition. My advice to you is as follows: should you see anyone walking on the water like a fish, walking through fire like a salamander, flying through the air like a bird, or, like Satan, traversing the East to the West, or vice versa, in a single night, serve him well and obey him, if he is true to religion, the law, tradition, and received opinion. If, however, you see him deviate intentionally even an inch from the law, tradition and received opinion, do not associate with him, for he is a demon leading the people from the true path into perdition. That is my advice.[20] [43]

9. The Shaykh Leaving the Mountain of Nâmaq for the Mountain of Bizd-e Jâm

Another time they asked the Shaykh al-Islam, may God sanctify his precious soul, "What was the reason for your coming down from the mountain to rejoin society?"

He said: After I had been on the Mountain of Nâmaq for twelve years, I heard a voice calling to me, "Ahmad, go live amongst the people and call them from the path of lust and heresy to the path of God and the law." This voice troubled me immensely because it was replacing heavenly companionship with human companionship.

> We make our salutations to the masses -
> This path contains the key to all our troubles

I prostrated myself and prayed, "O Lord, you know that I am not sure whether this voice I have heard is divine or satanic. I fear it could be a trick of Satan." Another voice called out, "What proof will you accept for the truth of this call?" I said, "I need a proof

---

[20] Compare what Shaykh Ahmad says here to the words attributed to Abu Sa'id-e Abu al-Khayr in *Asrâr al-towhid*, ed. M. Shafi'i-Kadkani (Tehran: Enteshârât-e Âgâh, 1366/1987), 1:199, lines 10-16. See also *Ferdows al-morshediyeh fî asrâr al-samadiyeh* (ed. Fritz Meier, 98), *al-Luma'* by Abu Nasr-e Sarrâj (324), and the article by Hellmut Ritter, "Die Aussprüche des Bayezid Bistami," in *Westöstliche Abhandlungen*, ed. Fritz Meier (Wiesbaden: Harrassowitz, 1954), 236.

with which Satan can in no wise tamper." The voice said, "Tell me what you want."

Now there was a large spring flowing down the mountain, so I said, "O Lord, if this is your heavenly voice and is true, command the water of this spring flowing downward to flow up the mountain, for none but You can perform this deed and such power is possible only for You. Satan cannot interfere with it."

I had not yet finished my prayer when the water of the spring turned upwards and reached the summit of the mountain by the power of God, the Exalted. I said, "O God, it is proven true. Tell me where to go and command the water to return to its own place. O Lord, the world is large and its peoples innumerable, tell me, then, where to go."

A bright light, like a torch, immediately appeared. The voice said, "Ahmad, follow this torch until it disappears." I followed the torch from mountain to mountain and plain to plain, up to the mountain of Bizd-e Jâm.[21] [44] On the spot where the light disappeared I built a mosque. I stayed in that mosque on that mountain for six full years. People would come and go from all parts and take away many things with themselves to all corners of the earth. They would bring written questions from Imams, Shaykhs and grandees of the world, and take back the answers to them. They would observe the grace and blessings of God, glorified and exalted be He, granted to this indigent servant.

And peace be with you.

---

[21] The name of this mountain and the village at its foot is given variously in the manuscripts of this book. We have been unable to find reference to it in other sources. According to the *Farhang-e joghrâfiâ-ye Irân* (v. 9) there are three villages named Bizkh, Bizg and Bizah, the first in the outlying area of Sabzevâr, the second in the district of Torbat-e Jâm and the third also in the area of Sabzevâr. The Bizd in our source may well be Bizg, which according to the *Joghrâfiâ-ye Irân*, is one of the villages of Miân-Jâm in the district of Torbat-e Jâm, near the city of Mashhad, located 20 kilometers to the northwest of Torbat-e Jâm, in a mountainous area with a temperate to cold climate. See 'Ali Fâzel, *Sharh-e ahvâl...Shaykh Ahmad-e Jâm* (Tehran: Tus, 1373/1994), 18-19, 30, etc.

10. Building the Mosque

Furthermore, when Shaykh al-Islam Ahmad, God sanctify his precious soul, took up residence on the mountain of Bizd-e Jâm, laid the foundation of that mosque—which today is still there—and began to build it up, his friends would bring stones and wood so the masons and carpenters could keep working. One of the beams was a little too short.

The carpenters said, "Sire, this beam is too short, we need another one." The Shaykh answered, "What sort of carpenters are you that you cannot lengthen wood?" They said, "We can make the wood shorter, but we cannot lengthen it."

He said, "Get the wood ready," and they did. When it was ready, they asked, "What now?" He said, "Put one end in place," and they did. Then they asked the Shaykh, "What now?" The Shaykh climbed on top of the wall and said, "Give one end [45] to me and put the other end in place and hold it firmly." The Shaykh then pulled on the end of the piece of wood in his hands that did not reach the wall, until it extended a couple of feet [*nim gaz*] beyond the wall, by the power of God, the Exalted.

This beam is on the eastern side of the mosque. When the construction was finished and he settled in there, people from all over the world came to see him. Many would come and witness his miracles and carry his repute to all corners of the world.

11. The Arrival of a Messenger from Imam Ilâqi and the Question of Transmutation of the Elements

One day a messenger arrived from the late Imam Sayyed Ilâqi[22] carrying a letter [and a message], saying "It has been reported to me that in your hands rocks, pebbles, dust and anything else turns to gold. According to what I know, in the hands of God's holy men gold turns to dust, not vice versa. If the report I have heard is

---

[22] Ilâq is a town 10 farsangs from the city of Châch in Central Asia. This figure may be the same Imam Ilâqi mentioned in the section on Alchemy in Shaykh Ahmad's *Epistle to the Samarqandians* (see Part Four). Later on in this same anecdote, the same Imam Ilâqi is also called by the title Amir.

correct and you have been given the power and authority to transmute matter, you should transmute the seal in this messenger's hand, without opening it, and send it back to me."[23]

The Shaykh al-Islam reached out and took the seal from the messenger and turned it over in his hand, saying:

> The day on which the works of fate were sealed,
> the lovers' gold was stamped from different mold.
> Your reason cannot fathom this impression -
> This gold was fashioned from beyond the mint

He then said, "He who can turn rocks, pebbles and dust to gold is also able to transmute gold to rocks, pebbles and dust. These rumors and confusions stem from the supposition that it is Ahmad who makes gold. It is not Ahmad, but *Ahad*[24] who does so. Ahmad is as helpless as anyone else, but God, the Exalted and Almighty, is All-powerful and He, by His power, does this through the hands of Ahmad."

He then gave back the seal just as it was and said, "Take this back so that they can see what has happened to the seal and what is inside it." [46]

The messenger reported:

He then handed the seal to me. I realized only that it was lighter. When I brought it before Amir Sayyed Imam Ilâqi, he handled it carefully and looked at it closely, and found it to be intact. A group of distinguished men were in his presence. When he broke open the seal, everything inside that was in one piece, had turned, like the seal itself, to stone, and everything inside that was small had turned to pebbles and dust. They were greatly amazed and all

---

[23] *Mohr* could be a ring or stone seal used to impress a signature on a letter, and also the impression left by the seal usually in wax. The text seems ambiguous about whether an impression of the seal or the seal itself is here at issue. Perhaps both a stone seal or stamp, and also the impression left by that stamp on the outside of the envelope or package, are intended.

[24] i.e., God. *Ahad* is a divine attribute, meaning the Single or Unique One (see, e.g., K112:1). In Persian or Arabic, as in English, it differs from the word Ahmad by a single letter.

of those distinguished men came to believe in and follow him,
acknowledging that this man was a saint of God.

12. The Onion and the Vinegar of the Shaykh and the Imams of Nayshabur

One day a group of the distinguished Imams of Nayshabur came
to visit the Shaykh al-Islam, who was sitting in the mosque. He
treated them very kindly and asked them about all manner of
things. Then he told his servant, "These Imams have just arrived
from a journey; bring whatever food you have for them to eat."
The servant went out but he soon came back, as there was no food.
The Shaykh told him, "You simple-hearted man, don't you have
any vinegar and onions?"

He replied, "I do, but I have no bread. What can I serve them
with?"

The Shaykh said, "The food is coming; you go and get the
vinegar and onions."

The servant spread the tablecloth, dumped some onions on it and
placed two bowls of vinegar in front of them. The Shaykh peeled a
few onions with his own blessed hands and handed one of them to
each person. As they started to eat, a ravenous appetite [*sharah-e
tamâm*] for onions and vinegar took hold of them. After a while a
lavish full-course meal was brought in and set before them. [47]
After helping themselves and eating a few morsels [of the food],
they gave up on it and returned to the onions and vinegar.

"We have never eaten anything more tasty, delicious and
delectable than this," they said. With ravenous appetite they ate
many onions and much vinegar.

13. How the Shaykh went to Sarakhs and Cured the Sick

The Shaykh, God sanctify his precious soul, also said:
After I had spent six years on the mountain of Bizd-e Jâm, one
night just before dawn I was praying in the mosque, beseeching
God, the Almighty, for the community of Mohammad, the
Chosen, may prayers and blessings be upon him. Suddenly a
heavenly voice called out, "O Ahmad, hurry hence and go quickly

unto Sarakhs[25] as a healer, for We have sent down an illness on
the people of Sarakhs and have invested your breath with its cure.
Now go, for in this there is a grand design [*ta'biyeh-hâ*], the
wisdom of which no one knows, except for Ourselves. Heed My
command and go."

I got up at once and set out for Sarakhs. No one knew where I
was going. When I arrived in the city of Sarakhs, I walked through
the bazaar every day, calling out loudly, "Doctor, here! Healing,
here!" [*tabibân, hakimân*], but no one paid attention to me.

Then one day a well-known noble of that city by the name of
Rashid al-Din Abu Sa'id saw me and said, "What sort of a con is
this you are running!"

I said, "What dishonesty do you see in this?"

He answered, "You wear a Sufi cloak and say such things?! If
you are a physician, where is your book, your medicines, your
instruments? If you are a surgeon, where are your surgical tools?"

I answered, "Sir, tell me why a physician is called to the bedside
of a sick person?"

He answered, "In order to treat the patient and make him better."

I said, "Have you taken me to the bedside of any patient who did
not recover, that you should ask for a book and medicines and
instruments from me?"

He answered, "Dervish, what lofty words you speak! [48] If I
take you to the bedside of a patient, will you come?"

I said, "That's why I have been sent here."

"Come on," he said.

He led me to the bedside of a patient who had been ill for a year,
one of the well-known citizens of Sarakhs. I sat at his bedside and
read the opening Sura of the Qur'ân [*Fâtiha*] over him and prayed.
I rubbed my hand on his chest and breathed over him. Then I said,
"Arise, by the will of God, the Almighty!" At that very moment
God sent His healing down upon him.

Then the Shaykh told him, "Put on your shoes and come out
with me."

---

[25] A city in Khorasan, east of Nayshabur, on the Harirud River, near the
present-day border with Turkmenistan. It was an important center of
mysticism in the twelfth century.

They said, "He has not been on his feet for one whole year; he does not have any shoes."

The Shaykh said, "Let him put on someone else's shoes so we can go out." He put on some shoes and came outside.

The news spread throughout the town. Many people turned to the Shaykh, for the number of the sick in the city of Sarakhs was large. The Shaykh al-Islam was taken to the bedside of all the sick people and God, the Almighty, sent healing down on them by means of his blessed breath, for God is the Healer.

14. The Shaykh and the Qâzi of Sarakhs

The wife of the judge of Sarakhs fell ill. An official from the court of justice said, "Your honor, a Shaykh has arrived in this city who instantly cures every patient whose bedside he is brought to. If the patient is a man, the Shaykh [makes him rise from his bed] and walk outside with him; if it is a woman, he has her walk to someone else's house. If you so desire, we will bring him."

The judge replied with harsh words. "Do you consider me one of the ignorant masses!? Aren't you ashamed to talk to me of such things?!"

The official from the court of justice fell silent. The patient grew worse, so bad that for seven days and nights no liquid went down her throat. The judge was extremely sad, for he loved this woman. Finally, the official said to him, "Your honor, they are taking the Shaykh to such-and-such place and he will pass by your house. Bring him to the bedside of your patient, if she is not cured, well, she will die and your agitation on her behalf will come to an end."

[49] The judge put on his cloak and his turban and waited at the door. When the Shaykh arrived, the judge came out and greeted the Shaykh. The Shaykh returned his greetings and said, "O judge, you have tarried too long at the door. We have answered your hesitation by coming forward Ourselves. Go and put a veil [châdor] on your lesser half,[26] for you have caused her much pain.

---

[26] 'Owrat, which literally means "private parts" or "genitals," but is used in Persian to refer obliquely to a man's wife. Ironically, it is considered more decent than saying the word for wife [zan]. Each reference to the woman in this story, as in many medieval and even

Since God, the Almighty, has vouchsafed her cure in the breath of Ahmad, what did you hope to accomplish?"

He went straightaway into the house and sat down at the bedside of the woman ['*owrat*], and said to the judge, "Give me your right hand." The judge held out his hand and the Shaykh al-Islam took the judge's wrist and rubbed his hand on the chest of the woman, recited the *Fâtiha*, prayed and blew upon her. Then he said, "O judge, would you permit your lesser half to remove the veil from her face, to say hello and to sit up? For God, the Almighty, has already cured her."

The judge was so overwhelmed with joy that he said, "There is no need even to ask, think of her as your own maid-servant." The Shaykh al-Islam said to the woman, "Take the veil off your face, woman, and sit up and say hello." So the woman reached up and unveiled her face and greeted them.

Then the Shaykh al-Islam told the judge, "She has grown very weak; give her a cane so she can walk to a neighbor's house." In his joy, the judge supposed that by cane he meant just that, namely his member! The Shaykh al-Islam said, "Put away that nightstick and give her a wooden staff to go to the neighbor's house." The woman went to the neighbor's house.

---

modern texts, is signaled by the word '*owrat*. As we see below, a male physician did not directly touch a female patient - who would remain covered by her veil - but used, at least in this case, the intermediary of her husband's hand to examine her.

15. The Shaykh's Dispute with Imam Mohammad-e Mansur of Sarakhs[27]

The Shaykh al-Islam and the judge left the house. On their way back, they passed by [50] the khâneqâh[28] of Imam Mohammad-e Mansur of Sarakhs. He was a learned man, and used to lecture while sitting on a chair. When they reached the door of the khâneqâh, the judge stopped the Shaykh and said, "A whole population of men and women have been healed by your blessed breath. Mohammad-e Mansur is a very great and learned man, crippled in both legs. They lift him up and put him in the chair and then lift him up and put back down again. If you look upon him favorably and God should heal him through your blessed breath, that would be a weighty matter. A handful of commoners could never accomplish what he has."

The Shaykh said, "He is a disagreeable man."

The judge answered, "I, too, doubted you. When I saw it with my own eyes, I was won over. Once he sees, he will be won over."

The Shaykh al-Islam said, "You were a doubter who was won over, after witnessing [a miracle] performed on a third party. He is

---

[27] An important figure in the development of Sufism in Khorasan, who flourished in the first decades of the 12th century. Sanâ'i has composed a number of poems for Mohammad-e Mansur, including a *qasideh* that may possibly allude to a reconciliation between Mohammad-e Mansur and the Shaykh al-Islam Ahmad (*Divân-e Hakim Sanâ'i*, ed. Modarres-e Razavi, 2nd ed., 262ff). Other than Sanâ'i, few sources make mention of Mohammad-e Mansur, though a book in Arabic entitled *Riyâz al-uns* is ascribed to him. This work has not been published, but manuscripts of it exist in the British Museum, at Leiden and in Munich (see Charles Rieu, *Supplement to the Catalogue of the Arabic Manuscripts in the British Museum*, 153, Nr. 236).

[28] A retreat and center of activities for a particular order of Sufis, similar to a monastery. The Sufis meet there to pray, listen to lectures, study, etc., and travelers from out of town might eat and sleep there as well. Sanâ'i wrote a dedication for this particular khâneqâh, which included a library and hospice. See *Divân-e Hakim Sanâ'i*, ed. Modarres-e Razavi, 2nd ed., 1074; an English translation of this poem appears in Franklin Lewis, *Rumi: Past and Present, East and West* (Oxford: Oneworld, 2000), 27-8.

a doubter who, having witnessed a miracle performed on himself, will become even more opposed."

The judge replied, "Even if what you say is true, it seems unreasonable to me that a person who has experienced such a miracle performed on his own person would become even stronger in his denial." He continued, "If I am right, please be gracious."

The Shaykh answered, "Judge, I will show you this very hour, and we will see whether you agree with me or not."

He turned around and entered the khâneqâh. [51] When the Shaykh's glance fell upon Mohammad-e Mansur, he said a prayer and breathed over him, saying, "Arise by the will of God. The Almighty God has cured you."

Imam Mohammad-e Mansur immediately stood up on his feet in the chair. A great commotion arose among the audience and they surged forward. Mohammad-e Mansur began stamping on the chair and shouting, "Be quiet!"

Before the crowd calmed down, the judge said to the Shaykh, "Come, let us go to the prayer sanctuary [*mehrâb*], for we cannot get out of this gathering."

The Shaykh said, "Sit right here and wait to see and hear what happens."

When the crowd quieted down, Mohammad-e Mansur said, "O Muslims! Know that God, glorified and exalted be He, has and will continue to have countless blessings on the outward and inward aspects of Mohammad-e Mansur. For a while He reproached me and kept me seated, until today He cast His glance of mercy upon me and made me arise. Let no one suppose that God, glorified and exalted be He, would perform such deeds as this through the words of any old two-faced, dishonest libertine."[29]

As he said this, the Shaykh got up and said, "Since you believe that God, in compliance with the request of His elite servants, won't do anything...." And here he clapped his hands, saying, "Sit down, be quiet and don't talk nonsense." Mohammad-e Mansur trembled on his chair and sat down, and he was struck dumb.

---

[29] For *abâhati-rang*, a term for a person who considers the breaking of religious laws and ordinances to be permissible.

The Shaykh al-Islam came out of the khâneqâh and Mohammad-e Mansur indicated with a nod of his head for his followers to go after him. When they came out they stopped the Shaykh and pleaded with him, "Do you believe it is proper [52] to leave him dumbstruck like that when his talks are of great benefit to the masses?"

In response to this plea, the Shaykh al-Islam returned to the khâneqâh, looked at Mohammad-e Mansur and said, "Speak and speak knowledgeably, but do not meddle in things of which you know not, for the works of God's holy men are not accomplished by the aid of your hands or those like unto you. But you will never rise again." And the Shaykh left the khâneqâh and went away.

That evening Mohammad-e Mansur sent someone to fetch the leaders of religion and the notables of the city and told them, "In this town of ours there has never to this day been heresy, hypocrisy or laxity in following the laws of religion. What has befallen you today, that you held your peace while a deceiver entered our town and led the people astray?"

The judge said, "Your honor, why are you talking against a person who, when he tells you to arise you cannot sit down and, when he tells you to sit down you cannot stand, and when he tells you to be quiet, you cannot speak, and when he tells you to speak, you begin talking? You have experienced all this on your own person, why then do you talk like this?"

Mohammad-e Mansur said, "Silence! You and he both!" And he rebuked the judge very harshly. After that one of the townspeople got up and said, "What would be the reward of a person who kills this Shaykh?"

Mohammad-e Mansur said, "He would receive the reward of one who kills ten atheists on the battlefield."

The townsman said, "Order that this be written down and handed to me and I will kill him tomorrow."

Mohammad-e Mansur ordered a fatwa[30] to be written in response to the question, "What do the leaders of religion say concerning a man who kills Ahmad Abu al-Hasan Nâmaqi? How

---

[30] A judicial decree issued by a religious leader (Arabic *fatwâ*, Persian *fatvâ*). For Sunnis, in modern times, only the highest judicial authority in a community, holder of the office of *mufti*, has the right to issue a fatwa.

much reward would he receive?" Mohammad-e Mansur wrote the reply, "The reward for shedding his blood would be equal to someone who kills ten atheists in battle." He then gave it to Sayyed Ziâdi[31] who wrote [53], "The response is approved."[32]

Then they gave it to the young townsman, who said, "So be it. Tomorrow I will kill him. Let there be no further debate about the matter."

Mohammad-e Mansur said, "Wait until we call a meeting. We'll summon him and have a final word with him. The moment we declare him an infidel, you kill him."

The next day they all gathered in the khâneqâh of Sayyed Ziâdi and sent someone to tell the Shaykh al-Islam, "You must come so we can speak with you." A group of the Shaykh's disciples were aware of what was happening and wept. One of them said, "O Shaykh, this is the situation and such is their plan. It would not be advisable for you to go."

The Shaykh said, "I have a King. As long as that King is here in town, I have no fear of agitation by anyone, and there is never a time when this King is absent.

> In town you won't see troubled agitation
> when the standard of that King comes marching in.

He then asked his servant to bring his shoes so they could go.

[The opponents] had agreed that none of them would rise to his feet when the Shaykh al-Islam came in or move from his place. When he came in and their eyes fell upon him, not one among them stayed in his place, except Mohammad-e Mansur who was not able to rise. The Shaykh al-Islam entered and sat down and asked, "Why have you summoned me here?"

---

[31] First mentioned here, he is called Ziâdin, but henceforth he is referred to as Ziâdi, without the final "n". Likewise, the *Kholâsat al-maqâmât*, 36, gives his name as Ziâdi, with no "n."

[32] *Sabaqa al-jawâb*, an Arabic phrase which appears to be a somewhat unusual expression. The reading we have given is proposed by the late scholar, Dr. Abbâs Zaryâb-e Khu'i, who suggests that Mohammad-e Mansur sent his ruling to Sayyed Ziâdi, another religious scholar or mufti, who confirmed it with this Arabic phrase.

The judge offered an excuse and everyone was saying one thing or another. Sayyed Ziâdi turned to those present [54] and said, "Why don't you speak up?...We, sir, have summoned you."

The Shaykh said, "Tell me why."

He answered, "We hear that you claim to know God directly, and anyone who believes so is an infidel."

The Shaykh said, "And I say that whoever does not say and believe likewise, he is the infidel."

"Wow [*hay hay*]!," said the Sayyed.

The Shaykh said, "Wow is no kind of answer for me. What is your view?" Three more times Sayyed-e Ziâdi repeated the same words, "Wow!"

Finally the Shaykh shouted at him, saying, "Silence, you impudent fellow. Your knowledge doesn't extend beyond the legs of a menstruating woman. How do you dare to talk of God's unity with Ahmad?" Then the Shaykh got up. The people who had drawn their knives and stood waiting to kill the Shaykh, dropped their knives and fell at the blessed feet of the Shaykh and cried out in repentance.

When the Shaykh left the khâneqâh, the father of Sayyed Ziâdi, who was still alive, [though] very advanced in age, stood in his way, holding his gray locks in hand and weeping. He said, "O Shaykh, upon the sanctified honor of Mohammad, the Prophet, prayers and blessings be upon him, spare the life of my son for my sake, for I have no other children."

The Shaykh leaned upon his cane for a while deep in thought. Finally he raised his head to say, "My dear Sayyed, God has spared the life of your son for your sake, but he will not enjoy knowledge anymore and no true fatwa will ever again issue from his pen, on account of the impudence he has displayed."

The Sayyed said, "I won't be satisfied until you lead him out of the khâneqâh."

In the khâneqâh only Sayyed Ziâdi and Mohammad-e Mansur were left [55] and the Sayyed kept on saying "Wow." The Shaykh went back into the khâneqâh. Sayyed Ziâdi and Mohammad-e Mansur were still there and the Shaykh called out to Sayyed-e Ziâdi. He came forward and bowed at the feet of the Shaykh, saying, "O Shaykh, I repent. Forgive me, for I was ignorant."

The Shaykh patted him on the back. "My good man,[33] didn't you know that the work of God's holy men is not accomplished by the aid of your hands? God, the Almighty and Exalted, forgives you for the sake of your father, but on account of the impudence you have shown, you will no longer enjoy knowledge and good works, and no true fatwa will be issued from your pen."

So that you know!

16. Sultan Sanjar Visits the Shaykh in Ma'd-âbâd

Now, because of the great commotion in the town of Sarakhs, the Shaykh al-Islam left and came to the mountain of Estâd near Zur-âbâd,[34] where he founded four monasteries in different locations [56]. All of them are still there today and flourishing. If we describe all of the conditions and works and miracles which occurred there, the story will grow long and lead to boredom.

After a while, he left that place for Ma'd-âbâd and settled there, and crowds of people from all over came to him and witnessed the works and miracles he performed. When word of the Shaykh reached Sanjar son of Malekshâh, the Sultan of Sultans, a messenger came from the city of Marv to see the Shaykh in Ma'd-âbâd near Jâm. Since the Sultan had earlier experience of the Shaykh's wondrous miracles, he wanted to find out whether it was the same person.

The Shaykh was informed that the Sultan was coming to visit him. "Fine," he said.

As the Sultan reached the door of the khâneqâh, where the carpenters had been sawing wood, he dismounted. The Shaykh got up, filled his sleeves with sawdust and left the khâneqâh. The Sultan was standing on one side of the street while the Shaykh stood, across the water channel, on the other. He threw open his arms, shaking his sleeves, and said, "O Sanjar, this is Ahmad's

---

[33] Shaykh Ahmad idiomatically uses a fictional patronymic here, *Bâ 'Isâ*, as a form of general address, "O Abu 'Isâ," probably with the sense of, "my good man." Though it occurs twice in this text (see also Story 27), it does not appear in other Persian texts.

[34] See "Ahmad's Career in Jâm and Khorasan" in the Introduction for details on these toponyms.

offering to you."

By the power of God, the Almighty, it had turned to pure gold. Some of it fell on the Sultan and some of it spilled in the channel and some of it in the street and some of it on the by-standers. And still today people find gold in that water, in the form of those wood chips.

17. The Shaykh and Toghrol Tekin

As Shaykh Ahmad, God sanctify his precious soul, was busy with the construction of the khâneqâh and the Friday mosque, he had ordered the people to bring lumber to the khâneqâh and mosque from the vicinity of Zur-âbâd. At that time Jâm was a fiefdom of the Seljuk Toghrol Tekin,[35] and he [57] was constructing his own estate in the town of Sâghu[36] in the district of Jâm, which was his seat of government. He wanted to obtain high-quality beams and columns, but could not find them.

A person in the governor's circle told him, "They have gotten good lumber for Shaykh Ahmad from the mountain of Zur-âbâd; someone should be sent to him asking for some of those beams and columns. They can get more for him." So he sent someone to the Shaykh al-Islam with this request.

The Shaykh refused and replied thus: "How can the lumber which is brought for the khâneqâh of Ahmad be taken to and used for the estate of the Amir?"

When the messenger returned and conveyed the answer, the person who had made the original suggestion was present. He said, "How strange! How can wood that has been taken from the domains of the king and carried by his subjects, be denied to the governor of his domain?"

The Amir grew livid at these words. He ordered that the drums be sounded and that the troops mount their horses. "Let us go and get the wood."

---

[35] The text literally states, "Toghrol Tekin the Sanjarite" [*sanjari*], indicating that he was a subordinate of Sanjar, the Seljuk Sultan. For historical information about Toghrol Tekin, see the section *Shaykh Ahmad and His Contemporaries* in the Introduction.

[36] See "Shaykh Ahmad's Career in Jâm and Khorasan," supra 11-15.

The one who had made the original suggestion grew fearful. He pleaded with the associates of the Amir: "This is not a wise move. What if things go wrong and someone is killed?"

The Amir asked, "Do you mean that someone would fight with me?"

The notables replied, "If that's not a concern, why then the troops and the battle drums? We can get the wood some other way."

The Amir said, "We absolutely must bring that wood from Ma'd-âbâd. Do it by whatever means you deem appropriate."

They said, "We will take care of it." They then provided a few men with rope and horses[37] and told them, "Do it such that the people remain calm. Enter the village, pick up the wood and head out."

When those men arrived in Ma'd-âbâd from Sâghu, the people had already performed the evening prayer and the Shaykh and his followers had gone home and were eating their supper. The wood was lying on the ground at the door of the Friday mosque, which was on the main road near the village gate. [58] They picked up two columns and three beams and headed out.

The Shaykh suddenly sank into thought as he ate. After a while he raised his head and smiled. The servant bowed and asked him why he smiled. The Shaykh al-Islam said, "At this moment thirty men arrived from Sâghu and loaded up five pieces of lumber, tied them on their horses and set off." A number of his followers rose from the table in order to chase them and bring back the lumber. The Shaykh said, "Calm down. If Toghrol should ever lean on those columns, Ahmad is very much mistaken."

One of the associates of the Amir was in Ma'd-âbâd and happened to be present. When these words were uttered, he wrote them down and quickly sent off a messenger to inform the Amir of the situation. He told the messenger, "Present this to the Amir," and he did so. Amir Toghrol grew more heated and commanded as

---

[37] The word used is *yarkh*, which does not appear in the dictionaries. It is probably a dialectical pronunciation of *yarâgh*, meaning a horse that has been broken in and trained. *Yargh* or *yarâq*, meaning equipment or accoutrements, might also be intended.

follows, "Get candles and torches and bring the masons and carpenters here and put them to work. By morning have the columns in place so that I can lean on them. The people will realize that everything Shaykh Ahmad says is a lie."

The masons set to work and the carpenters waited for the lumber, which arrived there in the morning. They tried very hard, but by breakfast time it was not completed, because the columns could not be raised without ropes. The Amir came in person and told them, "Bring some rope and raise the column right on this spot. Bring my throne and place it such that I can sit on it and lean back on the column, that everyone may know his falsehood."

When the column was in place and the Amir entered the hall and was about to sit on his throne and receive the offerings of gold scattered at him, a loud noise arose from behind the hall, such that all the people were greatly astonished. [59] The Amir was surprised and wondered what the noise was. Several smooth-faced young Turkish riders entered the compound of the Amir's estate. The perplexity of the Amir and those in attendance increased, not knowing who these riders were, where they came from or to what purpose. One of them dismounted, removed a lasso from his saddlebag, entered the hall and threw it around the Amir's neck, pulling him out and tying it to the saddlebag. He mounted and spurred on his horse. They went on for one league down the highway and then disappeared into the desert off to the right. Several of the Amir's horsemen put on their armor and followed after them. They followed one full league into the desert, where they saw the headless body of the Amir lying, and no footprints leading away in any direction.

They were stupefied. They sent someone to Sultan Sanjar informing him that, "An incident has taken place, a grave event, which no learned or wise man has been able to figure out. We have reported what happened, the rest is left to the king's royal judgement."

The Sultan was greatly angered at this and said, "If the people of Jâm do not figure out what has occurred, I will kill them all."

The people of Jâm were greatly perturbed. They turned to the Shaykh and said, "A grave event has taken place and no one can figure out who they were, from where they came or where they went. Now the Sultan has issued a decree and we are perplexed by this occurrence and cannot solve it. If you, by way of intuition or by seeing it yourself, are aware what has happened, lend a hand to these unfortunate folk and save them, for we are in great dejection."

The Shaykh explained who they were, from where they came, by whose orders they acted, why, and where they went. The people said, "Since [60] you know all this, perhaps you could come to our aid and respond to the Sultan, for it is not within our power to send this answer." The Shaykh said, "It is fitting that I write what the circumstances were and what happened."

Here follows the letter which the Shaykh al-Islam wrote to Sultan Sanjar:

> Should one of the chosen servants of the king go to one of the cities in the domain of the king, and should one of the officials of that city scorn him for no reason and look upon him with disdain, once the king found out about it, he would consider himself obliged to redress that offense with a thoroughly suitable punishment. [The king], a creature who is not self-sufficient, in order to ensure the well-being of the realm, would not fail to redress an insult to his chosen servant; how then, could the Creator, who is self-sufficient and sanctified from all need, fail to redress an offense against one of His own weak and needy servants? He would overlook thousands upon thousands [of sins] against Himself, but not a single one committed against His chosen servants.[38] For on that plane, it is a question of absolute self-subsistence, and on this, a question of abject need. Should an impudent person commit a treacherous act and then seek to discredit the words of one of God's chosen servants, making them appear false, how could God, Exalted be He, permit it to go unpunished?
>
> God sent several horsemen from the invisible world to punish that impudent hypocrite in a befitting manner. What sin can be attributed in this to the people of Jâm, and what could they have done to avoid it? Even the king, with his power and his troops, would be unable to ward off or amend it, let alone

---

[38] See the similar phrase in Shaykh Ahmad's "Epistle to the Samarqandians" in Part Four, below.

this weak and powerless lot. Beware not to think anyone other than that impudent hypocrite guilty in this matter. Such is my counsel.

When the letter of the Shaykh al-Islam reached Sanjar, he read it and asked [61], "What was the nature of this treachery and what statement has been discredited?" They told the Sultan the whole story of what happened and what was said. He wept bitterly and said, "Do not [oppose Shaykh Ahmad] and do not confront him, for I have witnessed major miracles from him." And so he treated [the representatives of] the people of Jâm with kindness, honored them with gifts and sent them back home joyful and happy-hearted.

And peace be with you.

18. The Shaykh's Miracle for the Learned 'Omar Elyâs

Once the learned 'Omar Elyâs from the area of Ghur and Ghazna was studying in the city of Nayshabur. He had finished [the study] of a certain book. His teacher asked him, "Now that you have finished this book, which book will you start next?"

He said, "My heart is heavy. I will not study anymore."

The teacher asked, "Why do you say this?"

He answered, "There are those among the students who have not memorized ten pages and yet they give talks on [learned] questions in meetings. I, on the other hand, have learned more than one hundred pages by memory and cannot say a word. Why should I take such trouble for nothing?"

The teacher said, "Take care not to talk like this or entertain such ideas, for you have worked hard and studied. God, the Almighty, will one day inspire your heart."

He said, "I am depressed. I think I'll go away for a while."

The teacher said, "If you want to go on a journey, go to Jâm, for they are saying that there is a man who works miracles there. If it is true, perhaps he will look on you with favor, and God, the Almighty, will open the door of knowledge to you through the blessings of his glance. You will gain great happiness, and you can also bring news to us of his doings and what he is like. If it is not true, at least you will have had a change of scenery and will be refreshed. You can come back to your studies so that God, the Almighty, will not render your efforts useless."

['Omar Elyâs] says:

When I decided to go see the Shaykh al-Islam and was on my way [62] to Jâm, everywhere I stopped along the way, I would hear amazing reports. Then I reached the village of Ma'd-âbâd and went to see him. I saw a large crowd of scholars and jurists and dervishes sitting there eating. I greeted him and the Shaykh said, "Greetings to you, learned 'Omar. Sit down right there and wait for the food to be taken away."

I was surprised; how did he know my name was 'Omar and that I was a scholar? When I looked closely, I saw a full spread of all kinds [of delicacies] in front of him. I thought to myself, "What kind of an ascetic is this?!"

Right away, the Shaykh called out, "Control your thoughts, you are not yet in the know."[39] He sent me some of the elaborate spread which was in front of him. When they finished eating and removed the spread, he called me forward and asked how I was. He comforted me greatly and asked about the Imams of Nayshabur. Then he said, "Now, as an offering from his journey [*rah-âvard*], the learned 'Omar will give a homily."

I had never studied homiletics and was deeply perplexed about what excuse to offer and what he would say. Then the Shaykh removed the cushion on which he was leaning and laid it before me, saying, "Knowledge demands loftiness, so sit on this cushion." There was no way I could respond and I sat down with hesitation on the cushion. The Shaykh asked me to lean forward and he spit in my mouth. Then he told the Qur'ân reciters, "Begin by chanting some holy verses before the learned 'Omar speaks, for such is our custom."

When the Qur'ân reciters finished the verses, through the aid and mental efforts and blessed favor of that great man of religion, God, the Almighty, opened the doors of eloquence to my heart. The sermon came out so well that the scholars who were present

---

[39] In Persian, it is literally, "you don't know" [*na-dâni*], but the Shaykh is suggesting that 'Omar does not have the other-worldly knowledge that the Shaykh possesses.

praised it effusively. From then on, God, exalted and glorified be He, through the blessings of [the Shaykh's] breath and saliva, showered knowledge upon me and opened to me the doors of knowledge and wisdom in such wise that [63] none will ever comprehend.

And it is God who bestows success.

19. The Imams of Nayshabur Test the Shaykh

When continuous reports, necessarily confirming the validity of the matter, reached the Imams, dignitaries and nobles of the city of Nayshabur about the spiritual feats and the miracles of the Shaykh al-Islam Ahmad, may God sanctify his precious soul, the leaders of the various Islamic rites[40] came to Jâm to investigate the matter and see for themselves the life, spiritual qualities and miracles of the Shaykh. When they arrived at the village of Ma'd-âbâd, the Shaykh treated them with kindness and humility. The Imams, likewise, out of their own magnanimity, showed him great respect, to the extent that some of them questioned why a Shaykh should be treated with such respect and humility. "After all, we first need to see some of the things we have heard that our hearts may be convinced and that we not act out of mere imitation,[41] for it is not befitting that the ulama should merely imitate [others]."

Three days later a group of followers from Amghân[42] came, bringing mounts with them, and requesting that the Shaykh bestow honor upon Amghân with his presence. The Shaykh al-Islam said, "We have received honored and distinguished guests, we cannot come."

The people of Amghân went to see the Imams with this request,

---

[40] i.e., the four canonical schools of Islamic law among the Sunnis (the Hanafi, Maliki, Shafi'i and Hanbali schools), as well as the legal school of the Shiites, and, in this text, the Karrâmites.

[41] At issue is the concept of *taqlid*, which in Islamic law, is the reliance upon the decision of another. The laity is expected to follow or imitate the legal judgements of the legal scholars ('*ulamâ*), whereas the high-ranking legal scholars of Islam are the authorities to be imitated in matters pertaining to religious life.

[42] A village 18 kilometers to the northwest of Torbat-e Jâm.

"You have come to see the Shaykh al-Islam. If you would suggest to him that he accept, along with you, our invitation, it would be a great blessing for us and it would do you no harm."

The Imams agreed and told the Shaykh, "We have come to attend you. Wherever you may be, we will go with you, so you should accept the invitation of these humble followers." [64]

The Shaykh accepted and they set out from Ma'd-âbâd. The Imams quarreled among themselves, saying, "We are riding behind the Shaykh by way of imitation, which goes against reason and knowledge. Shouldn't we have seen with our own eyes some token of the things we have heard about him?" It was the Imams of the Karrâmites[43] and the Shiites who were most opposed.

The Imam Zahir al-Din Bayhaqi[44] and the Imam Sadr al-Din

---

[43] The followers of Mohammad ebn-e Karrâm (d. 869 / 255 A.H.), whose unorthodox teachings became popular in Khorasan in the eleventh and twelfth centuries. The article "Karrāmiyya" by C.E. Bosworth in the *Encyclopaedia of Islam* (2nd ed.) now requires revision in light of the following brilliant articles by Mohammad-Rezâ Shafi'i-Kadkani: "Ravâbet-e Shaykh-e Jâm bâ Karrâmiân-e 'asr-e khwish," in *Yâdnâmeh-ye Ostâd 'Abbâs-e Zaryâb-e Khu'i*, in a special issue of *Majalleh-ye Dâneshkadeh-ye Adabiyât va 'Olum-e Ensâni* (Dâneshgâh-e Tarbiyat-e Mo'allem), new series, 2, 6-8 (Fall 1373-Spring 1374/1995): 29-50; "Nakhostin tajrobeh-hâ-ye she'r-e 'erfâni dar zabân-e Pârsi" in *Jashn nâmeh-ye Zarrinkub (Derakht-e Ma'refat)* (Tehran, 1376/1997), 431-62; "Chehreh-ye digar-e Mohammad ben Karrâm-e Sejestâni dar partov-e sokhanân-e now-yâfteh az u," *Arjnâmeh-ye Iraj* (Tehran, 1377/1998), 61-113; and "Safineh'i az she'r-hâ-ye 'erfâni-ye qarn-e chahârom va panjom" in *Jashn-nâmeh-ye Ostâd Zabih Allâh Safâ* (Tehran, 1377/1998).

[44] Perhaps this is the same Imam Zahir-e Bayhaqi (d. 1170 / 565 A.H.) who wrote the *Tatimmah siwân al-hikmah* and the *Târikh-e Bayhaq*, in addition to numerous other works. The description "one of the famous scholars of Islam and a prominent philosopher in his day" would not likely be applied to an unknown figure. This Imam furthermore alludes to philosophy (*hekmat*), specifically the science of the transmutation of the elements, which is again suggestive of an author and learned man. The passage also states that this Imam wrote a Qur'ân commentary; among the list of books which Yâqût attributes in his *Mu'jam al-udabâ'* (ed. Margouliouth, 5:208) to the well-known Bayhaqi (quoting from the latter's own *Mashârib al-tajârib*), there are titles which might well be

'Ali Haysam of Nayshabur were riding along together and discussing this matter. The Shaykh al-Islam was sitting on a donkey and all at once rode right in between them to say, "I've come to race my donkey with your horses."

They replied, "O Shaykh, it has never been the custom to race donkeys with horses."

The Shaykh said, "We will break with the custom." He then spurred on his donkey and they too spurred on their horses. However much they tried they could not overtake the dust of the Shaykh al-Islam's mount. He got so far ahead that they couldn't even see him anymore. They were greatly astonished. After a while they suddenly saw the Shaykh standing on a hill. He said, "Charge on, for I am waiting for you."

They all dismounted and asked to be forgiven. They said, "This was more than a miracle. The Imams all wanted to witness a miracle and this truly was a wondrous miracle you performed. This cannot and never will be outdone."

The Shaykh replied, "O pure-hearted men! You hold the grace of God, the Exalted and Almighty, bestowed upon His chosen servants so small and worthless?! Does the heavenly robe of honor remain hidden or can it be veiled from sight? Behold and see for yourself the evidences of God's grace."

The Imams looked and the entire plain—rocks, stones, pebbles, dust, plants, trees, and everything which their eyes fell upon—had turned to pure gold by the power of the Creator, and the fruits [65] of the plants and trees as far as they could see had turned to rubies

---

Qur'ân commentaries, such as *As'ilat al-Qur'ân ma'a al-ajwibah* [Qur'ânic questions and their answers] and *I'jâz al-Qur'ân* [The Inimitability of the Qur'ân]. Hâjji Khalifeh, in his *Kashf al-zunûn*, has listed similar titles under the rubric of Qur'ân commentaries.

Shaykh Ahmad-e Jâm died in the year 536 of the Islamic lunar calendar (1141 A.D.), whereas the famous Zahir-e Bayhaqi died in 565 (1169 or 1170). The fact that Mohammad-e Ghaznavi states that Imam Zahir-e Bayhaqi became a believer in Shaykh Ahmad-e Jâm some thirty-odd years [*si o and sâl*] after his death need not be understood literally, as it could easily be an estimate or a misremembrance on the part of the author. In any case, there is only a discrepancy of at most five years, insofar as the Persian *and* [odd] is usually used for between two to four years.

and pearls. All who saw this were bedazzled, amazed and stupefied, except for one servant of those Imams who had remained calm and picked up a stone and had thrown it in his bag.

When these men returned to their senses, the Shaykh told the Imams, "Each of you should have taken a stone as a souvenir and a blessing for your friends." The Imams in their hearts still did not believe it, thinking that this suggestion was absurd. God, the Almighty, revealed a thing and then returned it to its original state. If someone had taken a piece of it, how could it not have returned to its original state? What use would it have been to take any of it?

The Shaykh al-Islam, seeing their denial in his heart of hearts, asked, "What do the Imams think? The All-Powerful One who can do such a thing, is He, likewise, able to maintain it in the same fashion?"

They said, "He is." The Shaykh said, "Well, then, since it is within the realm of possibility and is not an inconceivable thing, can you say why you deny it?"

He then called their servant and said, "That stone which you picked up and put in your bag, bring it here." He brought it. By the power of God, the Exalted and Almighty, it was still made of gold, just as it had been. The Shaykh said, "You see! It was still the same. If you had picked up anything and kept it for yourself, it would still be the same."

The Imams, once again, [66] asked to be forgiven and repented. For a few days they stayed in Amghân with the Shaykh and returned home as convinced believers.

And through God comes success.

20. The Shaykh's Forty Day Vigil with Imam 'Abd al-Rahmân[45]

The Shaykh al-Islam, God sanctify his precious soul, went to Nayshabur where a large number of people were attracted to him and repented. Large crowds would gather. The learned Imam 'Abd al-Rahmân 'Âbedi rose against the Shaykh, denying and

---

[45] Cf. the story in Mohammad ebn-e Monavvar's *Asrâr al-towhid*, Book Two, Chapter One, about Shaykh Abu Sa'id and a Qur'ân reader (see the translation of John O'Kane, *The Secrets of God's Mystical Oneness*, op. cit., 216-18).

contending with him. He said and did all sorts of things, to the point that if their paths happened to cross on the street, he would go in a different direction.

Finally, they came face to face in the bazaar of the city one day. The learned Imam had nowhere to go and slipped into a grocer's shop. The Shaykh al-Islam went over and entered that shop. He said, "Peace be upon you [salâm 'alaykom]."

Imam 'Abd al-Rahmân said, "Not upon you and not peace, either!"

The Shaykh said, "Why do you talk like this and do such things? What have I done to you?"

He replied, "What could be worse! What more could you do than to take away all my followers, both the advanced and the beginners?"

The Shaykh of Islam said, "Well said! Have you no shame to talk like this?"

Imam 'Abd al-Rahmân said nothing and went away.

When the Shaykh went home, a learned man came with this message from 'Abd al-Rahmân: "They say that you boast of being an ascetic. Let us go on a forty-day vigil together."

The Shaykh said, "Does he mean a ladies' vigil or a real man's vigil?"

The man took the answer back to Imam 'Abd al-Rahmân, who said, "What sophistry! What, pray tell, is a ladies' vigil and what is a man's vigil?"

The Shaykh answered, "A ladies' vigil is reducing one's diet to the minimum for forty days. Women can do this as well as men can, and both men and women observe it. But a man's vigil, on the other hand, is performing the ablution, sitting in one place and eating two roast lambs with a corresponding full course meal twice a day. On the fortieth day [67] they perform the prayer, after having eaten the eighty roast lambs and the accompanying foods, in the same state of ritual purity.[46] That is the real man's vigil, from which women are excluded, for women cannot do it."

When this answer was conveyed to the learned 'Abd al-Rahmân, he became angry. "Just wait. This man is going to make a paradise

---

[46] That is, without having washed or answered the call of nature, since the first day.

for himself in this world. In this world it is not possible for someone to eat so much food and not rise from his place for forty days. Since he has made this claim, where will he hold this vigil, for I will sit with him."

They asked him, "How will you do it?" He said, "It is not I who have made the claim. I will eat but little and watch him. If he leaves the smallest morsel of that roast lamb or other food in front of him or gives it to someone else, I will denounce him. And if he eats it all, how can he not move from his place? If he gets up, the matter is settled and his claim is voided."

He sent someone to the Shaykh al-Islam, saying, "Where will you sit for this vigil, for I will sit with you."

The Shaykh sent back the answer, "For this vigil we need a supportive and generous host who can provide four roast lambs with all the trimmings every day, so that you and I can sit motionless with our minds at rest."

When this answer was brought to him, 'Abd al-Rahmân said, "He is trying to get out of it. I won't let him."

So, the Shaykh al-Islam sent for Karim al-Sharq[47] and said to him, "We plan to come to your house for a few days and have a private forty-day vigil." Karim al-Sharq answered, "It would be a great blessing to me and I would take great pride in it." The Shaykh al-Islam said, "It's not going to be one of those vigils with no food. It will be a vigil during which you serve us four roast lambs with all the trimmings—two each twice a day—and we will eat it."

Karim al-Sharq said, "If you order me to serve ten roast lambs everyday with all the trimmings man can provide, I'll do it." The Shaykh said, "Go on back and prepare your home. We will come in the morning."

The next day the Shaykh al-Islam went there in the early morning and sent someone to tell the Imam 'Abd al-Rahmân, "I am at such and such place, you must come." [68]

The Imam performed his prayers at the college and went to the Shaykh. At mealtime they brought four trays, two with roast lamb and two with all the trimmings. He put two trays in front of the

---

[47] This nickname means "The generous man of the East."

Shaykh al-Islam and the other two in front of Imam 'Abd al-Rahmân. The Shaykh told the servant, "Cut up this roast lamb and put it in front of me. Make sure you don't put a bite of it in your mouth, or I will be denounced. Your share is somewhere else and you will get it presently." The Shaykh finished all the food that was on these two trays.

As for the two other trays, the learned 'Abd al-Rahmân had eaten only a few bites. The Shaykh said, "We must help our friends out. Bring those two trays here."

The trays were put in front of the Shaykh. He said to his servant, "Here is your portion. Cut it up. Give [some] to me and eat [the rest] yourself." The Shaykh kept on eating until the food on these two trays was completely gone.

At the time of the evening prayer, they consumed four more trays in the same fashion. Imam 'Abd al-Rahmân was waiting for the Shaykh to get up any moment. The next day at mealtime, as agreed, they brought four trays. The Shaykh, as usual, finished his. When it came time for the noon-prayer, Imam 'Abd al-Rahmân's bladder was about to burst. By some means or other he held it in, thinking to himself, "This Shaykh has eaten six whole roast lambs and a lot of other food, and I am the one who has to get up?! This is a great shame."

After a while, the Shaykh al-Islam said, "Your learned honor knows that it is reprehensible to perform the prayer when you have to go.[48] [69] You ought to get up and renew your ablution, for I am at ease, and the proof of it is that I, in the evening, will eat two more lambs and again next morning, two more. When I have eaten ten, we will say our fond farewells. If you had the strength to continue, I would go on for forty days in the same fashion, but since you were not man enough for this deed, but were a man of denial, you will not measure up to it.

The next morning the Shaykh finished his breakfast and they departed from one another. The learned Imam 'Abd al-Rahmân asked, "Tell me, how could you manage this—where did all this food you ate go? I cannot figure it out at all, neither in theory nor in practice."

---

[48] See Story 246, for another instance of the topic of prayer and the call of nature.

The Shaykh al-Islam said, "Let me tell you something at the level of your knowledge and experience. Listen carefully, and put it into action, perhaps it will become clear to you."

The Imam said, "Tell me."

The Shaykh said, "Go back home and have them place an empty pot made of iron or copper on the fire and heat it up until the pot turns red hot. Then take an even larger pot, twice its size, and have them fill it with water. They should slowly draw water from it with their hands and sprinkle it on the smaller pot. That fire will keep burning until the larger pot is emptied and the smaller pot will not even get wet. Now, if the fire used in the physical world has such an effect on the elements copper and iron, would the fire of God's love have so little effect in the hearts of his servants that it could not consume a few morsels of food and make them disappear?"

[The Shaykh] is mixed with love from head to toe,
though made of meat and bones and veins and blood

21. The Shaykh's Commentary on the Sura of al-Rahmân

At this point, they departed. The Shaykh al-Islam returned home. After this, [70] the learned 'Abd al-Rahmân sent someone to the Shaykh with the message that "Such shenanigans [*tâmât*] will lead us nowhere. Knowledge is the only way to get anywhere. You write a commentary on a sura of the Qur'ân, and I will write one also. We shall see what the scholars say about them and which one they prefer."

The Shaykh answered, "You comment on any sura you want and I will comment on whatever sura you want me to."

Imam 'Abd al-Rahmân sent back the following reply to the Shaykh: "You comment on the Sura of *The All-Merciful* [49] and I will comment on *The Terror*."[50]

The religious leaders asked him, "What is your reason for choosing 'The All-Merciful?'"

He said, "In this Sura the phrase 'O which of your Lord's

---

[49] Surat al-Rahmân, Sura 55.
[50] Surat al-Waqi'a, Sura 56.

bounties will you and you deny?' is repeated thirty-one times. If he explains each one of them differently, it would be a transgression of the definition of the words, and he will be denounced. And, if he makes reference to [previous] commentaries, what ideas of his own will he have expressed?"

The Shaykh then commented on the Sura of The All-Merciful and he explained the phrase "O which of your Lord's bounties will you and you deny?" differently each time, in such a way that no one could find any fault with it. They took it to the religious authorities of Transoxiana, who all approved of and praised it. Many questions were sent to the Shaykh al-Islam from Samarqand and he answered them. Those questions and answers exist to this day, for your information.

Peace be with you.

22. The Story of How the Assassins Put a Dagger Under Sanjar's Pillow[51]

Once a person from the area of Qohestân came to Marv, introducing himself as Shaykh As'ad-e 'Erâqi, and initiated a long-lasting friendship with and won the full confidence of Abu al-Fotuh Jâmehdâr Ghâyati[52] who was among the trusted servants of the Sultan of the time, Sanjar son of Malekshâh, and was the chief of the servants in charge of the royal wardrobe.

One day this Shaykh As'ad revealed the following to Abu al-Fotuh, "I need a favor from you and appeal to your generosity. My hope is that you will not reject my request, but will fulfill it."

Abu al-Fotuh said, [71] "I would not withhold any help I can give you, in word or in deed, and would be grateful to do so."

He said, "If you swear not to tell anyone and to keep it a secret, I will tell you."

"Very well," he said, and swore, "I will not tell anyone what you

---

[51] See the introduction of this book on the Shaykh's relationship with his contemporaries. Compare also with *Târikh-e jahângoshâ-ye Jovayni*, 3:214 and *Habib al-seyar*, 2:486. Note that the Shaykh does not figure at all in Story 22, but does figure in the denouement to it in Story 23.

[52] Jâmehdâr was a title given to a servant responsible for keeping the royal wardrobe (*jâmeh*).

say to me."

Shaykh As'ad took out a knife and said, "The favor and request I want of you is that you put this knife under the Sultan's pillow."

Abu al-Fotuh said, "This I cannot do, for it is extremely dangerous."

Shaykh As'ad said, "How will the Sultan know that it was you who put it there? What harm could you suffer?"

He pleaded, but Abu al-Fotuh would not accept, until finally Shaykh As'ad promised to give him one thousand gold dinârs if he would do it. In the end the promise of gold seduced Abu al-Fotuh, who said, "Give me the gold and I will do it."

Shaykh As'ad gave him the gold. Abu al-Fotuh took the gold and in the evening, while he was preparing the bedclothes, he put the knife under the Sultan's pillow.

The next morning the king saw the knife under his pillow and was terrified. He asked Abu al-Fotuh, the keeper of the royal wardrobe, "What is this knife doing here? Where did it come from?"

Abu al-Fotuh said, "I don't know. I set out the bedclothes and left. I cannot say what happened after that."

The Sultan said, "Hold on to this knife and keep this matter secret. Let's see what will happen."

A while after this incident, a messenger came from Qohestân bringing many gifts to the Sultan. He said, "You should make peace with us and permit us to enter the province of Khorasan.[53] If you do not do so, harm will come to you and you will be unable to protect yourself against us."

The Sultan asked, "Why wouldn't I be able to? Who are you and on what account should I fear you?"

The messenger of the Assassins[54] said, "Why do you ask this?

---

[53] The Assassins were Ismaili Shiites responsible for a number of political executions among various Iranian dynasties in the 11th century. The mountainous region of Qohestân [from the Persian *kuhestân*] in the southern part of Khorasan was one of the major strongholds of Ismaili propaganda. The Seljuk Sultans were opposed to the spread of Ismaili doctrine, as is reflected in the *Siâsat nâmeh* of Nezâm al-Molk, who himself fell victim to an Ismaili Assassin.

[54] *Molhedân*, meaning literally "atheists." It is used in the sense of

Who do you think put the poisoned knife which you saw under your pillow last year? If the order to kill you had been issued, who could have prevented it?"

The Sultan ordered the knife to be brought and had it thrust into a dog. The dog immediately swelled up and died.

When the Sultan heard these words, a great fear seized his heart. He made a pact with them and treated them well. [72] He permitted them to enter the cities of Khorasan, where they began to move freely. When their numbers grew large, the Imams and rulers and notables and the common people all spoke out, saying, "They must be stopped. What business do these atheists [molhedân] have in the cities of Khorasan?"

When the Ismailis received word that the people were exaggerating the extent of their presence in Khorasan, they sent a propagandist [dâ'i] called Khatir Kaysâlâr, a well-trained[55] and knowledgeable Ismaili [molhed], who had a complete knowledge of medicine and astronomy and was extremely clever and deceptive. He suggested the following to the Sultan, "Gather all the Imams of Khorasan so that we may debate for what reason they would exclude us from Khorasan."

The Sultan gathered the Imams together and told them, "Either debate the matter or say no more."

The Imams said, "Let us consult together and we will follow what seems to us to be proper." After consulting, it seemed advisable to them to allow the Ismailis into the province, rather than to debate the matter. This was closer to the wishes of the Sultan, who feared the Ismailis on account of the knife he had seen under his pillow, the secret of which he had been unable to discover.

This is how they resolved the matter.

---

heretics and is here applied as an inflammatory term to the Ismailis (Ismâ'îlî).

[55] The manuscripts are unclear on the word. Here we are reading *motabahher* for *m-t-h-n*. See the note to the Persian text of the *Maqâmât*, 72.

23. The Shaykh Rises against the Ismailis in Marv

After a while the Ismailis had established a center for propaganda [*da'vat-khâneh*] in Marv and other places. No one was aware of this fact or how they worked. Then one day they were discussing the topic of the movement of the Ismailis in the presence of the Shaykh al-Islam Ahmad, God sanctify his precious soul, in the city of Nayshabur.

The Shaykh said these very words, "This matter has been revealed to me and I am being sent to Marv on a mission. If the Sultan and the Imams knew only a small fraction of what has been revealed to me concerning the harm which allowing the Ismailis, God curse them, to move about freely will cause in the affairs of the world and of religion, [73] they would never have consented to this and would have prevented it. Now I have been instructed to go to Marv to reveal this matter and to inform the Sultan and the Imams of the resulting evils, and to rectify the matter as needed, for it is a grave upheaval in the affairs of the world and of religion, the extent of which no one as yet knows."

The Shaykh then set off towards Marv. When he arrived, the Sultan and the Imams came out to greet him and accompanied him with full ceremony into the city, showing him great regard. The next day the Shaykh demanded that the Sultan account for [his treatment of the Ismailis]. The Sultan said, "Whatever I did, I did in consultation and with the backing of the ulama. Now you give us your advice, that we may follow it."

The Shaykh al-Islam said, "Gather the Imams and order them to have a debate with me so that I can demonstrate to you and to them the evil which has occurred and the harm that they have done. How can you allow yourselves to do this to Muslims and to Islam, to admit atheists into the cities of the Muslims? Do you have no fear or shame before God? Now, summon the Imams so I can tell them what needs to be done."

They fixed a date on which the Imams gathered in the court of the Sultan. The Ismaili preacher also came and sat among the audience and made a comment. Not one of the Imams responded to him, for they had agreed among themselves that none of them would undertake to answer that cursed Ismaili, so that the Shaykh could answer him. Since the Shaykh had started all the troubles, he should be the one to answer. The Shaykh al-Islam then turned to the Sultan, saying, "The Imams are ashamed to talk with this atheist dog. Hey, Nasrak, come here and give this dog his answer."

This Nasrak was the personal attendant of the Shaykh, responsible for his shoes, and he was standing at the entrance of the royal hall, the Shaykh's shoes in hand. Nasrak right away came in and knelt down next to the Ismaili, saying to him, "Tell me what you have to say for yourself." After he began his presentation and they had both offered their opening remarks, in the third rebuttal the Ismaili preacher was silenced. [74] The people of the city entered, lifted Nasrak up, and began beating drums, blowing trumpets and shouting. They carried him around the city of Marv, while the Ismaili preacher remained, head downcast, in the hall.

The Sultan was hesitant about having him killed, because he was afraid of the Ismailis. He asked the Shaykh al-Islam, "What would you have me do with him?"

The Shaykh said, "He follows a false creed and has been bested in debate. You should kill him right away, for we have other matters to attend to."

Being afraid of the Ismailis, the Sultan did not dare to kill him. He delayed, hoping that the Shaykh al-Islam would let the matter of his execution drop. After a while, when the Sultan had not signaled for him to be killed, the Shaykh said, "How very strange! Since you are well aware that you have been entrusted to my care, and that I have been protecting you with the support of God, the Almighty, and by His permission, and that I continue to protect you, as you have many times in many different places experienced, how is it that today you are so shaky in your faith and so disobedient? When a negligent person, in his ignorance, is seduced by gold, and has placed a knife under your pillow as a result of the deception and treachery of an atheist, you would become so fearful and terrified? Aren't you ashamed? As long as I am alive, do not be scared and have no fear of anyone. Have this atheist killed, that you may see what disturbances and evils they have incited."

The Sultan then ordered the atheist to be beheaded. After they had killed the Ismaili propagandist, the Shaykh said, "Are you aware what disturbances and evils they have initiated in Marv and other places?"

They said, "We do not know and have no idea."

The Shaykh said, "Summon the army commander [*sarhang*] who is called Mohammad-e Marvazi." The army commander, Mohammad-e Marvazi, was summoned. The Shaykh told him "Go take ten trusted officers [*sarhang*] [75] with you. In such-and-such quarter of the city, in such-and-such a street, and in such-and-such a house, there is, in the southern end of the courtyard, a stone bench. In front of the stone bench hangs a curtain. Behind the curtain, there is a domed building with its door closed. Open the door and enter. In front of the wall facing Mecca in that house hangs another curtain. Behind the curtain is a niche in the wall, and there is a locked box within this niche. Pick up that box and break the lock. Inside the box are some record books. Get them and bring them here, so that you may see the scandal of it all."

When those officers had set out, the Shaykh mentioned the name of several of the notables of Marv and asked, "Do you know these people?"

They said, "Yes, we know them."

The Shaykh said, "Their names are in the record books as Ismailis, and you will see the names of many others as well within the hour."

The Imams and the elders were much astonished, because a few of those mentioned by the Shaykh were well-known citizens. After a while the officers came in, bringing the record books with them. When they examined them, they discovered the names of those whom the Shaykh had mentioned, as well as the names of many others in the city of Marv and in other places.

When they saw things were like this, the Sultan and the Imams apologized profusely to the Shaykh al-Islam. They said, "You were right. We were entirely ignorant of these plots, unaware of these treacheries and without knowledge of these matters. Until this very moment we held many doubts about you. Now that we have witnessed and seen for ourselves, there is absolutely no room for denial, inward or outward."

Then the Shaykh said, "Bring all those whose names you have

found in these record books and offer them the opportunity to repent. Whoever repents and renounces that doctrine and creed and returns [to orthodoxy], let him [76] go free. Whoever rejects the offer and will not turn his back on that sect, torture him to death."

So, they brought all of them, explained everything and offered them the chance to repent, giving them the ultimatum. Some of them returned [to the fold]. Eighteen of them remained, who, though they tried their utmost and pleaded with them, would not return, but chose the sword, willing to give their bodies over to execution, but not to return. Finally they tortured them to death.

It is said that five of these eighteen persons were among those that the Shaykh al-Islam had mentioned, so that you know. But God is the Most Knowledgeable.

24. The Shaykh's Journey to Herat

Once Shaykh Ahmad, may God sanctify his precious soul, decided to travel to the region of Herat. A group of dignitaries attended him. When he arrived at the village of Shakibân,[56] they asked the Shaykh, "Will you enter the city of Herat?" He replied, "Not if they don't take me, for the old Shaykhs have called Herat the garden of the Ansâris,[57] and it has been left to them. We will not dispute their right."

The news of this reached Jâber, the son of 'Abd Allâh Ansâri, may God sanctify his precious soul. He said, "I will go and bring the Shaykh al-Islam to the city on my own shoulders."

He signaled for them to bring the litter of Shaykh 'Abd Allâh Ansâri, God have mercy upon him, out of the house. They all gathered in the city and called the ulama and the elders and the notables and the leaders of the city to all come out to greet Shaykh Ahmad of Jâm. They all turned up [77] and set out. When they reached the village of Shakibân and attained the presence of the

---

[56] Probably Eshkidhbân, mentioned by Yâqût in *Mu'jam al-buldân* and *Târikh nâmeh-ye Herât*, a village between Herat and Pushanj. See the footnote in the Persian text of the *Maqâmât*, 76.

[57] The followers of Khvâjeh 'Abd Allah Ansâri (1006-1089 / 396-481 A.H.), the most famous Sufi saint of Herat.

Shaykh, his blessed gaze fell upon them and they couldn't contain themselves and displayed overwhelming excitement.

The next day Jâber, the son of 'Abd Allâh, ordered them to prepare the litter, and they requested the Shaykh al-Islam in this fashion, "We have agreed to carry you into the city on our shoulders. Please be seated in the litter." The Shaykh al-Islam climbed into the litter and sat down. Shaykh Jâber, the son of Ansâri, and Qâzi Abu al-Fazl Yahyâ took the two arms in the front of the litter and Imam Zahir al-Din Ziâd and Imam Fakhr al-Din 'Ali Haysam took the two arms in the back, and they set out. The four of them would not hand over [the litter] to anyone else.

The Shaykh al-Islam remained quiet while they traveled on for a while. Finally he said, "Put down the litter, I have something to say." When the litter was set down, he asked, "Do you know what devotion [*erâdat*] is?"

They said, "Please tell us."

He asked, "Is devotion obedience?"

They said, "Yes, indeed."

He said, "Then, since they are the same, you get in, so that others can carry the litter, and that everyone may receive a share in this honor."

The Imams and dignitaries then got in so that others could pick up the litter, and they went on. From the city and the surrounding countryside so many people turned out in the plain that not all of them could have a turn to carry the litter. If we were to attempt to write down all that happened along that road—the spiritual states and miracles—the story would grow long.

When they reached Herat, the Shaykh al-Islam stayed in the khâneqâh of Shaykh 'Abd Allâh Ansâri, God have mercy upon him.

25. The Ascetic whom the Shaykh Persuaded to Break His Fast and His Sexual Abstinence

The next morning a pious man who was called Shaykh 'Abd Allâh the Ascetic came to the Shaykh. This man had kept the

"Fast of Union,"[58] and was well-known and respected by the people. Khvâjeh As'ad-e 'Attâr, out of his affection for this man, had given him authority in marriage over his daughter,[59] who had lived in Shaykh 'Abd Allâh's house for twelve years and was still a virgin. The abstinence [78] imposed upon the girl had benefited her more than the willful abstinence of this ascetic man had benefited him.

When the Shaykh al-Islam had come to Herat, this ascetic had told his wife ['owrat], "Go and get my clothes so that I can go to see Shaykh Ahmad, for they say he is a very great man. I want to see for myself what he is like."

That woman replied, "Beware, Shaykh! Do not go to him with the intention of testing him, for he is not the sort of man you have imagined. If you intend to obey whatever he tells you to do, then go. Otherwise, stay away from him. Stay here or you will regret it."

This ascetic shaykh said, "Go and bring my clothes. You know nothing about it."

When he arrived in the presence of the Shaykh al-Islam and greeted him, the Shaykh al-Islam returned his greeting and said, "Now that you have decided to come to see me and to greet me, recalling what that woman told you, will you obey me?"

The ascetic said, "Since you are speaking the truth, how could I do otherwise than to obey you? I will do whatsoever you tell me."

The Shaykh told him, "Get up and go back past the cobbled street [ku-ye sangin] to the shop of Mohammad-e Marvazi, the butcher. There is a juicy leg of lamb [bakhteh] hanging on a meat hook. Get it and also get some oil and syrup from the grocer. Carry it home in your own hands, for, as the hadith says, 'He who carries his own package is freed from arrogance.' Have a dish

---

[58] *Ruzeh-ye vesâl*, perhaps designating a fast undertaken to attain union with God, though it may also refer to chaste cohabitation with an eligible woman as a means of combating temptation, as this story details.

[59] *'Ajuzeh* is usually an old woman, but in Ghaznavi's text the word is used to mean "daughter" (Stories 25, 154 and 376; see the Persian text, 77, 187 and 304, as well as the notes to Nezâmi 'Aruzi's *Chahâr maqâleh*, ed. Qazvini and Mo'in, 614). Perhaps it reflects jocular and disparaging slang in the region of Herat.

[*qelyeh*] prepared with that meat and have some halvâ prepared with that oil and syrup. Break your fast, together with that woman, and then perform the duty which has been your obligation for these twelve years, but which you have neglected. Go to the public bath and perform a ritual ablution. If you do not immediately thereupon obtain the goal you have been seeking in vain these thirty years, come and complain to me that I may rectify the situation."

When the Shaykh al-Islam said this, the ascetic thought to himself, "He is ordering me [79] to do something which is not within my capability. During these many years, I have not found in myself the slightest vitality or stirring. How would I find the vitality to penetrate [*dokhul konam*] this virgin woman?"

The Shaykh al-Islam realized by way of miraculous insight what the ascetic was thinking. He said, "Go, it will be easy, don't be afraid. If you should need help, just ask me. Go, it will be easy. Do just as I have told you. Get on with the business and you will see." Those who were present heard the Shaykh's words and were greatly perplexed about what would follow.

The ascetic got up and left. A group of people followed after him to see for themselves about this juicy leg of lamb hanging in on the meat hook in the butcher's shop on the cobbled street indicated by the Shaykh. When they arrived, it was just as he had said—a juicy leg of lamb was hanging from the meat hook. They asked the butcher, "What kind of meat is this?"

He said, "It's lamb."

That group returned, moved to tears. The ascetic took the meat and went home, ordering that the meat dish and halvâ be prepared right away. That woman smiled and said, "Are you, indeed, going to obey him?"

He said, "Yes, hurry up, for he has promised strange things. Let us see what will happen."

When the food was ready, the ascetic and the lady [*khâtun*] broke their fast. As they were eating the food, the ascetic felt a stirring within himself, which was so overpowering that in the middle of the meal, he reached for the woman. The woman laughed, saying, "It's true what they say—'ascetics follow no set schedule.' During these twelve years I have lived with you, you have never showed any excitement. Now you will not and cannot even wait for the food to be removed!"

The ascetic was embarrassed and withdrew his hand from the woman. After they finished the meal, the ascetic turned his attentions to his wife. As he began to make love, he found he had no vitality and was frustrated. In his thoughts he addressed the Shaykh, "Didn't you tell me to seek your help if I needed it? Now the time for help has come."

The Shaykh al-Islam was sitting among a large crowd of learned men and dignitaries, all of them waiting to [80] see what would happen. Suddenly the Shaykh, at the center of that large crowd, smiled and said, "O ascetic, stick to it and do not be afraid, for the matter is about to straighten itself out."

Immediately thereupon the ascetic achieved his aim. When he was finished, he hurried off to the public bath. The instant that his ritual ablution was completed, everything within the four walls of that city was unveiled to his eyes, such that he could see all things. He cried out and ran off shouting in the direction of the Shaykh.

When he reached the Shaykh, the Shaykh said, "O ascetic, it is not my fault. It is because your potential [hemmat] does not exceed the four walls of this city. Otherwise, if [your potential] had been as wide as the four corners of the earth, all of it would have been unveiled before you."

Zahir al-Din Ziâd, the Mufti and Imam of the city, said, "We are aware that this ascetic, for more than thirty years, has kept the 'Fast of Union' and has abstained not only from things and actions which are legally uncertain [shobohât], but even those which are good [mobâhât] and those which are enjoined [halâlât], and has reined in his passions to the extent that his lawfully wedded wife up to this very day has remained a virgin. Though self-abnegations promote purity, we never knew what he gained from all these self-imposed hardships. But today, you ordered him to do something which we do regularly. Now, if the cause [of today's experience] was his self-abnegations, why did it not occur earlier? And if what you ordered him to do is the cause of it, why don't we, who do these things day and night, experience the same?"

The answer: The Shaykh al-Islam, God sanctify his precious soul, said, "The essence of man is like the essence of iron ore, and the essence of self-abnegation is like unto a mirror. If the mirror-maker wants to make a mirror out of iron, he will be unable to do so. Until the smelter melts the ore and the founders forge steel out of it, the mirror-maker cannot make the mirror. And even when these tasks have all been accomplished, these hard labors have been undertaken and the mirror-maker has made the mirror, it will not reflect a clear and sharp image until the burnisher has burnished it. [81] The ascetic had undergone many hard labors, making a mirror out of his actions. Still, it required my polishing for the mirror to reflect clearly and sharply. One cannot get iron without ore, nor forge steel without iron, nor fashion a mirror without steel, nor can the mirror be clear and sharp without burnishing. And this is my counsel."

26. Healing the Blind Child

Once the Qâzi Abu al-Fazl Yahyâ of Herat had invited [the Shaykh, who was] in the khâneqâh of 'Abd Allâh Ansâri, [to his home]. He went to accompany the Shaykh al-Islam to his home. When the attendant placed his shoes in front of him, our Master, the Shaykh al-Islam, said, "Wait a moment."

After a while, a Turkoman named Khezr, along with his wife, Khadijeh, came in. They brought with them a Turkoman child about twelve years of age, most handsome, well-attired and decked out. The mother and father came before the Shaykh and stood their child in front of him, saying, "O Shaykh al-Islam! God, the Exalted, has given us many riches—horses, camels, cattle, sheep, gold and silver. We have only this one child, and, as you see, the Almighty God has withheld nothing from this child, except eyesight. We have taken him all over the world—anywhere where we had heard of a great man, a physician or a holy shrine—but it was all in vain. Today we have brought him to you, as we have heard from many distinguished people that God answers your prayers, and whatever you ask of God, the Almighty, comes true. They have sent us to see you; if you will cast a favorable glance upon him and ask God, the Almighty, to give light to his eyes, we will devote all the money and property we have to your disciples, and will become followers and servants of you. If our need is not fulfilled, we will throw ourselves [82] to the ground right here in the khâneqâh and die, for we can endure no longer. The rest is up to you."

The Shaykh al-Islam said, "This is a difficult situation. Bringing the dead to life, curing the blind, healing the leper, these were the miracles of Jesus, peace be upon him. When has Ahmad ever done such things and how could he perform them?" Then he got up and they stepped out. The Turkoman and his wife fell to the ground and began beating themselves.

There were more than forty important religious leaders present, and countless numbers of others. When the Shaykh got to the middle of the vestibule of the khâneqâh, a complete change [*hâlat*] swept over his demeanor, such that all were frightened and backed away from him. Suddenly the words, "We shall do it," escaped from the Shaykh's blessed lips, loud enough that many of the great ulama heard it.

The Shaykh then turned around and went back into the khâneqâh. He sat on the edge of the stone bench and said, "Bring that child to me." They did so. He placed his two index fingers on the eyes of that child and withdrew them. He said in Arabic, "And now, by the will of God, the Almighty, open your eyes!"

Instantly, both eyes of the child were healed. A great cry arose from the crowd.

The Shaykh al-Islam then went to the house of Qâzi Abu al-Fazl Yahyâ. When they finished their food and the Shaykh retired to his own secluded room, the Imams gathered together and told the servant, "We have come to see the Shaykh al-Islam. Go tell him that the Imams want to see him for a while and discuss a few matters with him."

The Shaykh told him, "Have them come in to discuss the matter and receive my answer."

The servant showed them in and they sat down. They said, "A serious question has come up. We have discussed it much among ourselves without reaching a solution."

"Tell me what it is," he said.

They said, "A couple of Turkomans entered the khâneqâh and asked that their blind child be cured. From your blessed lips we heard that quickening the dead, curing the blind and the leper, were the miracles of Jesus, upon him be peace. This was a very legitimate and [83] extremely agreeable answer. When you got up and reached the middle of the vestibule of the khâneqâh, a change in your demeanor appeared such that all were frightened. The words 'We, We shall do it,' escaped from your blessed lips, loud enough for many of those present to hear. Then you turned back and asked to see the child, put your fingers on his eyes, and he could see."

"If anyone had related this story to us, we would have certainly dismissed it and given it no credit. Now that we have seen it with our own eyes, there is no room for denial; as the Arabic saying goes, 'the eye is honest and the ear a liar.' Now, if what you said at first was correct, what was this you did in the end? And if what you did in the end was correct, why did you say what you did in the beginning? Furthermore, what was this sentence that came out of your mouth, 'We, We shall do it?' Please explain this for our benefit."

The answer: The Shaykh al-Islam replied, "What I said at first— that quickening the dead and curing the blind and the leper were the miracles of Jesus, upon him be peace—is exactly right. Those were my words and I could have said nothing else. Concerning the words that came from my mouth, 'We, We shall do it;' when I got up and reached the middle of the vestibule of the khâneqâh, the following was revealed to my heart: 'Wait [bâsh], Ahmad! Was it Jesus who brought the dead to life? Was it Jesus who made the blind see and the leper whole? It is We, We who do that.'"

"I heard them calling me, saying, 'Go back, for we have entrusted the sight of that child's eyes to your breath and to your hands.' These words so overpowered my heart that it came to my lips. The first answer was in my own words and what I did at first was legitimate, but what I did in the end was the power of God, the Almighty, so that you know. Peace be with you."

27. The Miracles of the Shaykh in Herat and Khvâjeh Mowdud-e Cheshti's Conflict with Him

When the Shaykh al-Islam, God sanctify his precious soul, came to the village of Fashkân, in the district of Herat, he stayed there for several days. They told him that the ascetic, Khvâjeh Mowdud-e [84] Cheshti[60] is coming with a host of his followers to ride the Shaykh al-Islam out of town [velâyat]. The Shaykh's followers were hiding this fact from him, but he was aware of the situation, more than anyone else.

One morning they set out the tablespread. The Shaykh said, "Wait a while, because messengers are on the way to see us from Mâr-âbâd[61] and will arrive presently." After a while he said once again, "Set the table, because the food [hariseh] is calling to us to come and the messengers have arrived, as well."

When the servant spread the table, the doorman came to say that a group from Mâr-âbâd had arrived and were waiting at the door. The Shaykh said, "They are messengers coming to see us from Khvâjeh Mowdud-e Cheshti. Show them in." They were shown in and greeted the Shaykh. The Shaykh returned their greetings and said, "Sit down and have some food."

When they cleared away the table, the Shaykh al-Islam said, "Khvâjeh Mowdud has sent you. Will you say why you have come, or shall I?"

They said, "You [85] say it."

The Shaykh said, "Khvâjeh Mowdud has sent you to ask me what business I have in this area [velâyat], [and to tell me] 'Return in peace or, if you need sending away, we will send you away.'"

The messengers said, "That is exactly right, just as you have said."

The Shaykh then said, "If Khvâjeh Mowdud means by the area [velâyat] these villages, these lands are the property of the people, and are neither his nor mine. And if he means by velâyat the people themselves, they are the subjects of Sanjar, who is the Shaykh of all the Shaykhs. But if by velâyat is meant spiritual dominion[62] as I and the saints of God understand the word, by

---

[60] For further information on Mowdud-e Cheshti (d. 1133 / 527 A.H.), the head of the famous Cheshti Sufi order in Afghanistan and the sub-continent, see the article "Čestiya" by Gerhard Böwering in the Encyclopaedia Iranica.

[61] A small town near Herat. See the footnote to the Persian text, 84n2, for further details.

[62] The author is playing on different meanings of the word velâyat,

tomorrow I will show you how it is with the saints and spiritual dominion, and what *velâyat* really is." He said this and a great cloud appeared and it began to rain very hard. It rained for twenty-four hours straight, with no interruption.

The next morning the Shaykh al-Islam said, "Get the mounts ready for us to leave." Khvâjeh Abu Bakr-e Sâlehi, who was the deputy [*khalifeh*] [of the Shaykh], said, "It will not be possible, because it will rain again during the next two or three days and no sailor will be able to cross the flood waters."

The Shaykh said, "That will not be a problem. Today I will be the sailor." They set off into the plain.

The Shaykh looked and saw that there was a large group of armed men. He asked Abu Bakr, the deputy, "Who are these armed men? Where do they come from and where are they going?"

The deputy, Abu Bakr, said, "They are your disciples and servants, come to render you service." He said, "May God reward them well! Send them back."

The deputy said, "A large group opposed to you have gathered in the village of Mâr-âbâd. Why send these followers of yours away?"

The Shaykh said, "You send this group away, for arrows and swords are the business of Sanjar, not of this people. This people have a different kind of weapon and a different purpose."

The armed men went away and the Shaykh al-Islam set out with a few people until they reached the edge of the river. No one [86] dared to set foot in that body of water, as wide and deep as it was.

The Shaykh said, "It is arranged that today, I will lead us across the water. Gather here, all of you." When they gathered around, he spoke to them of mystical knowledge [*ma'refat*]. The hearts were so overjoyed [by his words] that all were amazed. He then said, "Close your eyes and repeat all together, 'In the Name of God, the Compassionate, the Merciful.'" This he repeated three times. Those who opened their eyes first, found their footgear wet, and those who opened them last found themselves on the other bank of

---

which can mean area, province, dominion and also sainthood, supernatural power or friendship.

the river with their footgear dry, by the will of God. No one could figure out how this happened.

After crossing the water in this fashion, the messengers went in great haste to see Khvâjeh Mowdud, some of them with footgear wet and others still dry, and there were ten of them all together who had come on the mission from Mâr-âbâd. They told Khvâjeh Mowdud, "Watch out, Shaykh Ahmad is arriving. The situation is that they have crossed the water and are coming here."

He said, "This can in no wise be, for such was the miracle of Moses, peace be upon him."

They said, "We don't know anything about the miracles of prophets or holy men. We only told you what we have seen. We saw it with our own eyes and have no doubt thereof. The rest is up to you." They got up and equipped a thousand men with arms and set out.

The Shaykh and his supporters had halted for a while at the hospice of Bisheh,[63] because the supporters were in a state of spiritual ecstasy. The rival groups came together and met at the hospice called Mâdar-e Amir.[64] All were amazed and looked on the spectacle, until the ascetic, Khvâjeh Mowdud, arrived with his companions. When the blessed gaze of the Shaykh fell upon him, he dismounted his horse and kissed the feet of the Shaykh. The Shaykh patted him on the back, saying, "My good man,[65] what do you think of velâyat now? Did you not know that the velâyat of true men does not reside in a crowd of attendants or in armaments? Go get on your horse, for you are but a child and [87] do not know what you are doing."

They all mounted and rode into the village. The Shaykh alighted at the street they call Qasr-e Khorâsân at a building which they call the red house, which is still there to this day. Khvâjeh Mowdud went to a neighborhood that was less prestigious [asfal], where he had been staying previously.

The next day the followers of Khvâjeh Mowdud said, "We came to drive Shaykh Ahmad out of the area [velâyat]. Now, today, he

---

[63] See the Persian text, 86n3, for information about this place.

[64] Literally, "the Amir's mother."

[65] bâ 'isâ, on which see the note in Story 15.

has entered the village with us and taken up residence. We must give more thought to this situation."

Khvâjeh Mowdud said, "It appears that the best thing for us to do would be to get up in the morning and go to greet him, seek his permission to leave and then go home, for it is beyond our power to tangle with him."

His companions said, "That cannot be done; it would not be right."

He said, "What do you think we should do?"

"Last night we consulted together about this," they said. "The thing to do is to send a spy to keep tabs on the Shaykh. When he is alone and goes to take a nap, a few of us, in company with you, will go and unexpectedly throw ourselves before him, immediately begin to perform a *samâ'*,[66] and pretend to be in spiritual ecstasy. In the midst of all this, we will strike him with something and leave. If he is killed, each one of us will give one dinâr, which will amount to two thousand dinârs. The expenses will not be greater than this[67] and the enemy will be repelled."

Khvâjeh Mowdud said, "This is not possible, nor is it right. He is a saintly man and performs miracles [*sâheb velâyat ast va sâheb karâmât*]. You, a thousand armed men, stood in the plain yesterday, when he had neither troops nor armaments with him. For the same reason you could not do this yesterday, it cannot be done today. His spiritual dominion [*velâyat*] and his miracles will defeat the stratagems that you and I devise."

They said, "You are but a child and you know nothing."

Afterwards, they waited for the hour of the Shaykh's nap when his followers would disperse. His valet stood in attendance, laying out his clothes. [88] The Shaykh al-Islam said, "Wait for a moment, something is about to come up." As they spoke, someone knocked on the door. The servant went to see who it was. When he opened the door, he saw Khvâjeh Mowdud with a large crowd. They came in, greeted the Shaykh and sat down. They

---

[66] A session of singing of mystical poetry and often dancing. This was a kind of moving orison practiced by many Sufi orders.

[67] The anticipated expenses are the payment of blood-money and/or fines for the murder.

immediately began a *samâ'* performance and started to cry out.

Our leader, the Shaykh al-Islam, looked around and said, "Hey, Sahlâ, where are you?" Sahlâ was a man from Sarakhs, one of the wise idiots,[68] always in the company of the Shaykh and one of his special disciples. He was a man who could perform miracles. He came instantly and yelled at them.

Leaving behind shoes and turbans, they began to flee. Khvâjeh Mowdud stayed behind. He got up and removed his turban and began to ask the Shaykh's forgiveness, saying, "O Shaykh al-Islam, you most certainly know that this time, I was not in agreement with what they did."

The Shaykh said, "That is true, but [89] why did you agree to come here with them?"

He said, "May God forgive me. I repent of it. Be magnanimous, for I have done wrong."

The Shaykh said, "I forgive you, go and send your people away. Keep two servants with yourself and stay here for three days."

When Khvâjeh Mowdud left the presence of the Shaykh al-Islam, in great shame and embarrassment he told the people, "I told you not to do this, but you did not listen. Now you go home; I will stay here two or three more days, and then follow after you."

The group departed and the next day Khvâjeh Mowdud came to the Shaykh and asked, "What would you have me do now? I will obey whatever you command."

The Shaykh said, "Put away your displays of piety [*mosallâ*] and go acquire some learning, for the devil laughs at the ascetic who lacks learning."

Khvâjeh said, "Okay. What else would you have me do?"

He said, "When your education is completed, you will renew the honor of your lineage, for your fathers and forefathers were great men and could work miracles."

Khvâjeh Mowdud said, "Whatever you command, I will act accordingly. Since you would have me revive my lineage, initiate me, through your nobility and benediction."

---

[68] *'Oqalâ-ye majânin*, a Sufi term for someone who deliberately utters words of social criticism or complaints to God, which make him appear to be mad. As a madman, this disrespectful behavior is excused. See Hellmut Ritter, *Das Meer der Seele*, 2nd ed. (Leiden: E.J. Brill, 1978), 159-180.

The Shaykh asked him to come closer. As he came, the Shaykh took his hand and seated him at the edge of his own cushion [*chahâr bâlesh*], in a place of honor. He repeated three times, "Only on condition of knowledge." He stayed three days after that in attendance on the Shaykh, benefiting greatly and experiencing many kindnesses. He went home in great joy, utterly content.

If all the things which we observed in the presence of the Shaykh during this trip were to be written down, it would take several volumes and lead to boredom. Thus we make do with [90] these few stories of his miracles. Each of these stories contains several miracles, as anyone who reads will see.

28. The Shaykh's Son, Borhân al-Din Nasr, and the Story of His Debt

Another story of the Shaykh concerns Borhân al-Din Nasr and his debt. It goes like this:

Once, when times were hard, Khvâjeh Borhân al-Din Nasr was residing in Kâriz-e Sâ'ed[69] and living beyond his means. His father, the Shaykh al-Islam Ahmad, God sanctify his precious soul, sent a servant to him [with this message]: "Nasr, look after yourself in whatever you do, lest you be unable to make ends meet." Borhân al-Din Nasr said, "The door which has been opened to the Shaykh al-Islam is not closed to us."

The servant returned. Then Khvâjeh Borhân al-Din regretted his reply and said, "This was wrong. This was not the message that I sent with the servant of the Shaykh al-Islam." He recited this poem:[70]

---

[69] For the location of Kâriz, see the introduction, "Shaykh Ahmad's Career in Jâm and Khorasan."

[70] The verb does not specify whether Borhân al-Din has composed the poem himself or has recited a poem he already knew. The last hemistich is a common proverbial phrase in Iran, quoted by Dehkhodâ in *Amsâl va hekam*, without attribution.

I'm one of no account – like the reedpipe
I am hollow, and yet am full of noise.
On the Day all deeds of men are reckoned,
I'm a speck of dust unworthy of account.

He wrote these verses down on paper, gave it to his own servant, and said, "Go and if you should happen to see the servant of the Shaykh al-Islam on the way, give this paper to him and say that this is the answer. 'Do not submit what I told you before.' If you do not catch up with him, just put this piece of paper next to my father's prayer carpet."

The servant of Borhân al-Din did not find the servant of the Shaykh. After the Shaykh's servant arrived and reported the son's message to him, the servant of Borhân al-Din came in and put that paper by the Shaykh's prayer carpet. When the Shaykh read it, he smiled and said, "Even though Nasr has apologized, he will come to see for himself!"

A few months later Khvâjeh Borhân had nothing left and his debt grew to a thousand dinârs. He was depressed and at a loss. He turned to [91] the Shaykh, thinking to himself that only the Shaykh could cure his ills. When he reached the presence of the Shaykh, he begged to be forgiven and apologized profusely. The Shaykh calmed him and said, "Do not worry, I will come and pay your debt and straighten out your finances. But, have you learned now whether the Door is open to you or closed?"

He then ordered them to saddle the mounts. When this was done, they set out for Kâriz. When they reached the river of Jâhenân, a group of his disciples in Kâriz came by. The Shaykh al-Islam alighted there for a while and began to speak of mystical knowledge. All were enamored and amazed and were overtaken by spiritual ecstasies. Then some of those disciples from Kâriz said, "Let us get up, we have to go."

The Shaykh al-Islam said, "I will not get up and leave this spot until I have paid the thousand-dinâr debt of Nasr. And the debt should be paid by just one person, and we will be the guest tonight of whoever pays that debt."

Among the crowd there was a man they called Bu al-Fotuh the

landholder [*dehqân*] from the village Rivandân[71] who had a thousand dinârs, which he had put away in a jug hidden in the wall. He thought to himself, "I should pay this debt." On further reflection, he thought, "My wife better not quarrel with me on this." And so, he remained silent and said nothing.

When news reached Amir Ebrâhim, the mayor of Kâriz, he immediately mounted his horse and rode to the Jâhenân river. He said to the Shaykh al-Islam, "If you would be my guest tonight, I will pay this debt."

The Shaykh said, "So be it, but I will not touch the food until you pay the gold."

The Amir said, "So be it." [92]

Our leader, the Shaykh, then bade him, "Return and prepare the feast by the time we arrive." Then they set off toward Kâriz.

When they arrived, a discussion was going on between the Amir and his Missus. The dispute concerned the payment of Khvâjeh Borhân al-Din Nasr's debt. The lady was saying, "I shall pay this from my father's inheritance," and the Amir was saying, "I will pay it from the taxes."

When the Shaykh arrived, the report of what each had said was given to him. He said, "Let the Amir pay the debt and the Lady can pay one thousand dinârs for the living expenses of Nasr."

The Lady said, "I accept, on condition that you be my guest tomorrow."

The Shaykh, "Very well, I will be there."

When Bu al-Fotuh the Landholder returned to his home, his bride said, "This gold you are keeping in the wall, what better use for it than this? Why didn't you spend it for this purpose? Go, now, perhaps he will accept it as payment of Khvâjeh Borhân al-Din Nasr's living expenses and will accept our dinner invitation for the following day." Khvâjeh Bu al-Fotuh left. When he arrived in the presence of the Shaykh and greeted him, the Shaykh said,

---

[71] According to Yâqût, Rivand was one of the outlying districts of Nayshabur, consisting of 232 villages. Sam'âni relates that Rivand had more than five hundred villages (see Minorsky, *Hodud al-'Âlam: Translated and Explained* [London, 1937], 326, as well as Le Strange, *Lands of the Eastern Caliphate*, 387). The suffix "*ân*" is probably a denotator of place. This toponym recurs in Story 112.

"This is the way, for my sake, that women quarrel with their husbands, not the way that you supposed back at the Jâhenân river. Go, now, and prepare for the guests, but do not take the gold out from the wall until we are there."

Khvâjeh Abu al-Fotuh prepared the feast. When the Shaykh al-Islam arrived at his house, he headed straight for the place where the gold had been hidden and said, "Look for the gold here." They took out the gold and, with the permission of the man^{72} of the house, they gave it [93] to Khvâjeh Borhân al-Din Nasr.

At this point the followers began to talk among themselves: "What! Has the power to transmute matter been taken from the Shaykh al-Islam?! If not, why did he need the gold of the Amir and his lady and Bu al-Fotuh?"

The Shaykh discerned what they were saying by miraculous intuition. He called his followers and said, "How do you know they have taken the power to transmute matter away from me?"

The followers said, "We know nothing about it. However, when, at the Jâhenân River, your blessed lips uttered the words, 'I won't leave this place until Nasr's debt and his living expenses have been paid,' the friends thought, 'If he would throw a few pebbles in the lap of Khvâjeh Nasr, the matter would be resolved, as we have many times witnessed.' But, since you took care of his problems in a different way, a different thought occurred to each one of us, and we didn't know what the situation was. Each one said something different, whereas God, the Almighty, miraculously made it known to you by the light of intuition."

As they said this, there was a visible change in the Shaykh's demeanor, such that all those present in the meeting were shocked and overwhelmed. There was a jug sitting nearby. The Shaykh reached out, snapped off that jug's mouth and handle, and hid it in his sleeve. He said, "Oh, yes, the power to transmute the elements

---

^{72} *Khasm*, literally meaning "enemy." In India, the word *khasm* is applied to the husband and man of the house, as is humorously reflected in the following verse of a poet called Qabul:
So harsh the boys of India treat their charges [*mardom*]
that women there call their husbands "enemy" [*khasm*]
See 92n1 of the Persian text of the *Maqâmât*, and also *Farhang-e Nezâm* and *Farhang-e Nafisi*.

has been taken from me!" Then he removed the piece of the jug from his sleeve. By the power of the Creator it had turned to pure gold, and he threw it before Borhân al-Din and then said, "Should I, by the will of God, the Almighty, throw stones and pebbles in to the lap of Nasr and redeem his debt and arrange his affairs, with what happiness will Amir Ebrâhim be blessed, and what honor will his Lady receive, and what victory will Bu al-Fotuh have won?"

What happened here on this journey of the Shaykh was more than just a single miracle; those who reflect upon it will see. And God is the Most Knowledgeable. [94]

29. How the Pearl Melted and Became Solid Once Again

Then there is the story of how the pearl melted and became solid once again, which goes as follows: Qâzi Abu al-Fazl Yahyâ of Herat and Imam Zahir al-Din Ziâd and Fakhr al-Din 'Ali Haysam entered the khâneqâh of Shaykh 'Abd Allâh Ansâri, may God sanctify his precious soul, in the city of Herat, while they were discussing the mystical oneness and knowledge of God, the Exalted and Almighty. The Shaykh uttered these words, "You are saying this by rote [*taqlid*]. How will one who merely imitates be able to verify the truth?"

They were greatly disturbed by these words and said, "Every single one of us knows a thousand proofs of the existence of the Creator, glorified be He, by heart, and you call us imitators? Who, then, do you say are true seekers [*mohaqqeq*]?"

The Shaykh said, "Even if each one of you has memorized ten thousand proofs, you are nothing but imitators."

They said, "We need a more convincing proof of what you allege than this."

He said, "So be it." He then told his servant, "Bring three pearls and a basin."

The servant brought the pearls and the basin. He said, "Give me the pearls and put the basin down." He then asked those learned men, "What do you believe these pearls were originally?"

They said, "The oyster has enclosed drops of the spring rain and God, the Exalted and Almighty, has, in His absolute power, turned them to pearls inside that shell."

The Shaykh then threw the pearls into the basin and said, "If anyone who has discovered the truth by his own efforts should turn his face to this basin and say, 'By the Name of God, the Compassionate, the Merciful,' these three pearls would melt and mix together in a liquid state by the power of God, glorified and exalted be He."

The men said, "Go ahead and say it."   •

The Shaykh answered, "You do it first, and then I, in turn, will do it."

Those three Imams pronounced these words but the pearls remained intact. When they set the basin before the Shaykh al-Islam, [95] a change occurred in his demeanor. He turned his face to the basin and said, "In the Name of God, the Compassionate, the Merciful." By the power of God, glorified and exalted be He, all three of the pearls melted and mixed together in liquid form, quivering in the bottom of the basin.

The Shaykh al-Islam then said, "Be still, by the order of God, the Almighty." By the command of God, the Almighty, the liquid turned into one solid, unbored pearl. They were greatly astonished and began loudly crying out in states of mystical ecstasy. They all acknowledged the truth of the Shaykh al-Islam and said, "Whatever you say is the very truth and reality itself. Nothing can be said to gainsay this miracle which has been revealed and there is no greater proof than this."

And God is the Most Knowledgeable.

30. Dividing a Few Dates and Almonds Among a Large Crowd

One night this exalted leader [Shaykh Ahmad] had been to a wedding ceremony along with a few of his followers. When they returned, they brought some dates and almonds. He said, "I have brought these that you may have a share in the banquet." I said, "Well, since it is here, let us share it." The Shaykh said, "That would be good."

There were thirty-seven of us. I asked, "How should I divide them up?"

He said, "Give everyone three of them."

I said, "There will not be enough to give three."

He said, "Give five." I became more concerned, since there were not enough to give five. The Shaykh al-Islam said, "O you of little faith [*sost-hemmat*]! You are not giving from your own purse. Give each of them ten."

"Perhaps our master, the Shaykh al-Islam, would divide them up?" I said. He reached forward and began parceling them out to me in groups of ten, which I passed out to the others, until each one of those thirty-seven people got ten of them. It was the exact amount, neither one too many nor one too few.

I have seen many such things with my own eyes, but the book will grow long [96] if I relate more than this one. So that you know.

31. Providing the Needy Dervishes with Wheat

The Shaykh was once in the home of 'Omar Farâforuzi in Buzjân. A learned man from the khâneqâh of Ma'd-âbâd came in. The Shaykh said, "Come in, for you have fled from Ja'far."[73]

He said, "Yes, indeed, for there has been a famine for several days now."

The Shaykh asked, "For how many days?"

"It is three days," he replied, "since the famine began."

The Shaykh then raised his head and looked at the heavens. His lips moved and then he said, "I have asked God, the Almighty, for wheat and God has given a thousand maunds of wheat. Take it with you tomorrow morning."

The next day we performed our morning prayers. Two Turkomans came and said hello, conveying the greetings of Amir Âqtimur.[74] They said, "Amir Âqtimur has sent some wheat for you. Tell us what you would like us to do with it."

---

[73] It would seem from the context that a place is meant, though this could also be a personal name. The basic meaning of the word *ja'far* (as per *Muntahâ al-irab* and *Farhang-e Ânanadrâj*) is a river, a brook, or a camel which gives abundant milk.

[74] We have not located an individual in historical sources to whom this might refer. The text actually reads Atimur, but Âqtimur seems a more likely reading for a Turkish title of rank or tribe.

The Shaykh asked, "How much wheat is it?"

They said, "One thousand maunds."

He replied, "That is exactly how much I asked for." He turned to the learned man and said, "Go take this and let the dervishes have it."

He got up, loaded his animals and brought them to the khâneqâh of the village Ma'd-âbâd.

32. How the Shaykh Cured the Author of This Book

Once in the summer, the very first year I had entered the service of the Shaykh, I fell ill. I grew extremely weak and emaciated. After some time had passed, the Shaykh was sitting one day with a group of his followers at the time of the evening prayer. He asked me, "How are you today?"

I answered, "I'm in pain and am unable to make mention of God, for there is no strength left in my body." [97]

The friends said, "Long live the Shaykh al-Islam! Pray that God will restore him to health, for through your power and offices [bâzâr], this can be accomplished."

The Shaykh said, "Last night I spoke of him while praying to God. A call came telling me, 'You always pray for God to keep your friends and companions well and to bestow upon them gifts [khel'at], graces and blessings. As soon as I send a gift, you apply yourself once again and intercede.' Now, I leave it to you, Mohammad [i.e., the author of the book]. If you wish, I will ask God to change your sickness into health."

"Yes, I do," I said. The Shaykh prayed.

Next morning, at dawn, that illness had been changed to health and my body regained its full strength, so much so that I thought I had experienced the illness in a dream rather than while awake. That very day I picked up a scythe and, along with some of those friends, harvested some wheat, for I felt not the slightest weakness in my body, thanks to the blessed breath of that noble man of faith.

33. The Shaykh Churns A Pot of Boiling Halvâ by His Own Hand With No Ladle

One day I was informed that the Shaykh was in Buzjân in a state of spiritual ecstasy, and had cooked halvâ with his bare hands without a ladle.

I was in Ma'd-âbâd, studying the book, *Tarjomân-e feqh*.[75] I got up and went to Buzjân and said to the Shaykh al-Islam, "They tell me that our Master, the Shaykh al-Islam, has made halvâ with his own precious hands, churning the boiling halvâ bare-handed. I have got to see this."

He said, "I have kept a portion of oil and syrup for you. I will make halvâ for you today, for you are partial to sweets [98]." They brought the oil and syrup and poured it in a pan. The Shaykh al-Islam churned it with his own blessed hands, until it was fully cooked. Likewise, he poured it with his own blessed hands into a bowl.

I saw all this with my own eyes and a hundred more things like it, though I mention only this much and will not mention them all, so that the book will not grow over-long.

34. The Shaykh's Promise of Salvation to this Author in Both Worlds

Once our leader, the Shaykh al-Islam, allowed me to travel to Nayshabur. I was telling someone a little bit about the miracles of the Shaykh, his virtues and his qualities, but he would not believe me. He kept saying, "That is impossible." I said, "These things have all happened and I have seen them with my own two eyes, and I swear by God that it is true."

When I returned from the city, the Shaykh asked me about the city and our friends there, and I answered his questions. In the midst of this conversation, he said, "You swore an oath and I overheard it. One must not make a habit of swearing oaths, for it is not in accord with the way of the Dervishes and righteous people."

He then said, "How was the actual journey there?"

I said, "I had no need on the trip there or on the way back to beg a piece of bread from anyone, thanks to your blessings and your power of prayer. God, the Almighty, watched over me with His grace."

---

[75] We have not been able to identify this book.

The Shaykh al-Islam then spoke these words, "You will be graciously blessed in both worlds."

It is now nearly twenty years that I am enjoying the blessing and riches of God, and I have never needed to take provisions on any journey. The first half has been fulfilled, hopefully the second half will also be taken care of—God, the Almighty, willing.

35. An Anecdote from the Life of this Author

One day I put on slippers and strolled about the khâneqâh of Buzjân. The Shaykh [99] noticed me and said, "What are you doing and what is it you have in mind?"

"I am leaving," I said.

"Where will you go?," he asked.

"To Ghazna," I said.

"You cannot go," he said.

"I have asked the permission of the Shaykh several times, but you did not permit me," I said. "This time I will go."

The Shaykh said, "So long as you are in my thoughts, you may not go. And if you leave, I will break your foot."

Audaciously, I set out. The moment I set foot out of the khâneqâh, right by the entrance gate. I heard a loud crack in my foot and one of the bones broke, so I came back. My foot had swollen so much that I could remove my footgear only by great stratagems. For nearly three months I was confined to the spot like that.[76]

When I was healed, I once again asked the Shaykh for permission to leave, which he did not grant. He said, "So long as my heart is fixed on you, O Mohammad, you will not be able to go. If you stay here, I will be obliged to you. It would be better

---

[76] A similar story is told about Jalâl al-Din Rumi and Borhân al-Din Mohaqqeq in the hagiographical treatise of Faridun b. Sepahsâlâr, *Zendegi-nâmeh-ye Mowlânâ Jalâl al-Din Mowlavi*, ed. Sa'id Nafisi, 121-2 (original edition as *Resâleh-ye Sepahsâlâr*, Tehrân: Eqbâl, 1325/1947), in which Borhân al-Din has an accident because he left Konya for Kayseri against Rumi's wishes. However, Rumi does not appear so vindictively responsible for the accident as does Shaykh Ahmad in the case of Mohammad-e Ghaznavi's "mishap."

than having God place fetters on you so that you cannot leave, and cannot receive my gratitude."

I said, "I will go." The next day my eye began to ache, in such wise that I had no hope that it would ever get better. It remained like that for nearly two years. Then the Shaykh said, "If you renounce your intention to leave, your eye will get better." "I renounce it," I said. The next day my eye was better, and I could again see with both eyes.

I went to Nayshabur and stayed there for a while. Then I came to Jâm, and from there, with the Shaykh's permission, left for Ghazna.

36. Changing Sugar into Pure Gold

When the Shaykh first came to Buzjân and married the mother of Hojjat al-Islam Borhân al-Din Nasr, he had them bring [rock] sugar for the marriage ceremony. "Why did you bring so little?," he asked. Shaykh Ahmad-e Bu 'Amr, hearing this, said, "This was [100] all we had." The Shaykh picked up some [rock] sugar in his own blessed hand and gave it to him, saying, "Take this as a sign [from me] and go to the grocer to get [rock] sugar."

As soon as Shaykh Ahmad Bu 'Amr took it, it turned into a piece of pure gold [*zar-e sorkh*]. He cried out and was dumbfounded. It is now twenty years later and he still keeps some of that gold.

37. Changing Sugar into Pure Gold

Upon my return from Ghazna, I was sitting one day in the home of the Shaykh al-Islam with the uncle of Hojjat al-Islam Borhân al-Din Nasr. I told him, "Ask your sister what miracles she has seen from the Shaykh, so that she can tell me about them."

He asked. From behind a curtain in the women's quarters of the house I could hear her voice saying, "How can I describe his spiritual states, since all of his words, deeds and states of mind in this house are in their essence miracles requiring much commentary and explanation? But since you ask, I will mention a few of them."

She said:
Once a group of opponents were blaming me on account of the
Shaykh al-Islam. They said, "He is not what you suppose him to
be. He is not one of the ascetics or the saints of God." They urged
me to ask him for gold, intending to test his abilities. So, I asked
him for gold. I said, "A few goats have been brought [to the
market for sale] and I need some gold to buy them for the Imam,
Khvâjeh Nasr." At that time, Khvâjeh Nasr was still suckling at
his mother's breast.

The Shaykh told me, "Look in the box where the comb is kept."

I looked in that box and there was nothing there. "There is
nothing there," I said.

He said, "God, the Almighty, is capable of turning that
nothingness into something, but for your own satisfaction, [101]
put something into that box. If your intentions about what you
have said are honest, God will endow it with the property [of
gold]."

I brought some sugar and threw it in the box where the comb is
kept and held the comb-box in my hand. The lips of the Shaykh al-
Islam moved slightly. I turned the box upside down and that sugar
had turned to pure gold. It fell right in front of me. When I saw
this, I was astounded and all those who were with me fell to the
ground, dumbfounded and shouting.

The Shaykh asked, "How much do you need?"

"Six dinârs," I said.

When I looked, I saw that there were six dinârs, neither more nor
less.

38. Changing Sugar to Gold

She also said:
A silk garment came on the market and they convinced me to go
ask the Shaykh al-Islam to buy it for me. I said to him, "I need
some gold."

"What will you do with it?," he asked.

I said, "A garment is being offered, I want to buy it."

He said, "I am a poor man, I wear wool. You must not get used
to silk garments."

I insisted that I absolutely must have some gold.

"I have no gold," he said.

I said, "It is said that if the holy men of God want, they can grab a handful of dust and it will turn to gold. That's what you should do."

A tray of sugar was standing there. He picked up a bit of that sugar in his own blessed hand and said, "Woman, it is as easy for God, the Almighty, to turn this sugar to gold as it was for Him to turn the cane into sugar. But one must not become attached to such things." He then took the sugar and sprinkled it on his hand. The sugar had turned to gold.

"How much do you need?," he asked.

"Eight or twelve dinârs, God knows best," I said.

He gave me some of it and put the rest on that sugar tray, [102] which turned back into sugar. And what he gave to me, when weighed, was exactly the right amount, neither more nor less.

39. Taking Gold Out of an Empty Pocket

She furthermore said, God have mercy upon her:

Another time when I asked him for gold, he told me, "You have gold in your pocket and you ask me for gold?"

I looked in my pocket and said, "I have no gold."

He stuck his hand in my pocket and gave me just as much gold as I needed, saying, "One must not become attached to such things."

40. Transmutation of Dust and Pebbles to Gold

When they were building the khâneqâh of Ma'd-âbâd, a man came with three reed mats. The Shaykh al-Islam bought them for half a dinâr and three pence,[77] and said, "Stay a few days until I can give you the money."

The man squirmed a bit, for he wanted the payment immediately. The Shaykh picked up a bit of dust from the ground

---

[77] *Tasu*; for details on this word, refer to the Persian text of the Maqâmât, 102n1.

and rubbed it in his palm. He told the man, "Take this." The man hesitated a bit, then took it.

The dust, pebbles and straw [giâh] had all turned completely to gold. There were nearly ten people there who all saw this and began to cry out, causing a commotion. We weighed that gold, which was equal to the price of the mats. Those present there all saw this with their own eyes, and all expressed their devotion, so that you know. [103]

41. Transmuting Stone into Pure Gold

When the Shaykh was on his way to the village Bizd, a man from Buzjân came to him. The Shaykh al-Islam asked, "What news is there from Buzjân; what are they saying about me?"

The man said, "They are saying—those disbelievers—that they will not give the girl in Buzjân that the Shaykh al-Islam has asked to marry until he pays the gold and the expenses [of the marriage]."

Upon hearing this report, the Shaykh grew worried. He thought, "O God, You had those people entreat me to stay here with the promise of giving that woman to me as a wife; they said, 'If a child is born, he will be a memento of you and a source of pride to us.' After the marriage contract was concluded, You put it into their heads to demand gold and withhold [the bride]. If gold should be given, You give it. I have no gold, You do. I am always boasting of Your treasure of generosity, magnanimity and kindness. Either give me gold or stop their tongues from caviling at me."

His heart was inspired with the following: "O Ahmad, what have you ever asked of Us that We withheld from you? We have granted you a thousand different spiritual blessings, the slightest fragrance of which has never reached the nostrils of anyone else, though the whole word longs for them. Why would We withhold gold from you, which is a worldly thing."

[The Shaykh related]: "After this intimate conversation, I was overwhelmed by spiritual ecstasy [vaqt] and a mystical state [hâlat]. There was a piece of stone in front of me. I thought, 'I will ask that He turn this stone to gold.' Upon further reflection, I decided to ask something that was befitting for such a King, [for] this [transmutation] is in keeping with my own lowly aim. A little further ahead there was a huge boulder [104] in the road. I thought I should ask him to turn that into gold. As this thought passed through my mind, that boulder turned to pure gold by the power of God and shone as brightly as the sun."

Those who were with him witnessed this and saw it. I heard this from reliable sources and from followers who were present there and saw it, so that you know.

42. Concerning Khvâjeh Borhân al-Din Nasr, the Shaykh's Son[78]

As the Shaykh al-Islam was concluding this marriage contract in Buzjân, they asked him, "Why do you want this wife?"

He answered, "It has been promised to me I will have a son by her who will be the leader of the people on the path to God, the Almighty."

When Khvâjeh Nasr, God have mercy on him, was born, God bestowed upon him graces the likes of which seventy year-old spiritual masters [pirân] dream. At the age of twenty, he became the leader of the masses and today he has a huge number of disciples and most of the nobles and the commoners of the city have turned to him. All those who are disbelievers he refutes, such that it galls his opponents and refreshes the hearts of his disciples, and his words quicken the spirit of his friends.

And the answer which the Shaykh al-Islam gave is retold in its entirety.[79]

43. The Celebration of the First Sermon of Borhân al-Din Nasr

The learned Imam Sadr al-Islam 'Ali Haysam, God have mercy upon him, came to Buzjân asking that Hojjat al-Islam Borhân al-Din Nasr, who was as yet only ten years old, give a homily. On

---

[78] Concerning him, see *Rowzat al-rayâhin*, 52-60.
[79] The text is not entirely clear and may be defective here.

Friday[80] in the congregational mosque, he gave a good homily [*majles*] that was praised by all the Imams and dignitaries.

The scholars obliged [the Shaykh] to host a celebration. The Shaykh al-Islam said, "With great pleasure, I will [105] host a feast, but it will not be a feast to which some are invited and others excluded."

[It was decided] to have the town-crier call out, "Citizens, tomorrow you are all to attend the feast of the Shaykh al-Islam." The call was given right away, and the next day all the people came—high and low, residents and strangers, alike—and he fêted them all.

At that time I was in charge of the table-service [of the Shaykh]. I had fifty maunds of bread and some meat. I asked our leader, the Shaykh al-Islam, "How are we going to have all these people here tonight?! What will we give them?"

He said, "Don't worry, everything will be available."

That day the people kept coming, wave after wave, to sit at the tablespread and partake of the food. It came about that all the people ate bread and meat and sweets, and all the necessities were amply provided.

44. The Shaykh Finds a Lost Donkey

Abu al-Hasan Salâh said:

A man of Ma'd-âbâd called Bu al-Hâres had lost a donkey. He came to the Shaykh and said, "One of my donkeys is lost. Would the Shaykh al-Islam look into this matter?"

The Shaykh said, "Your donkey is in the village of Tud near Bâkharz,[81] seven farsangs from here. There is a mountain with the same name along the way. Your donkey is there."

The man went there, found the donkey and brought it home.

---

[80] The traditional day of congregational prayer at the mosque, where an official sermon would be delivered to the assembled worshippers.

[81] Yâqût mentions two villages called "Tudh" [Tud], one near Samarqand, the other near Marv, but none near Bâkharz.

45. The Shaykh Finds a Lost Slave

Abu al-Hasan Salâh also said:
One day a man from the town of Sâghun[82] came, whom [106] they called Mohammad-e Abu al-Hasan. He brought five green melons to the village of Tâybâd[83] and placed them before the Shaykh al-Islam. He said, "A slave of mine has gotten lost. I can't find any trace of him."

The Shaykh had a pen in hand and was writing something. Without hesitation, he said, "Your slave was walking along the river bank when a man grabbed him. He is taking him to the village of Tuseh[84] in the environs of Mâr-âbâd."

It was sixteen farsangs from Tâybâd to that village. The man got up and left. [The slave] was there where the Shaykh had indicated. The slave was safely returned.

46. The Shaykh Finds Another Lost Donkey

He also said that two men came saying, "Long live the Shaykh al-Islam. A donkey of ours has been lost. Tell us where it is and where we should seek for it."

Without hesitation, the Shaykh immediately said, "Your donkey is near the village of Nâzh. There is an old wall in that village. Behind that wall is a stream. Your donkey is there, tethered with a strap of camels' wool."

They went and found the donkey exactly where he had said.

---

[82] See "Ahmad's Career in Jâm and Khorasan" in the Introduction.

[83] Tâybâd or Tâyâbâd, according to Yâqût in the *Mu'jam al-Buldân*, is one of the villages of the Pushanj district near Herat.

[84] So reads the manuscript, but Kuseh (also Kusu and Kusuyeh) may be intended. A text from several centuries later, the *Matla' al-sa'dayn va majma' al-bahrayn* of Samarqandi, reports on the visit of Amir Taymur-e Gurakân to the area. He arrives first in Kusuyeh, from where he makes a short journey to the village Tâybâd to see Mowlânâ Zayn al-Din Abu Bakr-e Tâybâdi, a great local Sufi. See Hâfez Hosayn Karbalâ'i-ye Tabrizi, *Rowzât al-jenân*, 2:560-61.

47. The Shaykh Distinguishes Lawful from Unlawful Melons by Intuition

Once we were in Nayshabur. The Shaykh al-Islam said to his servant, "Get a donkey-load of good melons tomorrow, because a number of dear ones are coming to visit us."

The next day the servant got the donkey-load of good melons. The Shaykh looked at them and said, "Five of these melons are lawful and the rest are unlawful [harâm]." The best and choicest melons he set apart and said, "These are all unlawful."

The Shaykh's followers called the servant in charge of the vegetable garden and reprimanded him, asking, "Why have you sold us unlawful melons?"

He said, "They are not unlawful."

They brought him before the Shaykh, [107] who told him, "Take care to tell the truth; how many of these melons are unlawful?"

He said, "To tell the truth, the owner of the garden and vegetable plot [pâliz] came everyday to take several melons and eat them. I said to myself, 'When he leaves, I will pick the good ones and put them aside to sell for myself.' Now, these are those same good melons."

It was established that this half of the melons was unlawful.

48. The Shaykh Discovers Unlawful Food by Intuition

Once the opponents in the city of Nayshabur said, "The Shaykh al-Islam can no longer perform miracles and can no longer tell [the unknown]. What he had has left him." The Imams and Shaykhs and notables of the city said, "Let's invite him to a feast where all the bread, meat and sweets are unlawful. Let us test him to see if he will eat it, so you will see with your own eyes."

They prepared a feast of unlawful foods, except for one piece of lawful bread and one bowl of lawful vinegar, which they placed at opposite ends [of the table]. The Shaykh looked upon that bread and said, "Pass that bread to me, for it is toasted [beryân] and agrees with my constitution. And pass me that bowl of vinegar, as well." As he ate, he talked about matters of religion ['elm]. Those present told him, "Eat some of these other things; why do you pass over all these wonderful delights [ne'mat] to eat just bread and vinegar?"

"I am out of sorts today," said the Shaykh. "If I eat of these other things, I might fall ill."

"As you please," they said.

When the meal was finished and the table spread was cleared [108] away, the Shaykh said, "One can only deal with the blind in this manner. Let it be known that he whose heart has been enlightened by God, the Almighty, and who has illumined vision, is able to tell apart an unlawful from a lawful morsel."

The whole assemblage apologized to him and became his followers.

49. Deposing and Appointing the Qâzi of Baghdad

One day, after the Shaykh had returned from his pilgrimage [*safar-e Hejâz*], the learned Imam Haysam said, "Your opponents in the city are saying that you no longer have [mystical] intuition and the [power to perform] miracles, as you used to." He said this several times.

The Shaykh al-Islam replied, "On the path of God, glorified and mighty be He, no adversity has overtaken me; the only thing I know is that the journey has left me with some fatigue."

Finally, they made this request of him, "If you still have your intuition and your powers, depose the Qâzi of Baghdad, Abu Sa'id."

"We have deposed him," crossed the precious lips of that exalted leader.

Not long afterward the news that the Caliph had deposed the Qâzi reached Nayshabur. The opponents said, "It is not such a big deal to depose someone from his position. If what you say is true, he who can depose someone can also restore him to his position and office."

The Shaykh spoke these words: "The office of Qâzi is granted to him once again."

And what the Shaykh had said came to pass.

50. The Shaykh has a Vision of the *Qotb*[85] on Mount Qâf[86]

Once it was said in the city of Nayshabur that the Qotb, who is the axis [*mikh*] of the world, was no longer alive, and his absence from this world was a sign of the Last Days. They repeated this in the presence of the Shaykh several times and asked him, "What is your opinion in this regard? Is the Qotb of the world still with us, or not?"

The Shaykh answered, "Nothing about this matter has been revealed to me. Should anything be revealed to me, I will tell you. Otherwise, I am just an individual like you."

The learned Imam pressed the point and [109] begged, "You must certainly inform me!"

Then one day, as the Shaykh was paying a visit to some graves in the cemetery of the city, he remembered this request and said, "O God, Mohammad the Prophet–the blessings of God be upon him–was supreme among humankind, [though] all could see him. Likewise, all the prophets and messengers lived amongst the people and could be seen by them. What harm would it do if you were to let me see the Qotb once?"

The Shaykh reports that, "I looked ahead in the direction of the west and saw him sitting on the slope of Mount Qâf. It seemed to me he was wearing a garment of light. I was about to go up to him and ask him to pray for me, [but] the following was revealed to me: 'O Ahmad, do not forget your aspiration! The whole world should come to you with their needs that you may be their intercessor. What have you ever asked of Us that was not fulfilled, that you should have recourse to anyone but Us?' I was ashamed and embarrassed because of this."

---

[85] In Sufi thought, the universe revolves around the greatest living spiritual master, who is called the Pole, or *Qotb*, and who is therefore considered the spiritual *axis mundi*.

[86] A mythical mountain which in Zoroastrian cosmology and Iranian mystical thought is given various spiritual significances, usually as the center of the spiritual cosmos. Interestingly, this story is followed by one about the door of the Ka'bah opening to Shaykh Ahmad. In Islamic cosmology, the Ka'bah in Mecca is sometimes considered to be the navel of the world. See also Story 170.

Peace be with you.

51. The Door of the Ka'bah Opens to the Shaykh

On the Shaykh al-Islam's [pilgrimage] journey to the Hijâz,[87] those who traveled along with him saw him perform many miracles. One of them was the following:

As they finished performing the rites of pilgrimage, the door of the House[88] was closed and no one was permitted to enter any more. One day the Shaykh sat near the Ka'bah with the Qâzi Bu Sa'd-e Nayshâburi. When the sun grew hot, they got up to go each of them to their separate lodgings.

The Shaykh said, "When I arrived at the door of the sanctuary, I remembered that my friends and followers had asked me to pray for them. I had not yet said any special prayers for them, and I thought that, being in the proper mood, it was now time to do so."

He turned around and went back to the door of the Ka'bah; they had closed it and departed. He was overcome by a spiritual trance [*vaqt-i va hâlat-i*] and said, "O God, if we [110] invite someone to our place, we would not allow ourselves to close the door of the house in their faces. Is it worthy of Your pre-existent hospitality to invite a guest and then slam the door in his face?"

The Shaykh went on, "It was revealed to my heart that 'The door of the House is open to anyone who comes to visit.'"

He then said, "I reached for the door of the House and it opened. I went inside and a feeling of bliss [*vaqt-i va hâlat-i*] swept over me. I asked what should I pray for on behalf of my friends and followers and my heart was inspired with this thought, 'Pray as follows: O God, the Creator! Make my friends and followers dear in this world and the next'" (a phrase that often issued from the blessed lips of the Shaykh).

The Qur'ân reciter Mohammad-e Kâshki relates: "I had gone to look for the Shaykh al-Islam. When I reached the door of the Ka'bah, I saw him coming out of the door, in a state of ecstasy and excitement."

---

[87] The region of Arabia in which Mecca and Medina are situated.
[88] i.e., the Ka'bah.

This event has been related about him and it is here duly recorded.

52. Sprinkling Water over Lifeless Creatures to Revive Them

In the first year after my return from Ghazna, I was in the service of the Shaykh al-Islam when he had been taken to a village by the name of Oshtu[89] near Bâkharz. The people of that village were repenting, great deeds were being done and it was just like a miracle. Then one day the people of that village said, "We have an underground aqueduct [kâriz] which is almost dry. We have the following favor to ask of you: Would the Shaykh al-Islam pass by it so that the blessings of his footsteps might cause the water in that underground aqueduct to rise?"

The Shaykh, in order to please them, went to the opening of their underground aqueduct and prayed. It was the time of the noon-prayer. I went looking for the Shaykh and saw him sitting on the edge of the pond, performing his ablutions. I went up to him. There was only a little water left in the pond. [111] There were some of those insects that live in the puddles of water that gather in the hoof-prints where beasts of burden have tread. Some of them were dead-dry and some were still clinging to life.

When the Shaykh al-Islam finished his purifications, he sprinkled a handful of water. Everywhere a drop of water fell from his hand, the insects came alive, and began to crawl and hop into the water. Some of them began wriggling in their place and the Shaykh kept splashing water over them, saying: "...and of water We have fashioned every living thing. Will they not believe?"[90]

He said this and left. I went into that pool and took a handful of that water, pouring it over the other insects. None of them were stirred or were revived by my hand.

---

[89] See "Shaykh Ahmad's Career in Jâm and Khorasan," in the introduction (supra) for further details on the location of Oshtu.

[90] Qur'ân 21:30.

53. Increasing the Water of the Underground Aqueduct and Irrigating the Vineyard

Abu al-Hasan-e Salâh has related:

There is an underground aqueduct in the village of Bizd. There was just a trickle of water in it. One night it was my turn to draw water. I was extremely worried and upset, calculating whether or not my share of the water that night would be sufficient to wet two or three rows of the irrigation ditch.

I had a friend who was called Hasan-e Rotbat. I delegated him to see that the vineyard was irrigated while I walked alongside the irrigation ditch, extremely worried over the shortage of water. All of a sudden something occurred to me. I beseeched God, the Almighty, upon the honor of the Shaykh al-Islam Ahmad: "Give me enough water tonight to wet my entire vineyard." I said this and continued walking along the irrigation ditch.

Khvâjeh 'Ali-ye Ra'is had an orchard, which had been filled with water. I looked down over the wall and saw that the orchard was filled like a lake. I was amazed and wondered where this water had come from. When I returned to my own vineyard, I saw that friend of mine weeping.

"What has happened?," I asked.

He said, "This vineyard filled up with water three times and was absorbed into the ground. Now, once again, it is entirely filled with water." [112]

All by the blessings of that great man of religion.

54. The Shaykh Wills a Foul-mouthed Man to be Struck Dumb

There was in Ma'd-âbâd a man whom they called Mohammad-e Sorkh. He was an insulting loud-mouth. Every night that it came his turn to draw water, he would raise a ruckus and use foul language all night long.

The Shaykh would hear this and was annoyed by it. Finally, the words "May you be struck dumb" issued from his sweet lips. "How long will go on raising such a ruckus?!"

The next day that man's mouth was stopped up and it remained so for nearly fifteen years, such that no one heard him utter a word. I saw him in this state myself and verified the truth of the matter.

55. The Son of the Lord-Mayor of the Village Dies at the Will of the Shaykh as a Lesson to the Sinners

The Shaykh al-Islam once got up in the mosque in the village of Ma'd-âbâd and said, "Know, O people, that the Lord Almighty sends one of His saints to a certain place that he may be a source of felicity to those people who look upon him with a respectful eye, and a source of abasement to those who look upon him with a disdainful eye. Until now you have shown respect in your lives, consequently you have witnessed abundant favors. Now, however, your disrespect has reached the point that you pass by the entrance to my khâneqâh playing flutes and acting lewdly. One of the most prominent members of the village will die before Friday in such wise that it will be a lesson for all sinners [mofsedân], recorded in the annals of history ['alâmati târikhi], or else you can disregard everything I say."

Two or three days later, the son of the Lord-Mayor of the village lost the power of speech, his complexion turned dark and he died. On the third day the Shaykh said a prayer at his grave. In the midst of the prayer he became disturbed and a feeling came over him that [113] bothered and vexed him all day. They asked him what had happened. He said, "I was upset because I caused that poor fellow pain and I have a bad feeling about what I have done to him. That is what made me upset."

56. The Shaykh Heals One of His Followers

We have a friend called "The Learned Shaykh." He contracted a fever and fell so ill that no one expected him to live. He grew so weak and emaciated that two people had to lift his head off the pillow and a third had to pour water, juice or food down his throat. Likewise two people were needed to lift him by the arms and take him to the toilet.

Then, one day, the Shaykh al-Islam returned from Jâm. He was informed that so-and-so is ill and in great pain. The Shaykh al-

Islam got up to go visit him. He took his hand, brought him to the khâneqâh and departed. After that he was no longer ill.
As we have seen, there were many other cases like this.

57. Changing the Entire Plain into Pure Gold

One day Imam 'Ali Haysam, God have mercy upon him, said, "Long live the Shaykh al-Islam! These Karrâmites[91] ask me, 'What have you seen from the Shaykh that you humble yourself like this before him, whereas you are famous and well-reputed in the world and have many of your own students? This is very shameful!' I related to them a few of your miracles. They do not believe it. Why don't you demonstrate something to them so that they will stop mocking me."

The Shaykh al-Islam answered, [114] "May God, the Almighty, show them, that they may realize. Otherwise I cannot perform a miracle for them to see at will."

Then one day the Shaykh al-Islam, together with the learned Imam, a group of scholars and nearly a hundred other people, was going from the village of Fesâvarz[92] to the village of Amghân. The Imam said, "Today there are many respected friends present. A miracle must certainly be performed." The Imam swore that, "If you fail to demonstrate a miracle today, I will leave now and never come back." He reined his mount in the direction of the mountain.

After he had gone a short way, the Shaykh al-Islam was inspired with the thought, "Call him back, for what he is asking for is correct." The Shaykh called him back, saying, "Now, you may

---

[91] Reading *valiân*, literally "saints," which is a moniker for the Karrâmites, the followers of Mohammad ebn-e Karrâm-e Sistâni (d. 869 A.D. / 255 A.H.), as demonstrated in M.R. Shafi'i-Kadkani, "Ravâbet-e Shaykh-e Jâm bā Karrâmiân-e 'asr-e khvish," *Majalleh-ye Dâneshkadeh-ye adabiyât va `olum-e ensāni* [Dâneshgâh-e Tarbiyat-e mo'allem], new series, 2, #6-8 (special memorial issue for 'Abbâs Zaryâb-e Khu'i; Fall 1373-Spring 1374): 29-50. The same word appears in Story 266.

[92] Perhaps this is Feshâvarz, as in story 359. There is no reference to such a place in the standard geographical dictionaries, but the *Nozhat al-qolub* refers to a place called Feshârud in the region of Qohestân. Perhaps Feshâvarz is a variant of this name.

request whatever you like, and it will come true." The Shaykh said this and the learned Imam, may God have mercy upon him, fell from his mount and the entire gathering fell off as well, and were dumbstruck.

When they came to, the Shaykh asked them, "What did you see?" They said that the entire plain—the stones, earth and thistles—was all changed into pure gold.

Later on, the Imam said, "Do it [again]." The Shaykh said, "The [power] which I had is gone. You should have asked at that moment." But I asked the Shaykh al-Islam [about it], and he said, "In that spiritual state which had come over me at that moment, if you had asked God, the Almighty, to change that donkey upon which you were riding into a horse, it would have turned to a horse. But that moment is gone."

58. Water Flows Upward

The Shaykh al-Islam was sitting on the bank of a river speaking with someone about the Sufi path [tariqat] and the blessings of the Almighty God, and the ample kindnesses He has shown to His lovers. Then he gestured toward the river and said, "If the lovers of Almighty God were to point and say, 'O water, [115] go back towards the top,' the water would head in that direction."

As he said this he pointed and the water went back and started flowing upwards. It went quite a ways. He pointed once again and the water returned to its original course and flowed on.

I heard this miracle from several older followers. I asked the Shaykh al-Islam about it. He said that it happened as reported.

59. Spring Water Rises and Floats into the Air

Once the Shaykh al-Islam was on the slope of the mountain. A man was looking for water to do a ritual purification. The Shaykh said, "You there looking for water! There is a spring at such-and-such place. Go there and perform your ritual purification."

This person did not know where the spring was. The Shaykh gestured with his finger, pointing out where the water was. At the command of Almighty God, the water of the spring rose up into the air and levitated. It rose three cubits in the air, such that everyone present saw it.

60. A Woman Who Looked in Through the Crack of the Door is Blinded

The Shaykh al-Islam asked for the hand of the one who would become the mother of Khvâjeh Shams al-Din Motahhar[93] and brought her home. Whenever he was alone together with her in private, someone kept coming to look through the crack of the door, as women are wont to do.[94]

One day the grandmother of Khvâjeh Imam Nasr[95] came to look. The Shaykh noticed. He said, "Who is there watching? May she be blind!" Immediately thereupon a pain began shooting through her eyes.

The next day she was blind in both eyes and remained so till the end of her life. She died blind because of her impudence.

61. Blinding a Relative Who Looked Through the Door

When the Shaykh al-Islam asked for the hand of the daughter of 'Omar Farâforuzi, as in the previous case, whenever [116] they were alone together in private, someone would look through the door. This annoyed the Shaykh al-Islam. The person looking on was one of his relatives. He appealed to her two or three times, saying, "Don't do this, for you will lose your vision over it, just as the grandmother of Nasr did."

She did not heed this advice and finally she went blind in both eyes and remained so the rest of her life.

---

[93] This rather amusing circumlocution allows the author to avoid using the words for woman or wife, which might be seen as too forward. The Persian literally reads "when the Shaykh asked for the hand of the mother of Khvâjeh Shams al-Din Motahhar," though this Shams al-Din was not to be conceived until after the marriage. Concerning Shams al-Din, see *Rowzat al-rayâhin*, 72-3.

[94] It appears that in the institution of polygamy, the womenfolk of the household, especially the co-wives, were curious to know how their husband behaved when alone with his other wives.

[95] She would be the mother of another of the wives of the Shaykh.

I, myself, saw both of these blind women.

62. A Wife of the Shaykh Who Went to the Vineyard with a Relative Becomes Housebound

The Shaykh al-Islam Ahmad, God sanctify his precious soul, had a kinsman from the village of Estâd near Zur-âbâd. Once it happened that the Shaykh had returned home from somewhere. When he entered the women's quarters of his house, that kinsman from Estâd had gone, together with one of the Shaykh's wives, to the vineyard.

When he returned, the Shaykh al-Islam said [to his wife], "Just wait; you are behaving like these other women who sometimes leave the house and sometimes go to the homes of friends and relatives. Don't you know that it is not proper for you to leave the house without the permission of your husband?!"

That veiled woman [*mastureh*] said, "That was wrong of me. I won't do it anymore."

The Shaykh answered, "Whether it was wrong or right, I am a liar if you should set foot out of this house ever again."

It is nearly five years that she has remained in the house. Whenever the Shaykh al-Islam is there, the Almighty Lord gives her enough strength that she can walk and wait upon the Shaykh. When he is away, that veiled woman is just like a disabled and paralyzed person, unable to move from her place.

63. The Shaykh Wills One of His Enemies to Die

Shaykh Abu al-Hasan Salâh recounts that there was an official in Buzjân called Abu al-'Abbâs-e Vakil. This man once went to the Amir of the city complaining about the Shaykh al-Islam. "O Muslims, God save us from this stranger who has come to [117] our city and is even now intent upon destroying it. He has been a cause of disputation and cliquishness in this city."

The Amir, not knowing who was meant, said, "Expel that person from the city." The camel driver of the Amir, who was standing there, said, "He means your godfather [*pedar-khvândeh*], the Shaykh al-Islam." The Amir reprimanded the official.

The news was brought to the Shaykh al-Islam, who was heard to say, "Either he will expel me from the city, or I him."

Three months passed, during which the Shaykh al-Islam did not see this official. Then, one Friday when the Shaykh was walking to the congregational mosque, he met the official and said, "I hear that you have said this and that about me. You can expel me from this city if you manage to make it this day to the Friday prayers."

He said these words in the presence of a large crowd of people and went on his way. At that moment the man fell ill with an aching stomach and was overcome by colic. He swelled up like a water skin.

His nephew came to the Shaykh al-Islam and said, "Give me something of yours to cover him with that he might be released from this pain." The Shaykh said, "If you cover him with my prayer rug he will shortly give up the ghost." The nephew agreed, the man's condition being so bad that all were resigned to his death.

The Shaykh gave him his own prayer rug, which they spread over the man, who then died. The following Friday they put him in his grave.

64. A Follower Dreams of the Shaykh Leading the Messenger of God in Prayer

Abu al-Hasan Salâh has related:

One night I saw the greatest [of prophets, i.e. Mohammad], the blessings of God be upon him, in a dream, with the four righteous caliphs [*chahâr yâr*], may God be pleased with them all, sitting to his right and the Shaykh al-Islam to his left. The greatest [of prophets], the blessings of God be upon him, was talking to his companions. When he was finished, I greeted him and asked, "Who is leading the prayers today? Whom should they follow in performing the prayers?"

The Messenger, upon him be the peace and blessings of God, pointed to the Shaykh al-Islam, Ahmad, saying, "The people of orthodoxy and tradition, the people [118] of orthodoxy and tradition, the people of tradition." Three times he pointed to the Shaykh al-Islam.

It came time for the prayers and the Messenger, upon him be the blessings of God, rose to his feet and took the hand of the Shaykh and led him to the prayer niche and followed his lead in performing the prayers. The companions and all the people performed their prayers behind the Shaykh.

65. The Shaykh with the Zoroastrians and How He Put His Hand in the Fire

In the early years when the Shaykh al-Islam used to come to Jâm, he wanted to go to the mountain of Kukuriân.[96] When he arrived at the village of Ziâd-âbâd, which is a Zoroastrian village, two of his friends and disciples were with him. It was in winter and the weather was cold. They gathered a donkey-load of tamarisk wood from the riverbed.

There was a mosque at the gate of Ziâd-âbâd. There they built a roaring fire. There were also a group of camel drivers there. Amongst them was a Zoroastrian, who entered the mosque. The Shaykh al-Islam said to him, "What business does a heathen have in the mosque? Why don't you leave?"

The Zoroastrian began to debate with him, arguing that a man's creed is his own affair. The Zoroastrian said, "In front of the gate of the mosque is a small pool filled to the edge with frozen water. Let us both get up and go in the water. Whichever of us has the true religion, he will emerge safely, and the one of us who has a false religion will perish."

The Shaykh al-Islam said, "You have issued the challenge; let us go into the water." The Zoroastrian said, "I don't know anything about the arguments you have learned; I need a demonstration that can be seen by the eye. Let us put our hands into this fire." [119]

The Shaykh al-Islam jumped up and, grasping the Zoroastrian's hand, thrust it, together with his own hand, into the fire. He kept them there just like that until a cry rose from the Zoroastrian. A few Zoroastrians came, intending to fight with the Shaykh, but the camel drivers reached for their clubs and beat the Zoroastrians, holding them back.

When they removed their hands from the fire, the hand of the Zoroastrian was burnt, but not a single hair on the hand of the

---

[96] According to Maqdisi (495), a prosperous village in Qohestân.

Shaykh al-Islam was singed, by the power of the Lord Almighty.

66. The Shaykh Discovers a Man's Hidden Gold

The Qur'ân-reciter Mohammad relates:
One day I said, "Long live the Shaykh al-Islam! I have nothing and no means of livelihood, and I am weak. Tell my father to give me some of his property that I might be at ease."
He said, "Qur'ân-reciter, you must not allow your heart to become attached to such things. You must be content."
"Content with what?," I asked.
"Haven't you got the slightest thing at all?," he asked.
I said, "I have absolutely nothing."
The Shaykh said, "First spend the gold that you have bundled up and put away in such-and-such place, that God, the Almighty, may grant you more."
I said, "What gold, how much?!"
He closed his blessed eyes and counted out eighteen dinârs on his fingers. He added, "There is half a dinâr more."
I went to look and there were eighteen and a half dinârs. I was ashamed.

67. A Sleeve that Does Not Burn in the Lamp-flame

'Ali Torshizi is a trusted friend. He relates:
One night I had a feast at my home and a lamp with three wicks was burning. When some of the guests had gone, my father held the sleeve of my overcoat in the flame of those three wicks for a while. I said, "O Lord, if You hold the Shaykh al-Islam Ahmad in esteem and he is one of Your holy men, protect this sleeve." By the command of God, exalted and glorified be He, not a single thread of my sleeve burned, and in the morning [120], when they compared this sleeve with the other, there was no difference.[97]

---

[97] The text does not explain why the father holds his son's sleeve in the fire; perhaps he is displeased that the son is wearing an overcoat that marks him as a disciple of the Shaykh.

68. The Shaykh's Cloak Does Not Burn in a Flame

The learned 'Abd al-Samad is a disciple, one of the earliest. He relates:

In the early days, the Shaykh wanted to go to the village of Barniân.[98] He stayed at my inn one night and left behind with me a cloak from among his blessed garments.

I held it in the flame of the lamp's fire one night and said, "O Lord, if You hold this man has any value and credibility in Your eyes, protect his cloak from this flame." I held it there a long time. Through the blessing of his name, not a single thread of it burned.

69. The Shaykh Reads Minds

He also relates, may God have mercy upon him:

In the early days the Shaykh al-Islam wanted to visit the town of Barniân after passing through Jâm, where the people were as yet unaware of his station. When he arrived in Buzjân, I was staying at the khâneqâh of Ostâd 'Osmân. He stopped there, in the middle of the city, like a traveler. A tear in his wool cloak needed mending, and he was sewing it up.

I saw this and had the impression that he was no ordinary traveler. I had some new trousers at home. I went up to him, set the trousers down before him, greeted him and stood there. He looked at me and a feeling came over me that nearly knocked me out. The Qâzi, who was my teacher, had made me promise, since I am fond of the Sufis, that if I should one day have the fortune of coming across a man [of God], I should let him know so that he might profit from the example of such a man. When this feeling came over me, I ran to see the Qâzi and I explained to him what had happened. [121] He immediately rose and, in the company of those who were with him, he set out to see that special man.

On the way there, they were saying to each other things like the

---

[98] The manuscript here and in the next story has the spelling Barniân, though in Story 189 and 190 from the Chester Beatty Library manuscript, the name assumes the form Barinân. Regardless of the spelling, no such toponym is found in the standard geographical dictionaries. For further details, see the Introduction, "Ahmad's Career in Jâm and Khorasan."

following: "There may be many saints and special men, but none of them can share the station and rank of our spiritual guide, Shaykh Abu Dharr, God have mercy upon him. None can compete with him." They also said, "If this man whom we are going to see is one of those men [of God], he should demonstrate the ability to work wonders [*maqâlât*]."

When they entered and sat down by him, the Shaykh al-Islam said, "You have come with a balance, intending to weigh me. But do you have stones enough to take my measure? The stones you have placed in the scale as a counter-weight may be heavy, but they cannot equal me. If you should set foot beyond the gates of Buzjân, you will cross the graves of many men like Shaykh Abu Dharr before you come to his grave. But God, the Mighty and Glorified, makes one man appear every five hundred years whom all must follow and to whom all must pay tribute."

He then repeated everything we had said on the way there.

70. The Shaykh Saves a Man's Crops from Locusts

Once there was a swarm of locusts in Jâm which had afflicted the whole area, inflicting damage. The Shaykh al-Islam was in the village of Ma'd-âbâd in the house of Khvâjeh Nasr. He had a small vegetable garden in the courtyard of the house, where Ahmad the Grocer was growing cotton of good quality.

Ahmad the Grocer said [to the Shaykh], "Please keep this garden under your protection that the locusts will not devour it."

The Shaykh replied, "Very well." The locusts devoured everything in the village, but did not touch a single leaf from that vegetable garden.

One day at the time of the noon-prayer the Shaykh al-Islam asked Ahmad the Grocer, "Would you be willing to sacrifice your garden if the locusts, every single one of them, were to leave these parts?"

He said, "I would."

The Shaykh al-Islam said [to the locusts], "O army of God! I give you leave to eat this vegetable garden and then to depart from this countryside."

In no time they reduced that vegetable garden to ruins. The next day [122] not a single locust remained in the countryside, neither a mature adult nor any pupae [*na savâr va na piâdeh*], by the command of God, the Mighty and Glorified.

71. The Shaykh Foretells the Coming of Locusts and the Destruction of a Certain Person's Wheat Crop

In the first year when the Shaykh al-Islam was in Jâm, the learned Abu Bakr Amghâni said one day, "Some of the nobles of Amghân are against him and deny that this distinguished leader experiences mystical states and performs miracles. Some miracle should be performed that they, as well as others, may see."

It so happened that the Shaykh al-Islam was coming from Sâghu to Amghân with a large crowd. Along the way there was a man sowing wheat. The Shaykh al-Islam called out to him, "Have you already planted the seeds, or not?"

"I have planted some, but am not yet finished."

The Shaykh al-Islam said, "I see wheat here, very tall and fine, with quite large spikes, but I can see several locusts perched on each spike devouring the crop, and I hear the sound of their teeth."

A number of those present denied this and some were greatly disturbed. What the Shaykh had said was widely reported and everyone, each according to his own belief, said something about it. The learned Abu Bakr reported this to a group of opponents in the village of Amghân. It did not sound plausible to the people and others waited for the wheat to ripen.

One day Mozaffar the Cutler came to the Shaykh al-Islam, agitated and upset, saying, "O Shaykh, I wish you had never mentioned a word about the locusts, for there are some who [because of their denial] will bleed their spirits dry."

"What has happened?," asked the Shaykh.

"They are gathered in the Friday mosque saying all manner of things."

The Shaykh al-Islam said, "Have they already stored the wheat crop?"

"No."

So the Shaykh said, "What they say is true if I do not measure up to what I have predicted."

The next day the locusts descended upon that plot of land which the man had sown and about which the lips of the Shaykh al-Islam had uttered their prediction. The following day there was nothing left of it, and nowhere [123] had the wheat grown as tall and fine as in that plot of land. When they had consumed that plot they flew away and left without harming a single blade in any other spot.

72. The Shaykh Foretells the Killing of the Vizier, Majd al-Molk Qommi

In the early years of the Shaykh's repentance he had a neighbor called Bu al-Qâsem Musâ the Scholar, who was a good calligrapher. He had been engaged by the Amir to work for him. He would always criticize the Shaykh al-Islam and used to, in his youth, invite misfortune upon himself.

He was in charge of two or three villages. Every now and then he would go to those villages and poke fun at the Shaykh while bragging about himself, for in his own eyes his function was most important.

One day the Shaykh al-Islam told him, "Several times you have come and made ignorant remarks. If you talk to me like that once more, I'll give you a slap."

The Scholar answered, "If you have power enough to go about punishing people, reveal to me some secret of current affairs, that I might repent and join you in the path that you follow."

"Do you solemnly pledge to do so?," asked the Shaykh.

"I do," he said.

He kept asking every day, "Reveal to me some secret," until one day a noticeable change came over the Shaykh, he grew pale, and he went into a trance for a while. When he returned to himself, the Scholar asked him, "What happened to you?"

"Something of the sort that you were demanding has been revealed to me, but a danger is involved; if you disclose it to anyone before twenty days have passed, your blood will be on your hands."

He promised he would not say anything. The Shaykh al-Islam

said, "They have killed Majd al-Molk."[99]

"When?," he asked.

"Just now," said the Shaykh. "I saw it with my own two eyes." [124] [....the Scholar asked where this had taken place]. "It is a very distant place," said the Shaykh, "where I have never been. I don't know where it is. If this news is confirmed as true within twenty days, then you repent. If it is not true, do not repent and go on your own way."[100]

On the nineteenth day word came that Majd al-Molk had been killed in Iraq,[101] nearly two hundred farsangs away. This scholar had occupied himself with his work for these twenty days. When this proved true, he abandoned his position and repented, staying in the company of the Shaykh, becoming one of his special disciples, and never returned to work.

---

[99] Shams al-Din Abu al-Fazl As'ad ebn-e Mohammad ebn-e Musâ Majd al-Molk Barâvastâni-ye Qommi was the Chief Treasurer of the Seljuk Sultan Malekshâh and the Vizier of Barkyâroq from 1096 (490 A.H.) until his death on 7 September 1099 (18 Shavvâl 492). For a description of how he was killed, see 'Abbâs Eqbâl, Vezârat dar 'ahd-e salâtin-e bozorg-e Saljuqi, 109 and 129-30. The poet Mo'ezzi has also composed three qasidehs and a tarji'-band for this patron (see Mo'ezzi's Divân, ed. Eqbâl, 638, 641, 732, and 750).

[100] bar sar-{p}ay-ye khvish bâsh; the word sarbi or sar-e pay (in this instance, though not in others in the text, the dot under the letter "b" is missing) is not listed in any of the standard dictionaries, though it occurs several times in the present text (Story 72, 92 [twice], 99, 147, and 189). The word sarb is given by Ânandrâj and Farhang-e Nafisi with the meaning of state, condition, mind or soul, though it is unclear if this is the origin of the word sarbi we encounter here, which seems to imply soundness of mind or the ideal state of mental or spiritual clarity. See also Montakhab-e Serâj al-sâ'erin, ed. 'Ali Fâzel, 230-236.

[101] That is in 'Erâq-e 'ajam, or western Iran.

73. The Emissaries of the Village of Nâmaq Go to Tabas and the Shaykh Recalls Them

In the days when the heretics were extracting the religious tax[102] from the province of Rostâq[103] and humiliating the people, Sultan Sanjar was also levying taxes and the people were very hard pressed. They said, "We are not able to pay taxes on two accounts and cannot endure this."

The Sultan was at that time on campaign, and the people of the village of Nâmaq sent two scholars (one was Abu al-Qâsem Musâ and the other 'Ali-ye Ja'far) to Tabas-e Gilaki[104] in order to straighten out their situation. Word was unexpectedly received that the Sultan [125] had come to Nayshabur and the people of Nâmaq found themselves in a very difficult situation. They said, "If he finds out that we have sent emissaries, we will get burned. We will all be in for punishment."

The mayor of this village was called Khvâjeh Abu al-Hasan 'Isâ, and he was one of the special disciples of the Shaykh. The mayor said to the Shaykh, "For God's sake, save us, for we are in difficulty. Deliver us from it and come to our rescue."

The Shaykh said, "They left here ten days ago, what can I do about it now?"

The mayor said, "You have the standing and rank to demand of God, the Almighty, to make them come back."

The Shaykh al-Islam bowed his head for a while and then said, "I have made them turn back; do not worry."

"Where were they?," he asked.

They had gone two stages into the desert past Torshiz. There

---

[102] *Khoms*; the *khoms* is literally one-fifth, or a double tithe. The heretics are the Ismailis, and like other Shiites, they took a twenty percent payment for the Shiite state or the Shiite community.

[103] An area in Khorasan near Nayshabur. See Ibn Athîr, 3:97.

[104] The city of Tabas was divided in two (the Arab geographers speak of Tabasayn, the two Tabas), and the part that was controlled by Amir Abu al-Hasan Gilaki, who established Ismailism and prevented brigandry in the area, was called Tabas-e Gilaki in his honor. See LeStrange, *Lands of the Eastern Caliphate*, 359-61 and Abbâs Eqbâl, *Vezârat dar 'ahd-e salâtin-e bozorg-e Saljuqi*, 281).

was a mound where they had left their donkeys and gone to sleep. One of them was sleeping on his stomach, his legs in the air. The Shaykh caught them around the neck with the lasso of God's wrath and then and there they came to regret [the decision to speak with the Ismailis] and they were turned back. They returned on the twelfth day.

The mayor explained the situation to them and described how they had been made to return. They said, "Your description is correct, but we cannot believe it. Although we have seen many of the Shaykh's spiritual states, still, this is a mighty feat. You would think, in truth, you were with us!"

These, who were disciples of the Shaykh and had seen many feats of this sort, expressed skepticism. It is no, wonder then, that any other person should deny it and might not believe. [126]

74. The Shaykh and Khvâjeh Rostam

There was a youth called Khvâjeh Rostam. The Shaykh al-Islam was sitting one day on the bank of the river. This Khvâjeh Rostam had been a companion of the Shaykh al-Islam in the wanton days [before the Shaykh's enlightenment], and because of this he would come to him often, acting very chummy, and would say, "Why did you spoil our fun and take all the joy out of life? Times were when we kicked up our heels."

The Shaykh al-Islam said, "God be praised that my life is a thousand times more enjoyable than it has ever been."

Khvâjeh Rostam said, "People talk a lot about you; it would be to your advantage if you demonstrate something [of your powers] to me."

The Shaykh replied, "Silence! [be-row] for you know nothing about it. I am not that which the people claim about me."

Khvâjeh Rostam begged and pleaded. As it happened, just then a viper, extremely terrifying, crawled out from the bushes. He said, "Get up and run, for a viper the size of a dragon is heading this way!"

The Shaykh al-Islam said, "I will catch it and hold it in my bare hands and you will repent, or else I will throw it at you."

He said, "This is no ordinary snake like the ones you've seen before! If it bit an elephant, the elephant would melt."

"Where is your sense of bravado?!," asked the Shaykh al-Islam. "If you speak to me in this fashion one more time, I'll throw the snake on you."

"Unless you demonstrate something of your powers to me, I will not change my mind."

The Shaykh al-Islam reached down and grabbed the snake. This Rostam fellow fled from the Shaykh's presence. The Shaykh ran after him a little ways, holding that heavy viper in his hands, and said, "So, do you repent? If not, I will throw it at you."

"I repent for God's sake! Put the snake down, my innards are all aquiver!"

The Shaykh al-Islam put down the snake and it crawled off. [127]

75. A Group of Heretics Try to Kill the Shaykh[105]

During the time when Esmâ'il Gilaki[106] was extracting the religious tax from the village of Torshiz, the Shaykh al-Islam was in the village Nâmaq. Thirty men were sent to that village by the heretics to collect the religious tax, and they were demanding three years of back-taxes, to a total of 7000 *dinârs* of pure gold.[107]

The people had firmly resolved to let the village fall to ruin. They went to the Shaykh al-Islam and explained the situation,

---

[105] See also Story 363, to which this story seems related.

[106] Esmâ'il-e Gilaki is the son of Amir Abu al-Hasan-e Gilaki, who established an Ismaili state in Tabas. Esmâ'il, who is graced with the following titles in this text—'Alâ al-Moluk, Hosâm al-Din, Abu al-Mozaffar, Shams al-Ma'âli—was one of the famous Ismaili leaders in Qohestân. Mo'ezzi has written many poems in his honor; see Eqbâl, *Vezârat dar 'ahd-e salâtin-e Saljuqi*, op. cit., 280.

[107] *Zar-e rokni*, literally gold Rokni dinârs, possibly named after Rokn al-Dowleh of Daylam. See Mo'in's edition of *Borhân-e qâte'* under the entry, "Rokni," where he quotes a line by Nezâmî. It is also suggested by Dozy (*Supplément aux dictionnaires arabes*, 1:556n2) that a "Ruknî" coin [*al-dirâham al-murakkanah*) was square in shape, first minted by Ibn Tumart al-Mahdî, the founder of the Almohad dynasty in North Africa and Spain.

saying, "We will abandon the village, for we cannot endure this. They have arrested one of your disciples, Abu al-Hasan-e Pârsi, beat him severely and humiliated him."

The Shaykh al-Islam sent someone to them with the message, "If you want money, why do you beat and humiliate people? Get up and leave this place in peace, or else I will drive you out by whatever means necessary."

When they received this message, their hostility increased a hundredfold and they replied, "We'll take care of that Shaykh of yours and all who follow him."

The Shaykh and his friends were in the home of 'Ali-ye Pârsi. There was a scholar by the name of 'Ali-ye Ja'far, who had invited the Shaykh's circle to a feast. The heretics thought, "The stage is set. Tonight, we will finish them off." They determined to get rid of them that night.

The tablespread had not yet been laid when three of [128] them entered, pretending to be completely drunk. The close companions of Esmâ'il Gilaki used to drink, but not the rest of the Ismailis. That night, though, all of them had drunk and had buckled their daggers about their necks. They entered the feast and began playing drunk. The Shaykh's followers were with him, and the scholars were there, as well. All of them fled. The Shaykh al-Islam remained with four men.

The heretics came in and drew their daggers, reciting this verse:

> We are true men and rule the world through manliness!
> Why should we bear injustice from unmanly men?
> Till well into the night we hold our shields on guard;
> The arrows fired by us cut clean through hardest stone.

This verse brought joy to the heart of the Shaykh al-Islam, who said, "Your arrows are useless, but watch how the arrows of God's holy men pierce your stony hearts." He began chanting the verse along with them. They stood facing each other, repeating the poem in turns, until things reached the point that the heretics tore their clothes open and began pulling their hair out. The others also came to help, until all had joined in the fray. All of them were falling at the feet of the Shaykh al-Islam, shouting and repenting and begging his forgiveness.

One of them was standing on the roof spouting nonsense and the Shaykh said, "You are talking nonsense, come down or else I'll bring you down." The fellow grew more angry and drew his dagger and came toward the Shaykh, intending to stab him, but he fell down the ladder and broke both his legs in pieces.

All thirty men left, letting the people keep their gold, and they never repeated their demands again. Those heretics converted and remained faithful. [129]

76. Predicting Heretics Will be Killed in a Far Away Place

When the people of Tabas saw this, a debate arose amongst them. Some of the people said that what the Shaykh says was true and others said it was deception.

One day two heretics came to the Shaykh and said, "If yours is the way of Truth, forty of our men have gone and cannot be found anywhere. If you can tell us where they are and in which direction they have gone, we will renounce all of this and follow your way and convert to your school."

At that time no one could pass from one village to the next because of the heavy snows. The Shaykh al-Islam bowed his head for a while and then said, "I see all of them, corpses."

They asked, "How many bodies are there?"

He said, "Let me count....There are thirty-eight corpses."

They asked, "Where is that?"

He said, "I have never been there, though I can see the place now. However, I see a man from the village of Râfeq going around amongst them removing their trousers and other garments."

They said, "Alas, that is a true sign, for they have gone in the direction of Kondestân."[108]

On the fourth day three men who had escaped returned from there and told the story. It was exactly as the Shaykh al-Islam had described. Those heretics called the Shaykh "the Prophet of Nâmaq."

---

[108] A village near Samarqand, according to Yâqût.

77. Predicting the Capture of Zuzan

Around the same time, the accursed Pâydâr and Monavvar had sent an army from the village Posht[109] [130] and it was late in arriving. They sent two people to the Shaykh al-Islam, promising, "If you tell us where we have sent the soldiers we dispatched, we will know for certain that your way is the true path."

The Shaykh al-Islam thought for a moment and then said, "Alas for the town of Zuzan!"

"What has happened?," they asked.

"Forty of your men have been killed, but they took the town," he replied.

A week later the news came that Zuzan had been captured and forty heretics had been killed, just exactly as the Shaykh al-Islam had indicated. Those dogs, however, did not change their way of thinking the slightest little bit.[110]

78. The Shaykh Describes the Appearance of a Woman Without Seeing Her

The learned Mahmud saw all of these events and was greatly astonished. He said to the Shaykh, "I know that there is no substance in such things, but I would like to pose a question to you; if you can answer I will believe."

The Shaykh said, "I leave it to you." The learned Mahmud said, "You should figure out and say what kind of woman my wife is and what clothes she is wearing."

The Shaykh al-Islam asked, "Do you permit me to look upon your wife?"

"Yes."

The Shaykh said, "She is a woman of olive complexion with a mole on her lower lip and she is wearing a white dress from Ghazna and a red veil covers her face."

---

[109] A county in the region of Nayshabur consisting of 226 villages. See Yâqût and the notes of M. Moʻin in *Chahâr maqâleh*.

[110] The capture of cities in Qohestân by the Ismailis, including Zuzan, is reported in Ibn al-Athîr's history, *al-Kâmil fî al-taʼrîkh*, as occurring in the year 1101 / 494 A.H.

The learned Mahmud went to his house and began violently beating his wife with a stick, saying, "You have been in the presence of [Shaykh] Ahmad and he has seen you."

"I have not gone to him and he has not seen me," the woman swore. The learned Mahmud obliged his wife to change her clothes and he returned to the Shaykh al-Islam.

The Shaykh said, "There was no call for beating that veiled one with a stick."

He said, "If you speak truly, then what is she wearing at this moment?" – for she had changed her clothes.

The Shaykh al-Islam answered, "Your wife is now wearing a [131] black cloak with an ornament on her left arm and a black veil covers her face."

The learned one said, "Now I am convinced that the genies [*pariân*] teach you this, for it is they who can do such things and traverse the world in an instant."

79. The Shaykh Foretells the Death of Amir Bozghosh[111] from a Distance

Another day the learned Mahmud was sitting there [in the khâneqâh]. Tears were pouring from the eyes of the Shaykh al-Islam and Mahmud asked him, "What has happened to you? Why do you cry?"

The Shaykh, attempting to conceal the matter, said, "It's nothing." Mahmud kept insisting and the Shaykh at last said, "Amir Bozghosh has just died; during his life there was much peace and stability."

The learned Mahmud said, "Get up, my noble man, and leave this place; you are going to ruin my khâneqâh. What is this that you are saying?!"

Ten days later word arrived that Bozghosh had died in Kenâr-e

---

[111] One of the generals of Sanjar and his field commander in the battle against Amir Dâd-e Habashi and Barkyâroq in Buzjân in 1100 / 493 A.H., which Amir Bozghosh won. He died in 1104 / 497 A.H. after defeating the Ismailis in a battle near Tabas. For further information, see the Persian text 131n1.

Âb,[112] which is more or less one hundred farsangs distant from where the Shaykh was when he described this matter. On the day when he described this event, they had noted the date. When the news was received it proved to be the very date he had announced.[113] [132]

80. The Shaykh Knows Who Has Taken His Sheep

In the early days of the Shaykh's repentance, he ate no meat because he suspected the sheep were unlawful. Whenever the Shaykh had a guest come visit, he would set a trap for game on the mountain and there was a man who would help set the traps for the Shaykh on the mountain. Wherever a wild sheep was caught in a trap the Shaykh would inform that man to go to such-and-such place in such-and-such valley and bring the wild sheep that had been caught there. He would go and bring the wild sheep from right where the Shaykh al-Islam had indicated.

Then one day the Shaykh said, "Go to such-and-such place, where a wild sheep is entrapped and has gotten tangled in the briers; [free it] or else it will die and go to waste."

The man went. The trap was there but there was no sheep. He returned and said, "There was no sheep, and I could not find its tracks anywhere."

The Shaykh al-Islam said, "Go to the main road [gozarestân] and wait there. Two men will bring a donkey-load of firewood. They have tossed that sheep on top of the wood. Take it from them

---

[112] Literally meaning "on the river bank," but this must be a place name of a village or town here.

[113] A quite similar story is told about Borhân al-Din Mohaqqeq of Termez and his Shaykh, Bahâ al-Din Valad (the father of Jalâl al-Din Rumi). In the middle of a talk he was giving in Termez, Borhân al-Din cried out that his master, Bahâ al-Din, who was in Konya, had just died. Borhân had the prayer for the dead recited and his disciples noted down the date and time. A year later, when Borhân reached Anatolia, the date and time proved to have been exactly correct. This legend appears about 120 years after Bahâ al-Din's death in Shams al-Din al-Aflâki's *Manâqeb al-'ârefin*, ed. Tahsin Yazıcı (Ankara: Türk Tarih Kurumu Basımevi, 1959), 56-8.

before they enter the village with it."

The man went and saw everything as the Shaykh al-Islam had described. He took the sheep and brought it to the Shaykh al-Islam, who rewarded him with a portion of it.

81. The Shaykh and the Dragon

There was a man by the name of 'Abd al-Rashid, the brother of Khvâjeh-ye 'Amid Ebrâhim-e Sâvardi, who collected the taxes in the village of Nâmaq. One day 'Abd al-Rashid said to Shaykh Abu al-Hasan-e Sahâqari, "Let's go visit the grave of Shaykh Bu Tâher, God rest his soul."

This was in the early days of the Shaykh al-Islam's calling. The Shaykh al-Islam agreed and the three of them went together.

There was a valley and meadow in the midst of the mountains where lived [133] a huge terrifying dragon, which could drag down a donkey just by sucking in its breath. It was well into the night when they arrived there. 'Abd al-Rashid and Abu al-Hasan were in front and the Shaykh was following behind them. Suddenly their horse began to rear up, threw off its riders and bolted.

The Shaykh al-Islam ran in front of the horse and grabbed it. When he reached those two, he saw that they were discouraged and afraid. He asked, "Why aren't you moving?"

Shaykh Abu al-Hasan Sahâqari said, "We are unable to go on. You are more courageous; perhaps you can walk ahead of us."

The Shaykh al-Islam went ahead and they followed behind. The horse kept startling and pulling away. They asked, "What is that black shape up there on the edge of the mountain in that reed bed? That is what the horse is scared of." The Shaykh al-Islam at first thought it was a burnt-out tree that looked black. He went in front and stood blocking the horse's view of it, so that the horse would move on.

In reality, it was a dragon. When the Shaykh al-Islam went forward and stood in front of it, that dragon raised its head over the shoulder of the Shaykh from behind and gazed into his face. The horse, seeing the head of the dragon above the Shaykh's shoulder, was afraid and would not go on. The Shaykh raised his hand and held it in front of the dragons' face. That creature moved its head over his other shoulder and gazed into the face of the Shaykh just like a lover. The Shaykh collected some reeds and wove them together into something the size of a camel's neck, holding it in front of the dragon so that the three of them could pass by. Then the Shaykh al-Islam showed his affection for the dragon, which responded in kind. For God is with him who is with God.

82. The Shaykh and His Spiritual Mentor, Bu Tâher

One time, when the Shaykh al-Islam went to see Shaykh Bu Tâher, he was accompanied by his brother-in-law, [134] the learned Abu Bakr, who kept reproaching him. "Why don't you do anything to earn your living? You cannot go on like this." He complained like this in front of Shaykh Bu Tâher and conveyed messages from the Shaykh al-Islam's mother and father asking that Bu Tâher advise him to take up a trade.

Shaykh Bu Tâher, God have mercy on his soul, turned to the Shaykh al-Islam and said, "Why have you left your trade, for I have heard from Khezr,[114] God bless him, that even if a person wears a deerskin and eats turtle eggs and sleeps in thorns and bristles, he is still of this world."

The Shaykh al-Islam answered, "Khezr would not say such a thing. And if he did say it, you tell him that he has planted a pomegranate tree by the spring with the intention of worshipping God in its shade. The tree did not let go its hold of you until it dragged you down to the rank of a common servant, and you have seen what came of that."

The Shaykh Bu Tâher was enraged: "Just wait! You have come to the point where you criticize Khezr?!" Many words were exchanged between the two of them until finally Shaykh Bu Tâher threw the Shaykh al-Islam out of his house.

The Shaykh al-Islam went to the mosque. He was fasting and had not yet eaten. He prayed to Almighty God, as follows, "O God, my mother and father and kinsmen and relatives have turned

---

[114] On Khezr, see the note in Story 5.

me away and driven me from the house. I had a mentor to whom I was close; he, too, has turned me away and driven me from his home. I no longer know who I am." [135]

[The Shaykh relates]: When a good part of the night had passed, Shaykh Bu Tâher arrived holding a tray of food in his hand. He knocked on the door of the mosque. When I opened the door he came in and fell at my feet, saying, "Forgive me, for I was ignorant and have failed in my duty towards you. I ask for your forgiveness."

The Shaykh al-Islam said, "What has happened to make you remorseful?"

He said, "Khezr came and reproached me, saying, 'You have no business interfering with the Shaykh al-Islam. He follows the right path and you must not interfere.'"

So that you know, and it is God Who is the Most Knowledgeable.

83. The Shaykh Makes Abu al-Hasan 'Isâ Mayor of the Village of Nâmaq

The Shaykh al-Islam said:

There was a man in the village of Nâmaq, a nobleman born to a noble family, called Abu al-Hasan 'Isâ. He went before the governor of Khorasan for a while and spent a great deal of money in hopes that the mayorship of the village of Nâmaq would be given to him. But it was to no avail.

Then one day he came to see the Shaykh al-Islam. "I have heard that you work wonders. I have been trying for some time to gain the position of mayor of the village of Nâmaq. If you give it to me, I will repent."

The Shaykh al-Islam asked, "Do you really mean that?"

"I do," he said.

The Shaykh said, "Go and call out for all the people of the village to gather in your house." He went and gathered all the people. The Shaykh al-Islam then said, "People, know that this Khvâjeh Bu al-Hasan has been made your mayor and you must obey his order and pay him due respect."

He told the previous mayor, "Don't worry. I have advised him to

say nothing against you or those associated with you, and to do no
wrong to you."
That Khvâjeh Bu al-Hasan then became mayor and he remained
the mayor of the village of Nâmaq as long as he lived.

84. A Thread from the Prayer Carpet Turns to Gold in the Shaykh's Hand

Khvâjeh Abu Bakr Kusavi[115] relates:
We went to see the Shaykh in the village of Ma'd-âbâd. [136]
The Shaykh al-Islam was sitting in the prayer niche of the
khâneqâh, in a trance [kâr-i va hâlat-i]. He pulled out a thread
from the prayer carpet on which he was sitting and wiped the
sweat from his brow with it. He twisted the thread with his
fingers. When he tossed the thread down it had turned to pure
gold. Those present saw all this.
There was an old irrigation channel in Ma'd-âbâd. The Shaykh
interceded and all contended that it was his. It still belongs to him.
[sic][116]

85. The Shaykh Works a Miracle With Some Flour

Brother 'Ali Asfarghâbadi[117] relates:
Once I filled two sacks of flour for the Shaykh al-Islam. The
amount of flour in these two sacks would last for twenty days. I
held a feast in honor of the Shaykh al-Islam, to which the Sadr al-

---

[115] That is, the town Kusuy or Kusuyah near the Herat River, north of
Khar-gerd, about one-third of the size of the neighboring city of Bushanj,
(see Le Strange, *Lands of the Eastern Caliphate, 358*). A person from the
town would be called Kusu'i or Kusavi. The toponym occurs again in
Story 113 and the same Hâji Kusavi appears in Story 193.
[116] Evidently a sentence or more is missing from the manuscript about
the ownership of the irrigation channel, as the passage in the last
paragraph bears no relation to the rest of the story about turning the thread
to gold.
[117] This toponym sometimes occurs in the form Asfarghâbadi and in
this case as Asfarghâbâdi; as mentioned in the introduction to this book,
Asfarghâbadi has been identified with the modern Samarqâveh.

Islam[118] from Herat came, along with one hundred of his people. There were another one hundred and fifty people who came with the Shaykh al-Islam. Bread was baked for all of them from those sacks, enough for two hundred and fifty people. After the feast, we continued to eat from it for four more days. We used the flour from that sack for four months.

Later, a detachment of soldiers arrived and billeted in the village. Members of my household moved that sack of flour in an effort to hide it. When the Shaykh saw me, he said, "The flour has been moved. They should not have done that, for they have harmed themselves."

When I came home, they had already moved that sack from its place. It still held nearly one hundred maunds of flour.

86. All Receive Equal Portions From the Shaykh

He likewise reports that:

The Shaykh al-Islam has told me on nearly a hundred different occasions to distribute something that belonged to him. Each time I asked, "How much of it should I give [each person]?"

He would say [137], "Give such-and-such amount to each." It happened that I always distributed things such that there was neither one too few nor one too many.

How wondrous was the blessing of God, exalted and glorified be He, over him!

87. The Shaykh Catches a Falling Child in Mid-air From a Great Distance[119]

Ostâd Imam Mohammad Shâd,[120] God have mercy upon him,

---

[118] Evidently a prominent judicial official.

[119] This story is similar to, and probably modeled upon, a miracle related about Abu Sa'id-e Abu al-Khayr in Mohammad b. Monavvar in *Asrâr al-towhid*, 58; *Secrets of God's Mystical Oneness*, 134-5.

[120] The name Mohammad Shâd is often found in connection with the Karrâmite sect, a heterodox Muslim sect subject to occasional harassment (for the latest research on the Karrâmites, see the articles of Mohammad-Rezâ Shafi'i-Kadkani mentioned in the introduction).

once told the Shaykh, "There has always been someone from our community endowed with intuition who would tie the hands and tongues of our enemies. Today you are the cynosure of the city of Nayshabur. Tomorrow the Faqih-e Ajall [the Supreme Jurist][121] will come to see you. How would it be if you perform some miracle for him or his children, so that we can remain with you, unharassed?"

The Shaykh al-Islam wanted to oblige Ostâd Imam and watched for an occasion to do so. The following morning he was sitting in a group of people in the khâneqâh of the learned Imam 'Ali Bayhaqi.[122] He bowed his head and suddenly jumped up, raising his arms in the air, saying, "Make smooth the way, make smooth the way!," his demeanor completely changed.

The people asked him what had happened and he said, "You will shortly see." They pressed him [for more information]. Eyes fixed on the door of the khâneqâh, he said, "Wait for a while." Then a youth came in the door of the khâneqâh. Before the youth spoke a word, the Shaykh al-Islam said, "Go and tell them not to worry, but to send a few maunds of bread and meat to every khâneqâh."

The people asked that youth what had happened. He asked, "Did anyone [138] come here before me?"

"No," they replied.

He said, "This thing which happened in our house—no one had any news of it and no one left the house before me. How did he know about it?"

They answered, "We don't know what has happened; we only know that a while ago the Shaykh al-Islam jumped up and raised his hands in the air, saying 'O Lord, make smooth the way.'"

That youth said, "The grandchild of the Faqih-e Ajall fell from the roof of the house of Khvâjeh Abu al-Hasan, the brother of

---

[121] The title of Abu al-Qâsem 'Abd Allâh ebn-e 'Ali ebn-e Eshâq, the brother of the famous Seljuk vizier, Nezâm al-Molk. He was a famous judicial scholar in Khorasan who died in Sarakhs in July 1106 (Dhi al-Qa'da 499). His son, whose relations with Shaykh Ahmad are described in a few stories in this text, was for a while minister to Sultan Sanjar.

[122] This man should not be mistaken with Zahir al-Din 'Ali ebn Zayd Bayhaqi, the author of the famous *Târikh-e Bayhaq*, who was not born until 1106 / 499 A.H., after the events in this story had taken place.

Khvâjeh Imam Shehâb.[123] It was as if someone caught her in mid-air and set her down upright on the roof. They were all determined to come see the Shaykh al-Islam today, but when this accident happened, they sent me to ask the Shaykh to keep them in his prayers and not to expect us. When I entered the khâneqâh, before I said a word, he addressed the situation."

Later they asked the Shaykh al-Islam, "What were you doing when you raised your hands in the air?"

He said, "When that girl fell from the roof, I reached out and caught her and set her down, in honor of the request of Khvâjeh Mohammad Shâd."

88. The Shaykh Predicts the Dismissal of Khvâjeh Imam Shehâb[124]

After the accident, Khvâjeh Imam Shehâb came to see the Shaykh. Imam Ostâd Mohammad Shâd had previously recommended that the Shaykh ought to display a miracle [139] which would cause the entire family [of Nezâm al-Molk] to

---

[123] That is Khvâjeh Abu al-Hasan Tâher, son of the Faqih-e Ajall. Concerning his brother, Khvâjeh Imam Shehâb, see the next note.

[124] Abu al-Mahâsen Shams al-Din Shehâb al-Islam 'Abd al-Razzâq ebn 'Abd Allâh, the son of the Faqih-e Ajall mentioned in the previous story, and one of the leading religious scholars in Nayshabur. He was the brother of Nezâm al-Molk, and the poet Mo'ezzi has composed eight panegyrics for him. He is also mentioned in Nezâmi 'Aruzi's *Chahâr maqâleh* in relation to Ferdowsi, and also in Imam Zahir-e Bayhaqi's *Tatimmah siwân al-hikmah* in relation to 'Omar Khayyâm.

Shehâb al-Islam was chosen by Sultan Sanjar to be his vizier, a post which he occupied from 1117 / 511 until his death on 7 April 1121 / 17 Muharram 515. The *Spiritual Feats* calls him Imam Shehâb al-Din (a title which Mo'ezzi also uses in relation to him once), but he is elsewhere known as Shehâb al-Islam. The *Spiritual Feats* indicates that he was partial to the Ismailis, which would account for Fakhr al-Molk's decision to have him imprisoned, probably in 1106 / 499. A rumor circulated that Shehâb al-Islam had been killed, and this supposedly precipitated the death of his father, Faqih-e Ajall, in July 1106 / Dhi al-Qa'dah 499. Shehâb al-Islam was released shortly thereafter, when Fakhr al-Molk was killed on 16 September 1106 / 10 Moharram 500.

believe in him. Khvâjeh Imam Shehâb said, "The great nobleman, Fakhr al-Molk,[125] is opposed to me and wants to get rid of me [dar nafy-e man mi-kushad]. Remember me in your prayers."

The Shaykh answered, "If you want to be safely out of his reach, stop the scholar who gives sermons in the square of the bazaar from making his allegations [against me]. Otherwise, they will come and remove you from office. I can see at this moment that they put you in a litter and are carrying you away. God only knows what will happen to you next."

Khvâjeh Imam Shehâb al-Din looked sharply at the Shaykh al-Islam and said, [140] "Look carefully at me. Am I not a good mayor for Nayshabur?"

The Shaykh al-Islam said, "Since Nayshabur was founded, it has never had a worse mayor than you. Do you think I don't know which sect [qowm] you are supporting?" The Shaykh gave him two or three examples which won for himself the complete confidence of Imam Shehâb.

The next day there was an old man called Khvâjeh Ahmad the Minter, whom Khvâjeh Imam sent, along with Hosayn Mohebb, to deliver this message [to the Shaykh al-Islam]: "Yesterday you said something that has weighed very heavily on my heart, but there was no opportunity to pursue it then. I'd like you to accept one of the villages that belong to me, that I might find a place under the shelter of your power."

The Shaykh al-Islam answered [those messengers]: "Which of you is stupider, the two of you or him?"

"What indications of stupidity do you see in us and in him?," they asked.

He said, "If he is in the shelter of my power, it is he who must receive his wages from me, not I from him."

One of them said, "This is so; you are quite right."

---

[125] That is, Khvâjeh Abu al-Fath Mozaffar, the eldest son of Nezâm al-Molk, and cousin to Imam Shehâb. Fakhr al-Molk was vizier to Barkyâroq, as well as Sultan Sanjar's vizier for a period of ten years. He apparently had Shehâb al-Islam imprisoned in the Fortress of Termez in 1106/499, probably on suspicion of Shehâb al-Islam having ties to the Ismailis. However, on 11 September 1106 / 10 Muharram 500, Fakhr al-Molk was assassinated by Ismailis and Shehâb al-Islam was released.

The Shaykh al-Islam did not accept the offer. Then they asked, "Is the news of his dismissal true?"

"Yesterday," he replied, "at the noon-prayer, they wrote the orders for his dismissal."

Not long afterwards the royal Altun Tâsh was sent to arrest him. Khvâjeh Shehâb pretended to be ill and kept the door of his house locked. Amir Altun Tâsh entered his house with fifty horsemen and, just as the Shaykh al-Islam had predicted, they put him in a litter and carried him off towards Termez. No one knew where they took him and, in the end, it was the Shaykh al-Islam who came to his rescue.

89. One of the Shaykh's Predictions

Ostâd Imam Mohammad Shâd advised the Shaykh al-Islam to display a miracle for them. The next day he went to see the Shaykh al-Islam to ask, "What happened in the end?" The learned Imam 'Ali Bayhaqi [was there and] described what took place. Ostâd Imam Mohammad Shâd said, "The Shaykh al-Islam will be the ruin [141] of us and we will no longer be able to live in this city if what he has said does not come to pass."

The learned Imam 'Ali Bayhaqi reported his words to the Shaykh al-Islam, who said, "If this is what you believed, why did you ask me to perform miracles?"

Twenty days later, news of what the Shaykh al-Islam had predicted was received and the matter became clear. Ostâd Imam apologized profusely: "Forgive me, what I did was wrong."

90. The Shaykh Gives Word that Imam Shehâb is Alive

When Fakhr al-Molk was the vizier and was on bad terms with Khvâjeh Imam Shehâb, and the royal Amir Altun Tâsh was taking Imam Shehâb to the army camp, Khvâjeh Imam Shehâb wrote a letter from Balkh and sent it via a messenger to the Shaykh al-Islam: "Help me, for the vizier is determined to kill me."

The Shaykh al-Islam prayed for him. Then the father of Khvâjeh Imam Shehâb, the Faqih-e Ajall, traced him to the army camp in order to pay a ransom to save his son's life. It was rumored among the people when the Faqih-e Ajall arrived that his son, Khvâjeh Imam Shehâb, had already been killed. Rumor had it that when he saw this, he dropped dead of grief. This story made the rounds and became the talk of the town.

At the time this rumor was spread, the Shaykh al-Islam was in the vicinity of Jâm. One day a group of soldiers came before the Shaykh al-Islam and gave him this news. When the Shaykh al-Islam heard it, he too was saddened, because Imam Shehâb was a friend and follower of the Shaykh al-Islam. When he heard the news, he reflected upon it and, by the vision which great men possess, he saw that a regiment of horsemen came to Khvâjeh Imam Shehâb on the banks of the Oxus and took him away.

Then the Shaykh al-Islam [142] turned to those who brought him the news and said, "Why do you report things which you cannot substantiate?"

They said, "O Shaykh, we were there when it happened and saw it with our own eyes."

He said, "You never saw such a thing. Just now he has reached the banks of the Oxus with several horseman and is safe and sound."

When the news of what the Shaykh al-Islam had said spread, a learned man from Buzjân whom they called Khvâjeh Imam 'Abd al-Rahmân, said, "This is nonsense, what the Shaykh al-Islam says. We have heard it from several people that Imam Shehâb was killed. The estate which he left behind must now be divided according to the laws of Islam. Shaykh Ahmad should not say such things, for it has a bad effect on the people."

When the Shaykh al-Islam heard him say this, he said, "What possible benefit could anyone have in saying such a thing?" And he swore that Khvâjeh Imam Shehâb was alive at that very moment. The learned 'Abd al-Rahmân noted down the date and he constantly asked all those who came from the army camp, who all confirmed that Imam Shehâb had been killed and buried along with his father in a grave off to the side of the road, as an admonition to all. All were agreed on this matter and they mocked the Shaykh al-Islam.

A while later it finally became known that Imam Shehâb was alive, safe and sound, for all to see.

91. The Shaykh's Prediction about Imam Shehâb Comes True

When they had taken Khvâjeh Shehâb al-Din to Termez and the rumor of his death had been bandied about, the Shaykh al-Islam said, "It is certain that they have not killed him; he is alive." To those who reported him as dead, the Shaykh swore that he was alive.

The news that the Shaykh al-Islam was saying this reached to Nayshabur. Those who believed in him said: [143] "If the Shaykh says so, then he is alive." An investigator was sent from Nayshabur to Buzjân to tell him, "They say that you have said he is alive; is there any truth to it?" The Shaykh al-Islam wrote a letter saying that it was true and that Khvâjeh Imam Shehâb was alive in the fortress of Termez. When the investigator returned, the Shaykh's opponents began to talk, saying there was no basis to it, that two hundred people had seen him dead. Everyone was saying something different.

When the Sultan of the world came to Dahaneh-ye Shir,[126] Ostâd Imam Mohammad Shâd was at odds with the Chief Qâzi, Bu Sa'id. Ostâd Imam took the Shaykh al-Islam with him to that place to intercede with the Sultan. The sister of Khvâjeh Imam Shehâb al-Din and a group of those dependent on him were there.[....][127]

"Many times they sent someone to see you, but you have many things to attend to, and we are veiled women and cannot go there. If you would out of your magnanimity pass by this way once so we could see you, it would be wonderful and a great blessing for us weak ones."

In order to bring happiness to their hearts, the Shaykh al-Islam

---

[126] Yâqût lists a place called Shirz as one of the villages around Sarakhs, explaining that the final "z" is an adjectival ending, so that the name of the village is in origin "Shir." There is a village near Sabzevâr [formerly Bayhaq] called "Dahaneh-ye Shir" [the mouth of Shir] listed in the *Farhang-e Joghrâfiâ'i-ye Irân* (v. 9), and it is perhaps the same location mentioned in our text.

[127] There seems to be a lacuna in the manuscripts here. The text continues with the female dependents of Imam Shehâb speaking.

went there with a few companions. The women said, "For the good pleasure of God, give us the true facts, for we cannot figure out what has happened. We have spent three thousand dinârs on account of the one thing you are reported to have said. We have likewise spent a great deal on Zayn al-Molk[128] that we might learn something with his help, but we have heard [144] nothing."

The Shaykh al-Islam asked, "You still haven't heard anything about him?" They said, "No." The Shaykh reflected deeply on this matter, thinking, "These people have spent so much money and a full year has passed and they have not received any news, whereas I have seen him a number of times and he is alive." He was lost in this thought when a voice once again told him that Imam Shehâb al-Din was alive and that he would break the fast of Ramadan together with them.

The Shaykh al-Islam said, "Do not worry, for he is alive and will break the fast this year together."

Having heard this, they each cried out loudly and fainted. This was on the sixth day of Ramadan.

Imam Shehâb al-Din arrived on the evening of the twenty-eighth, and they broke their fast together the last day of Ramadan for all to see.

92. Epilogue to the Story of the Shaykh and Imam Shehâb

When Khvâjeh Imam Shehâb returned, they told him everything that had happened, and his faith in the Shaykh grew one hundred-

---

[128] Shams al-Din Abu Sa'd Zayn al-Molk Hendu ebn-e Mohammad ebn-e Hendu-ye Qommi, the Royal Treasurer of Sultan Mohammad, the Seljuk, from 1104 (498 A.H.). In 1106 (500 A.H.), when Sa'd al-Molk was killed, Zayn al-Molk was also arrested and jailed. In 1110 (504 A.H.) he was released and became head of the Treasury once again. In 1112 (506 A.H.) the Sultan, at the instigation of rival courtiers, turned him over to Amir Âltun Tâsh, who had him hanged. Historical reports accuse Zayn al-Molk of being ignorant and taking many bribes; his excessive greed brought about his downfall. Mo'ezzi has composed a couple of poems in his honor (see the poem beginning "*do chashm-e to hastand fattân o jâdu*" in *Divân-e Mo'ezzi*; at Zayn al-Molk's request, as reported in the *Chahâr maqâleh*, Mo'ezzi composed a poem in imitation of Rudaki's famous ode in the radif *âyad hami* about Bokhara).

fold. While the Shaykh al-Islam was in Nayshabur, Imam Shehâb would go to visit him every week. Some of the scholars and opponents of the Shaykh went to Imam Shehâb and said, "Why do you put such faith in him, for he is no longer at the top of his form."[129]

Imam Shehâb replied, "My faith in him is not such that you can [145] destroy it with your talk. Even if what you say is true, still a handful of opponents like you are no match for him."

Then one day Imam Shehâb said to the Shaykh al-Islam, "Your opponents are saying such-and-such. I need you to show them some sort of a miracle now, so that all people can clearly see it and their claims will be refuted."

The Shaykh al-Islam said, "One must pay no attention to them."

Imam Shehâb pleaded. "I need something which can be grasped by no mortal mind, something that has never been done before and will never be done again."

After much pleading, the Shaykh al-Islam said, "Go prepare yourself to become the vizier. When you have made the necessary arrangements, the office of vizier will be given to you."

Imam Shehâb said, "That's impossible, with all of Nezâm al-Molk's offspring still alive. Besides, I have no desire for it, as the costs of attaining the office are too heavy."

The Shaykh al-Islam said, "You made a request of me. I have told you the inspiration that came to me."

Khvâjeh Imam did not believe it, so he went off to report this exchange, by way of renunciation, to the faction who were saying that the Shaykh al-Islam is no longer at the top of his form.

The Shaykh al-Islam was informed of the matter and grew sad. He said, "There is no question but that he will be punished."

At that time Imam Shehâb was the mayor of Nayshabur. He was dismissed from office. He came to the Shaykh al-Islam and fell at his feet, telling him: "You were promising me to be vizier, and now I have been dismissed from the mayorship."

The Shaykh said, "Do you not know that you will be punished for denying my word?"

---

[129] *Bar sar-e pay nist*, on which, see the note on the word *sar-e pay* in Story 72.

He wept bitterly and said, "I repent."

The Shaykh said, "Go now, you bastard.[130] Not for your sake, but in order to fulfill my promise, I am granting you both the office of mayor and of vizier. Now you will see just how lacking you are in discrimination."

The mayorship was restored to him the very same week. As for the vizierate, the Shaykh told him, "Unless you resolve to stop promoting that sect and to purify your heart of the thoughts that you now entertain, you will not become vizier." [146]

"What thoughts are those?," he asked.

The Shaykh gave several examples of what he meant, revealing the sect that Imam Shehâb was partial to, and all that he had in mind. He told him everything just as it was, though none was apprised of what was in Imam Shehâb's heart, except for the Imam himself and Almighty God.

Imam Shehâb went to make all the arrangements for the viziership. Before all the arrangements had been completed, someone came looking for him and took him to the army camp, where he was made vizier. These events are as well-known as the sun in the sky.

93. The Shaykh's Prediction about a few People from Nayshabur

There was a feud once in Nayshabur between the Qâzi Sâ'ed, the Imam Ashraf,[131] and Bu Sa'id, the Chief Qâzi, and their kinfolk. There was a disagreement about pious endowments for the college and about the Friday Mosque and its official preacher.

---

[130] Reading *hiz*, as per the Nâfiz Pâshâ manuscript, rather than *hamin*, as given in the Chester Beatty manuscript.

[131] Imam Ashraf could ordinarily be understood as an honorific - the respected Imam (Emâm-e ashraf) - modifying Qâzi Sâ'ed. However, the title Imam Ashraf Abu al-Ma'âli is used in Chapter Three without reference to Qâzi Sâ'ed, and the name Qâzi Sâ'ed appears in Story 116 without the title Imam Ashraf. In the present story, Abu Sa'id sends a message to the Shaykh al-Islam which appears to distinguish a separate individual, Imam Ashraf, from Qâzi Sâ'ed. Therefore it must refer to another individual.

Both families went to the army camp. The learned Ahmad Zâvahi was with the Imam Ashraf, God have mercy upon him, and told him, "You have many enemies who actively [oppose you][132] and I don't see that you have any means or any followers with which to confront them. What will happen?"

"I proceed with the backing of the Shaykh al-Islam Ahmad," he answered, "for I have many enemies and I find no followers nor any means, but in him I have a mighty refuge. I have complete faith in his prayers and spiritual power."

Ahmad Zâvahi went to the Shaykh al-Islam and informed him. "Khvâjeh Imam Ashraf has been saying such things about you in public. Keep an eye on him."

The Shaykh al-Islam replied, "Because of his faith in me, God Almighty will not allow his efforts [147] to fail."

On the twenty-seventh of Ramadan they were reciting a sura of the Qur'ân to close the service at the old Friday Mosque, when a messenger from the Chief Qâzi, Bu Sa'id, arrived, informing everyone that the endowments for the college and for the official preacher of Nayshabur had been placed in the trusteeship of the Chief Qâzi and that Khvâjeh Imam Ashraf had been arrested and detained.

The people of Nayshabur were saddened by this news. There were more than four thousand men in the Friday Mosque and within one hour's time the whole city had learned of it. The kinsmen of Chief Qâzi Bu Sa'id took the podium of the pulpit to the assembly grounds[133] three days before the Festival of Ramadan, and made arrangements for the sermon to be given there.

The Shaykh al-Islam reflected about this for a while, and it was revealed to him that a change in the current circumstances had been ordained. He sent a messenger to the Chief Qâzi, Bu Sa'id, telling him, "It would be no source of pride for you to give the

---

[132] The text is defective here, but perhaps should read *doshmani mi-varzand*.

[133] *Khoruj-gâh*, literally "place of going out," a word not listed in standard dictionaries. It appears to refer to a location outside the city gates where large assemblies could be held.

sermon, and no cause of shame if you did not. It has been revealed
to me in this regard that there has been a change of affairs."

The Shaykh told [his messenger], Khvâjeh Imam Abu al-Hasan
Mos'abi, to take this message to the Chief Qâzi. He replied, "I
cannot tell him this, for it would not be right."

The Shaykh al-Islam said, "If you don't take this message, the
reputation[134] of Chief Qâzi Bu Sa'id will at stake, for the decree
in favor of Khvâjeh Ashraf will arrive during the interval between
the two sermons, which will only harm his reputation."

Khvâjeh Imam Abu al-Hasan said, "It is impossible that the
Chief Qâzi would accept this message." The Shaykh said, "Just go
and tell him," which Abu al-Hasan did.

The Chief Qâzi did accept the message, thinking, "I know he
would not lie." However, he sent someone back with this message
for the Shaykh, "If you say this because of your friendship with
Ashraf, and the truth is otherwise, I will be greatly offended. But
if you know this to be the truth, then someone should be sent to
the Qâzi Imam Sâ'ed[135] so that he can give the sermon."

The Shaykh al-Islam said, "It is undoubtedly true," [148] and he
sent a messenger to Imam Sâ'ed informing him that, "You must
give the sermon tomorrow, for it has been decreed that the office
of preacher is yours."

Word spread throughout the city and the people said, "Why does

---

[134] "Reputation" for *âb-e b-sh-d-li*. The word /*bnt*/-*sh-d-li* is not
attested in any of the standard Persian dictionaries, though it appears clear
that something similar to *âb-e ru rizi*, or loss of face, is meant.

[135] A descendant of Abu al-'Alâ 'Emâd al-Eslâm Sâ'ed ebn-e
Mohammad ebn-e Ahmad ebn-e 'Abd Allâh, a pious and ascetic man who
was a great Hanafi legal scholar, and functioned for some time as a qâzi in
Nayshabur. He died in 1041 (432 A.H.), but his descendants continued in
the profession of qâzi, at least until the middle of the 12th century
according to the *Ketâb al-ansâb* of Sam'âni (see under the rubric
"*Ostovâ'i*"). The founder of the family, Abu al-'Alâ, was well respected at
the Ghaznavid court and is mentioned several times in *Târikh-e Bayhaqi*.
For further information, see *Ma'âref-e Bahâ-e Valad* (ed. B. Foruzânfar),
4:309. According to 'Attâr, Qâzi Sâ'ed was an opponent of Shaykh Abu
Sa'id-e Abu al-Khayr and tried to test his mystical powers, which caused
embarrassment for Qâzi Sâ'ed, who then dropped his opposition. See
Tazkerat al-owliyâ (Leiden, 1905-7), 2:334.

the Shaykh al-Islam say and do such things, which only cause enmity between the people?" As it happened, the Shaykh al-Islam and Khvâjeh Imam Shehâb met in the assembly grounds on the day of the Ramadan festival. Khvâjeh Shehâb said, "I hear you saying such-and-such."

The Shaykh said, "Yes, I have said so."

The Khvâjeh said, "What if it isn't true—our enemies will be delighted, as your opponents have for some while longed for an occasion to find fault with you."

The Shaykh al-Islam asked, "Don't you believe in me anymore?"

He replied, "The preacher has assumed the pulpit and there is yet no sign of what you have predicted."

The Shaykh said, "I have said that it will happen between the two sermons."

The moment that the preacher had finished delivering the first sermon and was about to begin with the next, a clamor arose and two decrees in favor of Khvâjeh Ashraf were brought. They were hung on both sides of the pulpit so that all were able to see it. When the prayers were finished, on the way back into the city, the glance of Imam Abu al-Hasan Mos'abi fell upon the Shaykh al-Islam. Abu al-Hasan, in front of all the people, raised his finger in the air and cried out three times in a loud voice, "We believe, we believe, we believe."

Most of the inhabitants of the city are aware of this matter, so that you know.

94. The Shaykh Predicts a Food Shortage

When the Shaykh al-Islam went on his pilgrimage journey to the Hijâz, the Chief Qâzi Bu Sa'id of Nayshabur, may God have mercy on him, was with him. His sons were disciples of the Shaykh al-Islam, and the [149] Chief Qâzi would sometimes reproach them, saying, "What have you seen in him that you are constantly going to visit and keep company with him?" When the two of them happened to be traveling in the same company, his sons told the Shaykh al-Islam that, "The Chief Qâzi, our father, reproaches us on account of you. It is our desire...how would it be if you demonstrate something miraculous to him, so that he will leave us alone?"

One day it was revealed to the Shaykh that there would be a shortage of food. The Shaykh al-Islam told the Qâzi, "Bring some provisions with you, for there will be a shortage of food in the desert." This is what the Shaykh told the Qâzi. The Qâzi thought, "This knowledge is hidden to us [*ghayb ast*], and none knows what is hidden except for God, the Almighty."

On the day when they arrived in Tha'alabah,[136] a dinâr, which used to fetch thirty maunds of bread, was now buying a hundred maunds. The Chief Qâzi laughed mockingly and asked his sons, "And you believe that this Shaykh is clairvoyant?"

The Shaykh al-Islam had stated, "I can see the Chief Qâzi coming to ask me for bread, which I give to him." This was reported to the Chief Qâzi and it displeased him greatly.

On their journey back home, there was a shortage of bread, such that one dinâr was fetching only four maunds. The Shaykh had several maunds of flour hanging in a sack on his camel. That day the Chief Qâzi came to see him. He was hungry and said, "O Shaykh, I am heavy-hearted about the provisions. Have you any bread?"

The Shaykh replied, "I have—I've got a few maunds of flour," and he gave him two pieces of bread.

The Chief Qâzi said, "He undoubtedly can see the future!"

So that you know.

95. The Shaykh Predicts Someone's Death

When the Shaykh al-Islam was in Nayshabur and the learned men and nobles were coming to ask all sorts of questions from him, there was a certain Khvâjeh Imam Zaki Bu Sa'd-e Sarrâji, one of the Mozakkis,[137] who would come very often and ask questions of the Shaykh.

One day the Chief Qâzi [150], Bu Sa'id, told him, "Why do you go [to the Shaykh] so often? You are a scholar and it is harmful to

---

[136] A place in the Arabian desert.

[137] It is not clear whether the name of a family, a religious sect or of a particular profession is intended.

your rank and reputation. Have you ever seen him perform any kind of miracle?"

He said, "I have never seen anything like that, but he is a righteous man, and it is said that he has knowledge of the unseen. Perhaps I will see some example of it."

The Qâzi said, "I don't believe in this. But you keep going; perhaps you will see something."

One day Khvâjeh Bu Sa'd-e Haysam, who was extremely ill and could eat nothing, was brought before the Shaykh al-Islam in a litter. The Shaykh al-Islam asked him, "What is your desire? Death or a bit of bread?" The Shaykh al-Islam prayed for him and he was carried home.

The people asked the Shaykh, "What will become of him? Will he live?"

He said, "No. As I was saying the prayer, it was revealed to my heart that on the day a fresh crop of rhubarb comes to the market, he will die."

Khvâjeh Imam Bu Sa'd-e Sarrâji came and told Qâzi Bu Sa'id that "I have heard from him today what I was waiting for." The Qâzi said, "Wait and see what happens," and left.

The day when fresh rhubarb came to market, Imam Bu Sa'd went to the Qâzi to say, "There was no substance to what he said, for today I saw rhubarb in the market square."

"I was surprised that you gave credence to such talk," the Qâzi said. "Don't you know that God, alone, has knowledge of the unseen?"

As they were talking, someone came in to say that Bu Sa'd Haysam had died. [151] They stared at each other in amazement and said, "We confess that this cannot be gainsaid and there is no [proof] greater than this. This man is one of God's saints."

Peace be with you.

96. Turning Water into Food

Once a number of scholars were guests of the Shaykh. When it came time for the meal, there was only bread. The Shaykh al-Islam asked his servant, "Don't we have any food?"

The servant said, "I can't find any."

After a while, the Shaykh said, "If there is nothing, we should at least fetch a ewer full of water and pour it into a bowl."

No one said anything. For the third time, the Shaykh said, "Do you not have faith in your own teacher [*pir*]? Do you suppose that the Lord God cannot change water into food by his hands? What a waste [*harâm*] it is to spend time with you!"

After his sweet lips had spoken for the third time, I went to the brook with a ewer in hand and brought the water myself. I took three bowls from the room, filled them with water, and placed them before the Shaykh. He sprinkled a dash of salt in each one. As each of them dipped the bread into [those bowls] and ate, they were deeply stirred and cried out, as though in spiritual ecstasy.

The Shaykh al-Islam asked me, "O Mohammad-e Ghaznavi, won't you have some food? Our goat gives wonderful milk, better than the goats of Ghazna."

I dipped a piece of bread in that bowl and put it in my mouth. It tasted like milk, warm and sweet, as if it had been freshly milked! The guests were in a state of great commotion, rocking back and forth on the portico until well into the night.

And peace be with you.

97. The Shaykh Punishes the People of Ma'd-âbâd

Once a fight broke out between the people of Ma'd-âbâd and Kâriz, and a man was killed. [152] They proceeded to the army camp to lodge a complaint and returned with a horseman, and an order was issued to do what the Shaykh al-Islam thought best. The Shaykh al-Islam offered his advice, but the people of Ma'd-âbâd did not follow it and accused the Shaykh al-Islam of being partial to the people of Kâriz. He kept silent about it.

Then one day a group of people from Ma'd-âbâd came, saying, "Your oldest son is living here with us, and your other sons also come here to stay. Take them away from here, we cannot bear to have them here, for they abuse us. If you will not take them yourself, we will ride them out of town ourselves."

The Shaykh al-Islam was enraged and said, "You have the gall to concern yourselves with my sons? Fine then, either you throw my children out of the village or I will throw you out. Within twenty days you will be expelled from the village in such wise that you will beg to die, or else you can expel my sons."

Twenty days had not passed when the Stable Master of Sultan Âq Sonqor came with twenty royal pages, bringing with them the order to punish the head of the village and to exact seven thousand dinârs of pure gold from the citizens of Ma'd-âbâd. Half of the populace fled and came to the Shaykh al-Islam, falling at his feet, apologizing and repenting.

In the end, the Shaykh al-Islam came to their rescue and they agreed on a payment of five hundred dinârs. Thus he saved those people from bloodshed and resolved the matter in the best way possible.

98. The Shaykh Punishes a Man who Drinks Wine

Then there was the time the Shaykh was in the village of Bizd. They told him that 'Osmân the Mayor [*Ra'is*] broke his [153] fast with wine, and it was the eve of the Festival of Ramadan. The Shaykh was disgusted by this.

The next day 'Osmân came to greet him. The Shaykh al-Islam said, "You miserable wretch! I hear that you broke the fast last night with wine? How long will you persist in sin? I will make of you an admonition for the world to see, or else do your worst."

'Osmân the Mayor left and [subsequently] said, "How long will you keep up your threats and boasting? Do what you will."

This statement of 'Osmân was reported to the Shaykh al-Islam, who said, "No sooner said than done."

Just then 'Osmân the Mayor was seen in the hospice, spread out unconscious on the ground with blood trickling from his mouth. When the prayers were finished, Field Commander 'Omar took the Shaykh al-Islam to his home. A man came in to say, "I just now saw 'Osmân the Mayor spread out on the floor of the hospice. He might die. It was so awful I couldn't bring myself to go inside the hospice."

Some people took 'Osmân to his home in such condition that none had hope he would live. He was the son-in-law of the village elder, Mohammad, as well as brother-in-law[138] to one of the son's of the Shaykh al-Islam.

Village Elder Mohammad came to plead with the Shaykh [on behalf of 'Osmân]. "He has small children. I appeal to your magnanimity to restore him to me and to his children."

The Shaykh said, "I accept your plea, on condition that he repent." Mohammad went and told this to 'Osmân, who said, "I will do as the Shaykh al-Islam commands."

However, he did not do so. The illness went on for two months, and his condition became so bad that no one had any hopes of his recovery. Then the Shaykh al-Islam went to see 'Osmân, and held his hand until he repented. He soon recovered and got on his feet.

99. The Shaykh Punishes a Rude Man, Making Him Repent

Once a group of people came from Amghân to the aid of the Shaykh. The Army Commander 'Omar and a number of noblemen of Bizd were standing just inside the door of the Friday mosque. A man came in and said, "A large group of the people of Amghân have arrived and they mean to do mischief [bi-adabi]; if they should spill into the streets of the village, it will be an affront [154] to our honor."

Everyone there fell to discussing the matter. The Field Commander 'Omar said, "No one has the gall to enter this village, and should anyone do so, I'll beat his head to a pulp with this club."

The Shaykh al-Islam was disgusted by this remark and said, "How could anyone dare to frown upon someone coming to Our aid? If anyone of you oversteps his limits, he will see."

Right there and then the hand of Field Commander 'Omar began to ache and he went home. The pain continued to increase and he lost all use of his arm. They went to a physician, who treated him, but to no avail. Finally, someone told him, "It is the heart of the Shaykh al-Islam which has wounded you. Recall the cause of it, and he will cure you."

---

[138] The word for brother-in-law occurring here is *self*, which describes the relationship between men married to two sisters. The husband of one's wife's sister is one's *self*. See also Story 377.

He said, "I am ashamed now, because I have offended him."

Some people intervened and interceded on his behalf. The Shaykh said, "Repent of wine and promise never to touch another glass, and then you will be cured."

He repented. The Shaykh al-Islam reached out and touched him with his blessed hand. He got better and returned to health by the blessings of the breath and touch of that great man of faith.

100. The Shaykh Cures a Sick Man

This same Field Commander 'Omar had an older brother called Khvâjeh 'Ali. He had taken ill and was lying on his deathbed. There was no hope for him.

Then one day the Shaykh al-Islam went to visit him and saw him in that state. His mother, father and the rest of his family were crying. Right away the Shaykh al-Islam had a vision about him and asked his father, "How much would you pay to save his life?"

"A thousand pure dinârs," he said.

The Shaykh replied, "It's not worth a thousand dinârs. Will you give a hundred?"

"Yes, I will," he replied.

The Shaykh then said, "It's not worth even a hundred dinârs. Just give ten dinârs, but it must be paid in cash."

[155] They went and came back with seven dinârs and five pieces of canvas cloth. The Shaykh al-Islam told the learned Bu al-Qâsem, "Take it, and if he is cured, bring it to me. I will tell you what to do with it. If he doesn't get better, give it back to them." He further advised, "Take it, and I'll recite a prayer for him."

He said the prayer as 'Omar was on the verge of death. The Shaykh touched him and took him by the hand. 'Omar opened his eyes and the Shaykh said, "Rise!" They sat him up and he showed renewed signs of life. By the next day he was all better, restored to health.

101. The High Price of Grain

[Ostâd Imam 'Ali Tâybâdi] said:
One day we were strolling in the gardens. The Shaykh al-Islam

told me, "There is trouble ahead for you." The next day he said, "Buy five hundred maunds of millet and put it in a hole in the ground in my name, so that the troubles do not overwhelm you."

I had no money at home. I thought, "There is a little bit of canvas on the spinning wheel.[139] When it is finished I will exchange it for the grain."

A few days later the locusts came and the price of grain went up to seventy maunds of wheat per dinâr. I then became worried. I took a lamp stand, its cover [*maqbur*] and a pair of rings and bought with them around seventy maunds of wheat.

The Shaykh al-Islam was in a village called Hayânân[140] and I went to see him. The first thing he said when he saw me [156] was: "Didn't I tell you to buy five hundred maunds of millet and save them in my name? You didn't do it and now you are in trouble."

102. Prophesy About the Price of Grain

On another occasion we were sitting talking about the price of grain. Everyone said, "It has gone very low—a dinâr will get three hundred maunds of grain."

The Shaykh al-Islam predicted, "It will come down to two hundred maunds per dinâr."

Four months passed and the price fell to two hundred maunds per dinâr and it remained that way for some seven or eight years.

103. A Dream of Hell-fire and the Friends of the Shaykh are Saved

Ostâd 'Omar said:

I saw in a dream that I went into a hole and there were terrific flames there. "Where are we?," I asked. I heard a voice say, *"Not one of you there is, but he shall go down to it. That for thy Lord is a thing decreed, determined."*[141]

When I heard this voice I knew I was in hell. "If this is hell," I

---

[139] Literally, *bar kâr ast* = in preparation.

[140] No such toponym has been located in the geographical dictionaries.

[141] Qur'ân 19:71.

thought, "how come it does not burn me?"

I heard a voice saying, "Upon the power of My majesty, the fires of hell do no harm to the friends of My friend." Or perhaps the phrase I heard was, "The fires of hell do no harm to the Shaykh al-Islam and his friends."

104. The Shaykh Distinguishes Between Lawful and Unlawful Food

Abu Bakr-e Lâlaki[142] once said:

In the early days of the Shaykh al-Islam's calling, I invited him for meat stew. He did not touch what I offered him. The following night, the learned Ostâd 'Osmân-e 'Âref invited him, and he ate none there either. The next night, Shaykh Ahmad-e Bu 'Amr invited him, and he ate none there either, though he did eat eggplant and bread.

I had bought a lamb and slaughtered it. 'Osmân-e 'Âref had taken one-fourth of it, [157] Shaykh Ahmad-e Bu 'Amr another fourth, and I had kept half of the carcass for myself.

It so happens there was a constable called Sâroqcheh, a military man and official of the governor. He invited the Shaykh, and the Shaykh ate everything he offered, though there was no doubt about its unlawfulness.

The people of Buzjân wagged their tongues about the Shaykh al-Islam. "How pious a man! He eats the food of Sâroqcheh!"

The Shaykh al-Islam got wind of this, and so he asked "What do you think of Ostâd 'Osmân-e 'Âref and Abu Bakr Lâlaki and Ahmad-e Bu 'Amr?"

They answered, "They are God-fearing men, all three."

He said, "All three invited me and in all three places the meat was completely unlawful. That's why I ate none of it there. On the other hand, what Sâroqcheh offered was all lawful."

We investigated and found that the sheep which I had slaughtered was stolen by a Turkoman and given to a third party. This third party sold it to us and the three of us prepared the meals with that meat. On the other hand, the people of Tahr-âbâd had

---

[142] Mentioned also in Story 218 as Lâzaki.

baked bread and given it to Sâroqcheh, in hopes of the Shaykh al-Islam's blessing. Sâroqcheh had borrowed a lamb from someone else's flock and prepared the meal with it. That meat was lawful and the others' meat was unlawful, so that you may know, and leave your doubts behind.

Peace be with you.

105. The Hostility of a Family Member of Abu al-Ma'âli Imam al-Haramayn towards the Shaykh

One day the learned Mas'ud came up and said:

There is a scholar nicknamed The Hyena, who had asked for the hand of a granddaughter of one of the relatives of Abu al-Ma'âli Imam al-Haramayn.[143] [158] Through her, he had achieved [*bordeh*] some degree of standing and respect. This learned "Hyena" insulted me. "I'll have that turban of yours tied round your neck [and drag you through the streets][144] for all to see."

The Shaykh al-Islam looked at me and said, "Everything he has threatened to do to you, I will do to him, or else let him tie your turban around your neck and do whatever he likes."

Ten days after this, the Hyena's turban was tied round his neck and they did to him whatever he had threatened to do to Mas'ud. News of it spread about town and word reached the ears of

---

[143] There is a famous Abû al-Ma'âlî 'Abd al-Malik Abû Muhammad 'Abd Allâh ibn-i Yusif ibn-i Muhammad al-Juvaynî entitled Imam al-Haramayn, a famous Shâfi'î scholar and teacher at the Nizâmiyyah in Nayshabur who counted the Imam al-Ghazzâli among his students. He died in 1094 / 487 A.H. It is uncertain whether this is the same Imam al-Haramayn mentioned in the present story, because his association with Shaykh Ahmad would present chronological difficulties. Shaykh Ahmad himself is also referred to as Imam al-Haramayn in Story 173. However, it is likely that the compiler of the text, who is more concerned with the reputation of Shaykh Ahmad than historical fact, had in mind the famous Imam al-Haramayn (a title, meaning the Imam of the two shrines, namely Mecca and Medina) in this story. For further details see the Persian text of the *Maqâmât*, 157-8n2.

[144] There is apparently a lacuna in the text at this point, which merely gives *to mo'âmalat....* We have rendered the assumed meaning of the rest of the phrase within brackets.

Khvâjeh Imam al-Haramayn. His kinsmen [159] were all talking about it and threatening to tear down the Shaykh al-Islam's khâneqâh if [the Imam al-Haramayn would agree].[145] They made many threats and the townspeople were terrified.

Then one day, the Hyena[146] was walking along in a group of people. The townsfolk assumed that he was going to the Shaykh al-Islam's khâneqâh to do some mischief. So they went to the Shaykh al-Islam and informed him that so-and-so is coming to do some mischief. The Shaykh al-Islam said, "They cannot do anything."

As they got near the khâneqâh, the Shaykh al-Islam, with his inner powers, set to work and struck a blow. Later it became evident that they were not intending to do anything. When they passed by the khâneqâh of the learned 'Ali Bayhaqi, the Shaykh said, "The Hyena is finished."

Less than a week later, The Hyena passed away and all his scheming proved to be his undoing.

106. An Impudent Woman Gets Her Due

Shaykh 'Omar-e Luk relates:

The mother of Yusof-e Rangi, Zar-sati[147] by name, has told the following story. The wife of Ahmad the Weaver,[148] was one of those who did not believe in the Shaykh al-Islam.

['Omar] went on:

Once she was mocking the Shaykh al-Islam and this Zar-sati

---

[145] There is apparently another lacuna in the text at this point, the presumed gist of which we have given within the brackets.

[146] The subject of this sentence is not specified by name. It is remotely possible that Imam al-Haramayn is intended, but it would presumably be beneath his dignity to engage in such behavior. Therefore, we have assumed that The Hyena is intended.

[147] A name meaning "Golden Dame." It is morphologically similar to the name Gowhar-sati given by Anvari (*Divân*, ed. S. Nafisi, 427) and Dorr-sati given by Nezâmi (*Haft paykar*, ed. by Ritter and Rypka, 60; in the edition of Vahid Dastgerdi, 78) and Mah-sati, the famous poetess (See F. Meier, *Die schöne Mahsati* [Wiesbaden: Franz Steiner, 1963], 43ff.).

[148] That is, Ahmad-e Julâh.

reproached her: "Have you no shame, wagging your tongue about such a man?! Aren't you afraid that the Almighty God will afflict you with some calamity?"

The Weaver's wife, in her [160] ignorance, said, "The Almighty God can grow a donkey's penis from my vagina for such a great Shaykh!"

It was not long after that the Weaver's wife fell seriously ill.

Dame Zar-sati reports:

I went to pay a visit to her and asked what had happened. She showed me the troubled spot. A growth in the exact shape of a donkey's penis had appeared on her vagina. I said, "Didn't I warn you to watch your mouth with respect to him? You didn't listen!"

In the end, she died from that affliction.

107. The Shaykh Treats a Man who was Struck Dumb on Account of his Opposition

Once the Shaykh al-Islam received word that those who disbelieved in him in Buzjân were saying rude things about him. He said, "They will not repent of their opposition unless God, the Almighty, makes an example of one of them."

One day a group of people were sitting and mocking the Shaykh al-Islam. One of them, called Hâmed the Scythe-Maker—who was a glib talker—said mockingly, "The Shaykh al-Islam has called down a punishment on those who speak ill of him. So where is this punishment?"

As soon as he said this, God, the Almighty, tied his tongue. He turned mute and his face was disfigured. He remained like this for a while until they brought him before the Shaykh, his tongue mute, and his face all disfigured and deformed. The Shaykh al-Islam, being a compassionate man, looked upon him and said, "Repent and you will recover."

Hâmed shifted hesitantly a while and finally, through gestures, made a vow and repented, falling at the feet of the Shaykh and [kissing] his hands. The Shaykh muttered some words over him and blew in his mouth. Immediately thereupon his tongue regained its power and he was cured.

All of us saw this, and all the people of the village and all around Buzjân know about it, [161] for they saw it with their own eyes.

108. The Shaykh Reveals the Location of Some Gold

Hâji Surâni,[149] who is a reliable man, relates:
I had some gold which I had buried in the ground. At that time,
the Shaykh al-Islam was in Bâkharz and crowds were seeking his
blessings and repenting. They were saying that he is a miracle
worker.

One night he was at my home. I wanted to test whether what the
people were saying was true or not. I said, "Long live the Shaykh
al-Islam. I had some gold and hid it somewhere, but it's no longer
clear for me where I put it."

He said, "It's right there where I slept last night. Go look."

Indeed, I had put it where the Shaykh al-Islam said.

109. The Shaykh Discovers a Thief

Once the Shaykh was in Farâmad-âbâd.[150] A man came up to
him and said, "I dropped fifty dinârs of pure gold in the house of
so-and-so. Someone has taken it and, in order to recover the gold,
many people will be greatly inconvenienced. If you would tell us
[who has taken it], good Muslims would be spared of trouble and
you would be doing a good deed."

The Shaykh said, "I am not the spy of the land!" This man
pleaded and begged abjectly. The Shaykh al-Islam said, "I will tell
you on one condition. You must keep it a secret until the objective
is achieved."

After the man accepted the condition, the Shaykh told him, "Go
and find a certain young man of such-and-such features and such-

---

[149] A man apparently from Surân, a city near the Jaxartes (Syr Daryâ)
river, and a center of trade between Muslims and the Ghuzz tribes of
Central Asia.

[150] No such place is mentioned in the standard geographical
dictionaries. Yâqût does mention a village called Farand-âbâdh, near
Nayshabur, but Farâmad quite possibly is a variant of the name
Faryumad, a well-known district and village in the area of Sabzevâr, and
the birth-place of the poet Ebn-e Yamin.

and-such build. Tell him that the Shaykh Ahmad says [162] 'You picked up the gold that dropped from his belt, went into the woodshed, separated the gold into two parts and hid it in your waistband. Return the gold to its owner, or else I will have them do such-and-such to you.'"

By the time this ignorant man, Mozaffar, reached Tâybâd,[151] several people had warned him [the thief]. The young man denied everything. Though he received a hundred blows of a stick, he did not confess.

The people then began to gossip about [the Shaykh], saying all sorts of things. Finally, the Shaykh al-Islam said, "This man will not return the gold, since the people's gossip has led him into defiance."[152]

A group of the Shaykh's opponents gathered together to consult and they told the man to go to the Sultan and say, "A huckster has come along and is spreading lies like this; he should be dealt with."

The Shaykh al-Islam replied, "That is all completely baseless. That man has all of the gold, but he will not give it back. Keep an eye on him. When he leaves this place, he will take the gold with him. Send someone to follow him and strip the gold from his belt."

They kept an eye on him until one day he left the village. Two people trailed after him. They grabbed him and stripped him of all that gold.

110. The Shaykh and a Sick Youth who Repented Falsely

One day the Shaykh al-Islam was sitting in the mosque of Farâmad-âbâd in a large crowd. A man came in with a boy who could not move and said, "This boy has been paralyzed for some time and we do not know what we can do for him."

He was a young man. The Shaykh al-Islam told him, "Repent so

---

[151] The text actually has Tâbâd, but it probably intends the village in the district of Pushanj, near Herat, otherwise named Tâybâd, or Tâyâbâd in this text.

[152] *Tabâh*, literally ruin or destruction, but here persistence in his wayward behavior is intended.

that, when you are better, you will remain pious and not fall back into sin." He repented.

The Shaykh al-Islam muttered some words over him. When he was better, the Shaykh al-Islam asked him, "Now that you are better, you will not return to your former ways?" [163]

"No," he said.

The Shaykh al-Islam massaged his legs and arms and muttered some words over him. "Move your arms," he said, and the boy did. They returned to normal. "Move your legs," he said, and the boy did. The Shaykh said, "Now you are well. Take heed to keep far away from sin, or else you will lose your life."

The man thought to himself, let me make merry for a while longer—after all, I'm still young—then I will repent.

The Shaykh al-Islam looked in his eyes and said, "Have you no character!? What are these thoughts you are harboring? You have cut your own throat." The Shaykh told him, "Move your arms." No matter how hard he tried, the man could not move his arms or legs. He had relapsed to his former state.

A few days later, due to these thoughts, he lost his life. There are many similar cases—we have seen them ourselves.

111. The Shaykh Heals a Crippled Turkoman Boy

Another time, a Turkoman brought his son before the Shaykh al-Islam and said, "I have only this one boy, and he was crippled. I spent much money on his treatment, but to no avail."

The Shaykh al-Islam asked, "Will you repent if your son is cured?"

"I will," he solemnly promised.

The Shaykh al-Islam muttered something and told the man, "Do not let him get up for a while."

A while passed and the Turkoman said, "My boy says he wants to get up. Should I let him, or not?"

The Shaykh said, "No, if he gets up, he will remain crippled. Let me go see him." The Shaykh al-Islam went to see the boy and said, "Do you think you are strong enough to get up and stay on your feet?"

"I do," he said.

"Wait a little while longer," said the Shaykh, and muttered some words over him. Then he said, "Get up, now, and walk."

The boy stood up. The father let out a loud cry and fell to the ground in amazement. When he got to his feet to help his son mount the camel, the Shaykh told him, "Don't touch him; let him walk on his own for a farsang." The father got on the camel and [164] the boy held the reins, and they went off in good health.

112. The Shaykh Heals a Girl with a Crippled Arm

Another time, a girl from Rivandân[153] was brought to the Shaykh. One of her arms was so badly crippled that she couldn't put on her head veil [*meqna'*]. If you hit her arm with a heavy rock, she would feel nothing at all. She had been like that for eight months.

Since the girl had reached the age of maturity, the Shaykh could not lawfully touch her. He said, "I cannot treat such problems at present."

She and her relatives withdrew from the Shaykh, doubting his powers. They said, "Do you see! His pretense is exposed!" This statement was repeated to the Shaykh al-Islam, who kept the girl and her mother and sent the others away.

On the third day, the girl's arm was sound enough that she could pleat yarn with it. On the fourth day she began to spin with the spool. On the fifth day, she began to bake bread and she was as good as she had ever been.

The Shaykh said to her, "My girl, in return for your treatment, I expect you to give a good sock in the mouth to whoever it was that said 'His pretense is exposed,' so that he will not say such things again."

The girl did as she was told and they went home in good health.

113. Treating a Dreadfully Ill Boy

Another time a man came to Kâriz-e Sâ'ed with a fourteen year-old boy from Kuseh.[154] [165] He was so ill that if the wind ruffled

---

[153] See the note in Story 128 on this toponym.

[154] Probably the same village, Kusu, that Hâji Kusavi, mentioned in

the shirt on his back, he would let out a cry of pain. Of course, no one could touch him. For two days the Shaykh al-Islam did not even mutter anything over him. He said, "I don't plan to treat such cases any longer."

Finally, though, he asked, "Where do you come from?"

The man said, "From around here. I am from Kuseh, so-and-so's brother."

The Shaykh said, "Why didn't you say so in the beginning?! He is my friend and disciple, one of my followers." That man then brought the boy to the Shaykh al-Islam, who took hold of his leg and muttered something over him for a while.

There were many people sitting there. The Shaykh said, "What would you say if this boy were to get up right now and stand on his own two feet?"

They said, "That would be amazing," along with other phrases that were even more impressive.

The Shaykh al-Islam said to the man, "Get up and pull the boy to his feet."

The boy was screaming. The Shaykh said, "Don't be afraid; put your feet on the ground." He placed his feet on the ground, but they were still dragging.

The Shaykh al-Islam said, "Walk!" The boy began to walk. Right then and there he set off walking around all the mosques. It caused a great commotion among the people who were present.

The boy got up and walked throughout the whole village that very hour, climbed the minaret, and recited the call to the noon prayer. No trace of pain remained.

114. Curing a Blind Girl

On another occasion a blind girl from Zur-âbâd was brought to the Shaykh. At that time, the Shaykh al-Islam was in Estâd. He asked when she had become blind. They said, "She was still small. Now she has reached the age of maturity."

The Shaykh al-Islam muttered something over her and the girl

Story 84, hails from.

left. Some while later, she could see with both eyes; she made a sash and sent it to the Shaykh. [166] The people were greatly surprised by this and said, "She could not have made this."

The next day, she made a scarf [sotrah] with a beautiful insignia on it and sent it to the Shaykh. Her eyes had been cured by the command of the Almighty God.

Peace be with you.

115. The Shaykh's Prayers Bring Rain

Khvâjeh 'Omar 'Ali-ak related the following:

One time when we left Sarakhs, the whole world appeared dry and lacking vegetation. The people were worried about this and everyone was talking about it, hoping that perchance, with the blessing of the Shaykh al-Islam, the rains would come.

Shaykh 'Omar Farâforuzi said to the Shaykh, "Long live the Shaykh al-Islam! Pray for us, that the rains might come."

He said, "Fine, I will."

As we approached Buzjân, some people came out to complain about the drought. The Shaykh al-Islam said a prayer and a cloud immediately appeared, and God, the Almighty, bestowed heavy rain.

They said, "It's going to get us wet! Ask for a short respite so that we can make it to the village."

The Shaykh prayed once again and the clouds parted and the rain stopped. When we came closer to the village, some of the people complained once again. The Shaykh al-Islam said a prayer and the rain resumed once again.

We were headed in the direction of Ma'd-âbâd. The Shaykh al-Islam said, "Let us stop at Buzjân and tomorrow we will go on to Ma'd-âbâd."

We said, "Ask for a short respite so that we can make it to the village."

The Shaykh prayed again and the rain stopped. When we reached the gates of Buzjân, the rain fell once more. By the time we reached the door of the khâneqâh, we were all wet. Many people know of this event.

When the rain stopped, the Shaykh al-Islam told 'Omar

Farâforuzi, "Go get the shovel and attend to your fields."
'Omar told me, "When I reached my field, the riverbed was full
of water. I diverted it into my field and drenched the land." [167]

116. The Shaykh's Prediction about Amir Onar[155]

Amir Onar used to boast of his devotion to the Shaykh al-Islam.
He would say to him, "If you say that day is night, I will believe it
is night. And if you say that night is day, I will say it is day. Please
remember my belief in you, and watch over my affairs." Because
he was a true disciple, the Shaykh al-Islam watched over his
affairs until the time when the Shaykh set off on pilgrimage.

The Imams and Qâzis and the notables of Nayshabur told him,
"We will not let you go this year." They were agreed in this and,
indeed, did not let him go. Four months passed.

One day the Amir Esmâ'il Gilaki was to arrive in the city and
Amir Onar and all of the notables went out to welcome him. The
Shaykh al-Islam was displeased by this, because Esmâ'il was well-
known for his heresy.[156] When Amir Onar came before the Shaykh
al-Islam, the Shaykh reproached him for welcoming Esmâ'il.

Amir Onar said, "I was ordered to do it."

The Shaykh had some [harsh] words for him and for those who
had given him the orders. [168] News of this reached Esmâ'il,
who began devising stratagems against the Shaykh.

---

[155] There are two Seljuk military commanders with this name. One was
in the service of Barkyâroq. In 1099 / 492 he rebelled against the Sultan
in Rayy and was killed. (See Ibn Athîr, under the events of the year 492
A.H., and Râvandi's *Râhat al-sodur*, pp. 144-5). The second Amir Onar
was in the service of Sultan Sanjar and figures in a few of the stories
about Shaykh Ahmad in the present text. This Amir Onar led the conquest
of Ghazna in 510 or 1116-17 / 511 and was dispatched by Sanjar at the
head of an army to Gorgân in 1119 / 513, during the uprising of Sanjar's
nephew, Mahmud (See Ibn Athîr, under the events of the year 513).
Likewise, there is a story in *Majâles al-'oshshâq* about a love affair
between Shaykh Ahmad and the son of Amir Onar, which is certainly
untrue (Hagia Sophia, Ms. 4238, folios 60-63).

[156] *Elhâd*, literally atheism, but what is meant is his affiliation with the
Ismaili sect.

Qâzi Hammâd and Qâzi Sâ'ed came up to the Shaykh in the Friday mosque after the congregational prayer and said, "We hear that you are once again planning to go [on pilgrimage] to Mecca. We cannot possibly let you go."

The Shaykh said, "I must go, for if I do not go, much trouble will result. There are difficulties ahead for me and Amir Onar and for you, Qâzi Hammâd. The remedy for my difficulty is to go away, and the remedy for yours is your own concern."

They said, "But knowledge of such things is hidden."

The Shaykh replied, "Hidden or not, I'm telling you, and now I'm going to leave. Convey this message to Amir Onar."

Qâzi Hammâd said, "If he has the same regard for predictions of the future that I have, then it is better not to say anything to him."

The Shaykh said, "Tell him anyway. When the willows turn green, be on your guard." This was in the middle of winter.

When the Shaykh al-Islam left and the time he had specified arrived, Qâzi Hammâd was arrested on some pretext and the case against him became serious. He realized what had happened and sent two maunds of wheat, gold and meat to the house of the Shaykh al-Islam and expressed regret that he had looked so contemptuously on the prediction of the Shaykh. "As a result, I have fallen into trouble."

As for Amir Onar, he was sent to Farâmarzan and was arrested there. At the time, the Shaykh al-Islam was crossing the open plains [bâdieh], along with Khvâjeh Eqbâl, who had several times made the remark, "You should show me some kind of miracle, that my faith in you may grow."

That day in the wilderness, the Shaykh said to him, "Amir Onar has been arrested." One of Amir Onar's servants was accompanying Khvâjeh Eqbâl, and the Shaykh al-Islam told that servant to pray for Amir Onar because he had been arrested.

The servant turned to Khvâjeh Eqbâl and said, "This Shaykh Ahmad pretends to be a friend of Amir Onar. Look what he says."

Khvâjeh Eqbâl said to the Shaykh, "If this prediction proves to be correct, it would be an unquestionable miracle. If it turns out to be false, you will have cut your own throat."

Word of this reached the ear of the Sultan and the entire populace. When the Shaykh al-Islam and Khvâjeh Eqbâl reached

Hamadan, they learned that Amir Onar had been arrested the very day [169] the Shaykh had made his prediction.

117. Prediction of Amir Onar's Defeat in Ghazna

When the Sultan of Islam [Sanjar], may his dominion last forever, was moving on Ghazna, he sent Amir Onar on ahead of him. Amir Onar's retinue passed through the town of Buzjân. Amir Jâveli[157] was in his entourage, and the Shaykh al-Islam asked Amir Jâveli to tell Amir Onar that he would be unable to accomplish his objective.

When Amir Onar heard this, he said, "If that is what the Shaykh al-Islam has said, it must be the case, but I am under orders and have no choice but to obey them."

Amir Onar proceeded and came back in defeat.

118. The Shaykh Forbids Amir Onar from Proceeding to Gorgân and Predicts his Defeat

After the Sultan had returned from Ghazna, he sent him on a campaign to Gorgân. When he arrived in Buzjân, he went to see the Shaykh al-Islam and said, "I have been sent on a campaign to Gorgân; do you think it will turn out well?"

He said, "The only thing you will accomplish by going there is a loss of face."

Those who were accompanying Amir Onar said, "This is hidden knowledge and none knows the future except God, the Almighty."

---

[157] Amir Jâveli Saqâvu was a Seljuk commander who ruled for a while in the provinces of Khuzestân and Fârs and eradicated a large number of Ismailis in that area in 1101 / 494 A.H. Sultan Mohammad gave Mosul and the surrounding areas as a fief or land-grant [*eqtâ'*] to him in 1106 / 500 A.H. He continued to participate in military campaigns and conquered many cities in the province of Fârs, which he plundered. He died in 1116 / 510 A.H. (see Ibn Athîr, under the events of that year). If this same Amir Jâveli is the one intended by the present story, it is a chronological error on the part of the narrator, as the Amir died the year prior to Sanjar's conquest of Ghazna, which took place in 1117 / 511 A.H. He appears again in Story 211 and 269.

The astrologers who were with him said, "What the Shaykh al-Islam says is nonsense."

Amir Onar did go on the campaign and suffered great humiliation before he returned. The Sultan reproached him: "When such a pronouncement was made by the Shaykh al-Islam, why did you proceed? You have on many occasions experienced [that his predictions came true]." [170]

119. Amir Onar is Killed

The Shaykh al-Islam heard that Amir Onar had been slandered in the presence of the World Ruler, Sultan Sanjar, by his detractors, and that the Sultan had waxed angry with him. The Shaykh sent a letter to Amir Onar in Gorgân warning him, "Stay away from here, if at all possible. Don't come even if the Sultan summons you." Within two or three days he arranged for the letter to be delivered.

Two or three months later, word came that Amir Onar had arrived in Râyakân.[158] The Shaykh al-Islam said, "Alas, he has cut his own throat."

Some people said, "Amir Onar is a true disciple. Figure out a way, if you can, to rescue him."

When Amir Onar arrived in Sarakhs, the Shaykh said, "This makes matters very difficult." His followers said, "If we can do something for him, we will go." The Shaykh said, "It will not help. Even if I were to go, it would not help. Let us see what will happen."

[Even so] some of them got up and set out with the Shaykh toward Sarakhs. When they were within one stage of Sarakhs, word arrived that Amir Onar had gone in the direction of Marv. The Shaykh al-Islam said, "This makes matters even worse. Let us turn back; there is no longer any point in going on."

Some of the companions said, "Since you have undertaken a mission, we must go on to Marv." The Shaykh, following their suggestion, went to Marv.

They arrived at the army camp and the next day Amir Onar

---

[158] This toponym is not attested in any of the standard geographical dictionaries.

learned of their presence. He went to see the Shaykh al-Islam, saying, "I am very surprised you have come all this way. Why did you come? Last night the World Ruler was asking me if I knew why the Shaykh al-Islam had come to town."

The Shaykh said, "I have come for your sake. Didn't you receive my letter?"

"I did," he said.

"Then why did you come here?" asked the Shaykh.

Amir Onar said, "Had I not come, much trouble would have resulted."

The Shaykh said, "What could be more trouble than your being killed?"

He replied, "They cannot kill me, because everyone has pledged fealty to me."

The Shaykh al-Islam protested, "Whatever happened to your faith in me?"

Amir Onar swore, "My faith in you is as strong as ever, [171] but I know that they are unable to kill me."

The Shaykh al-Islam said, "I have done my part; the rest is up to you." He got up, paid a visit to the Sultan and returned.

Ten days later, they killed Amir Onar.

120. Transmuting Threads into Pure Gold

One day the Shaykh had a few threads [*muy*] from his own prayer carpet in his fingers, and was playing with them. Shaykh Bu 'Amr said, "Give me those threads." Ebrâhim of Kâriz reached out and took them. They all turned to pure gold through the power of the Creator, Magnified be His glory.

121. The Shaykh Witnesses the Capture of Jerusalem and the Slaying of Muslims

In the days when the Shaykh al-Islam was in his own village, there was a certain scholar named Mohammad whose father, Khvâjeh Mansurak, was extremely opposed to the Shaykh. He would call the Shaykh al-Islam and his own son, Mohammad, libertines. He would reproach his son and tell him to stay away from the Shaykh, but it was useless.

One day this Mohammad the Scholar made a vow and said to the Shaykh, "How would it be if you performed a miracle for my father of the sort that he could not deny; perchance his opposition will be changed into faith in you."

Then one day the Shaykh al-Islam got up in great pain and distress. There were a few drops of blood on his feet and shoes. One of his disciples took the shoes to be washed. The shoes were all bloody inside.[159] [172] Those present asked him, "Where did this blood come from?"

He said, "This is not your business. Call Mohammad the Scholar."

They brought Mohammad to the Shaykh, who said to him, "Concerning what you asked of me, I have seen something which no one will believe of me." Mohammad the Scholar asked what it was, and the Shaykh said, "The infidels have taken Jerusalem and killed so many souls that none knows their number. This was revealed to me and I saw myself amongst them. That is how the blood got on my shoes. They are still fighting and the killing continues, but the armies have dispersed. Go and inform your father and make him solemnly vow not to speak of this to anyone for five months, for it is happening very far away."

Mohammad the Scholar went and told his father and made him promise. Five months passed and there was no hint of this event, for the roads were unsafe. One day this Mansur told his son, "Now I have just cause to curse you with words that one wouldn't even say to a dog." Mohammad said, "Wait a while for the promise to come true." Mansur said, "I wrote down the hour and the day. Look, see for yourself!"

Mohammad relates:

I read the note and the allotted time had passed. I went and told the Shaykh al-Islam, who said, "It has indeed happened, but you must wait to see when news of it will arrive. Tell him to wait one more month."

---

[159] The similarity between this story and the tradition of the stigmata in Christianity are obvious. This motif is quite rare in Islamic hagiography, though its appearance in this story about Christians and the Crusades, reflects a knowledge of the tradition of the stigmata on the part of the author and/or the source of the story.

This Mansurak was a muezzin. One day he went to the mosque and saw a man sitting there speaking Arabic. Mansurak asked, "Where do you come from?"

"From Jerusalem," he replied.

Mansurak asked, "When did you leave there?"

He said, "Six months ago. I left the day the disaster occurred."

"What disaster was that?" asked Mansurak.

"Haven't you heard that Jerusalem was sacked and the Muslims were killed?," he said.[160]

It was precisely as the Shaykh al-Islam had indicated. Mansurak came to the Shaykh in tears, expressing his repentance, and never said another word against him. [173]

122. The Shaykh Describes the Appearance and Inner Thoughts of an Old Man whom He Has Never Seen[161]

The learned Mohammad-e Ghaznavi[162] relates:

There was an Imam in Ghazna called Jurist Abu al-Fath Kalâ'ji, God have mercy on him. One day he asked me: "When you go to see the Shaykh al-Islam, give him my regards and tell him that if I were able, I would have put on my turban, taken my cane in hand and come to see him. But I am feeble, so please excuse me." He also sent word of three different events with this message.

When I returned, the Shaykh al-Islam had gone to his own

---

[160] This occurred in 1099 / 492 A.H. Ibn Khaldûn estimates that 70,000 people, including a number of the 'ulamâ, were killed. See the article "al-Kuds" in *Encyclopaedia of Islam*, 2nd ed.

[161] This and the following three stories are expressly attributed to the author of the book, Mohammad-e Ghaznavi. Evidently, they were written down by someone else after the author's death and added to the text of Ghaznavi's *Spiritual Feats*. See also "Manuscripts of the Spiritual Feats" in the Introduction, and Story 298.

[162] The text reads *Faqih* Mohammad-e Ghaznavi. Though elsewhere in the text *Faqih* is translated as "Jurist," we have not done so here. *Faqih* typically denotes someone who has completed a formal course of study of Islamic law, but it seems somewhat doubtful that Ghaznavi held such rank in his lifetime. We rather suspect it may be a title bestowed upon him by later followers of the Shaykh in order to magnify his importance.

village. Later on, when I saw him, he asked me to report about the province of Ghazna. I gave him the message from Abu al-Fath and he told me, "He is an old man, thin and tall, with a long beard." This described him exactly; you would think that the Shaykh was looking at him as he gave this description. He then said, "He is now in the station of fear.[163] In that station is the seed of failure. If he is confirmed and makes it from that station to the station of hope, it will turn out well, otherwise his efforts will be to no avail."

123. The Brother of the Author is Captured by Afghans

The same Mohammad-e Ghaznavi relates:

Once my brother was captured and carried off by Afghans,[164] and I was extremely sad. In the middle of the night I once got up and performed a ritual purification and a two-prostration prayer.[165] Then I put the rolled-up prayer carpet on my shoulder [pas sajjâdeh dar gardan kardam], weeping bitterly as I got to my feet, and calling upon the Shaykh al-Islam to intercede with God on my behalf. It seemed as if a voice said in my ear, "Do not have a heavy heart, [174] things will turn out in accordance with your desire."

Then, on Friday, I went to see the tribe where he was. They were demanding 100,000 silver coins.[166] God, the Almighty, inspired them with such kindness that they gave him back to me and removed the shackles from his feet. I returned home safe and sound and all were much surprised, for none had ever achieved

---

[163] For a description of the station of fear [khawf], see Qushayrî's *Risâlat*.

[164] The text here transcribes as A-W-GH-âniân, and would be read either *Owghâniân* or *Avghâniân*. The usual Persian word would be Afghâniân, but this may reflect an older pronunciation preserved in Khorasan. It appears in the *Hodud al-'âlam* in this form, and there is also a 6th century Sanskrit text, *Brhita Samhita*, which calls the Afghans "avagâna."

[165] This is the number of prostrations required by the dawn prayer.

[166] The text has *deram*, meaning *derham*, or dram. This was less than the dinâr.

such success as we did.

124. The Shaykh Hears the Tearful Cries of the Author

He further related:
When I returned from the province of Ghazna, the Shaykh told me, "One night I heard your tearful cries, as you wept bitterly. I was very worried until I could intervene on your behalf."
I told the Shaykh al-Islam the story of what had happened.

125. The Author Crosses the Border of Ghazna without Papers

He related further:
I was coming from Ghazna. They were checking papers at the Ghazna frontier on the road to Ghur. The local head of the Royal Post and Intelligence[167] was sitting there, watching with extreme care over the traffic. It was inconceivable that they would allow anyone to pass [without papers].

When I arrived there I was very upset, thinking I might have to return, because in the time it would take me to get a pass [*javâz*], I could have been in Khorasan. I begged of God forty times, in the name of the Shaykh al-Islam, to come to my aid, and plowed on ahead.

I passed right by all those army officials and guards. Great God! The Almighty Lord closed the eyes of every one of them. No one asked me where I was coming from or where I was going.

When I arrived in the presence of the Shaykh al-Islam, [175] he told me, "I saw one day that you were lost in the dark. I held your hand and led you out of it."
I asked brother 'Ali Asfarghâbadi[168] how many days ago this was. I counted the number of stages and it was thirty-seven days

---

[167] *Barid*, on which, see the article "Barid" by C.E. Bosworth in *Encyclopaedia Iranica*.
[168] The text actually reads Safarghâbâdi, which must be an error. In Story 126, his name is given as Asfarghâbâdi, but elsewhere it occurs as Asfarghâbadi, which is the correct form. See the Introduction ("Ahmad's Career in Jâm and Khorasan") for the location of Asfarghâbad.

since the day when the Shaykh al-Islam had seen this.

126. The Shaykh and the Partridge

One day the Shaykh al-Islam was sitting in Zohd-âbâd. A partridge came along and sat down next to the Shaykh. The Shaykh said, "He must be fleeing from an eagle or something," and gave it to 'Ali Asfarghâbâdi to take it outside and let it go. It came back and stayed for several days.

A while passed and it came no more. They thought that something must have killed it.

Two months later, however, it came one day bringing its brood of chicks. They stayed there for a while, until there were two hundred of them. Now they have moved to the garden and live there.[169]

127. The Tree which Bore Fruit Three Times in One Year

Once they were planting trees in the garden of Zohd-âbâd. There was one very large tree which had been uprooted two or three days earlier and was all shriveled up. Everyone was saying, "It won't grow [if we re-plant it], it is too large."

The Shaykh al-Islam said, "The way I plant is not the usual way of the people."

All the trees blossomed. The big tree showed no signs of budding. Some people began to ridicule [the Shaykh]. The Shaykh al-Islam fixed his gaze upon that tree and, after a few days, it blossomed.

That very year it gave fruit three times, by the power of God, the Almighty, and his followers ate of it.

128. A Man Comes to Kill the Shaykh

Once Khvâjeh 'Amid-e Sâlâr told the Shaykh al-Islam, "You

---

[169] Note that Shaykh Ahmad, when a youth of fifteen, began raising partridges as a hobby and loved them more than anything else. See the section "Shaykh Ahmad-e Jâm, the Colossal Elephant," in the Introduction, supra, 8ff.

must come to our village." The Shaykh said, "I will come."

When he set out, a man was walking out in the middle of the plain. The Shaykh said, "This man intends to kill me. There are two people coming for this purpose." This man [176] kept approaching and when he got close to the Shaykh al-Islam, he recognized him. When the Shaykh reached his lodgings, that man followed him inside. The Shaykh said, "He is the one who intends to kill me." The people were perplexed about it; they looked the man over and saw no sign of any threat. They thought, "Perhaps the Shaykh is mistaken."

The next day this man came up to the Shaykh al-Islam, who asked him, "Where do you come from and what is your business here?"

He said, "Being a young man,[170] I wanted you to help me to repent."

The Shaykh said, "Give me your hand."

He held out his hand to the Shaykh and repented.

The Shaykh then told him, "You have not come to repent. You are using this repentance to entrap me," and the Shaykh revealed why the man had come and who had sent him.

The man said, "O Shaykh, you are suspicious of me?"

The Shaykh said, "If I reveal the signs you have on your person, will you confess?"

He said he would. The Shaykh said, "You have two marks on your right arm, one the size of a silver coin or larger, and the other smaller than a silver coin."

Still, the man did not confess. The Shaykh al-Islam said, "Search him and see."

The man would not permit this. The Shaykh said, "Throw him down." They did and examined him. It was exactly as the Shaykh had said.

The man said, "I was an infidel, but I hereby pronounce myself a Muslim. Set me free." They set him free and he told the truth about who had sent him and why.

---

[170] The implication being that in the ardor of youth, one is more inclined to sinful behavior than in old age.

129. The Shaykh Exposes the Intentions of Two Men Who Come to Kill Him

One day the Shaykh al-Islam was sitting in his home in the village. The mayor of that village was one of his true disciples. The Shaykh al-Islam told him:

"Know that two of the heretics [Ismailis] have left their fortress to come kill me. They will arrive here at the next prayer and will ask you where the house of Shaykh Ahmad is. 'We must see him,' [177] they will say. Bring them to my house."

Two companions arrived at the time of the next prayer and told the mayor they must see the Shaykh. He brought them to the Shaykh al-Islam. When the Shaykh saw them, he addressed them gruffly, saying, "You wretches! Have they pulled the wool over your eyes, then? I will tell you now why you have come here."

They said, "Why have we come, then?"

The Shaykh al-Islam started at the beginning and related the whole story to them of how long they had been on their mission and that at first two others wanted to come, but they were natives of the area where the Shaykh was. "Then you were chosen and sent here," said the Shaykh, and he told them what they had said to each other along the way.

One of the men said to the other, "He [the Shaykh] has knowledge of many things, and if he knows why we have come here, I hope he will not kill us."

His companion said, "He won't kill us, for they say he is a righteous man."

[....The Shaykh said:][171] "If you renounce your heresy now, I will let you go. Otherwise, I will chop off your heads this very minute."

Both of them admitted that everything the Shaykh said was true. They repented and returned to their homes safe and sound, where they related this story. As a result several of the heretics returned to [the true] Islam.

---

[171] There is a lacuna in the manuscripts at this point. It is evident from the context that the Shaykh is now speaking.

130. The Shaykh's Conversation with a Zoroastrian

In the early days of the Shaykh al-Islam's ministry in Jâm, Khvâjeh Sâlâr sent the scholar Mohammad Sani'i with a Zoroastrian to invite the Shaykh to his home. The Shaykh al-Islam said, "You send a Zoroastrian to me?!"

The Zoroastrian said, "And what is wrong with that?"

The Shaykh said, "I don't even want [178] to see your face."

The Zoroastrian said, "We, too, are following a path [*mâ niz bar kâr-im*]."

The Shaykh al-Islam said, "Come, let me prove to you that you are not followers of any path."

The Zoroastrian came in and they entered into a discussion. The Zoroastrian said, "You realize I will not abandon my religion just because you argue better. I need to see a sign."

The Shaykh al-Islam said, "Will you accept Islam if I tell you what you were thinking during our debate?"

"I will," said the Zoroastrian. They agreed on this.

The Shaykh said, "When the discussion reached such-and-such point, you thought, 'Let me embrace Islam.' Then you thought further, 'If I become a Muslim, my relatives will take my belongings away from me.' When the discussion reached such-and-such a point, you thought, 'Man, what do I need belongings for? Let me convert to Islam and things will work out right.' Then the thought of circumcision held you back."

The Zoroastrian said, "You are right, and I know for a certainty that your religion is true, but let me wait until tomorrow to convert to Islam."

As he slept that night, Satan led him astray. The next day, the Zoroastrian fled, saying, "I am afraid of this man."

131. The Heretics' Blade Fails to Harm the Shaykh

One day the Shaykh al-Islam was at home in his village, Nâmaq. There were some ten to twelve heretics debating with him, but the Shaykh bested them.

They said, "We have to kill this fellow." One of them stabbed at him. The Shaykh al-Islam said, "Things are not such that God, the

Almighty, would deliver me into your hands."

The man stabbed at the Shaykh, but the blade did not cut. He stabbed again, and again the blade did not cut. He stabbed a third time and the blade bent like a bow.

The heretics said, "We will follow your path, for it is the path of truth," and they returned to Islam.

132. A Heretic Stabs at the Shaykh and then Repents

Once a group of heretics came before the Shaykh al-Islam and argued with him. [179] When they were unable to win their point, one of them, by the name of Lays the Infidel [*Layth-e Kâfer*], rose up, drew his sword and aimed it at the Shaykh. The point of his sword hit the wall and the blade bent into a circle. The man fell on his own blade and cut his knees.

He then drew his dagger and lunged at the Shaykh. The Shaykh al-Islam looked at him and he dropped the dagger, falling at the feet of the Shaykh and saying, "I place myself at your service and will do whatever you command. If you permit, I will return to my own folk and preach to them."

The Shaykh al-Islam gave him leave and he went and preached to them. He recanted his former beliefs and did many good works for the cause of Islam.

133. The Shaykh Turns Rowan Berries into Rubies in the Hands of some Zoroastrians

Once the Shaykh al-Islam went to the village of Ziâd-âbâd, where there were some Zoroastrians living. The Shaykh preached Islam to them and they argued with him. In the end, they said, "Among the people of Islam, you are a leader and a great man, well-respected, and they say you perform miracles. One of us will hold something in his hand and if you can say what it is, it will convince us of the truth of your religion." He said, "So be it, but only on condition that two Muslims witness what you have in your hands, so that you may not deny it and make excuses."

They left the room and picked up something in their hands in the presence of two Muslims. It was reportedly a rowanberry [*senjed*]. They came before the Shaykh al-Islam and asked what it was. The

Shaykh said, "It is a ruby."

The Zoroastrians were delighted, thinking, "His claims are disproved and we have prevailed." The two Muslims were downcast. When they opened their hands, the rowanberry had turned into a ruby, as the Shaykh al-Islam had said. The Almighty Lord had changed the quality of that substance into something else, so that the proof would be greater and the miracle more remarkable.

What has been mentioned about the mystical station and the miracles of this great religious figure who is peerless in this age— the Shaykh al-Islam, may God sanctify his precious soul—[180] is but a token of many more. Whoso is aware and enlightened and has happened to attain his presence and to be in his company, has viewed all his spiritual states and acts and sayings as miraculous, but the pen is unable to recount them all.

134. Changing an Almond in the Hand of a Zoroastrian into a Locust

Khvâjeh Imam Zahir-e Bayhaqi,[172] may God have mercy on

---

[172] Perhaps this is the same Imam Zahir-e Bayhaqi (d. 1170 / 565 A.H.) who wrote the *Tatimmah siwân al-hikmah* and the *Târikh-e Bayhaq*, in addition to numerous other works. The description "one of the famous scholars of Islam and a prominent philosopher in his day" would not likely be applied to an unknown figure. Furthermore, this Imam alludes to philosophy (*hekmat*), specifically the science of the transmutation of the elements, again suggestive of an author and learned man. The passage also states that this Imam wrote a Qur'ân commentary; among the list of books which Yâqût attributes in his *Mu'jam al-udabâ* to the well-known Bayhaqi (quoting from the latter's own *Mashârib al-tajârib*), there are titles which might well be Qur'ân commentaries, such as *As'ilat al-Qur'ân ma' al-ajwibah* [Qur'ânic questions and their answers] and *I'jâz al-Qur'ân* [The Inimitability of the Qur'ân]. Hâjjî Khalîfah, in his *Kashf al-zunûn*, has listed similar titles under the rubric of Qur'ân commentaries.

Shaykh Ahmad-e Jâm died in the year 536 of the Islamic lunar calendar (1141 A.D.), whereas the famous Zahir-e Bayhaqi died in 565 (1169 or 1170). The fact that Mohammad-e Ghaznavi states that Imam Zahir-e Bayhaqi became a believer in Shaykh Ahmad-e Jâm some thirty-odd him, was one of the famous scholars of Islam and a prominent philosopher in his day, and the author of a Qur'ân commentary. Some thirty-odd years after the death of the Shaykh al-Islam, he became a believer. The reason for his belief was that he had zealously collected numerous sayings of holy men and stories about their miracles. While learning about the spiritual state [*hâl*] of the Shaykh al-Islam, the following story made his greatness apparent to Imam Bayhaqi:

Once a Zoroastrian unknown to the Shaykh came to him, secretly holding an almond in his hand. He said, "If you tell me what I have in my hand, I will believe in you."

The Shaykh reflected and said, "You have a locust in your hand."

The Zoroastrian laughed and said, "Can't you tell the difference between an almond and a locust? How could I believe in you?!"

The Zoroastrian then opened his fist, and the almond in his hand had turned into a locust, by the power of God, the Almighty. Those who were present were astonished and that Zoroastrian stranger embraced Islam.

This is why Zahir al-Din became a believer in Shaykh al-Islam Ahmad. He said, "According to philosophy, the transmutation of matter is not possible except for God, the all-Glorious. Therefore, this man cannot be other than a man of truth [*haqq*]."

By whatsoever touchstone his spiritual state was tested, it always proved pure and true. God sanctify his precious soul, and peace be with you.

135. Conjuring Up Tarantulas and Putting an Army to Flight from Buzjân

Once an army arrived in Buzjân and let their horses graze on the crops. The people of the town warned them, "Do not do this, or else we will tell our lord to send an army against you." They came to the Shaykh al-Islam and reported the situation. The Shaykh al-

---

years [*si o and sâl*] after his death need not be understood literally, as it could easily be an estimate or a misremembrance on the part of the author. In any case, there is only a discrepancy of at most five years, insofar as the Persian "*and*" [odd] is usually used for between two to four years.

Islam said, "All right, I will send an army." [181]

Presently a host of tarantulas—that is to say poisonous spiders[173]—appeared and began biting the men and horses, killing them on the spot. The entire army fled in no time and the crops remained safe.

This miracle has been reported by Khvâjeh Abu al-Qâsem, the son of Shaykh Abu al-Mo'ser.

136. The Shaykh and the Hungry Dragon

I heard from several trustworthy disciples of the Shaykh al-Islam that while he was on the mountain, there was a spring of water which he would use for his ablutions. He would perform his prayers at that spot.

One night it happened that a group of caravan travelers had come to stop near that spring. When it grew dark, the Shaykh al-Islam came to the spring, as was his wont, to pass the night wakeful in prayer. He saw a crowd of people camping there, and a huge, terrible and horrifying dragon was crawling amongst them, snapping up and eating leftover breadcrumbs and bones. Still hungry after this, the dragon made for the caravan travelers.

The Shaykh al-Islam yelled at him, "You crude and ill-mannered fellow! Have respect for the guests."

The dragon pointed with his head in the direction of the travelers and said in clear words, "I am hungry. My meal tonight is on them."

The Shaykh al-Islam went up to the dragon and placed his tongue into the mouth of the dragon. That beast sucked on the Shaykh al-Islam's tongue a couple of times and said, "I am full. For the next month I will not eat anymore." The dragon left and the group of people was saved from harm by the blessings of the Shaykh al-Islam. [182]

---

[173] The two Persian words used here, *daylamak* for tarantula and *ghondeh* for poisonous spider, are now obsolete, having been replaced by the Arabic-derived word *rotayl*. They are attested in the *Borhân-e qâte'*, however, and the word *ghondeh* occurs in the poetry of Kasâ'i in the 10th century.

137. Fifty Men Eat Dinner in the Home of the Shaykh

Imam Shams al-Din relates another story:
I never saw a person as firm of heart as him. One day we left Ma'd-âbâd, heading to the town of Sâghu with the Shaykh al-Islam. His house was in Sâghu and we were close to fifty people, all of whom were going to stay in his house that night. The Shaykh neither went on ahead of us, nor did he send anyone on ahead, nor did he ask for anything to be prepared, nor did he send any message. We arrived there as the setting sun glowed orange on the horizon [âftâb-zard], and there was of course no sign of any preparations for a feast.

[But] that night, God, the Almighty, prepared the means for all, and we all ate supper in his home and were full, by the blessings which God, the Almighty, bestowed upon the meal.

138. A Large Crowd Filled by a Small Amount of Food

He also relates the following:
One day the Shaykh al-Islam was in the home of 'Ali the Tailor in Amghân. I went there with a group of his followers. 'Ali the Tailor said, "O Shaykh al-Islam, I have only a little and the guests are many."

The Shaykh asked, "How much is there?" There was no more than five maunds of bread and some two to three bowls of food.

The Shaykh al-Islam recited something over the food and blew upon it, and all of us—twenty people—ate our fill of it, and still there was a little left over, from which the household ate for several days.

139. Changing a Piece of Bread into Pure Gold

It is reported by the learned Esmâ'il-e Oshtavi that one day a man came to the Shaykh al-Islam. The Shaykh al-Islam gave him a piece of bread from his own table and the man wrapped it in his waistcoat and left.

The learned Imam Esmâ'il reports:
I heard that man say, "I took out the piece of bread from my coat along the way to eat it. By the command of God, the Almighty, it

had turned to pure gold."

140. Changing a Prayer Carpet Thread into Silver

Brother Ahmad the Hacker [*So'âl*] was one of the special disciples. He said:

Once in the village of Ma'd-âbâd [183] in the home of Mohammad the Turner, a gathering was seated at the feet of the Shaykh al-Islam. He pulled a thread out from his prayer carpet and the thread turned to silver for all to see. I saw a light shining from the face of the Shaykh al-Islam, now on to his face, and now on to his beard. When he got up, the children picked up the silver, and they still have it to this day.

141. The Shaykh Wipes his Brow and the Grime Changes to Pure Gold

Khvâjeh 'Ali-ye Yahyâbâdi relates:

Once the Shaykh al-Islam was coming from Mâlin.[174] He reached Bizd and sat down in the Congregational mosque. A state of bliss came over him and he wiped his hand across his brow and the grime from his forehead changed into pure gold between his fingers. I picked some of it up. Some time later I asked him what state he had been in.

He said, "This thought occurred to me: 'How is it that in Ma'd-âbâd the earth turned to gold in my hands? The disbelievers said that it was gold from the mountain. I hope what they said was not the case.' My heart was assured [by the thought] that if that is how they explained that case, how would they explain this one?"

142. The Shaykh Knows the Dream of Another and the Words God has Spoken to Him

Ostâd Imam 'Omar-e Ma'd-âbâdi said:

I dreamt that God, exalted and glorified be He, spoke a few

---

[174] Mâlin was the administrative center of Bâkharz, and a fertile agricultural area, famous for its melons. See Le Strange, *Lands of the Eastern Caliphate*, 357.

words with me. When I woke up, my whole being was joyful with this thought, but I had forgot what He said to me.

The Shaykh al-Islam was in Buzjân. I got up and went to see that great man of religion and told him about my dream. He told me [184] the whole story of what I had dreamt and the words that God had said to me. He revealed them to me one by one, adding nothing and leaving nothing out.

As the Shaykh al-Islam has said in a poem:

He was I and I He; now He filled up the cup, now me.
Till morn we drained the mystic wine, goblet upon goblet.

143. Someone Sees the Messenger of God and the Shaykh in a Dream

Khvâjeh 'Ali-ye Yahyâbâdi further relates:

In a dream I saw the Messenger, the blessings of God be upon him, building the mosque of Zâhed-âbâd. When my eyes fell upon his blessed beauty, he sat down in the prayer niche. I said, "O Messenger of God, put your hand on my chest."

He put his hand on my chest. I grew bold and said to him, "O Messenger of God, is the tradition that a demon cannot show himself in your image in a dream true?"

....[175] and he recited this tradition three times.

Then I saw the Shaykh al-Islam sitting there in the same place. I was very surprised that just then the Prophet had been there and now the Shaykh al-Islam was sitting in his place, reciting the same tradition that the Messenger had recited.

I heard a call saying, "He is We and We are He. It is therefore no surprise."

---

[175] The first phrase of the Prophet's reply appears to be missing here.

144. The People Believe the Shaykh is the Qotb

He further relates what was said:[176]
I heard the scholar Jebrâ'il Barnuri the Turkoman, God have mercy upon him, say: "It was midday. One of the nobles asked me, 'What do you think of the Shaykh?'"
Jebrâ'il said, "I believe he is the Qotb [spiritual pole] on earth."
The noble replied, "That is true, I believe the same thing."

145. The Shaykh Knows the People's Intention

The same scholar[177] relates that Jebrâ'il also said:
I wanted to go [185] to see the Shaykh al-Islam with the intention that he put a morsel of food in my mouth with his own blessed hand.
It was three days journey from my house to his. When I arrived before him, the table had been spread. He dipped a morsel of food [*nân*] in the salt and whispered in my ear, "If this is what you desired, take this morsel of food."
He put it in my mouth and I obtained what I had desired.
Peace be with you.

146. The Shaykh Directs a Jug of Water to Dance

Khvâjeh 'Ali-ye Yahyâbâdi relates that Shaykh Mohammad-e Haddâd-e Oshtavi said:
One day the Shaykh al-Islam was at my house. He was speaking. A drink was set in front of him, and a jug of water was standing there. The Shaykh al-Islam motioned with his hand [to the jug], and the jug of water began moving, revolved and started to dance, such that the people who were there all saw it. It caused a great

---

[176] Literally, "He also relates what he said: I heard the scholar Jebrâ'il Barnuri the Turkoman...who said:" For the first "He" we may assume it intends Khvâjeh 'Ali-ye Yahyâbâdi. No subject is specified for the second "he".

[177] One might assume that the phrase "the same scholar" alluded to Jebrâ'il Barnuri in the previous story, except that he now appears as the one whom this "same scholar" heard.

commotion and many shouts came from the crowd.

147. The Shaykh Cures a Turkoman Girl

'Omar Kushak said:
They brought a Turkoman girl before the Shaykh al-Islam. One of her arms had been paralyzed for two years. The opponents of the Shaykh in Bizd said that the Shaykh al-Islam had given up his claims and the performance of miracles, and that he was no longer at the top of his form. [But] the Shaykh al-Islam muttered something over her and said, "Move your arm and go fetch that skin coat."

She went and got the skin coat and was fine right away, such that she never again had any trouble with her arm for the rest of her life.

148. The Shaykh Cures a Blind Turkoman with His Spittle

He also relates that:
Once we went to Sâghu and a Turkoman, blind in both eyes, was brought to the Shaykh. He said, "My son passed away and I cried so much I have gone blind."

The Shaykh al-Islam [186] rubbed spittle from his own mouth on the eyes of the Turkoman. The following day, he could see with both eyes, by the power of God, the Almighty.

149. The Shaykh Restores the Vision of a Girl with His Spittle

He further relates that:
There was a girl in our village, whose vision was obstructed, as if by a veil, such that she could see neither right nor left. One day she came before the Shaykh al-Islam, who smeared spittle from his own mouth on her eyes. The following day, she opened her eyes and was restored to health, such that her vision was never dim again.

150. The Shaykh Cures a Sick Man with His Spittle

Abu Bakr the Singer [Moghanni] tells the following about the Shaykh al-Islam:

I went to see him once, when I had a lump the size of a melon on the back of my neck. I was afraid it would kill me. The Shaykh al-Islam muttered something over it and within three days it had completely disappeared and was all better, through the blessing of the spittle of that great man of religion.

151. Curing the Legs of a Fourteen Year-Old Boy

He also relates:

Once they brought a fourteen year-old boy before the Shaykh al-Islam. His legs were bent together, as if in the shape of a symbol ['alâmat-i]. The Shaykh al-Islam muttered something over him and laid his hand on the boy. Right then and there his legs were healed and he began to walk.

152. Curing a Crippled Girl

He further relates:

Once a girl who was crippled and could not move was brought before the Shaykh al-Islam. The Shaykh muttered something over her and laid his hands on the girl. Right then and there she was healed and began to walk. No trace of her ailment remained.

153. Curing a Mad Woman

'Omar 'Ali-ak relates that there was a woman lunatic in the city of Sarakhs who had lost her mind [187]. She was brought before the Shaykh al-Islam, who caressed her and muttered something over her, covering her with his own shirt. Right away the woman calmed down and went to sleep for a while.

She had a small child and when she awoke, she nursed it. Her husband said, "She has not been still and quiet for a whole month, nor has she nursed the child."

God, the Almighty, cured her through the blessings of the

Shaykh al-Islam.

154. Healing the Burned and Crippled Knee of a Girl

When the Shaykh al-Islam was in the village of Sâghu in the beginning of his ministry, a woman[178] held a feast. After the meal was finished, Shaykh Mozaffar the Cutler brought a twelve year-old girl before the Shaykh al-Islam, saying, "Her mother has arranged this feast in the hope that you will heal this girl."[179]

The Shaykh al-Islam asked what was wrong with her. He said, "All around her knee-cap was burned in the fire and the veins and tendons are all wasted away. Her knee is fused motionless to her thigh and it has been almost two years she is like this."

The Shaykh al-Islam looked it over and said, "Only Jesus, the Prophet, the blessings of God be upon him, can heal this." This he said and went. As he turned to go, his heart was inspired with the thought, "Do you believe it is you who brings healing to all these others, that you feel powerless to heal this one?"

The Shaykh al-Islam turned back and said, "Bring that child to me," and they brought her. He laid his hand on her knee and left. Later, word came that the girl was all better. The Shaykh al-Islam did not believe it and said, "Bring her to me." After she arrived, he saw her playing with the children. [188]

155. Curing an Ailing Turkoman

A Turkoman was gravely ill. He had not been able to move for nearly a year. The Shaykh al-Islam saw him and gave him a lump of sugar to eat and wrote an amulet[180] for him to pin on himself. The soldiers had confiscated his camel, taking it from Tâyâbâd[181]

---

[178] *Sar pushideh'i*, literally a "a covered one," that is a veiled person, or woman.

[179] *'Ajuzeh*; see the note to this word in Story 25.

[180] *Ta'viz*, which appear also in Stories 157, 333 and 337. On the use of amulets in Islamic praxis, see Rudolf Kriss and Hubert Kriss-Heinrich, *Volksglaube im Bereich des Islam, Band II: Amulette, Zauberformeln und Beschwörungen* (Wiesbaden: Otto Harrassowitz, 1962).

[181] Spelled thus here in what was undoubtedly its original form, but

to Kâriz. The sick man heard this and set off for Kâriz in search of his camel. He came back from there to Tâybâd with his camel and took it home. Through all of this, he felt no pain at all.

156. Curing a Crippled Arm

The brother of [the scholar Mohammad Esmâ'il-e Sâghu'i],[182] Mohammad Mehin-e Sâghu'i, said:
A man lost the power to open his right hand. He was crippled like this for nearly a year. They brought him to the Shaykh al-Islam, who muttered something over him. Right then and there, he opened his hand and went away all healed.

157. Curing a Turkoman Boy who Could Neither Move nor Speak

Hosayn ebn-e Abu al-Qâsem-e Sanjari relates:
Once the Shaykh al-Islam went to the hospice in Ba'nân.[183] A Turkoman brought a nice twelve year-old child who was paralyzed and could not move. For nearly a year he had been unable to speak. The Shaykh al-Islam muttered something over him.
Right then and there the power of speech returned to him. The Shaykh wrote a talisman and hung it on him. The child got up and began to walk. [189]

158. The Shaykh Punishes a Man for Coveting a Muslim Woman

Brother Mohammad the Turner relates:
There was a time when, if twenty women came to my house to buy something, I would not look upon any of them. One day I came out of my house and saw a girl standing at my door. She

---

otherwise appears in this text in the shortened, spoken form as Tâybâd.

[182] Story 160 precedes the present story in the Chester Beatty Library manuscript, and is narrated by Mohammad Esmâ'il-e Sâghu'i. The possessive pronoun in the Persian phrase, *barâdar-e vay* [his brother], must therefore refer to this man.

[183] The same place is mentioned in Story 217.

looked beautiful to me. I thought, "What a shame that I have never taken any notice of her!"

Instantly a pain shot through my eyes and I could not see at all. I went and got on a donkey and went to the Shaykh al-Islam. When his blessed gaze fell upon me, he said, "Such is the punishment of whosoever covets Muslim women."

He smeared some of his spittle over my eyes, which got better right away.

159. Curing a Lunatic

Once a lunatic was brought from Bâkharz. It took five people to restrain him. He came in with tied arms and made obeisance before the Shaykh al-Islam. He bit into the flesh of his leg and tore out a piece.

The Shaykh al-Islam caressed him and said, "Let go of him and let him come closer." They let him go and he came closer. There was a skin coat which he bit and held in his teeth by the corner, ripping it in half. He chewed on it and swallowed it.

The Shaykh al-Islam placed his headgear on the man's head. That night the man rested peacefully. The next morning, he was well and no trace of his lunacy remained.

160. Curing a Turkoman Lunatic

The learned Mohammad Esmâ'il-e Sâghu'i said:

I saw a Turkoman brought before the Shaykh al-Islam and learned that he had been mad for a couple of years. When he was brought near, the Shaykh al-Islam asked him, "Why have they bound you like this?"

He said, "I don't know."

The Shaykh al-Islam put a lump of sugar in his mouth and then gave it to the man, telling him, "As soon as you eat this, we will untie your hands and legs."

[Someone] said, "You cannot undo his madness" [*to na-dâni band az vay bar-dâsht*].

The Shaykh said to the man, "Wash yourself [190], for you have an unpleasant odor."

The man went and washed and returned. The table was spread

and the man ate much food, becoming alert and rational. Then he left. Along the way he passed by a village where they were harvesting. He thought, "I have no provisions at home." He picked a bagful of wheat clusters, ground them to flour and took them home.

161. The Death of the Shaykh's Father

He also relates that the Shaykh al-Islam said that once, when he had gone to the countryside on the mountain slopes near the town of Nâmaq, his father, Khvâjeh Abu al-Hasan, fell ill. For nearly a month or more, he was unable to get up.

They informed the Shaykh that his father was at the door of death. The Shaykh al-Islam got up and hurried back home. As he was about to sit down at his father's bedside, the father's eyes were still open. By the time he took off his footgear, the father was done for.

They bound his chin[184] and the people gathered around. The Shaykh al-Islam got up, performed ablutions anew and said his noon prayers. He came and sat by his father's deathbed, and stood to pray: "O Lord, I had not expected of You to take my father when I was not present. I do not know whether he was in a state of repentance or not, nor whether he has affirmed the Muslim creed or not, and I therefore do not know the state of [his soul] when he died."

The Shaykh stood there saying this until the time came for the prayer [for the dead]. He was afraid the women would begin to wail in [ritual] lamentation. All of a sudden his father moved as the Shaykh was praying to God, the Almighty. The Shaykh reached down and untied his father's chin.

After a while, the father opened his eyes and began to speak. He first said, "I have witnessed the states of my son." He then said, "All ought to do as my son does." Again he said, "I ought to do exactly as my son does." He next said, "I hold the same beliefs that my son does. O son, tell me then, what I must do." [191]

---

[184] At the time of death, Muslims traditionally tie the chin to close the mouth of the deceased.

The Shaykh al-Islam said, "Father, first repent." He repented and uttered the Muslim creed.

He lived for six more days after this, just as the Shaykh al-Islam had asked and as it behooved the father. He died on the seventh day.

162. The Shaykh's Prayers Bring Riches to a Poor Man

Khvâjeh Imam Abu al-Fath[185] relates:

We were going to the Hijâz [on pilgrimage]. When we arrived along the way in the town of Bastâm, we went to visit the grave of Shaykh Abu Yazid.[186] A penniless dervish came up, greeted the Shaykh al-Islam and begged from him, lamenting his poverty. The Shaykh al-Islam gave him a little something and said, "Do not worry; I was in a state of spiritual ecstasy and God, the All-Glorious, has led you to me. I know for certain that my prayers on your behalf have been answered."

When we reached the town of Bastâm on our return, the same man came up and prostrated himself before the Shaykh al-Islam. He said, "God, the Almighty, has granted—through the blessings of your prayers on my behalf—riches enough for me and seventy descendants."

We asked him, [but] he didn't explain how this had come about. We realized that he must have found something valuable.

---

[185] According to 'Ali Buzjâni in the second chapter [*maqsad*] of his *Rowzat al-rayâhin* (62), this would be Jamâl al-Din Abu al-Fath, the son of Shaykh Ahmad, who accompanied his father on his pilgrimage to Mecca and Medina. This Abu al-Fath is the source of this story, and Stories 353 and 355, as well as several other stories related in the *Rowzat al-rayâhin*.

[186] This is the famous Sufi Shaykh Bâyazid (Abu Yazid) Tayfur ebn-e 'Isâ ebn-e Sorushân-e Bastâmi (d. 848 / 234 A.H. or 875 / 261 A.H.), known for his ecstatic utterances [*shathiyât*]. He lived most of his life in Bastâm (or Bestâm), a small town in the province of Qumes (modern Semnân). His followers continued to function at his tomb in Bastâm through the 10th-11th centuries and the Il-Khanid ruler Uljâytu erected a dome over his tomb in 1313 / 713 A.H. See the article "Bestâmi, Bâyazid" by Gerhard Böwering in the *Encyclopaedia Iranica*.

163. How a Child of the Shaykh is Saved from Famine

The Shaykh al-Islam said:
When my son, Shaykh Abu al-Hasan, was born, there had been famine for several years, and no woman who gave birth that year could give milk to her child. His mother had grown frail and the child was left to waste away. We feared he would die.

Every day without fail a handful of wheat would appear in his crib, an amount less than a [192] pound. For four months they made food for him from this. When the wheat was harvested, it appeared no more.

164. The Shaykh, His Child and the Tray of Sweets

In the early days of the Shaykh al-Islam's ministry, when he had come to Amghân, he was sitting once in the home of the scholar Abu Bakr with a tray of sweets[187] and various fruits set in front of him. The Shaykh al-Islam said, "Put this tray of sweets on the ledge and I will tell you what to do with it later."

"Why?," they asked, and he said, "I have a son who is between five and six years-old; I heard his voice asking for some of these sweets in front of me here."

There was a scholar by the name of Pâydâr. The Shaykh gave him what was on the tray and instructed him to take it to his son. Pâydâr left.

The Shaykh's family were in the village Bars [?] in the district of Rokh.[188] The child in question was named Abu al-Hasan, whom

---

[187] *Forâteh*, a kind of sweet made from almonds or walnuts covered in a syrup of grape juice, starch and flour, which is first boiled and hardened. Today it is often called *Bâsluq*.

[188] Rokh or Rokhkh, also commonly called Rikh according to Yâqût, was part of the district of Zâveh, in the eastern part of the province of Torshiz. The center of that district was Bishak or Zâveh. Hamd Allâh Mostowfi describes Zâveh as having a mud fortress and fifty dependent villages in its surroundings. Zâveh is today known as Torbat-e Haydarieh (Le Strange, *Lands of the Eastern Caliphate*, 356). The shrine of Shaykh Qotb al-Din Haydar, who flourished in the early 13th century, is located here. Ibn Battûta visited Zâveh in the 14th century and reports that his

they called "Shaykh." When he saw the Learned Pâydâr, he told him, "Give me what my Papa has sent." When the package was produced, they asked him, "Abu al-Hasan, do you know what [193] is in it?" Bu al-Hasan said, "It's like halvâ, but it isn't halvâ." Pâydâr took out the sweets and gave it to him.

They said to him, "The Shaykh al-Islam never used to send anything. How is it that he sent this?"

Pâydâr said, "On such-and-such day they had placed this in front of the Shaykh al-Islam, who said, 'Take this and set it aside, because my son, Shaykh al-Islam Abu al-Hasan, called out to me asking for it.'"

They reckoned the date and it was the same day that Shaykh Abu al-Hasan had said, "Something like halvâ has been placed in front of my father and he is eating it." We told him to ask for some. He cried out, "Papa, give me some of what you have in front of you." That very moment the Shaykh heard the cry and set aside the sweets for him.

165. A Prince Carries Hod for the Khâneqâh of the Shaykh

A prince of Ghazna by the name of Halim came along with five thousand of his horsemen to Sultan Sanjar. Someone had told him about the exploits of the Shaykh al-Islam, and he had come to see the Shaykh al-Islam in a college in the village of Ma'd-âbâd in order to test him.

The Shaykh al-Islam gazed most thoughtfully into his face. The prince was overcome with feeling and a sense of belief in the Shaykh. He begged his lordship [the Shaykh al-Islam] not to hold him back from what he wanted to do. His lordship said, "Please, go ahead."

They were laying the roof of the khâneqâh on that day. The prince got up and, in his royal attire, he laid a hod full of mud over his shoulder and carried it up on to the roof. When he came back down, the Shaykh al-Islam asked him, "Why did you do that?"

---

followers, the Haydariyyah, pierce their ears, hands and necks with iron rings as a sign of their piety and asceticism. Shaykh Haydar could supposedly walk through fire in summer and snow in the winter without harm. In Story 369, Bar is said to be five farsangs from Nâmaq.

He replied, "Because I know of no better means of salvation at the divine threshold. When, on the day of Resurrection, they will ask me 'Who are you?,' I will say, 'I am the hodman of Shaykh Ahmad,' and I believe that will be my salvation."

And, indeed, it is so.

166. The Shaykh Receives the Mantle of Abu Sa'id-e Abu al-Khayr

Near the end of his life, the Shaykh al-Islam Abu Sa'id-e Abu al-Khayr, God have mercy upon him, [194] revealed his last wishes to his disciples and gave them each a task to do. To Bu Tâher he said:

O my son, take heed to tread the path of the law of religion and to serve the people. I reveal to you that a few years after my death, a youth with the first growth of beard on his cheeks, tall in stature, and ruddy of complexion, by the name of Ahmad, will enter your khâneqâh. You will be in the midst of the disciples in the khâneqâh. Make sure to surrender my mantle to him and to serve him as if he were your master.

Bu Tâher answered, "I will do as you command."

When Abu Sa'id's days were coming to a close, Bu Tâher and the others who were present each longed to be appointed the saint for a given territory. Bu Tâher had hoped that Abu Sa'id would entrust his own dominion to him. Shaykh Abu Sa'id, in the throes of death, opened his eyes and said, "O Bu Tâher and other friends of mine! That dominion which you covet has been entrusted to someone else and the banner of my Shaykhdom has been raised over a certain khâneqâh [*kharâbât*]. My mission and that of all the Shaykhs of the past has been entrusted and delivered to him. It is he who has been chosen."

No one knew what it all meant. Several years later, Shaykh Bu Tâher was sitting one day and a youth came in through the door of the khâneqâh. Shaykh Bu Tâher showed him great respect—all the signs which the Shaykh Abu Sa'id, God have mercy upon him, had given were apparent in this youth.

Just the night before Shaykh Bu Tâher had seen his father in a dream, hurrying along with a group of disciples. Abu Tâher had asked, "Father, where are you going, and why all this hurry?" The father replied, "You come, too, for the spiritual pole [*qotb*] of the saints is arriving." [Bu Tâher said:] "I was about to go with them, when I woke up."

The next day this youth came into the khâneqâh and Bu Tâher realized he was the one. He thought to himself, "How can I give the mantle of my father away?" The youth said, "O Bu Tâher, one must not betray the trust which has been placed in him." Bu Tâher was pleased by this. He brought the mantle and set it before the youth, who put it on. That youth was the Shaykh al-Islam Ahmad of Jâm, God sanctify his precious soul.

It is said that the mantle belonged to Abu Bakr, the Caliph, may God be pleased with him, [195] who left it as a legacy for the Sufi shaykhs, down to the day when it reached the Shaykh al-Islam Ahmad.

When the Shaykh al-Islam, God sanctify his precious soul, returned to the mercy of God, he left behind fourteen sons. These sons tore up the mantle and each of them took a piece of it as a token of blessing. Those pieces are still in the hands of his descendants and the infirm and the ill make pilgrimage and God, the Almighty, through their blessings, grants them a speedy recovery. Any sick or ailing one, any epileptic who puts on that mantle is cured and delivered from his suffering through the mantle's blessings.

So that you know.

167. A Flock of Game Animals Keep the Shaykh Warm

He himself, God sanctify his precious soul, has related:

One night it was extremely cold. When I finished with my devotions, there was a round stone, three fingers high, more or less, on which I lay my head. A feeling of warmth came over me. When I opened my eyes, I saw a flock of game animals gathered around me, sleeping. Their breath had made me so warm that sweat was pouring from me.

"God is with him who is with God."[189] Choose to serve God and all creatures will serve you and make you their leader.

---

[189] A famous *hadith*.

168. A Man has a Vision of the Candelabras of God's Throne Room[190]

Razi al-Din 'Ali ebn-e Ebrâhim ebn-e Elyâs-e Tâybâdi[191] relates:

I heard it directly from him, may God sanctify his precious soul, as follows:

There was a man well-versed in the traditions of the Prophet [*az ashâb-e hadis*] who had toiled greatly and expended immense effort, as a result of which his eyes were blessed with miraculous vision over all things on earth. One day I told him, "Look at the province of Nimruz, around [196] Sejestân. What do you see there?"

He bowed his head for a while and looked in those environs. He then raised his head and said, "A wondrous vision of one of the spiritual states of the Imam of Zâhedân, Abu 'Abd Allâh Mohammad-e Karrâm,[192] may God be pleased with him, which had previously been unknown [to me]. It was this: In the vicinity of Sejestân there was a house from which light was shining all the way up to the skies. I asked what place is this and was told, 'It is the birthplace of the Imam of Zâhedân. The light which shines from it is in honor of him.'"

---

[190] This story also appears in *Kholâsat al-maqâmât* (ed. Ivanow), 43 and in *Rowzat al-rayâhin*, 40 (#34).

[191] In the Chester Beatty Library manuscript, this story follows Story 173, which is related by 'Ali Ebn-e Ebrâhim-e Tâybâdi. The Persian text of the story is simply introduced by the phrase *digar goft* ("He also relates"), but in view of the order of the stories as given in the Chester Beatty manuscript this should refer to 'Ali-ye Tâybâdi. Stories 169-170 and 173-4 are apparently all related by this same source, as was Story 101. In the Chester Beatty Ms. there are a total of 27 stories related by this Razi al-Din 'Ali ebn-e Ebrâhim ebn-e Elyâs-e Tâybâdi, who collected many stories about the Shaykh and is buried in Buzjân (see *Rowzat al-rayâhin*, 40). The Nâfiz Pâshâ Manuscript, however, gives only three stories related by him, two of which do not explicitly mention him. See "Manuscripts of the Spiritual Feats" in the Introduction.

[192] The founder of the Karramite sect (d. 869 / 255 A.H.), concerning whom see the note in Story 19, and the articles by Mohammad-Rezâ Shafi'i-Kadkani.

This was the answer to what the Shaykh al-Islam had asked him, and this man was able to see miraculous events only on the face of the earth. He asked the Shaykh, "Reveal to me something of the miraculous events in the heavens."

The Shaykh said, "You lack the strength to bear such things."

The man begged and insisted. The Shaykh al-Islam, God sanctify his precious soul, reports as follows:

> I spoke with him for a good while and then told him, "Look up." He looked up, gave out with a shout and fell to the ground. Later on I asked him, "What did you see?," and he said, "My eyes lit upon the candelabras of God's throne room. I could not withstand the vision of it." Following this experience, the man lived for seventeen days, started to bleed and died.

169. The Shaykh has a Vision of the Torments of Hell

He also relates the following:

I heard the Shaykh, God sanctify his precious soul, say: "For two years following my initial repentance every one of Hell's torments was visible to me, until I prayed and God, glorified and exalted be He, hid them from my sight."

Peace be with you. [197]

170. The Shaykh Has a Vision of the Spiritual Pole on Mt. Qâf[193]

He also relates the following:

I heard the Shaykh, God sanctify his precious soul, say: "I wanted to see the Qotb [spiritual pole]. He was made visible to me, standing on Mt. Qâf enveloped in so many circles of light that I could hardly see him."

171. A Locked Door Opens Before the Shaykh

The Shaykh al-Islam, God sanctify his precious soul, relates: When I was in Nayshabur, one day it happened that we went to

---

[193] See the notes to the title of Story 50.

visit the graves of Ostâd Eshâq and Ostâd Imam Ahmad of Bejestân. When we arrived at the door of the mausoleum, it was locked. I said, "O learned Ahmad, if you are alive, open the door." The door opened instantly.

172. The Shaykh Speaks of His own Rank and Station

The Shaykh's followers once said to him, "May God give you long life. We have heard much about the spiritual stations of the Sufi masters, God sanctify their precious souls, and we have been taught about the successive generations of these masters, but we have never heard the likes of your spiritual states before. The Shaykh al-Islam ought to edify us about why this is."

The Shaykh al-Islam said, "God's holy men do have such spiritual states. During the period when I practiced feats of asceticism, I practiced every kind of feat that I knew the holy men of God, glorified and exalted be He, had done in times past. And I added to and surpassed what they had done. God, the Almighty and Exalted, through His grace and bounty bestowed upon me, Ahmad, the total sum of what He had bestowed separately to those others. Every four hundred years one man like Ahmad appears and when [198] he appears, the signs of God's grace towards him are such that the whole world perceives them."

[As the verse says]: This is of my Lord's bounty.[194]

173. The Miracles Related by Razi al-Din 'Ali Ebn-e Ebrâhim-e Elyâs Tâybâdi[195]

Khvâjeh Imam Razi al-Din Jamâl al-Eslâm 'Ali Ebn-e Ebrâhim-e Elyâs Tâybâdi, God have mercy upon him, has related the following miracles and divided them in three categories—those he has heard from the Shaykh al-Islam, those which he witnessed himself and third, those which he heard narrated by reliable followers of the Shaykh and by the pious leaders of religion:[196] Among the things which I heard the Shaykh al-Islam, exemplar to

---

[194] Qur'ân 27:40.
[195] See the note on him in Story 168.
[196] See *Rowzat al-rayâhin*, 40.

the saints, cynosure of all sects, the Imam al-Haramayn,[197] Abu Nasr Ahmad ebn-e Abu al-Hasan of Nâmaq and also of Jâm, God sanctify his precious soul, say [was this]:

> Before I repented, God, may He be glorified and exalted, showed me three miracles. The first concerned a boulder in the village of Nâmaq which forty men together could not budge. I went forward and by the confirmation of God, the Almighty, I threw it several paces. The second was when I was on a tall roof with a glass in my hand. It fell and hit the ground. I said, "God!" The glass remained in tact with no damage. The third was the incident of the donkey which I led to the wine jugs and the voice I heard.

The latter incident is written in the beginning of this book.[198]

174. Wheat Appears in the Cradle of the Shaykh's Infant Son During a Famine

I [Razi al-Din] also heard the following from him:
In the days of the famine for a period of seven days and nights, my household had nothing in the way of food. I had children, one an infant in the cradle. Every day, under the child's covers, enough wheat appeared to provide sustenance for the whole day.[199]

175. A Deaf Man Sees the Shaykh in a Dream

Brother [*Akhi*] Shaykh 'Ali of Nayshabur, who was one of the special disciples of the Shaykh al-Islam, said: [199]
My mother had been deceased for thirty years and I had never during this time had a dream about her, though I very much

---

[197] A prestigious title, meaning the Imam of the two shrines of Mecca and Medina.

[198] See Story 1. Obviously, Mohammad-e Ghaznavi had access to this book of Razi al-Din of Tâybâd and recorded some of the stories found here from it.

[199] See the end of Story 2, which has slight elaborations.

wanted to see her in a dream. Then one night I dreamt I was walking in paradise. I saw my mother sitting in a lofty place with several jugs filled with water, all set in a row. I looked in the distance and saw a mountain and a great pavilion around which were pitched many tents.

I asked, "Mother, whose pavilion is that?"

She said, "That is for Shaykh al-Islam Ahmad and his disciples. They will arrive very shortly to go on pilgrimage. I've prepared this sugar-cane water for them to drink."

All at once royal heralds appeared, as if clearing a path for the king. One group was clad in blue and another contingent wore white, and a third green. Then the Shaykh al-Islam arrived, sitting upon Burâq,[200] light shining all around him. I went forward and greeted him. When I came close to him, I embraced his blessed knee. He spoke to me and I said, "My ear has gone deaf."

"Which ear?," he asked.

I placed my hands on my head, indicating both ears. He placed his hand on my right ear and I awoke.

I had been afflicted for eight months and both ears had grown deaf, but I was healed. I now hear with my right ear, but not with the left.

176. The Shaykh Predicts the Future and the Date of Death of One of His Disciples[201]

There is also the following story concerning the same Shaykh 'Ali of Nayshabur. Several reliable followers of the Shaykh and pious leaders of religion have related that the Shaykh al-Islam had some followers in Zohd-âbâd who were building a wall around the town garden.

There was a certain special disciple of the Shaykh al-Islam called [200] 'Ali of Nayshabur. He was an efficient man and

---

[200] A mythical beast, half ass and half angel, which carries the Prophet Muhammad to the heavens according to the legendary elaborations upon a Qur'anic verse.

[201] This story, as well as Stories 177-179, appear in Manuscript C mingled with the stories related to the period after the death of the Shaykh.

worked very hard, and was a firm believer in the Shaykh al-Islam. The Shaykh was pleased with his work ethic and praised him. He asked him, "Shaykh 'Ali, what would you like? Make a wish and it will come true."

'Ali said, "Long live the Shaykh! I need to know what will happen to me in the next world."

The Shaykh al-Islam, God sanctify his precious soul, reflected for a while and then lifted his head and said, "Twelve years after my death two individuals will come from Lahore bringing you true news of your state [in the next life]. You will know them because they will take hold of your thumb and give you a message. At that time your death will be imminent, for if I reveal anything to you now, people will reject it and that would have bad consequences for them."

The Shaykh al-Islam lived for six years after the construction of that wall. Twelve years had passed from his death, may God sanctify his precious soul, when two Sufis came from Lahore to Ma'd-âbâd and asked for Shaykh 'Ali of Nayshabur. When they saw him, they took hold of his thumb and said, "Your spiritual master, Shaykh al-Islam Ahmad, sends you greetings and, by the sign that we are holding your thumb, says to you, 'Concerning the question which you asked me, do not worry. Know that all those who have, with firm faith, greeted me or one of my disciples, God, the Exalted and Glorified, will, for my sake, reckon them within my fold.'[202] Let this be a glad-tiding to you and to them."

This Shaykh 'Ali fell down unconscious and within a short while he was gathered to the Lord. Most of the inhabitants of Ma'd-âbâd personally witnessed this event, so that you know. Peace be upon you.

177. The Reward of the Shaykh's Friends and Followers

The Leader of the Dervishes [*Esfahsâlâr-e darvishân*] in the village of Andâd said:

For some time I had been [201] wondering about the circumstances of the Resurrection and how our reckoning, as

---

[202] *Hameh râ dar kâr-e mâ kard*, i.e., God will treat them favorably and forgive their sins because of their relation to the Shaykh.

followers of the Shaykh al-Islam, would be. Then one night I dreamt of the Resurrection and saw the plain of Resurrection, a huge mass of people and two banners coming in my direction. I looked and saw the Shaykh al-Islam and his followers.

I went up and took hold of the stirrup of the Shaykh and walked alongside of him a ways. There was a man called Abu Bakr-e Abu Sahl, who was not one of the Shaykh's followers. I asked the Shaykh, "Why have you stopped?"

He said, "I'm waiting for Abu Bakr to catch up with us."

I said, "But he has neither served you nor has he shown any inclination to you."

The Shaykh al-Islam said, "One day he placed my son's shoes before his feet. I cannot go to paradise without him, for it would ill beseem me."

So that you know.

178. The Shaykh's Influence in Distant Lands

The following was related by the nephew of Khvâjeh Bu Shahd of Boshkân,[203] who was the son of Vajih al-Din Mobârakshâh, Mohammad ebn-e Abu al-Qâsem:

> While on the way to India we passed through Ghazna. We were both small boys and were afraid, being strangers in a foreign land among infidels. This nephew of Vajih, Sam'ân,[204] told us, "Undo your braids and wherever you go, if anyone comes up to you and asks you who you are and where you come from, tell them you are from Jâm; and are a follower of Shaykh Ahmad. Then You will pass freely and no harm will

---

[203] Possibly the same place called Poshnegân or Boshneqân in *Asrâr al-towhid* 1:266 and 2:735.

[204] There seems to be some confusion in the manuscript about the relationship between Vajih al-Din Mobârakshâh, who we are told at the beginning of the story is the father of Bu Shahd of Boshkan. It is the nephew of Bu Shahd who is said to relate this story. But at this juncture, the manuscript now refers to a Sam'ân, "this nephew of Vajih," who has not otherwise been introduced so far. A few lines further on we find reference to a Vajih, the brother of Sam'ân.

come to you."

The two of us went on like this until we came to a place where we saw a number of human skulls scattered about and the remains of countless bodies that had been killed. Three naked Indians came up to us, each of them with an iron spear in hand. We thought they would kill us on the spot. They first asked us, "Where do you come from?"

"We are from Jâm and are followers [202] of the Shaykh al-Islam Ahmad," we said.

When they heard this, they put down their spears and took us to their homes as a blessing. They brought food and remained standing, jugs of water in their hands, until we had finished our meal. The entire region paid service to us on account of the blessed words "We are from Jâm," for they had heard talk about the Shaykh al-Islam and had believed in him. Such is God's blessing on behalf of those who love him—that both Muslims and infidels submit to and obey them.

The reason this happened was that Vajih, Sam'ân's brother, was the owner of a large enterprise in India and the Hindus had faith in him. He would speak to them about the Shaykh al-Islam and told of his spiritual feats. And those foreigners had resolved that since he had been from Jâm, they should serve anyone coming from that place. That is the explanation of this story, so that you know.

179. The Shaykh at Eighty Takes a Fourteen Year-old Girl to Wife

Towards the end of his life the Shaykh al-Islam Ahmad, God sanctify his precious soul, asked for the hand of the daughter of the mayor of Sâghu, explaining that he had foreseen that she would bear him a son. The girl's mother would not agree, saying, "He is an old man." But the Shaykh al-Islam would not give up.

One night the mother and father of this girl had a dream that an individual came and began to dig with a shovel under the foundation of their home. He lifted up their home and said, "Either you give your fourteen year-old girl to Ahmad, or I will turn your house upside down." They said, "We will give her, we will give her!" The individual set their house back down.

When they awoke, the mother said, "There is no way I will consent! An eighty year-old man and a small child? How can I give her to him?"

The next night they both had the same dream of that same individual who came and lifted their home from its foundation with a shovel and said: [203] "Will you give your daughter to Ahmad?" They said, "We will give her."

When they awoke, the mayor said to his wife, "Give the girl to Ahmad. Don't do this. Listen to me and give the girl to him, or else a tragedy will befall me. It has been twice revealed to us."

The wife said, "Of course I will not give this girl to him. How could I give a fourteen year-old girl to an eighty year-old man?" However much the mayor insisted, his wife would not listen and did not give consent.

Then, on the third night, both the mayor and his wife dreamed once again that this same individual came and drove his shovel in the ground under their house and lifted it into the air and said, "Will you give your daughter to Ahmad?" They said, "We will give her." The man turned the house on its side and set it back down. The mayor and his wife woke with a start. The room in which their daughter was sleeping had collapsed. The parents cried out.

The Shaykh al-Islam was in Sâghu, waiting with a lighted candle. He told his servant, "Take the candle and let us go to the home of the mayor, for there is a girl under the collapsed room. We will dig her out and marry her this very night."

The servant went ahead carrying the candle and the Shaykh al-Islam walked behind. The mayor and his wife were coming from the other direction. When they reached the Shaykh al-Islam, they fell to the ground at his feet, writhing in the dust and crying out.

The Shaykh al-Islam asked, "Will you now give your daughter to Ahmad?"

They said, "O Shaykh, what daughter? She is trapped under more than a thousand tons of rubble!"

The Shaykh said, "If your daughter should emerge unscathed from this rubble, will you give her to Ahmad?"

They said, "We swear by God, the Almighty, and the Prophet,

Peace be upon him, that if our daughter emerges from this rubble alive, we will ransom her to you."

The Shaykh al-Islam went to the house and the room which had collapsed over the sleeping girl. The Shaykh motioned to a certain spot, indicating that a path be cleared. A path was cleared. A wooden beam had remained leaning on the wall and the girl had not even stirred from sleep. The mother told the Shaykh, "You and her nurse go down together and bring the girl out alive [204] and well, but don't make any noise, lest the girl take fright."

They went and got the girl. Not a single hair on her head had been harmed. When the girl awoke, she took fright and had a fit brought on by yellow bile.

The next night, the Shaykh al-Islam asked for her hand and she was legally married to him. That night he entered her sixty times. He said, "It might have endangered [your] life, otherwise I would have carried it out a hundred times so that your mother would no longer say that Ahmad is too old."[205]

Exactly nine months later, a son was born to her, whom they named 'Abd Allâh. Everyone in the district of Jâm knows about this situation.

We have witnessed many such miracles, for his whole life and everything he said were miracles in themselves. But we have written down only one in a thousand, so that his followers, disciples and friends will read and rejoice, while his enemies will waste away and his opponents burn. May both camps receive in abundance what they deserve:

> Flames for the enemies and glory for the friends!
> Let both last till the horn of Resurrection sounds.

---

[205] The prototype for an old man fathering a son is, of course, the Biblical Abraham and Sarah, but a closer parallel can be found in the story told by Aflâki in *Manâqeb al-'ârefin* (ed. Tahsin Yazici, 449-50) about Jalâl al-Din Rumi. His wife, Kerrâ Khâtun, complained that he was so involved in asceticism that he no longer displayed any sexual attention to her. The same night, Rumi "entered her seventy times" like a "wild roaring lion," until she fled from him, with him hot in pursuit. The story concludes with Rumi observing that the men of God are capable of accomplishing whatever they want.

180. The Cloister Weeps Over the Shaykh's Death[206]

There are miracles which occurred after the death of this great man of religion, God sanctify his precious soul, the first of them as follows:

When God, the Almighty, called the Shaykh back to him, the Shaykh was in the village of Ma'd-âbâd in a khâneqâh named after him on a cloister which is still there, on the northern side of the building.

A large crowd was present. His blessed frame, God sanctify his precious soul, released his pure, sanctified soul. That cloister wept just as that crowd of people wept, such that water as pure as tears dripped from the bottom of every brick of the ceiling. For many years after his death the marks left by that water were still apparent for all to see, until they repaired the building of the khâneqâh and the whole area was covered with clay, [205] like the rest of the building, because they were unaware of the cloister's history, and those marks disappeared.

A few thousand people could clearly see this in the past and were greatly stirred by it due to the love and devotion which they held in their hearts and souls for that great man of religion, the Shaykh al-Islam Ahmad of Jâm, God sanctify his precious soul.

***

O Lord, bestow upon us a portion of Your friendship and bestow upon us the friendship of those who are Your friends. Grant us affection for those things which would strengthen our love for You, and make our love for You stronger than the desire of a thirsty man for cool water. For we have hope of Your generosity, o Generous one, o Compassionate one, through Your mercy, o most Merciful of the merciful. And blessings upon Mohammad and all of his family—those who are pure and righteous.

---

[206] Compare the story of the "moaning pillar," which weeps after the death of the Prophet, Muhammad, as related in the *Masnavi* of Jalâl al-Din Rumi, lines 1:2112ff. A shortened version of this story appears in the Chester Beatty manuscript under the rubric of the miracles which occurred after the death of the Shaykh.

[CHAPTER SEVEN]

Further Miracles of Shaykh Ahmad
From the Chester Beatty Manuscript of the
Spiritual Feats

The preceding 180 stories were taken from a manuscript of *The Spiritual Feats of Shaykh Ahmad* copied out in June or July of 1422 (Rajab 825 A.H.). This copy made its way to the Nâfiz Pâshâ Library (#399) in Istanbul, where it was discovered by Hellmut Ritter in 1938 and then edited and published in 1961 by Heshmat Moayyad as *Maqâmât-e Zhandeh Pil.*

The 189 stories which follow do not appear in that Nâfiz Pâshâ manuscript of *The Spiritual Feats of Shaykh Ahmad*, but are related in two other manuscripts of the work. These stories appear in Moayyad's second edition of the Persian text of *Maqâmât-e Zhandeh Pil*, published in 1967.

STORIES 181 TO 184
These four stories are found only in the manuscript of the Berlin Preussische Staatsbibliothek (Ms. Or. oct. 3784).

STORIES 185 TO 369
These one hundred and eighty-five stories are found only in the Chester Beatty Library Manuscript in Dublin (ms. 352), which was probably copied out sometime around 1570.

The Berlin manuscript preserves only a portion of Ghaznavi's *Spiritual Feats*, just 37 stories, and was perhaps intended as a selection. The four supplemental tales (181-184) found only in the Berlin manuscript probably derive from a source other than Ghaznavi's *Spiritual Feats*, perhaps one of the collections of posthumous miracles of Shaykh Ahmad.

It is, however, more difficult to explain the difference in size between the Nâfiz Pâshâ manuscript (180 stories) and the Chester Beatty Library manuscript (365 stories) of Ghaznavi's *Spiritual Feats of Shaykh Ahmad.* Perhaps the Nâfiz Pâshâ manuscript is incomplete, and the Chester

Beatty Library manuscript represents the full collection of stories compiled by Ghaznavi. Alternatively, stories 185-369 may reflect the work of an unknown later compiler, who inserted stories collected from other sources to supplement the work of Mohammad-e Ghaznavi and gather all the miracles of Shaykh Ahmad into a single volume. Indeed, some of the stories that follow (e.g., Story 244, 298) would seem to date to some time after the death of Ghaznavi.

In any case, the following 189 tales do not deviate from the style of the first 180 stories, and occur in the Chester Beatty Manuscript mingled in with the other stories, not simply added at the end of the manuscript. They must therefore have been composed, if indeed they are later additions, as a complement to Ghaznavi's work, deliberately following his style.

***

181. The Difference between Shaykh Ahmad-e Jâm and Khvâjeh Abu 'Ali Fârmadi[1]

The Shaykh al-Islam Ahmad, God sanctify his precious soul, in the beginning of his ministry, was a follower of Shaykh Abu Tâher. Eventually things reached the point that Shaykh Abu Tâher said, "I am the disciple of Shaykh Ahmad and he is my guide [*pir*]."

The religious authorities, may God be pleased with all of them, have stated, "Forty people who followed the example of Shaykh Abu Sa'id Abu al-Khayr, God sanctify his precious soul, became saints." One of them was the Shaykh al-Islam Ahmad, and another, Khvâjeh Abu 'Ali.[2] Both of them became well-known in

---

[1]   The anecdotes related here appear in virtually the same words in Jâmi's *Nafahât al-ons*, ed. Mehdi Towhidipur (Tehran: Mahmudi, 1336/1957), 359. It is highly likely that the account given here has been taken from Jâmi, or vice-versa.

[2]   This almost certainly alludes to Shaykh Abu 'Ali Fazl ebn-e Mohammad-e Fârmadi, known as the Shaykh al-Shoyukh of Khorasan. According to Jâmi's *Nafahât al-ons*, op. cit., 368-70, Abu 'Ali-ye Fârmadi was a student of the famous Imam Abu al-Qâsem Qoshayri in preaching and homily, and of Abu al-Qâsem Gorgâni of Tus in the Sufi path. But Jâmi also quotes a purportedly autobiographical anecdote in

the world, but, according to Pir Mohammad-e Hâzem, though Abu 'Ali had been granted the power to read minds, he was not permitted to reveal what he knew. The Shaykh al-Islam Ahmad, on the other hand, had both been granted the power to read minds and authority over the people's behavior [bar zâher-hâ hâkem], and he was permitted to reveal what he knew. Mohammad-e Ostâd said, "The Shaykh al-Islam Ahmad's saintliness was such that all were commanded to follow him [hameh râ be-khedmat-e u farmudand]."

And so it remained for the rest of his life, God sanctify his heart.

182. A Story about the Shaykh's Asceticism

Reliable sources whose word can be believed have reported that the Shaykh al-Islam Ahmad, God sanctify his precious soul, during his withdrawal from society—the few years he spent on the mountain practicing [210] self-renunciation and worshipping God, the Exalted and Almighty—was bothered and vexed by carnal desires, every now and then, which the Shaykh al-Islam would overcome through prayer and fasting.

One day the following thought occurred to him: "Let me go and cut off this organ of desire and make myself such that I will be free of its evil." When this idea came to him he took a knife and was about to cut off his organ when, suddenly, a voice [hâtef] called out, "O Ahmad, the blood of thirty-nine holy men of God will be on your hands. We want to produce thirty-nine saints from your seed."

When the Shaykh al-Islam heard this voice, he abandoned the

---

the words of Abu 'Ali-ye Fârmadi himself, which states that when he was a youth in Nayshabur, Shaykh Abu Sa'id-e Abu al-Khayr came from Mehneh to Nayshabur and Abu 'Ali became his disciple (see also *Nafahât*, 359). When Abu Sa'id left Nayshabur, Abu 'Ali then studied with Qoshayri, and finally with Gorgâni. Abu 'Ali-ye Fârmadi is also noted as a disciple of Abu al-Qâsem Gorgâni in Hâfez Hosayn Karbalâ'i-ye Tabrizi's *Rowzât al-jenân va jannât al-janân*, ed. Ja'far Soltân al-Qorrâ'i (Tehran: Bongâh-e Tarjomeh va Nashr-e Ketâb, 1349/1970), 2:344.

idea. In the last years of his life he kept taking wives until thirty-nine sons and three girls had been fathered by him.

Shaykh 'Omar-e Sarrâji says that the Shaykh al-Islam Ahmad, God sanctify his precious soul, produced thirty-nine saints, some of whom became known in this world and some only in the next. On the day of Resurrection thirty-nine sons of the Shaykh al-Islam will be assembled under his banner.

One of the notables of religion has indicated: "The children born to the Shaykh al-Islam Ahmad, or to his children or to his children's children all the way until the Resurrection, will be holy men and leaders."

This is the special blessing of the Shaykh al-Islam, God sanctify his heart. And through God comes success.

183. The Shaykh Knows the Minds of Others

Another miracle was when three of his opponents came to see the Shaykh al-Islam to test him. Along the way they made a plan: "Let us agree here what food we want the Shaykh to give us when we are in his presence."

One of them said, "Let him give us bread and syrup." Another said, "Let him give us bread and vinegar." The third said, "Let him give us bread and yoghurt."

When these three people entered the door of the khâneqâh and greeted the Shaykh al-Islam and sat down, the Shaykh al-Islam motioned to his servant to bring some food from the bazaar [211] for the travelers to eat. The servant got up and said, "What shall I bring?"

The Shaykh al-Islam said, "Bring bread and vinegar and syrup and yoghurt."

When the servant prepared the spread and placed the food in front of them, the Shaykh al-Islam said, "Here we have what all three of you wanted."

These three people threw themselves at the Shaykh al-Islam's blessed feet and asked forgiveness. "O master, we have been impudent and ignorant! Forgive us through your generosity."

All three of them went back as believers and disciples in the Shaykh. And through God comes success.

184. The Shaykh and the Ghost of Abu Sa'id-e Abu al-Khayr

Shaykh 'Omar-e Fârsi relates on the authority of the notables of religion that when the Shaykh al-Islam Ahmad, God sanctify his precious soul, resolved to visit the grave of Abu Sa'id Abu al-Khayr, he got up and set out alone. When he reached the mountain of Bazâvandaqân,[3] he was thirsty. He saw an old man coming from out of nowhere with a bowl of cold water in his hands, which he gave to the Shaykh.

That day the Shaykh al-Islam kept company with that old man until evening. It was Khezr, blessings upon him. The next day the Shaykh al-Islam left that place.

The spirit of Abu Sa'id Abu al-Khayr, God sanctify his precious soul, came to greet the Shaykh al-Islam and they told one another all their secrets. It is believed that one of the secrets was this: the enemies want to destroy the religion of Mohammad, peace and blessings upon him. The pure spirit of Shaykh Abu Sa'id informed the Shaykh al-Islam of the fact that he had been destined to fight against them. "Be valiant," he said.

Later it became clear that this was true, for four hundred heretics, Jews and Christians were killed through the miraculous powers of the Shaykh al-Islam, and those who survived all became Muslims.

What could be more miraculous? God alone knows. [212]

185. The Shaykh Preserves his Followers from Harm

This same "Learned Shaykh"[4] also relates that at the time the Shaykh al-Islam was building the congregational mosque at Ma'd-âbâd, he—the learned Shaykh—was on top of the dome handing baked bricks to the foreman. His foot slipped and he fell off the dome. The Shaykh al-Islam was standing there and said, "In the

---

[3] We have not found his place name (*b-zâ-v-n-d-qân*) in any other source.

[4] This is the same "Learned Shaykh" referred to in Story 56. In the Chester Beatty Manuscript, this story follows Story 56 of the present text.

name of God, rise to your feet unhurt."

The dome was nearly fifteen cubits high, and below it they had made a pile of baked bricks. He fell on his head and neck upon the baked bricks and got up with no broken limbs, except for his arm, which was slightly wounded.

This was due to the blessings of the Shaykh al-Islam.

186. Punishment for Changing the Writings of the Shaykh

Khvâjeh Mozaffar-e Jowrmadi[5] relates the following:

One day our master, the Shaykh al-Islam, told me, [213] "Bring me your *Ons al-tâ'ebin*,[6] so I can see how you have copied it" When I took it to him, he looked it over and said, "Have you changed anything in this book?"

I had copied it out hastily, thinking that the more condensed it was, the better. Now, when he asked if I had changed it, my eyes immediately grew dim. I was almost blind, as if a veil were covering my eyes. I couldn't see the sky or the ground. I thought I am now going to be dishonored in the presence of that assembly. I knew where I had removed my shoes, since it was my own house. I slowly backed away, slipped on my shoes and groped my way outside and sat down, greatly distressed and in pain.

The Shaykh al-Islam cried out, "Khvâjeh Mozaffar, come here. Don't be worried, you have written down the gist of it!" When I entered the house and my gaze fell upon that blessed beauty, the veil of darkness was lifted, my sight grew bright again and returned to normal.[7]

---

[5] The manuscript gives Jowrmadi, though the toponym Jowrmadi/Jormad is known only from this story and Story 354. A village called Jowrbad near Esfarâyen in the district of Nayshabur is, however, attested in Yâqût and in Jovayni's *Târikh-e jahângoshâ*, 2:223 and 278, and perhaps that is the place intended, though Story 187 would seem to suggest that this village is only 10 farsangs from Zâhed-âbâd.

[6] This is a book written by the Shaykh al-Islam (see the Introduction, "Works of the Shaykh"), of which Khvâjeh Mozaffar has made a handwritten copy for himself.

[7] This story is also related in *Rowzat al-rayâhin*, 28, but the name is given as Mozaffar-e Hormozi and the Shaykh reprimands him for

187. The Shaykh Wills and Get Walnuts

One day in Zâhed-âbâd, a group of veiled ones [*masturât*, i.e., women] had come from the village of Sorkh asking for walnuts. They said, "We must have walnuts for the blessed month of Ramadan."

The Shaykh al-Islam, God sanctify his heart, said, "Walnuts cannot readily be bought in any town or market around here. Be patient for a while until they arrive, for they are one the way."

The following day Khvâjeh Mozaffar-e Jowrmadi arrived with a sackful of walnuts. The Shaykh asked him, "How did this come about?"

He said, "I felt like I should bring some walnuts to the Shaykh al-Islam, God sanctify his heart."

The very moment when the Shaykh al-Islam, God sanctify his heart, needed the walnuts, Khvâjeh Mozaffar had set out from his home. He arrived the following day at the noon-prayer. It was ten farsangs from there to his village. [214]

188. The Pear's Desire for the Shaykh

Khvâjeh Moqri-ye Sanjari relates:

Once the Shaykh al-Islam had a sore throat in the winter. He asked, "Moqri, have you got any pears like this?"

"I have two or three," I said. I went home where there were a number of pears hanging on a rope in the storeroom. I decided to take three or four of them and leave the rest. There was a particularly good one that I decided to keep. I reached out and pulled down three or four. The rest of them fell, as well, hit the ground, and were smashed.

In short, I picked them all up and went to the Shaykh, putting them in front of him. He said, "Moqri, you meddled in this matter." He picked the most beautiful pear and said, "You did not want to bring this one, but it wanted me and rolled after you so you would bring it."

Moqri said:

---

having changed the book.

I put the best one on a board and when I reached the door of the house, it rolled off the board all the way to the door of the house, where I picked it up.

189. The Punishment for Unbelievers

The Shaykh al-Islam had gone to the mountain of Barinân and saw the learned Mahmud,[8] and they spoke together of many things. The learned Mahmud said, "You are not at the top of your form." There was a man by the name of Rashid sitting there near the Shaykh al-Islam, repeating some of the words of the learned Mahmud, such as, "Alas for the days when they told stories about you; now things are different."

The Shaykh al-Islam answered, "My powers have not weakened; the bounties and gifts of my Lord to me are ever on the increase."

Rashid got up to leave and the Shaykh al-Islam said, "Where are you going?"

He said, "I want to go out."

The Shaykh said, "Don't go just yet, for if you go now, you will be arrested, slapped on the neck and beaten with a club."

The learned Mahmud said [to Rashid], "Be on your way, anyway. I'm sure his so-called 'powers' of mind-reading will become evident."

As soon as he got out of the door, some horsemen seized him and clubbed him and took him away, slapping him on the back of the neck. They took some ten people along with him to the mountain of Barinân and what the Shaykh had said proved true. [215]

190. The Shaykh Gives Instructions on How to Free Captive Villagers

There was a woman known as Âgah. She had a fiefdom which included the mountain of Barinân. She was an acquaintance of the Shaykh al-Islam, whom she had met in Nayshabur, and on this basis she came to see him.

"O Shaykh!," she said. "Some of the people have been deported

---

[8] He also appears in Stories 78 and 79.

from here. If they are not returned, there will be no way to make amends for this humiliation. Not a soul will remain here, they will all go and this village of ours will be ruined."

The Shaykh al-Islam was resting [khofteh] on the roof of the mosque. In answer to Âgah, who was the village lord, he said, "Dispatch one hundred men to the village of Barinân and release the people from the building there."

She said, "It is not possible to enter the village of others; it may result in even greater trouble and someone might even be killed."

The Shaykh al-Islam said, "Do not worry. I would not instruct you to do something if I had not had a vision about it. Do dispatch the men."

That woman was certain of the Shaykh, having seen and recognized some examples of his spiritual susceptibilities [ahvâl]. She immediately commanded the men to go. Outside the village there was a building where the people had been detained. The ruler of the village was hosting a banquet, to which he had invited the military officers [sarân]. The contingent she sent smashed down the door and led the captives out, returning them safely to their village. Horsemen followed after them, but could not engage them, for fear that someone might be killed.

191. The Shaykh Predicts an Assault by Horsemen

Then there was the time the learned Mahmud was in the village of Nâmaq and had gathered all kinds of wares to take to Nayshabur, where he lived. He told the Shaykh al-Islam, "You stay awake tonight, so that you can wake me at dawn and help me to load the pack animals so we can set out."

The Shaykh al-Islam went home and had a vision that a calamity was awaiting him [the learned Mahmud] on the road, so he did not wake him. When they performed the morning prayers, Mahmud said, "You woke up nice and early!"

The Shaykh said, "There is difficulty [mashghuli] ahead. I did not want you to go today."

Mahmud asked, "What is it?"

The Shaykh al-Islam said, "I had a vision that horsemen will

come after you in such-and-such a place [216] and strip the
donkeys of their loads and carry away with them whatever they
want. I also saw some people's books strewn on the ground or
carried away by the wind."

Khvâjeh Imam Mahmud said, "This knowledge is hidden to us
and I don't believe the future can be foretold." He ordered the
loads to be packed on the animals, and they set out.

When they reached the place the Shaykh had spoken of,
horsemen came and stripped the donkeys of their loads and took
whatever they needed. The books fell into the dirt and some of
them were carried off by the wind. At that point they remembered
what the Shaykh al-Islam had said.

192. A Mountain Goat Becomes Carrion

However often the learned Mahmud would see this kind of
thing, he still wouldn't believe it. One day he told the Shaykh al-
Islam, "You know your way on this mountain very well. I have
some friends who need canes. Could I trouble you to take my
friend with you so he can get a few canes?"

The Shaykh said, "Very well." He went out and waited for the
friend to come out. When the friend came out, the Shaykh asked,
"What took you so long? You have made the sheep go to waste."

Khvâjeh Imam Mahmud said, "What do you mean, 'go to
waste'?"

The Shaykh said, "If you had not taken so long, we would have
caught a mountain goat. Now, by the time we arrive there, the goat
will be nothing but carrion."

Khvâjeh Imam Mahmud called his learned friend and whispered
something in his ear and they left. When they had gone a little
way, the two sheep came down from the mountain. This learned
friend said, "Well, well, here we have those *sheep* you were
talking about!"

"Didn't I say a mountain goat!?," replied the Shaykh. "These are
ewes. We are still a half farsang away from the place I was talking
about." When they reached that place the Shaykh told the learned
friend, "Go over there and look; I saw it among these trees. But be
careful, there is a leopard there."

That learned friend said, "You are mocking me."

He said, "Not at all; it's just so that you know and can tell Khvâjeh Imam, so that he will know that the friends of God, the Mighty and Glorious, have other powers besides the ones you know of." [217]

That learned friend went in and called out, "Bring a knife; it's still alive!" By the time he got the knife, the sheep[9] was already dead.

That learned friend was astonished. He said, "Had I not seen it with my own eyes, I would not have believed it."

193. Bread and Meat to Feed Unexpected Guests

[Khvâjeh Abu Bakr Hâji Kusavi][10] also relates:

The year when the Shaykh al-Islam was on the mountain top, I hosted a feast. There were fifty people in the company of the Shaykh al-Islam. I had a twelve-maund crop. As they sat down to the table, Qâzi Bu al-'Alâ of Fushanj came by with more than forty people. This made about ninety people and I grew worried.

The Shaykh al-Islam saw this and called me over to him. He said, "Don't worry. Bread and meat will arrive—we have sent bread...."[11]

There was enough for all and nothing was lacking. I was still eating it a week later.

---

[9] The text gives *gusfand*, a sheep. Although the Shaykh did, indeed, first indicate that a sheep had been wasted, the second time he mentions his prediction, he says a mountain goat, *boz-e kuhi*, had been wasted.

According to Islamic law, it is not permissible for a Muslim to eat the flesh of an animal which has not been ritually slaughtered. This, then, is the reason for the Shaykh's impatience over the delay caused by the learned friend; had they arrived a few minutes earlier, they would have been able to ritually slaughter the animal and eat it.

[10] The same figure also appears in Story 84.

[11] There is apparently a lacuna in the manuscript here.

194. An Epileptic Child is Healed

Khvâjeh Abu Bakr, the son of the Shaykh al-Islam, may God have mercy upon him, said:

A child from the village of Zarashk[12] was brought to the Shaykh al-Islam one day. He was epileptic and could not function. The Shaykh al-Islam gazed at him and said, "It's not serious. He has been hurt by the 'earth creatures,'[13] many of whom are my disciples. I will tell them to leave him alone."

He turned in the direction of the child and asked out loud: "What do you want with him? Leave him alone, for he is my friend."

Instantly the child opened his eyes, came to his senses and left happily. [218]

195. Purity of Motive

Ostâd 'Ali Tâybâdi, who lived in Bizd, relates the following:

The first time I saw the Shaykh al-Islam, I had sincerely resolved to see him merely for the sake of God. Then I thought, I asked for the hand of a certain girl but have not yet [succeeded in] bringing her to my house. I should ask him to pray that my problem may be resolved.

When I saw him in the village of Sâghu, I asked the following: "If a person has to attend to an important matter and he says the 'Prayer of the Needy' and asks God, the Almighty, to help him, will he forfeit purity of motive?"[14]

The Shaykh said, "It would be just like the case of your visit to

---

[12] This village is also mentioned in Stories 211, 356 and 362. In every case, it is given as *Z-r-sh-k*, though in *Rowzat al-rayâhin*, 40 and 67, it appears as *Z-r-sh-t-k*. The standard geographical dictionaries, however, do not mention such a toponym in either of these forms.

[13] The text gives *mardomân-e zamin*, "the people of the earth," by which is apparently meant (mythical) creatures like the *jinn*, which were sometimes believed to be the cause of epilepsy.

[14] When a Muslim performs his prayers, his motivation must be purely to conform with the Will of God, and not to demand things of God.

me."

I said, "Wait, haven't I come with purity of motive?"

He said, "Your motive was pure, but when you allowed the thought of your bride into your heart, the matter changed. Otherwise, you would have received so many honors [khel'at] that it would have sufficed you for the rest of your life."[15]

196. The Shaykh's Apparel

The same source relates:

The first day, before I had seen him, I imagined that he would be dressed in coarse tatters or felt. When I saw him he was dressed in a white robe, like a worldly person.[16] I thought to myself, this is not an ascetic man. At that very instant my stomach began to burn with a pain I had never before experienced. The following day it was somewhat better.

I told the Shaykh, "Something has happened to my stomach and I don't know what it is."

He said, "Yes, it was quite bad yesterday, but today is a little better."

That was exactly so, and it was a secret between me and the Almighty God, and no one else knew about it.[17]

197. The Shaykh and the Reading of Anti-Mu'tazili Books

He also relates:

Once Khvâjeh Imam Ebrâhim, my brother, told me the following: "They say that the Shaykh al-Islam has the power to read minds. It would be nice if he would show me an example of it."

Then one day [219] both of us brothers were sitting in front of

---

[15] See the same story in Rowzat al-rayâhin, 36.

[16] Bar sân-e 'âlamiân. In the version of this story given in the Rowzat al-rayâhin, 36, it is rather 'âlemân, in the manner of the religious scholars.

[17] The version in Rowzat al-rayâhin, 36, adds a further explanatory sentence to this story.

the Shaykh. I said, "Long live the Shaykh al-Islam! Khvâjeh
Imam, my brother, would like to see an example of your
miracles."

He said, "Do you believe in the truth of this verse, where the
Almighty God says, *'And whoso has done an atom's weight of
good shall see it, and whoso has done an atom's weight of evil
shall see it?'*"[18]

My brother said, "I do."

The Shaykh then said, "You take this book written by certain
Muslims with you [...] and read it? Don't you know that it is
forbidden?"

My brother asked, "What sort of book is that?"

The Shaykh said, "The book vilifying the Mu'tazilis,[19] in
several quires stitched together, with no cover, the first quire of
which has been worn from much handling."

My brother said, "That is the book, but it is in square format
[?]."[20]

The Shaykh said, "Even so, it is still forbidden."

My brother said, "You speak the truth, it is so."

198. The Shaykh Helps a Newly-wed Groom

He also relates:

When I brought my bride home I faced a serious problem, which
even made one person wonder if I was impotent. The problem
lasted five days, at which point I appealed to God in the name of
the Shaykh al-Islam, saying, "O God, by the esteem which this
man holds at Your threshold, [I ask] that you inform him of this
charitable [*hasan*] deed and spare me from this [affliction], for I
fear that I will lose my bride."

That night the Almighty Lord relieved my difficulty. The next

---

[18] Qur'ân 99:7-8.

[19] An early school of theological thought in Islam. See the article
"Mu'tazila" in the *Enyclopedia of Islam*, 2nd ed., by D. Gimaret.

[20] The meaning of the word given here, *m-r-b-'*, apparently to be read
as *morabba'*, is normally "square," here perhaps in the sense of
"codex." One might also read *mari'*, meaning "fruitful," though this
adjective is usually used for land or gardens, not for books.

day I went to see the Shaykh al-Islam and said, "In recent days I have faced a serious problem. Through your help it was resolved." He said, "It was not in recent days, it was several days ago that I became aware of your problem and I prayed for you. Praised be God that you are now free of it." [220]

199. The Words of a Vengeful Man are not Persuasive

He also relates:
In the beginning of his ministry, when I had come to the village of Bizd, Ostâd Imam Esma'il Oshtavi was also there. There was a long-standing dispute between us. Twenty gatherings [to debate the matter] were arranged. He would have three days to speak and then I would have three days.

The day the Shaykh al-Islam came it was my turn to speak. Though a large crowd from the surrounding areas had come and the Shaykh al-Islam was present, my talk did not spark the audience's interest. The next day Ostâd 'Omar told [the Shaykh], "You give the talk today."

He excused himself, saying, "Let Imam Esma'il give it," which was contrary to my desire.

When Imam Esma'il sat at the lectern [korsi], I got up and went home. At the afternoon prayer, I returned and sat next to the Shaykh al-Islam, who said, "He gave a good talk today."

I said, "My speech this morning did not go well because I have not lectured for quite some time."

The Shaykh said, "No, it's because you harbor a grudge against the Imam Esma'il in your heart."

I said, "Since you have become aware of this, please beseech my Lord to remove it." He rolled his eyes heavenward and from that instant there was no longer any grudge or any hard feelings [in my heart].

The next day when I began to speak there was a warm feeling in the audience and, due to the Shaykh al-Islam's spiritual concentration, the relationship between myself and Imam Esma'il became almost like that of father and son [pesar khvândegi va pedar khvânedgi].

200. An Ecstatic Vision

In the beginning of the Shaykh al-Islam's ministry I had no sympathy for the Dervishes and their practices. One day I asked the Shaykh al-Islam, "From the time of the Prophet, peace upon him, until today, people have practiced repentance of their blasphemy and sin, but no one has ever behaved so mysteriously and done such things as they do today."

The Shaykh was replying [to my thoughts, and I argued the point with him. Suddenly I saw a light descending from the throne of God, which attracted my heart].[21] Because there was much excitement there, I didn't hear anything; it was just a light coming down from the throne of God, attracting my heart, as if all veils had been rent. It was as if I was in the presence of the divine [*moshâhedeh*, 221]. I leapt up and tore open the brand new cloak[22] I was wearing.

When I returned to myself there was a [tray] of black mulberries sitting in front of me. The Shaykh said, "Eat them, so that your yellow bile will subside."[23]

I asked him, "What were you thinking about when your head was bowed?"

He said, "I was praying to God, the Almighty: 'O Lord grant him a share of the spiritual fortitude of the Dervishes, so that he will not destroy himself.'"

---

[21] There is a lacuna in the text here of perhaps several lines, probably omitted accidentally by the scribe. This same anecdote, with slight variation, is related in *Rowzat al-rayâhin*, 37, which supplies the text of what is given in brackets here.

[22] *Dorrâ'eh*, for which see the lexicon at the end of the article "Clothing" in the *Encyclopaedia Iranica*. The Persian text has *dorrâ'eh chahâr*, which might mean four cloaks, or the word four may perhaps indicate the quality of cloth or price of the garment.

[23] Mulberries are traditionally believed to prevent excess of yellow bile in the balance of the body's humors.

201. Struck Dumb at the Sight of the Shaykh

Once I and a student walked barefoot from Bizd to Sâghu in order to visit the Shaykh al-Islam. When I saw him, a feeling came over me that struck me dumb.

When I came to my self again, he said, "Brother! In the end I took pity on you, for you could not have endured more than that, or the same thing would have happened to you that happened before."[24]

202. The Shaykh Grants a Metaphysical Experience

He also relates:

The Shaykh al-Islam was in Amghân. We went to see him in a group. When it was time to go, I said, "Long live the Shaykh al-Islam! It is the month of Ramadan, and in this month the commoners break their fast at the table of their superiors, and we are the servants of the commoners of this assembly. It is our hope that you will not leave us bereft of your gifts and attentions."

He said, "Very well."

After we departed, along the way a state came over me in which I could not tell if I was in the air or on the earth. Until the end of the month, every time that a spiritual state came upon the Shaykh, we felt its impact here on us, though we never experienced spiritual states at any other time.

203. Some Disciples Make Pilgrimage to the Shaykh

He also relates:

On the evening of 'Arafeh[25] I thought to myself, "The pilgrims have gone to the House [i.e, the Ka'bah] and are performing the pilgrimage rites [ziârat]. Let us go to visit [ziârat] the Shaykh."

---

[24] This is a reference to what happened to the narrator of this story, 'Ali Tâybâdi, in Story 200. This story also appears in *Rowzat al-rayâhin*, 37.

[25] The ninth and perhaps principle day of the pilgrimage ceremonies, on which the pilgrims stop at 'Arafât, before re-entering Mecca.

We went in a group.

The Shaykh al-Islam had foreseen that we were coming [222]. They were eating melons and he had said, "Keep the melon rinds, because the friends in Bizd are coming, and their mounts can eat them." When we arrived there he said, "Indeed, you have come on pilgrimage. Is there not also a desert to cross before you reach the door of his Ka'bah? You have suffered much crossing this desert."

The distance was so great that we walked all night long and arrived there only at breakfast time.

204. Repelling a Plague of Locusts

Once locusts had descended upon the whole region of Jâm, except for Amghân, and had wreaked much damage and destruction. One day the people of Amghân came and [asked the Shaykh] to intercede. "They have wiped Jâm clean and now they are heading for Amghân. For God's sake, help us!"

The Shaykh al-Islam said, "Bring some alms to the hospice at Golzhin." The locusts had reached there, as well.

The Shaykh al-Islam was about to go to Sâghu. He said a prayer and then turned around to head off in the direction of Sâghu. The locusts turned around with him so that not a single one of them entered the fields of Amghân and they all dispersed.

205. Reciting Poems and Dancing in the Presence of the Shaykh

He also relates:

Once the learned Bu Moti' had come to the village of Bizd. He had some ill feelings with respect to the Shaykh al-Islam, and used to tell me, "One should not dance and [yet] they recite poems before the Shaykh and dance."

That night I saw the Shaykh al-Islam in a dream. He was speaking harshly to me. About twenty days later I went to see him and said, "The other night I had a dream about you in which you were speaking harshly to me. I don't know what the reason was."

He said, "It was not the other night, it was when the learned Bu Moti' was here. I told you, 'Give him a firm reply; take heed not to cower before him.'"[26]

206. A Manly Excercise of the Spirit

He also relates:
Once when I went to see the Shaykh al-Islam, I was engaged in a spiritual exercise—[223] I was consuming bread without liquid and drinking no water. He looked at me and said, "If you really want to excercise your spirit, do it like a man. This is nothing."[27]

207. Punishment for an Adversary

He also relates:
There was a certain Hâji in Buzjân, who was the mayor there, who had a quarrel with the followers of the Shaykh al-Islam. He had arrested two of the Shaykh al-Islam's followers, saying, "I will extract a thousand dinârs from the disciples of this Shaykh al-Islam Ahmad."
The Shaykh retorted, "If he himself is not compelled to give a thousand dinârs, then let him come and take it from my followers."
A little while later a person came to the mayor and arrested him and took a thousand dinârs of pure gold from him.

208. A Medicine for the Eyes

The "Learned Shaykh,"[28] God grant him peace, relates:
Once I had a growth the size of a pea on my eye. When I closed my eye, it would bulge out, and it caused me great pain. People were telling me, "If you [go] to a big city, there are experts to remove this with their skilled hands. Otherwise you will lose your eye to this growth."
I was waiting for the Shaykh al-Islam, who was in Tâybâd, to come. When he came to Buzjân, I went to see him there. He said,

---

[26] See also *Rowzat al-rayâhin*, 38.
[27] See *Rowzat al-rayâhin*, 38.
[28] See Stories 56 and 185.

"Come closer!" I stepped up to him. He rubbed some of his saliva on it and three days later no trace of it was left.

209. The Shaykh Knows the Doings of Others

He also relates the following:
One day I was tearing down an old wall in Ma'd-âbâd. The next day I went to Buzjân, where the Shaykh al-Islam was. The Shaykh al-Islam told me, "Yesterday you were tearing down a huge wall. You had a shovel in hand, and the tip of it was broken." [224] What he said was the exact truth.

210. The Shaykh Bestows a Son on One of His Followers

He also relates:
Six girls in a row had been born to me, and not a single son. I and my wife[29] longed for a son.
One day the Shaykh al-Islam told me, "Mohammad Asfarghâbadi, who is not married, has had a dream. I grant [the fulfillment of] his dream to you, so that you may have a son."
My wife was pregnant at the time. After six months she bore a son.

211. The Shaykh Produces a Pomegranate from his Pocket

Ahmad-e Hableh-bori,[30] relates:
When the Shaykh al-Islam first came to the village of Zarashk

---

[29] Though not recorded in any dictionary, *qowm* (which usually means tribe, people, or kin) clearly means "wife" here, and in the next occurence in this story, as well as in several other stories in this book (224, 256, 331, 366). *Qowm* also occurs in this meaning in *Asrâr al-towhid*, ed. Shafi'i-Kadkani, e.g., 81 and 278.

[30] The name occurs in the text as *Hamleh-bari*, but the correct form, which also appears in Story 215, may be *Hableh-bori*. In Story 216 the verb *hableh kardan* occurs, the meaning of which is unattested. Instead of *Hamleh-bari*, we have preferred *Hableh-bori*, which may perhaps be a compound of *hableh*, meaning grapes, and *boridan*, to cut or pick. The compound would hence mean a grape-picker, though the *i* at the end of the word is somewhat problematic.

we went to see him there. The Commander, Amir Jâveli Soltân, and Amir Jâveli Jeb[31] came to pay obeisance. The Shaykh al-Islam treated them with consideration and offered them some advice.

When they rose to leave, Amir Jâveli Soltân told Jâveli Jeb [?], "Hand that pomegranate to this pious man so that he may say a blessing over it and we can take it to the Sultan." Amir Jâveli Jeb reached into the front of his cloak and pulled out two pomegranates and gave them to the Shaykh al-Islam.

The Shaykh al-Islam said, "The Sultan deserves a better pomegranate than this." He delved into his pocket and brought forth a large fresh pomegranate and said a blessing over it, as well as the two others, and handed them to the Amir—though prior to this, the Shaykh had no pomegranate in his pocket, nor is it customary for men to keep pomegranates [225] in their pockets.

This was seen by everyone, and it stirred up much commotion and a great cry arose.[32]

212. The Shaykh Knows the Doings of Others

The "Learned Shaykh," God grant him peace, relates that:

The Shaykh al-Islam was once in Amghân. I went to see him. I had brought three loaves of bread from Ma'd-âbâd with me [for the journey]. After travelling a part of the way, I sat down and consumed one of them. I gave another one to a passer-by. On the way a pleasant feeling came over me and I cried a little.

When I reached the presence of the Shaykh al-Islam, he knew what had happened to me. "You had a pleasant feeling along the way, the intoxicating traces of which are still visible in your eyes. When you gave the bread to that passer-by, you did an extremely good deed."

---

[31] The name given here, *J-b*, is not attested in dictionaries, and because the Arabic script does not record short vowels, it is therefore not clear whether this word should be read Job, Jab or Jeb, or if indeed, this is a scribal corruption.

[32] Cf. the version of this story given in *Rowzat al-rayâhin*, 40-41.

213. Treating an Eye-ache

Ostâd Imam 'Omar said:

Once I had a severe pain in my eyes, such that at night [...I could not sleep].[33] But when the morning came and I stood to pray, I felt as if someone splashed cold water in my eyes. The pain immediately subsided and went away.

At that moment they had told the Shaykh that my eyes were hurting. He had prayed for me and immediately the pain subsided. God, the Almighty, healed me on account of the blessed breath of the Shaykh.

214. Rain Clouds Appear at the Shaykh's Behest

Mohammad-e Shâhvâr relates:

Once we wanted to go to Kâriz-e 'Omar. We came to a remarkably beautiful field, which, however, would soon be marred by lack of water.

Shaykh 'Ali of Abivard said, "Long live the Shaykh al-Islam. You won't leave this spot before watering the field, will you?"

The Shaykh al-Islam said, "You are right."

Immediately a cloud appeared and everywhere was filled with water. [226]

215. The Shaykh Enjoins Harmony at Home

The learned Ahmad Hableh-bori relates:

I went by the door of the mosque once and Ahmad-e Bu 'Omar[34] was sitting next to the Shaykh al-Islam. The Shaykh said, "Why do you quarrel at home? Go on home and show some consideration to them [i.e., his wife or wives] and bring joy to their heart."

---

[33] There is a lacuna in the manuscript at this point, though one can assume the gist, as we have done in the brackets.

[34] In this story, as well as in Stories 219 and 247, all appearing in the Chester Beatty Library manuscript, this name is given as Ahmad-e Bu 'Omar. In Stories 36, 104 and 120, however, he is referred to as Ahmad-e Bu 'Amr.

Bu 'Omar got up and left the mosque. I sat down in his place next to the Shaykh al-Islam, who turned to me and said, "You are in the same position that Ahmad-e Bu 'Omar is in. You go on home, as well, and bring joy to their heart and make peace." The night before I had quarreled at home, though no one knew of it. I got up and did exactly as he had instructed.[35]

216. The Shaykh Always Provides for his Followers

He also relates:
Once we were in the village of Bizd near Jâm. The Shaykh al-Islam told 'Ali Asfarghâbadi, "Call for seventy or eighty men to go with us to Zâhed-âbâd and work on a building." To me he said, "Get that basket of dates and come along."

'Ali Asfarghâbadi said, "The Shaykh should work as hard at gathering food as he does at gathering men."

I said, "Show some respect for the word of the Shaykh."

He went and gathered [*hableh kard*] the seventy men and I took the basket of dates and went to Zâhed-âbâd.

They worked until the noon-prayer and everyone felt hungry. The Shaykh al-Islam said, "Shall we pray first or eat first?," though there was no food.

As I sat down a Turkoman came up leading a donkey on which sat his daughter, who was ill. He had brought with him a bundle of food, including a roasted lamb. He set it before the friends—and there were nearly a hundred of us—and we all ate our fill.[36]

217. An Example of the Shaykh's Powers of Healing

While we were on our way to Kâriz-e 'Omar, fifty people [of the Shaykh's company] had made a stop at the hospice in Ba'nân.

---

[35] See *Rowzat al-rayâhin*, 41, which relates the same story with minor variation.

[36] *Rowzat al-rayâhin* (41) relates this story with some important variations. In that version, they are building in a garden, whereas in Story 143 of the present book, there is mention of a mosque being built at Zâhed-âbâd.

There were [227] five of us with the Shaykh al-Islam, and those others had gone on separately.

The Shaykh al-Islam said, "Run ahead, for something has happened to them." We went on ahead and sat waiting in the shade of a boulder. They came along dazed and helpless, most of them with stomach aches and diarrhea.

When we arrived at Kâriz-e 'Omar, we alighted at an orchard. The Shaykh asked for a pitcher of water, which we gave to him. He drank a little and said a blessing over it. He then said, "Give it to them."

It was given to them and as each of them took a sip, they opened their eyes and came alive again. They all recovered right away and what happened only God, the Mighty and Exalted, knows.[37]

218. Shirts Offered to the Shaykh Should be New

Shaykh Abu Bakr-e Lâzaki[38] relates:

The Shaykh al-Islam was in Nayshabur. A group of people agreed to go to Nayshabur to see him. I agreed to go along, as well.

Two new shirts had been sewn for me for the New Year ['id]. I had worn one of them on New Year's day and had never worn the other. I thought to myself that I should give the better shirt to the Shaykh as a gift. On the way, I changed my mind, thinking to keep the better made shirt, which I had not yet worn, for myself and to give the other one to him.

When I laid that other shirt before him, he said, "To fail to deliver what is entrusted to you is a sin."

I said, "What do you mean, 'entrusted?'" He said what he had to say [goft âncheh goft] and I remembered the promise I had made.

---

[37] The text of this story is slightly confused and presents some grammatical problems; nevertheless, the gist of the story seems to be as we have presented it here.

[38] In Story 104, this name appears as Lâlaki. In the region of Khvâf in Khorasan, there was a town called Lâz, mentioned only in the work of Yâqût (see Le Strange, *Lands of the Eastern Caliphate*, 358). A person from Lâz would, however, be called Lâzi and not Lâzaki, though Lâlak is perhaps a dialectical variant or a scribal error for Lâzak.

"Here," I said, "I will take this shirt off now, so that you may wear it."

"You do that," he said, "so that your promise will be fulfilled."

[228]

219. The Shaykh Knows What Others Possess

He also relates:

Once we were coming from Ma'd-âbâd. Ahmad Bu 'Omar said to me, "You downplay your wealth. It is not true that you don't have two or three hundred sheep."

I said, "I have no more than a hundred."

He said, "You do so have more."

We argued for some time. I said, "The Shaykh al-Islam knows that I do not own as much as you say."

Ahmad-e Bu 'Omar said, "He has more than he admits."

"Long live the Shaykh al-Islam!," I said. "How many sheep do I have?"

He paused for a moment and said, "You have ninety-two sheep."

When I went over to my flock later to shear [boresh kardan] the sheep, there were ninety-two sheep.

"Are there any more?," I asked.

"No," I was told.[39]

I said, "The Shaykh al-Islam said, 'You have ninety-two,' and I know the Shaykh would give the exact number."

"He was right," they said.

220. The Shaykh Bestows a Son on Another Follower

Mohammad-e Asfarghâbadi relates that there was a scholar in Nayshabur called the Learned 'Ali Bayhaqi. He asked the Shaykh al-Islam to grant him a child. The Shaykh al-Islam agreed and asked when would be a good time. "So be it, it will come to pass."

Now, it happened that the sister of the Learned 'Ali delivered twin girls. Those who opposed and refuted the Shaykh raised a

---

[39] Evidently by the shepherds or other servants in charge of tending the animals.

clamor about it, saying, "The Shaykh al-Islam promised a son to Mr. so-and-so, and twin girls were born!"

The Learned 'Ali asked, "Long live the Shaykh al-Islam. What will my child be, a boy or a girl?"

"Which did you want?," asked the Shaykh.

He said, "A boy [*farzand*]."

The Shaykh al-Islam said, "So it is."

One day the Shaykh al-Islam [was resting]. With closed eyes he said, "Go give the Learned 'Ali the glad-tidings that he will have a son."

[The Learned 'Ali] got up and went all about the town telling everyone that the Shaykh al-Islam had given him the glad-tidings of [229] a son. "Those girls were my sister's."

Three days later, a son was born to him.

221. The Shaykh Cures a Sick Man

Brother[40] Mohammad Asfarghâbadi relates:

Once the Shaykh al-Islam was in his own home in Buzjân. A man who was paralyzed and unable to work was brought before the Shaykh al-Islam sitting in a litter. The Shaykh recited something over him and placed his hands upon him. The sick man was cured right away and stood up.

222. The Shaykh Strikes a Selfish Preacher Dumb

The Learned 'Ali Israel [*Esrâ'il*] relates:

A preacher by the name of As'ad-e Bar-âbâdi [?] was once giving a sermon in Tâybâd. They told him, "There are many Shaykhs and notables here and the Shaykh al-Islam himself is present. Be careful what you say, or you might be in for a shock."

He said, "I will put them in their place" [*foru namâyam*].

---

[40] The title *Akhi*, literally "my Brother," was often used among the young men's guilds, the *ukhuwwat* or *futuwwat* orders, which had a code of chivalry and sometimes played a quasi-martial role in town affairs (see *Encyclopaedia Islam*, 2nd ed., s.v. "Akhi," and "Futu-wwa"). This title occurs elsewhere in the present text, e.g., 229, 289, 332, etc.

He began the sermon by making some good points, but, reflecting upon his own situation, he all of a sudden said, "I'm not the sort of scholar that anyone can scare or silence."

As soon as he said these words, the Shaykh al-Islam gazed upon him and said, "Is that so?" [*chonin*].

Immediately, his tongue froze, he was rendered speechless and was unable to say another word. At this point Khvâjeh Imam Mohammad-e Haysam stood at the foot of the pulpit and offered excuses on his behalf.

223. Finding a Lost Donkey

Khvâjeh Mohammad-e Shâhvâr relates:

Once the Shaykh al-Islam was being taken to the army camp. He said, "Rent me a donkey."

I said, "But I have a good donkey."

"You are a poor man," he said, "I wouldn't want your donkey to get stolen."

"It wouldn't bother me," I said. I put the donkey at his disposal and together we left. Three days after we reached the army camp, the donkey was stolen.

"You should go stand on the bridge," I was told. "Perhaps you will see some trace of the donkey."

I went and told the Shaykh al-Islam, who smiled and bowed his head awhile. Then he said, "Don't worry. They will bring it back, themselves [230]." I waited unperturbed.

When I returned, the skeptics made biting remarks. One day Khvâjeh Imam Abu 'Âsem, God have mercy upon him, told me: "You claim to be a disciple of the Shaykh al-Islam, and yet he took your donkey and rode it to the army camp, where it was stolen and sold for drinking money. So why doesn't he tell you who has taken your donkey?!"

I reported this incident to the Shaykh al-Islam. He said, "Go along and if your donkey is not returned to you in the next two or three days, I will pay for it."

I came to Buzjân, where I was told that my donkey was there, being kept at the house of so-and-so. I went there and retrieved my donkey.

224. A Strange Light in the Wind Tower[41]

Shaykh 'Omar-e Hâji:
Once I invited the Shaykh al-Islam to a banquet. When it came time to sleep, I spread bedclothes for the guests in the middle of the house. I, with my wife [*qowm*], went to sleep on the roof.

In the middle of the night, there was a strange light in the house. I went to the edge of the roof to see what it was. I saw a flame, like the flame of a candle, on the door of the wind tower. The whole inside of the house was illuminated by its ray.

225. The Healing Effects of the Shaykh's Prayers[42]

(Shaykh 'Omar, who was one of the Shaykh al-Islam Ahmad's designated disciples [*az kholafâ-ye Shaykh*] and lived in the town of Buzjân,) has related:

I was once very ill, such that I had no hope of recovery. The Shaykh al-Islam was in Amghân. When he came to Buzjân, he heard that I was about to die. He came to visit me and asked after my health and returned home.

One of the opponents said [231], "The Shaykh al-Islam is always talking about miracles. Why doesn't he cure his own designated disciple?"

This talk reached the Shaykh al-Islam, who went into the khâneqâh and performed a two-prostration prayer, turned around and said, "I have asked for 'Omar and they have granted him to me."

---

[41] *Bâdgir* is a traditional architectural feature of some houses in eastern and southeastern Iran. A tower-like structure, it captures wind and funnels it down inside the home to cool it. See the article "Bâdgîr" by S. Roaf in *Encyclopædia Iranica*.

[42] The scribe has mistakenly transcribed the beginning two lines of Story 106 (An Impudent Woman Gets Her Due) and then, at the words, "he said, 'Once...', continued with this story, which is also given in *Rowzat al-rayâhin* (38), from which the portion of the text in parentheses is taken.

Right away my body was restored to health and I was fine.

226. Thread Touched by the Shaykh Does Not Burn

The learned 'Abd al-Samad relates:
The first time that the Shaykh al-Islam came to Buzjân, I took him home with me, where he stayed for three days. One day he took off his clothes to have them washed. His footgear was in need of repair and he took out some thread from his pocket to sew it up. I brought him new footgear, set it before him and took his, together with that piece of thread.

One night, after he left, I was thinking about him. I got that piece of thread and held it above the lamp. "O God," I said, "if this man is Your friend, protect this thread from the fire."

Though I held it [over the flame] for a while, neither the thread nor my finger were burned.

227. The Healing Effects of the Shaykh's Cloak

He also relates:
I was carving a mold [kâlbod] and a chip flew into my eye. It was very painful and I had no hope of ever seeing again.

I got the Shaykh al-Islam's cloak and rubbed my eye with it. I lost consciousness. It seemed to me as if I were asleep and in that unconscious state, someone was asking me, "How is your eye?" "I rubbed it with the Shaykh al-Islam's cloak," I said, "and it got better."

When I came to, my eye was better and it did not hurt at all.[43]

228. The Shaykh Gives News of a Birth Before it Occurs

One day Ostâd Imam Esma'il, God have mercy upon him, was giving a sermon in the village of Oshtu. In the middle of his sermon, the Shaykh al-Islam told him, "A son has been born to you. Call him Yahyâ."

Someone [232] came in through the door of the mosque. Ostâd

---

[43] Cf. the version of the story given in *Rowzat al-rayâhin*, 39.

Imam Esma'il asked, "Has a son been born to me?" The fellow said, "No."

When the sermon came to an end, a man came in to say: "Glad-tidings to you, for a son is born to you." He named him Yahyâ, who became a great Imam through the blessings of the Shaykh.

229. A Cure for Nightblindness

Brother 'Ali-ye Shâyegâni relates:

There was a man in our village named Hosayn. Once we went, he and I, to Buzjân. It happened that this Hosayn had been afflicted with nightblindness and couldn't see a thing at night. One evening we went to see the Shaykh al-Islam.

After we had eaten dinner, Hosayn said, "I have been visited by nightblindness again![44] I don't know how I will be able to find my way out of here."

The Shaykh al-Islam, God sanctify his precious soul, said, "Come here by me, young man."

He went to the Shaykh, who rubbed the blessed water of his mouth in his eyes. When we left that place, I said, "Here, give me your hand."

"There is no need," he replied. He returned to his master and never again were his eyes afflicted by darkness.

230. The Shaykh Knows his Grapes

One of the Shaykh al-Islam's followers in Amghân came to see him. He went into the interior of the house to bring some grapes for the Shaykh al-Islam. There were some grapes hanging on a strap, nice black ones.

His wife said, "Don't take those, because the little child keeps asking for grapes all the time."

This man reports, "To spite the woman, I took down the strap and put it in a basket and filled the rest of it with white grapes. I returned to the Shaykh al-Islam."

When I set the basket in front of him, he ate the white grapes and set aside the black ones in the basket.

---

[44] Literally, "that visitor has come again," *ân mehmân bâz âmad*.

231. The Seed of a Son in a Date

Abu Bakr, the Tailor of Oshtu [*Darzi-ye Oshtavi*] relates:
One day the Shaykh al-Islam gave me two dates [233] and said,
"Take these that you might have a son." I took them and we ate
them.[45] A son was born to me.

232. The Shaykh's Disciples Keep their Hair

He also said:
The first time that I went to see the Shaykh al-Islam I said to the
preacher of Bizd, "I am afraid that he will shave my head."[46] I
pinned my hair up under my turban.
When I went before him, they spread food before us and we ate
a meal. I went and sat in the corner. The Shaykh al-Islam asked the
preacher, "Where is the fellow who came with you?"
I said, "I'm over here."
The Shaykh said, "Do not worry, no one is going to touch your
hair."

233. A Disciple Must be Sincere

'Ali Shâyegâni relates that once the learned Ahmad Bosti was
giving a sermon in the village of Oshtu. After he finished with his
sermon, he stepped down and sat near the prayer niche and folks
began to talk behind the Shaykh's back. There was a man from

---

[45] Though the text has *be kâr bordam* (I consumed it), it must mean
that Abu Bakr ate one date and gave the other other to his wife to eat.

[46] *Muy-e man bâz konad.* This individual fears that his visit will be
taken as a sign of formal discipleship to the Shaykh, and his locks
shorn. It was a practice among many Sufi orders for the novitiate's head
and face to be shaved. Shams al-Din-e Tabrizi relates how potential
disciples would come before Jalâl al-Din Rumi and ask for him to give
them a cloak of discipleship (*kherqeh*) and cut their hair. See *Maqâlât-e
Shams-e Tabrizi,* ed. Mohammad-'Ali Movahhed (Tehran: Khwârazmi,
1369/1990), 756.

another village who [even] made an insulting remark about him which the learned Ahmad tolerated and did not refute.

Ahmad later happened to meet with the Shaykh al-Islam, who told him, "I was once considering which of the scholars speak honestly about me and which of them speak uncharitably. When my thoughts turned to you, I realized you sometimes act like my disciple and sometimes seem to waver in your [devotion] and to side with my opponents. I do not know why."

"God forbid!" he said. "I have never doubted you."

The Shaykh said, "You fool! On such-and-such day in the village of Oshtu, you gave a fine sermon and sat down in the prayer niche and people started talking. There was a man who was not from that village, wearing a dark-blue gown with a colored patch sewn in the front. He was mocking me and you did not stop him, but tolerated his remarks."

The Shaykh related the whole incident. [234]

234. One Must be Candid

Shaykh 'Ali Shâyegâni also relates:

Once I was in the village of Arzaneh. A scholar from the village of Narshâd came and said, "I need some wood to build a khâneqâh." The Shaykh al-Islam ordered some wood for him. When he was about to leave, he ceremoniously asked the Shaykh al-Islam, "Would you permit us to bring a mount for you so that you could come together with us and set foot in our village to bless it with your presence?"

The Shaykh al-Islam said, "One should not talk nonsense. One should speak what is in his heart."

The scholar said, "My words are true to my heart."

The Shaykh al-Islam said, "After you left your village with your group of companions, you came to a cemetery. You sat at the foot of the wall of a dome. Your companions suggested, 'We should bring the Shaykh al-Islam [to our village] that we, too, might profit from his blessed fortune.' You, however, said, 'We should not, it would not be advisable, because if he were to come, the people of Mâlin would turn against us.' You all talked for a while in this vein."

That scholar was stunned and said nothing.

235. The Shaykh Knows the Hearts of the Hypocrites

The Eminent Khvâjeh Ahmad Ebrâhim-e Kârizi relates:
Once I accompanied Amir Taymur and a group of Turks on a visit to the Shaykh al-Islam. When we reached Kâriz-e Ma'd-âbâd, the Amir got off his horse.

The Turks said in Persian:[47] "The Eminent Khvâjeh Ahmad Ebrâhim [was wrong][48] to lead us ten farsangs out of our way for this visit." They were all mocking me, and the Amir chimed in, himself.

When we reached the presence of the Shaykh al-Islam, food was spread before us and we ate a meal. He counselled the Amir Taymur, saying, "If Amir Ilakdi[49] finds out that you have come here, accusations will be made about you. [235] But you must take care not to become close friends with them, for it would be harmful for you."

"No one dares to say anything against you in front of me," he said. "Never have I, nor anyone else in my presence, spoken ill of you."

The Shaykh said, "Don't talk nonsense. Did they not, just now, standing in the shade of that wall, speak against me?"

He explained the circumstances of everything that had been said.

236. Curing a Painful Joint

He also relates:

---

[47] Literally *'erâqi*, or the language of Iraq. *'Erâqi*, by which is meant *'erâq-e 'ajam*, "Persian Iraq," or the central provinces of greater Iran (including Isfahan, Tehran and Hamadan), is sometimes used as an epithet for the Persian language.

[48] The Persian text simply has the verb *kard*, but it appears that the scribe has left out a word that goes with it (e.g., *bad kard*).

[49] The text has *y-l-k-di*, which we have transliterated as Ilakdi. No such name appears in any of the Persian historical sources and may perhaps be a corruption of a Turkish title.

Once I had pain in my joint [*ostokhvân*] which lasted for nearly two years. I tried every remedy I knew of, to no avail.

One night I heard that the Shaykh al-Islam had come to the village of Kâriz. I performed a major ablution and stood behind him for the morning prayer. Afterwards, I told him, "This pain is really bothering me."

He said, "It will get better," and he said a prayer.

"You should look more closely at the problem," I said.

"Come here!" he said.

I went over to him and he rubbed a bit of his saliva on the spot and laid his hands over it. In an instant it seemed to me as if I had never had any pain at all.

237. The Shaykh Prevents the Divestiture of Property

He also relates:

Once the Sultan had decreed that Amir Ok-Taymur[50] should divest Khvâjeh Hosayn Ahmad-e Hosayn of his property. We were very upset about this.

One day I went before the Shaykh al-Islam and reported to him the situation. He said, "I will look into the matter this evening." The next morning, after performing our prayers, he told me, "Don't worry, he will never be able to do it."

Having heard this, I returned home heartened. The Lord Almighty removed the bad feeling from his heart and he asked for [236] only a few silver coins [*deram*].

238. The Shaykh is Aware of an Unseen Event

He also relates:

One day a group of horsemen were riding along. Amir Mozaffar

---

[50] This name does not appear in historical texts, but in the *Târikh-e mobârak-e ghâzâni* (ed. Karl Jan, 1940), 18, the name Kur-Taymur occurs, for which Ark-Taymur is listed as a manuscript variant. This latter name is quite similar to the one in the present text, which might also be a variant of Âq-Taymur. It is probably the same Taymur referred to in Story 235.

was [....]^{51} By the time we passed through the city of Sarakhs, we had already performed the morning prayer. Everyone was talking against the Shaykh al-Islam and mocking him.

All at once the leg of his horse broke through the surface of the bridge. It was so bad that the horse could not get up again and it died.

I said, "We performed the morning prayer; you should have said a rosary [*verd*] but you go on mocking the saints of God, the Almighty. You can expect no less than this."

They said, "This is your 'blessed' doing! You have been associated with him for too long."

When we returned from Sarakhs, the Shaykh al-Islam recounted the event in exact detail.

239. The Shaykh Knows What his Ill-wishers Say

He also said:

One night the Amir Ilakdi had had a little to drink with Amir Ok-Taymur, and they had been mocking the Shaykh al-Islam. In the morning we returned to the village of Delshin^{52} and sat at the foot of the fortress wall. They were still suffering the after-effects of drinking. The Amir began to prattle, giving advice to the Shaykh al-Islam.

Later, we went to see the Shaykh al-Islam, who told me, "You and the Amir were sitting at the foot of the fortress wall of Delshin, mocking me." He described it to me truly.

240. The Shaykh Knows the Dreams of Others

He also said:

One day the Shaykh al-Islam was sitting in the mosque in the village of Tâybâd. There was a scholar who was called Bu Bakr-e Ja'far. He pretended to be a friend, but always held a grudge against the Shaykh in his heart.

---

^{51} There is a lacuna here in the manuscript.

^{52} The toponym *d-l-sh-y-n*, which we have transliterated as Delshin, is not mentioned in the classical geographical sources.

One day he came to see the Shaykh al-Islam, who told him, "How long will you continue to come see me with [237] a grudge in your heart? If I tell you what you dreamt last night and interpret it for you, will you let go of your grudge?"

"I have been expecting that kind of a thing," he said, "for a long time."

The Shaykh said, "Before anything else, tell two people whom you trust what you dreamt last night, so that you cannot later deny what it was."

He secretly told two people of his dream. Then the Shaykh al-Islam recounted the dream. The two people were astonished and said, "He has recounted your dream for us; from his description we understood it better than from yours."

That scholar got up and repented. Two months later he was back to his old ways.

241. The Shaykh Predicts Sanjar Will Be King

At the time of Sultan Malekshah's demise, God's mercy upon him, Shaykh Bu Tâher, God sanctify his soul, said, "From among Malekshah's sons, it will be Barkyâroq."[53]

The Shaykh al-Islam, trusting the prediction of Bu Tâher,[54] began to pray for Sultan Barkyâroq. One night a traveler[55] warned him to pray for Prince [*Malek*] Sanjar. "He for whom you pray is supporting the Ismailis. Behold!" The Shaykh al-Islam looked and saw two pavilions—one pavilion on the right, another on the left, facing one another. He was told, "One of those two pavilions belongs to Barkyâroq, and the other to the Ismailis. Both of them are intent upon the life of Prince Sanjar. Pray for him, for through him great comfort will come to the Muslim community. These others will meet their demise and Sanjar will endure."

---

[53] That is Rokn al-Din Abu al-Mozaffar Barkyâroq (r. 1092-1105 / 485-498 A.H.), the eldest son of Malekshâh, who was only thirteen years old at the death of his father. See the article "Barkîâroq" by C. E. Bosworth in *Encyclopædia Iranica*.

[54] That is Abu Tâher-e Kord, the Shaykh's mentor. See Stories 5 and 82.

[55] For *âyandeh*, concerning which, see the note in Story 6.

Shaykh Bu Tâher had had a contrary vision. He said, "How could this be?" [His followers] said, "There is no mistake in the prediction of Shaykh Bu Tâher. Maybe it was the devil who showed you this vision."

Yet another night, it was revealed to the Shaykh al-Islam that the vision of Bu Tâher was not correct. [238] It came to pass as had been revealed to the Shaykh al-Islam and not as Shaykh Bu Tâher had said.[56]

242. The Shaykh Warns Sanjar not to Retreat from Battle

Some time later the Shaykh al-Islam was sitting in a vineyard. A man whom the Shaykh al-Islam did not know came in and said, "Prince Sanjar has been entrused to you. Why are you not looking out for him."

"Who am I," said the Shaykh, "that Prince Sanjar should be entrusted to me?!"

"Were you unworthy," he said, "he would not have been entrusted to you. Get up and rush to his aid, for the Ismailis are on the verge of conquering the world."

[The Shaykh relates]:

> "What am I to do?," I asked. As soon as they had said these words, I saw myself in a river which I had never seen before. I saw horsemen galloping along the river banks. They were galloping in the manner of a routed army and the horses looked exhausted.

The man who had led the Shaykh al-Islam there said, "Go take the reins from that man and make him turn back. Tell him, 'Where do you think you are going? The army of the Ismailis has fled!'"

The Shaykh al-Islam went forward and took the reins from Prince Sanjar, saying, "Where do you think you are going? Turn back and have courage, for the Ismailis have fled." Sanjar at first said, "Let me go," but when he heard the news, he did turn back.

---

[56] Cf. the modified version of this story given in *Rowzat al-rayâhin*, 30.

The Shaykh al-Islam relates:
> At this point, a trance overcame me and I found myself
> back in the same vineyard I had been in before. I told
> this to no one except for Shaykh Abu al-Hasan
> Sahâqari, who said, "Keep quite about this, or people
> will laugh at us."

Ten days later, the news of this rout reached us, just as the
Shaykh al-Islam had said. It was the talk of the town and everyone
learned of it.

Years later the Shaykh was going to the village of Kusu. He
recognized the river and said, "It was here that I made Prince
Sanjar turn back."

From the village where the Shaykh had been to Kusu was a
distance of forty-eight farsangs.[57] [239]

243. A Preacher Begs the Shaykh to Pray for Him

When the Shaykh al-Islam set out on his pilgrimage journey
[*safar-e Hejâz*], the city dignitaries came along to bid him
farewell, but he sent them all back home. The learned Imam 'Ali,
God have mercy upon him, accompanied the Shaykh all the way
to the opening of the underground aqueduct [*kâriz-gâh*]. When it
was time to turn back, he prostrated his head to the ground and
some yellowish water that had trickled from a pile of dung wetted
his beard. When he raised his head, some of it dripped from his
beard on to his clothes.

The Shaykh al-Islam felt sorry for him and asked, "What can I
do for you to requite this display of humility?"

He said, "I wish my sermon at Sar-e Pol [*S-r-p-l*] to be well-
received."

The Shaykh replied, "So it shall be."

---

[57] The order of the sentences in the Persian text appears to have been
scrambled by the scribe, where two sentences began with the same
phrase [*ba'd az ân*]. This final paragraph of the translation occurs a few
lines earlier in the text, but we have preferred this order in the narrative,
which is more sequential and is confirmed by the version of this same
story as given in *Rowzat al-rayâhin*, 31.

When the Shaykh returned from his pilgrimage journey, Imam 'Ali asked him, "Did you pray for me at all?"

He said, "I certainly did."

Imam 'Ali asked, "Why wasn't the audience larger?"

He said, "It is dependent upon my presence in the meeting."

On the day of the next sermon, the Shaykh al-Islam went to attend the meeting. So many people were gathered around that one could not make headway through the crowd, and Imam 'Ali's popularity never decreased.

244. The Secret of Successful Business Transactions

Mohammad-e Ghaznavi, God's mercy on him, related that:[58]

The Shaykh al-Islam was sitting in my house in Sarakhs. A man came in and set a strap of dates in front of him and said, "I'm from Nayshabur and I've brought some merchandise, but there is not much market for them. I am at a loss; for God's sake say a prayer that I may unload these."

The Shaykh al-Islam said, "You went into the bazaar and tried to strike several deals, until finally you bought these two maunds of fruit. First you said, 'I'll buy these,' then you said, 'I'll buy those, because they are cheaper.' If you keep to this method in buying and selling, you will come by much gold."

He said, "It is exactly as the Shaykh al-Islam recounts."

The Shaykh then said a prayer and the man left. Two or three [240] days later, he returned. He had sold all of his inventory and brought some gold coins and set them before the Shaykh al-Islam, saying, "For you! Everthing is now all right."

---

[58] This and the following story come after Story 125 in the manuscript of the Chester Beatty Library, but do not appear in the copy-text, the Nâfiz Pâshâ manuscript. The Chester Beatty Library manuscript groups several stories related by the author, Mohammad-e Ghaznavi, which could not, however, have been part of his original text of the *Spiritual Feats* (Stories 122-25 and Stories 244-45). It is clear from the introduction to this particular story and the phrase "God's mercy upon him," that Mohammad-e Ghaznavi is no longer alive at the time of writing. See also Story 298.

The Shaykh al-Islam said, "Take it with you and go in peace."

245. Sustenance from the Unseen World

Once we were eating supper in the home of the Shaykh al-Islam in Buzjân, but other than bread, there was no food. The scholar [*faqih*] Khvâjeh Mohammad-e Sani'i[59] said, "Go to my house and bring the jug of syrup so we can have it with our bread."

The Shaykh al-Islam said, "It's raining and the roads are muddy."

After a while Khvâjeh Mohammad said, "They have prepared a meal at my house and we are eating dry bread here."

The Shaykh answered, "If you will only be patient, food is on the way."

At exactly that moment two people from Amghân came in carrying a whole load of foodstuffs. We ate the rest of the bread with the food.

246. A Man Should not Pray on a Full Bladder[60]

One day, in the beginning of my association with the Shaykh al-Islam, he was speaking. The time to say the evening prayer arrived and my bladder was full. I thought I would miss the congregational prayer if I went to the lavatory, and so I performed the prayer.

When I was finished, the Shaykh turned around to me and said, "The way one of you prayed, it was as useless as if he had stood in prayer with a leather flask of wine on his back. The next time you have to go, don't say your prayers. Otherwise you will be put to shame, as I will reveal who I am talking about."

247. A Four Thousand Dinâr Penalty for Four Dinârs

Ostâd 'Ali Bizdi said:

---

[59] The manuscript reads *Mani'i* here, but the same figure is mentioned in Stories 130 and 368 as Sani'i.

[60] Cf. Story 20, in which the call of nature is likewise said to invalidate the prayers.

A group of us from Kâriz-e Sâʻed were walking along. Someone [241] from Buzjân came up to us and said to the Shaykh al-Islam, "The people of Buzjân bought a cow for four *dinârs* to sacrifice in your honor. Abu al-ʻAbbâs Mostowfi[61] took it from them and threatened them."

This upset the Shaykh al-Islam. The next day he told Ahmad Bu ʻAmr, "Go tell Abu al-ʻAbbâs to bring the meat of that cow to the bazaar on his own shoulders or else he'll have to answer for that four dinârs with four thousand."

Ahmad-e Bu ʻAmr went and came back. Abu al-ʻAbbâs had said, "I cannot do that—bring it into the middle of the bazaar—but I will pay for the cow."

"I will not accept it," said the Shaykh.

A few days later Abu al-ʻAbbâs was to be married. They had gone to great expense for his wedding and decorated several tents for the ceremony. Four of the Sultan's soldiers [*gholâm*] came to extract gold and ransacked the building and the decorated tents. They remained there for a while.

The brother of Abu al-ʻAbbâs, Khvâjeh Mohammad-e Mostowfi, sent word to the Shaykh al-Islam: "For the sake of God, the Almighty, our losses have reached a full four thousand dinârs. For God's sake, forgive us!"

248. Turning Gold to Dust

He also relates:

Once the people of Mâlin had said, "It's nothing but tricks, what he does. And if he claims that dust turns to gold in his hand, that is no great feat. If he is telling the truth, we will send a donkey load of dust for him to turn to gold."

The Shaykh sent this reply: "Turning dust to gold is easy and has been done many times. You bring me one hundred dinârs of gold. I will turn them to dust in my hand, or else call me a trickster."

There was a scholar called Ebrâhim Mohammad-e Ebrâhim

---

[61] The name Mostowfi suggests he may have been a tax collector or official treasurer.

from Sanjân. He said, "I was sitting in a group in front of the Shaykh al-Islam, thinking how can he turn gold to dust in his hand? [242] I saw a gold shaving in front of me and picked it up. I thought to myself, 'I will use this to buy something for my companions to eat.'"

I rolled it in my hand for a while. The gold began to change. I rubbed it a bit more and it turned completely to dust between my fingers and poured on the ground. The Shaykh al-Islam fixed me in his gaze and said, "If you do not believe me, this is how gold turns to dust."

249. You Have Made the Shaykh Appear Foolish

He further relates:

I was sitting in a circle with the Learned Sohayl and the Learned Abu al-Qâsem of Sanjar,[62] God have mercy upon them, in front of the Imam, God have mercy on him, in a corner of the mosque. The Imam said, "You make extremely exaggerated claims on behalf of this Shaykh Ahmad. You have made him look foolish. What do you mean by this? You will lose [respect][63] on his account and the religious scholars will have none left either. Mind what you are doing."

Khvâjeh Imam Esma'il said, "I am surprised at you. There was a time in Nayshabur when you would rise on his account from the street where you were and follow him all the way to 'Âsem street. We are your students and follow your lead."

Later, when we returned, the Learned Abu al-Qâsem went to see the Shaykh al-Islam in the village of Ma'd-âbâd. The Shaykh said, "What were you saying there in that corner of the mosque, at the foot of that stool? The learned Imam said such-and-such and Ostâd Imam Esma'il gave such-and-such reply and the learned 'Ali lacked the courage to contradict you and so stayed silent."

He recounted everything exactly as it had happened.

---

[62] The same person appears as narrator of Stories 157, 292 and 356.

[63] A word has apparently been dropped by the scribe at this juncture, but we infer it may have been *âb-e ru* or something to that effect.

250. A Spineless Man

He also said:

One day I was sitting in Bizd with the Learned Imam, God have mercy upon him. He said something insulting about the Shaykh al-Islam, to the effect that the Shaykh sometimes says things that are not exactly right. I said nothing.

The Shaykh al-Islam was in Buzjân and told Ahmad Bu 'Amr: "Look how spineless that Learned 'Ali is! He lacks the courage to speak up when they mock me in front of him. He just keeps quiet."

251. "O Lord, Fill Our Stomachs with Grapes"

[243] Once the Shaykh al-Islam was going to the hospice of Sohayl. Fifty of us accompanied him. Along the way he said, "There is some trouble for us ahead. I don't know what will happen."

We went on for a while, lost our way and got separated from one another. We were all worried. There were about ten of us going along with the Shaykh al-Islam. As the day grew warm, we got thirsty. He told Hosayn [...],[64] "Go look under that tree to see if there is any water there."

He did so and reported, "There is none."

The Shaykh went there, rubbed his hand over the pebbles two or three times and crystal clear water, more tasty than the purest water, appeared. He drank and the ten of us drank. He then said, "Clear a path for it." We cleared a path for it and it flowed by. He said, "This water will bring much vegetation."

When we had gone a little further, he said, "O Lord, fill our hearts with light and our stomachs with grapes." Right away a tree turned up that was laden with ripe black grapes. We picked the grapes and consumed them and our hearts were satisfied.

When we got to the other side of the valley, our friends rejoined

---

[64] There is a word here, perhaps part of Hosayn's name, which is unclear in the manuscript and cannot with certainty be reconstructed, other than the fact that it begins with the letter "R" or "Z" and ends in the letter "M."

us. There was running water there and we were extremely hungry.
A Turkoman appeared bringing three loaves of fried bread and a
bowl of milk. The Shaykh al-Islam stood up and broke off a piece
of bread for each one of us with his own hand, dipped it in the
milk and gave it to everyone. He gave everyone one piece and
then another and then a third. We were all sitting down. We all
grew full, so much so that we could not touch the food which was
brought to us that evening in the village.

252. Mediation Between God and His Creatures

He relates:
The people of Bâkharz have said, "The repentance of the people
of Jâm will do no good. The Shaykh al-Islam may use his tricks
over there, but it will not work in the area of Mâlin."[65]
The Shaykh al-Islam had once said, "If [244] I go there one day,
just let them try to keep their curly hair and their robes."[66]
On the return from Sohayl's hospice, we came upon a village in
the district of Bâkharz called Kâheh. We stayed there that night
and performed the evening prayers. I reminded the Shaykh about
what he had said in reply to the people of Bâkharz. He said, "If
that is what I said, then that is what will happen."
He turned to the people and said, "When there is conflict
between two friends and offense is taken, a mediator is needed.
Now then, is there anyone who has taken offense at the Almighty
God, that we might mediate for him?"
A cry arose and they began to repent. The following day the
whole district repented and shaved their hair.

---

[65] The text gives Mâlân, which is the same as Mâlin or Mâlan. It is
the principle city of the district of Bâkharz. Hamd Allâh Mostowfi,
writing in the early 14th century, described it as a large and pleasant
town. See *Nozhat al-qolub*, ed. Le Strange (Leiden, 1915), 188.

[66] That is, they will pull out their hair and tear open their robes as a
result of the spiritual excitement they will experience through the
Shaykh.

253. It is God and Not Food that Gives Strength

Once we were with the Shaykh al-Islam during the month of Ramadan. They set out the tablespread, but there was only a loaf and a little something to go with it. I thought to myself, "What good will this do? How will we keep the fast tomorrow after such a meal?!"

The Shaykh said, "Do not worry, it is God and not food that gives strength." That night it happened that they they brought the pre-dawn meal [*sahar*], but the call to prayer arose, and the food was left unfinished.

In the morning I asked permission to go to the village of Bizd, which was five farsangs away. I was on foot. I did not get tired, nor hungry nor thirsty, and thus I learned that strength comes from the Almighty God, and not from food.

254. Melons as a Cure for Ear-ache

He also said:

My ear was aching. Sometimes it would become intense and I would be in extreme pain. One day I went from Buzjân to visit the Shaykh al-Islam in Ma'd-âbâd. Melon was served. I thought that if I were to eat melon for lunch, my ear would grow worse and I would perish.

He told me, "Have some melon, and do not be afraid. The pain will go away."

For his sake, I ate some. Just then I left and came to the village. At home they brought melon. I heeded the advice of that shaykh and ate my fill.

At night I started vomiting and I was purged of that malady and never had any earache again. [245]

255. The Shaykh's Healing Hand

Once my back was aching and I was in great pain. I couldn't rest at all.

One day the Shaykh al-Islam passed his hand through my sleeve over my arm and to my back. He put his hand right on the spot that

hurt without my telling him where it was. No sooner did he put his
hand there, than the pain went away.

256. Giving Alms Saves the Donor from Trouble

He also said:
At the holiday, the Shaykh al-Islam told the wife [*qowm*] of
Army Commander 'Omar, "Things can happen when you are
away from home."
She gave alms in large amounts for her husband's sake. Later on
it became known that, at that very moment, Army Commander
'Omar had fallen from his horse in Gorgân. His condition was
such that he had to be carried to his lodgings on a stretcher [*bar
jâmeh*]. There was no hope that he would live.
When the alms were given, he got better. It was truly a wonder.

257. The Shaykh and the Mountain Sheep

This is about when Prince Arghun[67] plundered Nayshabur. They
took some sheep and the flocks dispersed. From that time on for
seven years the Shaykh al-Islam ate no meat, as there was
considerable doubt about its legality.[68] During that time, for the
sake of his guests—so that they would not be left unprovided
for—he would set traps on the mountainside, and he would eat
[from this game] himself.
One day a sheep was caught in the trap. The Shaykh al-Islam
was aware of this. He got up and set out after the sheep. When the
sheep saw him, it shrunk away from him and threw itself off the
hilltop. There was nowhere for it to go. By the time the Shaykh
climbed up to where it was, the mountain sheep [*boz*] had reached
another peak more precipitous ['*azim tar*] than the first.
It was time for the noon prayer. The Shaykh thought, "If I go

---

[67] This may perhaps be Mozaffar al-Din Alp Arghun ebn Yarnaqosh,
one of the governors of the Seljuk Sultan Mohammad ebn-e Mahmud
(r. 1105-1118 / 498-511 A.H.).

[68] That is to say, it was not clear who was the rightful owner of any
sheep and it therefore could not be ascertained if the meat was lawful to
a Muslim.

after it, I'll be late for my prayers. And if I say my prayers, the sheep will die." He kept calling out to the sheep, "Come here, let me remove the fetters from your leg."

He[69] relates: The sheep came back from where it had gone and turned in the direction of the Shaykh, running towards him. [246] When it came up to him, the Shaykh reached out and took hold of the trap. The sheep began to flail about and the Shaykh forgot what he had told it earlier. The Shaykh killed it and when he remembered [what he had promised] he was extremely upset. He said, "My deed has made this meat unlawful to me."

And so he no longer trapped game after that.[70]

258. Punishment for a Lecherous Amir

When the Shaykh al-Islam came to Buzjân, a number of people repented and many good things happened. It was no longer possible to do sinful things in public and all the musical instruments [asbâb-e malâhi] were smashed. A grudge developed in the heart of an Amir there and his relatives, and grew until they openly denied the Shaykh. Some of the scholars also sided with him.

One day this Amir had said, "The Shaykh has tied my friends' hands."

Someone answered, "It is the fault of your Excellency for not saying anything about it."

The Amir said, "I will evict him from this city or the fault will be mine."

---

[69] Perhaps 'Ali Bizdi is meant; he narrated Story 247 through 250, and may be the authority meant by "he relates" or "he also said" in Stories 252 to 256. However, the compiler of the text or the scribe may have mistaken this 'Ali with the Imam Ostâd 'Ali, probably Imam Razi al-Din 'Ali ebn Ebrâhim Elyâs of Tâybâd, who relates Story 271ff.

[70] Cf. the similar version of the story told in Rowzat al-rayâhin, 32. Interestingly, this is one of the few stories that show the Shaykh as negligent or unmindful in any way. He atones for his broken promise to the entire species of sheep, by forswearing their meat and thereby sparing their lives. See also Story 301.

This situation was brought to the attention of the Shaykh al-Islam. One of the Shaykh's disciples, whose name was Ovays, was one of the elite chamberlains [of the Amir]. The Shaykh, through him, sent a message to the Amir: "Several times I have overlooked [your behavior]. Now you are really bragging. Let us see whether you will throw me out of the city, or I you."

Before the year was out, the fiefdom that had been granted several generations back was taken from him [the Amir] and his situation grows yet worse day by day.

259. The Shaykh Wills the Removal of the Amir

This same Amir came to visit the Shaykh al-Islam one day. The Shaykh said, "If there has been an alteration in your attitude [toward me], I will pray [*be-guyam*] to the Lord Almighty to return your fiefdom to you. But if you still feel the same way as before, take care that you do not lose everything else on that account."

He said, "I am no longer following that path." [247] But he was not telling the truth, for his companions threw him off course.

Some time passed and the Shaykh al-Islam grew dissatisfied with the Preacher in Bizd, who was removed from office [and a new preacher was appointed]. The Amir was the governor of Bizd and he sent a decree [*manshur nevesht*] against the [new] Preacher to spite the Shaykh al-Islam [*be-ta'assob-e Shaykh al-Islam*]. Word reached the Shaykh that, "The Amir has removed your Preacher from office."

The Shaykh al-Islam replied, "No matter, we have removed the Amir from office." Some people laughed at these words.

Two months later the village was removed from the control of the Amir and the governorship was taken from him.

260. The Shaykh Knows the Thoughts of Others

A messenger once came from Ghazna and the Sadr al-Islam[71] was about to pay a visit to him. The Shaykh al-Islam said, "Give a message to him from me."

---

[71] An official who has authority over religious matters.

The Sadr al-Islam said, "Very well."

The Shaykh told him what to say. The Sadr al-Islam went to see the messenger and returned. The Shaykh al-Islam asked, "Did you deliver my message to him?"

"I forgot," said the Sadr al-Islam.

The Shaykh said, "You forgot!? You said such and such and he said this and that. You received the answer you wanted. Four times you intended to give him my message, but you didn't. You were afraid that he would not be pleased, and so you did not tell him."

The Sadr al-Islam said, "Indeed, that is exactly what happened." [248]

261. Opening a Locked Door

One day the Learned Imam, God have mercy upon him, was standing in Fasâvarz with all of the saints[72] at the door of the house of the village Lord. They said in jest, "Open the door and we will plunder his house."

They tried with every possible tactic to open the door, but could not. One of them said, "Miracles are good for just such occasions. We need to work a miracle to open the door."

The Learned Imam looked at the Shaykh al-Islam. "It's you they are asking for."

The Shaykh said, "Very well, open the door!"

They said, "We cannot."

He said, "Put your hand on the door." They touched the door and it opened.

262. A Closed Door

One day they were trying to open the door of the Mausoleum of Ostâd Eshâq in Nayshabur, which is where the learned Ahmad

---

[72] *Owliâ*, the Arabic broken plural form of *vali*, saint, or "friend [of God]." Elsewhere in the text, the Persian plural *valiân* occurs, apparently in the technical sense of the followers of Mohammad ebn-e Karrâm. See Stories 57 and 266.

Bajestâni is also buried. However hard they tried, they could not open it. Someone said, "This door will not open."[73]

263. How A Little Bag of Gold Appears Before the Shaykh

One day the learned Imam 'Ali, God have mercy upon him, was gathered with Khvâjeh [249] Imam Bu al-Hasanak Dibâjeh and a few more of the Imams and nobles, along with a hundred other people, at the tombstone of Ostâd Mohammad Shâd. The Qur'ân reciters asked that something be donated to build a tomb.

One of them said, "Each one of you could give something."

The Reciter Hosaynak said, "There is a person here who can pick up a stone and it will turn to gold, so giving gold is not much of a problem." He said this with sarcasm.

Everyone then gave a little someting until the turn of the Shaykh al-Islam came. He was greatly embarrassed, because he had nothing. Ostâd Imam Esma'il was sitting next to him. He said, "If you have no coins, I'll give you some. How much do you need? Tell me."

The Shaykh al-Islam said, "O God, will you thus put me to shame?"

A purse of pure gold appeared in front of him, and he said, "There is no need for gold. If we ought to give gold, here, take this!"

The Shaykh gave the purse to him, unopened.

264. Spit in Exchange for Cloth

When he was in Tâybâd, he once bought some cloth [for veils] for his children. He paid in gold, but needed a half-dinâr more, which he did not have. Someone said, "A miracle would be perfect for a day like this."

The Shaykh al-Islam said, "You are right, it just now occured to me." He spit in the pan of the scale and said, "Weigh it."

---

[73] The story must be incomplete, though this is all that the manuscript gives us. It would make more sense for this story to come at the beginning of Story 261, in place of the jest to plunder the village lord's house.

They weighed it and it was even.[74]

265. The Shaykh Makes Gold with a Glance

Once he was in the house of Village Lord Mahmud of Bizd. They were weighing gold. They were one and a half drams [*dâng*] short. Two or three times they jiggled the scale this way and that, but it came out one and a half drams short.

They said, "You need this much more gold."

The Shaykh gazed upon the gold and motioned for them to weigh it again. They weighed it and it came out to be exactly the right amount!

266. You Cannot Outfox the Shaykh

One day the Learned Imam, God have mercy upon him, gave a sermon. He wanted to mention the Shaykh [250] in his prayers, but he did not do it because the Karrâmites[75] were hostile to the Shaykh, and the Imam was concerned about his own reputation. When the Learned Imam met the Shaykh al-Islam afterwards, he made flattering remarks and said, "I forgot [to mention you] on the lectern [*korsi*]."

The Shaykh al-Islam said, "Oh yes, that's true. When you came to such-and-such point in your talk, you were about to praise me, but your pride [*heshmat*] would not allow you. And behind my back, in your circle with so-and-so and so-and-so in the mosque, you spoke of me thus. Now, when you come before me, you whisper praises in my ear. This is very foxy behavior, but you can't outfox me."

He said, "You are so right!"

267. Protection From Locusts

Once locusts descended upon the area surrounding Nayshabur

---

[74] Either the tale implies that the spit turned to gold, or it is intended sarcastically.

[75] *Valiân*; see the note in Story 57 for this word, and also Story 261.

and a village which they call Ja'far-âbâd. They took the Shaykh al-Islam there. He walked all around the perimeter of the village. The locusts came and devoured the areas all around them, but did not harm a single spike of their wheat.

268. How to Combat Locusts

The people of Jâm once came to Nayshabur and asked the Shaykh al-Islam, "Will there be locusts this year or not?" He said, "If you will do as I say, I will tell you."

They said, "To hear is to obey!"

He said, "Over there"—and he described three places where they had made nests [*khâneh*]—"If you first dig up that ground and turn over the soil and plow it, you then plant seeds. If not, all your efforts will be lost [251] and they will consume your crops."

They went back and related this story. Some of the people said, "That's meaningless. Only God knows what is hidden." They didn't believe him, saying, "We have never seen any locust nests! How could he see them from forty farsangs away?"

Eventually locusts appeared in such numbers in the place he had described that the whole region was lost because of them.

269. Punishment for the Ill-wishers of the Shaykh

There was a man in Buzjân called Hâji Turkoman. At first he was a disciple of the Shaykh al-Islam, but later turned against him and began to quarrel with him. One day [they were building] the wall of the silver manor[76]...He told the brickmaker, "Raise [*n-sh-v*] this wall well, and I will plaster it and whitewash it. Then I will bring your Shaykh and hang him from this wall, to show how pretty he looks on this wall."

Word of this reached the Shaykh al-Islam, who said, "If he gets the chance to live in that manor and he remains on the face of the earth, let him hang me, or worse."

What the Shaykh al-Islam had said was conveyed to the Hâji. He got up and went to the army camp seeking an order to proceed and

---

[76] *Kushk-e sim*; there appears, however, to be a lacuna in the manuscript here, and several words may be missing.

hang the Shaykh. The Hâji was in the service of the Amir Jâveli Soltân and had control over the entire city. Whatever he wanted, he could certainly have.

Off he went and here we are still waiting for him to come back with the order. What became of him is an admonition for all the peoples of the world. He turned black and took on a monstrous aspect. His children were never able to live in that manor and he, himself, never saw it again.

270. A Wife Wants Her Husband to Die

While the Shaykh al-Islam was in Amghân, there was a woman who worked in his house as a servant. [252] One day her husband came and said, "Long live the Shaykh al-Islam! It has been nearly a year that this woman is working at your house. Because she is in your service, I have not objected. I am a poor man. No matter what I tell her, she will not come back home. If you would send her back home, I would be very obliged."

The Shaykh al-Islam went in the interior of the house and said [to his own wives]: "Why don't you send this woman home?"

They said, "We tell her to go, but she will not."

The Shaykh said, "Woman, get up and go home, for this situation will result in much gossip."

She saw no recourse and said, "Long live the Shaykh al-Islam! As you know, I have faithfully served this household [*marâ haqq-e khedmat ast*]. For God's sake say a fervent prayer for me."

The Shaykh said a prayer to cheer her heart: "O God, fulfill her hopes." He was sure the prayer had been answered, and asked, "I have prayed and it has been fulfilled. What was your desire?"

The woman put her lips to the ground and gave thanks to Almighty God. The Shaykh asked, "What was it you desired?"

She said, "That the Lord Almighty would take the life of my husband so that I might be freed."

He said, "You fool! His blood is on your hands!" The Shaykh al-Islam said some things to the woman and then he told the man, "This woman has spilled your blood." He told him the story in the presence of nearly fifty people, more or less, in that house. The man got up and went outside. He collapsed in the middle of the village and gave up the ghost.

271. The Shaykh's Kindness toward the Hostess

Ostâd Imam 'Ali[77] relates:
One day my sister held a banquet in Tâybâd for the Shaykh al-Islam. The guests were seated. The Shaykh, a piece of bread covered with meat sitting before him, looked at me and said, "Take this and give it to the mistress of the house." He had never seen my sister.

I went to the kitchen, but did not find her there. I gave the meat to my mother and other sisters, and returned.

The Shaykh told me, "My, how trustworthy you are! I told you to give that to the mistress of the house and you gave it to others." Once again he gave some meat for me to give to her, which I went and did. [253]

272. The Shaykh's Vast Knowledge about the Transmission of Hadith

He also relates:
I learned a tradition and began a sermon with it one day. I forgot one man in the chain of transmission. When I was finished, I asked the Shaykh, "How was my sermon today?"

He said, "You speak well and knowledgeably. If there is an occasional oversight and you leave out one of the names [in the chain of transmission], since the meaning of the tradition is not changed, there is no harm done."

If I had recited this tradition before a hundred Imams and Hadith scholars, it is inconceivable that they would have noticed.

---

[77] Probably Imam Razi al-Din 'Ali ebn Ebrâhim Elyâs-e Tâybâdi (see "Manuscripts of the Spiritual Feats" in the Introduction). Several of the anecdotes from Story 261 to this point in the manuscript pertain to events involving "Imam 'Ali," though they are not narrated by him. This is not absolutely certain, however, as there are other Ostâd 'Alis given as authorities for some of the stories (see the note for "He relates" in Story 257), though they do not seem to be Imams.

273. A Rosary Missing Beads

He also said:
Khvâjeh Imam, peace be upon him and the mercy of God, was called to God. He had willed that his cane, knife and rosary be given to the Shaykh al-Islam. The servant in the khâneqâh took six beads and gave three of them to an old woman, keeping the other three for himself. He brought the rest of the rosary, along with the cane, and placed them before the Shaykh al-Islam.

The Shaykh al-Islam said, "There should be six more beads in this rosary."[78] The servant stuck his hand in his pocket and gave the three beads he had there to the Shaykh, who said, "There should be three more."

The servant said, "An old woman has them."

274. The Shaykh's Knowledge of the Dead

He also said:
[The Shaykh] was walking in the cemetery of Tâybâd visiting the graves. I pointed to one grave that had a heap of dirt on it. He paid no attention and kept walking along till he reached the head of my father's grave. He had never been there nor had he heard it was my father's. When we came back home he told me, "He was a truly good man, the one buried under that heap, and a great man, too, and forebearing, was your father." And, in truth, that was the case. [254]

275. The Shaykh's Healing Glance

An ugly and completely crazy man was once brought before the Shaykh. He was so crazy he could not be restrained by chains and fetters. He remained like this until the eyes of the Shaykh fell upon him. He immediately came to his senses. The Shaykh al-Islam recited something over him and he went away happy.

---

[78] Since the number of beads in a rosary was fixed by tradition, this feat is quite calculated, and hardly miraculous.

276. The Shaykh Has Control Over Hail

He also relates:
Once there was hail [*zhâleh*] in Estâd and it nearly caused great damage. They cried out for help to the Shaykh al-Islam. He cast his gaze across the skies and muttered something. Right away the hail turned to rain and no more hail fell for several years after. [....]79

One day I was thinking, "If hail stops because of someone's spiritual concentration, well, in India children drive away the hail. It's no great wonder if one can do likewise in the Islamic realms." These doubts passed through my mind and I swore an oath [to God to drive away the hail (?)], but it was useless. Where the Shaykh al-Islam was, hail had fallen and then stopped.

He saw me the next day and asked, "Why did you drive away the hail?"

I said, "You are the constable in these parts, not me."

He said, "I just did what I could."

277. It Is Wrong To Build A Khâneqâh With Illicit Wood

He also said:
I was in the midst of renovating this khâneqâh. One day I went to the Shaykh al-Islam, who told me, "What do you think about this verse: '*Whoso has done an atom's weight of good shall see it and whoso has done an atom's weight of evil shall see it*'?"80

I said, "It is the truth."

"Then why are you using illicit wood in this khâneqâh?," he asked. "Don't you know that no good will come of it?"

"Let me look into the matter," I said.

I looked into the matter. Someone had given me a tree. I cut it down. Later on it became apparent that it belonged to his [255] wife. I went and asked for her forgiveness.

---

79 There may be a lacuna in the manuscript at this point, for the subsequent paragraph seems to assume a return of hailstorms to the area.

80 Qur'ân 99:7-8

278. Insincere Friends

In the beginning of the Shaykh al-Islam's ministry, my brother, 'Abd al-Salâm, did not believe in him. Then one day he was giving me this advice: "You must show regard for the Shaykh al-Islam and faithfully support him, for he now holds sway and in these parts everyone is his disciple. In order to further your best interests, you have no choice but to show him due regard."

Later on, I took a group of people to Ma'd-âbâd one day to help the Shaykh al-Islam, who was building the khâneqâh. As we sat down to eat, he turned to his followers and said, "My special friends! Do you still look after me for ulterior motives and help me out of your own self-interest?" He divulged his knowledge of everything we had said.

279. Lights in the Sky Over Ma'd-âbâd

He also said:
One night we went to visit the Shaykh al-Islam. We saw five lights like torches high up in the sky. We saw them all night long hovering over Ma'd-âbâd until morning came and we performed our prayers. Several trustworthy followers saw it as well.[81]

280. The Shaykh Dismisses the Village Mayor

He also said:
When the Shaykh al-Islam granted the mayorship of Amghân to Khvâjeh As'ad, the people repeatedly tried to have him removed. No one was able to dismiss him. One day his brother came before the Shaykh and the Shaykh said to him: "The people are complaining about your brother. [256] He should be more careful about what he does, or I will dismiss him."

The brother said, "No one can dismiss him."

The Shaykh al-Islam said, "I have dismissed him!"

At that moment, he was dismissed. Later a letter came from

---

[81] This constitutes perhaps the first description of a UFO-like phenomenon in Persian literature!

Amir Qomâj[82] dismissing him.

281. Treating A Sick Horse

The distinguished Khvâjeh Bu Sâleh of Amghân said:
Once there was a man from Pâshân on the outskirts of Herat who had a horse that was extremely sick. He brought a knife to kill it, as there was no hope for it.
The Shaykh al-Islam passed by and the man said, "Look at this horse for a minute."
The Shaykh looked the horse over and put his foot on its back and said, "Rise!" The horse got up and went off in good health.

282. The Death Of Mr. Insolence

He also relates:
I once said in front of the Shaykh al-Islam, "Khvâjeh Eqbâl is always[83] very insolent and he accuses the Shaykh of abandoning religion and becoming a sectarian."
The Shaykh bowed his head for a moment and said, "[Fate's] arrow has struck him and it is only a matter of time before he falls."
Ten days later, he fell ill and died.

283. A Bite Of Halva Rewards An Honest Word

One day 'Ali Abu Nasr of Amghân was in the company of some people who were mocking the Shaykh al-Islam. 'Ali said, "He is said to be a great man."
The next day the Shaykh al-Islam gave him a bite of halvâ, saying, "Eat this 'Ali Bu Nasr. You said one good word and I give you one bite. Had you said more, I would have given you more."
[257]

---

[82] The chamberlain of the Seljuk Sultans Malekshâh, Barkyâroq and Sanjar. He had many fiefdoms, was quite powerful and participated in many military campaigns. See the index of Râvandi, *Râhat al-sodur*, for information about him.

[83] Reading *nahmâr* for *n-h-m-â*.

284. The Shaykh's Expenses On Pilgrimage

Shaykh Ya'qub of Hasanâbâd[84] said:
I went with the Shaykh al-Islam from Nayshabur on the pilgrimage journey. We had only one and a half gold dinârs. When we reached Bastâm, our friends calculated that they had spent seven dinârs along the way. The Shaykh said, "Mark it down in my account, and I will pay. The expenses are on me all the way up to Baghdad."

When we arrived in Baghdad, the accounts showed that he had spent one hundred twenty dinârs on the camels, provisions, pack animals and equipment he had bought.[85]

285. Amir Onar's Gift Of A Camel

He furthermore said:
When we left from Nayshabur, Amir Onar was returning from the hunt. He saw the Shaykh al-Islam and said farewell.

We went off and halted after a distance of seven farsangs. The Amir was instructed in a dream to send a camel for the Shaykh, and so he sent a camel. The Shaykh al-Islam would not accept it. The Amir's Imam [sic] said, "He had a dream in which the Best [of Creatures],[86] the blessings of God upon him, instructed the Amir to send a camel."

The Shaykh said, "Well, since the Best [of Creatures] has commanded him, I will accept." The Shaykh took the camel, but gave him a knife [tigh] he had in return.[87]

---

[84] The manuscript actually appears to read Hasâbâd, but since no such toponym exists, this most likely represents a scribal error for Hasanâbâd, of which there were two in the area surrounding Jâm. One of them is mentioned in Story 326.

[85] Cf. the different version given in *Rowzat al-rayâhin*, 34, and also the less mysterious version given in Story 288.

[86] *Mehtar*, literally "the greater/greatest," but here an epithet for the Prophet Muhammad.

[87] Cf. the version of this story in *Rowzat al-rayâhin*, 33.

286. Predicting the Birth of a Boy

'Ali Asfarghâbadi relates:
Once we were riding down the road and the Shaykh al-Islam said, [258] "Keep your donkey a little further away!"
I said, "Grant me a son."
The Shaykh said, "I have granted you a son."
I said, "I believe you," and the Shaykh said, "I have named him 'Omar."
"So be it," I said.
I thought, "I have no wife, how will this come about?"
Later, when we arrived in Buzjân, he told me, "Your son has arrived!" I went home and on the fourth day afterward, a boy was born to my sister, who named him 'Omar.

287. The Shaykh Grants a Son

Bu Hafs Kusu'i related:
I had no children. I asked the Shaykh al-Islam for a son. He said, "I grant you a son." A little while after that a son was born to me.

288. How the Shaykh Provides Food

Hâji Ya'qub related further:
Our provisions ran out in the desert. When we arrived in Medina, the Shaykh gave me three and a half dinârs. I bought sixteen maunds of wheat and we lived on that. Whenever we ran out of flour, I would boil a bit of that wheat and the Shaykh al-Islam would serve it to us with his own hands. We would eat it and remain full until the same time the following day. We ate nothing else all the way to Baghdad, and there were six of us. That sixteen maunds was enough food for us for nearly two hundred and fifty farsangs.[88]

---

[88] Cf. *Rowzat al-rayâhin*, 34. This story is also clearly related to Story 284.

289. Reprimand for a Foul-mouthed Man

Brother 'Ali Asfarghâbadi has said:
Abu al-Hasan Hakim-e Buzjâni spoke ill of the Shaykh al-Islam.
Then one day 'Ali[89] came and said to the Shaykh al-Islam, "I
heard Abu al-Hasan say such-and-such about you."

The Shaykh al-Islam said, "If he ever says anything like that
about me again, on that day you will know that he is a man and I
am his woman. Is there no one to deliver this message to him?"

'Ali Asfarghâbadi relates:
I went and delivered the message. He said, "Indeed, either of
these is [259] a possibility" [âri mi-bovad az har guneh].

'Ali Asfarghâbadi told him: "Go and apologize to him that you
may avoid [the consequences]." He laughed and went on his way.
What happened to him three days later was an example to those
who denied the Shaykh.

290. The Seed of a Son within a Date

He also relates that:
The Lord of the village of Tohrâbâd asked the Shaykh al-Islam
for a son. The Shaykh gave him several dates and said, "I have
enclosed your son in these dates." Exactly nine months later, a son
was born to him.

Afterwards he said something impertinent about the Shaykh al-
Islam. The Shaykh said, "Do not do that. Just as the boy has been
given on my account, he can be taken away."

The village Lord went away and continued with his
impertinences. Two months later the son died.

291. The Shaykh Denounces a Scholar

He also relates:
One day the scholar 'Abd al-Rahmân, in the midst of a lecture,
criticized the Shaykh. A veiled one [a woman] conveyed this

---

[89] The manuscript actually indicates that Abu al-Hasan came, but this
is clearly a scribal error.

information in a gathering of the Shaykh, who was very insulted.

The following Friday the Shaykh al-Islam was present as 'Abd al-Rahmân's lecture was about to begin. They performed the Friday prayers and then the Shaykh al-Islam got up and said, "This lectern was not put here for people to speak of God, the Exalted and Glorified, anthropomorphically. If anyone ever speaks from this lectern again, then you can shave my face clean [*mu-ye ru-ye man forud ârid*] and believe whatever negative things have been said about me."

'Abd al-Rahmân lived for seven years after that, but was never able to lecture from that lectern.

292. The Shaykh Describes the Features and Words of His Opponents

The learned Abu al-Qâsem of Sanjar said:[90]

He sent me to Mâlin on a mission, saying, "Go to Mâlin. Four people were sitting around a little pool there—a certain Khvâjeh Hosayn and a [260] Khvâjeh Adib, a man of medium height with a beard that curls upward [*gusheh-rish be-bâlâ va miâneh*]. If you find him to be as I have described, then what I have said is true; otherwise it must be a demon who revealed it to me."

Hosayn Zaynab and I saw this man after the evening prayer, just exactly as the Shaykh al-Islam had described. Well, I told him the Shaykh had given a description of him. He laughed in disbelief and we fell to arguing.

I asked him, "Weren't there four of you yesterday around the little pool?"

They [sic] said, "There were four of us."

"Didn't you mock the Shaykh al-Islam?," I asked.

"We did," he said.

I said, "Did you not debate among yourselves what discipleship and faithfulness consist of?"

He said, "We did."

I said, "Does not Adib fit such-and-such description?"

"He does."

"So, what do you say now?"

---

[90] He appears in the next story and also relates Stories 157 and 356.

He said, "Nothing."[91]

293. The Shaykh Promises to Ward Off Calamity in Exchange for a Camel

He also relates:

The Shaykh al-Islam was about to go on pilgrimage to the Hijâz. He told me to convey the following to Shojâ' al-Molk Ahmad: "I see trouble ahead for you. I saw a flood carrying off your camel. Load up a camel and send it to my house in Sâghu that you might be spared this calamity."

The Shaykh went from Ma'd-âbâd to Sâghu. Shojâ' al-Molk went there in person, taking fifteen pure gold dinârs[92] with him, which he placed before the Shaykh, saying, "Abu al-Qâsem of Sanjar gave me your message. I have followed your instructions and am bringing money for a camel, as there were no camels available."

The Shaykh al-Islam smiled and said, "There is no need for your gold; the reason for the camel was rather that all who saw it might pray [for you] and that the calamity might be warded off." He did not accept the gold, saying, "Do not fret, that which has been ordained shall come to pass." The Shaykh set out on his journey.

The son of Shojâ' al-Molk and the Governor of the village (grew hostile to one another and a skirmish broke out).[93] The Governor hit Shojâ' al-Molk with an axe,[94] inflicting a life-threatening [261] wound. The constable came and took ten camels from Shojâ' al-Molk, which he saw neither hide nor hair of again. He also had to pay nearly a thousand dinârs in taxes in order to stay in his house.

---

[91] The text of this story may be incomplete.

[92] *Zar-e rokni*; see the footnote in Story 75.

[93] There is a lacuna in the manuscript at this point. The text in parentheses is supplied by *Rowzat al-rayâhin* (33), which also relates a version of this story.

[94] The manuscript has *tir*, an arrow, but *Rowzat al-rayâhin* (33) supplies *tabar*, an axe, a reading which we have preferred. The two words are distinguished one from the other by a single dot in the Persian script, so the possibility of scribal error is high.

294. A Cord of Wood as a Gift for the Shaykh

He also relates:

We had gone one day to Ma'd-âbâd to see the Shaykh al-Islam. Along the way I said, "One cannot go before him empty-handed. Let us cut some firewood and take it with us."

We loaded two donkeys, one of which ran away. We had great trouble getting him back again. He had thrown off his saddle pack and broken the straps.

We went before the Shaykh. Before he even saw my friends or the firewood, he came out of his room, saying, "I have been waiting for you a long while. You were gathering that firewood and the donkey slipped away from you and the straps broke and it was a lot of trouble for you." He recounted everything that had happened.

295. An Apple For the Shaykh's Guest

He also relates:

I told my son, "Go pick some apples from that tree so we can take them to the Shaykh." He went and picked them. We left the village and had reached the fields when a friend came up and fetched me to come back to attend to a contract. I went and sealed the contract, and then set out.

When we reached the Shaykh al-Islam, the donkeys with their loads were still behind us. The Shaykh al-Islam said, "I have been waiting for you for a long time; I could have used those apples, as Khvâjeh Eqbâl was our guest—he's still here, over there in that garden."

The apples were still with the donkeys, but the Shaykh revealed why we had turned back and delayed for an hour, and then come back. He recounted the entire adventure.

296. A Qur'ân Reciter With Overtones of Women in His Voice

Once the Shaykh al-Islam was in the village of Asfarghâbad. I went to see him. I asked Abu al-Hasan [262] the Washerman [*Gâzar*] where the Shaykh was. He said, "He is sleeping over there, and cannot be disturbed." I was about to leave town and was set on seeing the Shaykh before hand. The Shaykh stuck his head out of the window and said, "Who is it who is looking for me and has three times shaken me and disturbed my sleep? Let him come in."

I went in and saw him for a while. The Qur'ân reciter [*moqri*] of Torshiz came in and chanted a verse of scripture. The Shaykh said, "Have you asked for some girl's hand in marriage?" He said, "No." The Shaykh said, "Go contract a marriage in order to preserve your chastity."

When he left, the Shaykh told Abu al-Hasan the Washerman, "That Qur'ân reciter is sluggish[95] and his chanting reeks of women."

Abu al-Hasan said, "It is his habit to brag on and on and to hover around the ladies whenever possible."

297. The Shaykh Hears the Complaint of the Dead

He also relates:

Ostâd Imam Abu al-Qâsem of Asfarghâbad had been given a sheet of cloth [*châdor-i*] by his mother, Lady [*Kadbânu*] 'Âyesheh. She said, "I spun this when I was a child. Make a shroud with this half [*sheqqeh*] for your brother, the Imam Qâzi, and keep the other half for yourself." Abu al-Qâsem complied with her will.

When Abu al-Qâsem was called to God, his half [of the shroud] was in the hands of a servant girl and the people, not knowing about it, [263] buried him.

Some time later the Shaykh al-Islam paid a visit to his grave and said, "This Imam is complaining because they have not wrapped him in his half of the mother's sheet of cloth. He is very upset because of this." The Shaykh al-Islam had never heard of this sheet of cloth, as it was a secret between mother and son.

298. The Shaykh Feeds a Multitude with a Basket of Dates

He also said:

---

[95] i.e., in taking a wife. Cf. Story 361, below.

I went once to pay a visit to him at Ma'd-âbâd and I asked permission to leave at the time of the noon prayer. He said, "It is too late now." It was morning then. When night fell he told me, "I wish I had given you leave to go. We have no food on hand today."

I said, "I am not so fortunate as to go to bed without supper;[96] I already ate somewhere else."

The Shaykh withdrew. He had a basket of dates in the house and he instructed the learned Mohammad-e Ghaznavi to portion them out. He asked, "How many should I give each person?"

He said, "Give ten to each."

Mohammad-e Ghaznavi said, "I am not the one who can do that..."[97]

The Shaykh al-Islam put one of them in his mouth and portioned out the rest, ten to a person. There were thirty-seven people there. He gave a full portion to all. Nine were left for himself, and one of them he had already put in his mouth. And God is the Most Knowledgeable.

299. Boneless Chicken

Also related by him:

Once I went to the village of Sâghu to visit him. At supper time they brought a little barley bread, but nothing of curds or whey.[98] A man came along and placed three loaves of [wheat] bread and a chicken before him. The Shaykh pulled the chicken apart with his own hands and set it on three pieces of bread which he placed in three separate places.

There were seventeen people. Six people sat at one of the plates and my children at the other two. I had [264] four mouthfuls of that bread and chicken—none of it with any bone.

---

[96] A pious or ascetic person would have considered it a blessing to fast through the night or live in poverty.

[97] Evidently, this story was not compiled by Mohammad-e Ghaznavi, who appears as one of the main characters in the narrative. He also appears as a 3rd-person character in stories 122-125 and 244.

[98] *Dughineh*; this would go with the bread to make a meal. Barley bread would be cheaper, and less tasty, than bread made of wheat.

The next day I asked my companions about it. They said, "We thought that only ours had been like that."[99] And each of them had received four or five mouthfuls of bread and chicken.

300. The Shaykh Speaks Bluntly and Punishes Insolence

Khvâjeh Imam 'Ali of Bizd has related:
One day the Shaykh al-Islam went to the home of Village Lord Mohammad, where he found Army Commander 'Omar. The brothers and servants of 'Omar had wounded Village Lord Mohammad with their swords. He was bloodied and in a condition near death.

The Shaykh al-Islam then said, "You have acted cruelly toward Village Lord Mohammad."

Army Commander Shojâ' al-Molk 'Omar was offended, as he considered himself a member of the Shaykh's inner circle. The Shaykh al-Islam did not hide the truth, even though 'Omar was a member of the Shaykh's inner circle.

Following this incident, Shojâ' al-Molk took to arguing with the Shaykh and would speak ill of him. One day they held a drinking party right in the middle of the village of Bizd and then went to Amghân for a wedding. The Shaykh al-Islam was in the village (Bizd), and they acted without regard for him. The Shaykh's lips pronounced, "They will receive a punishment for this insolence."

This Shojâ' al-Molk went to the army camp and stayed there for some while. He spent one hundred gold Nayshaburi dinârs there, in order to buy the office of commander, but they did not give it to him.

301. Trapping Sheep

Khvâjeh 'Ali of Yahyâbâd recounts in his own scrapbook[100] that

---

[99] That is they each thought that only their own portion had been full of tender meat and that the others had been stuck with the bone.

[100] The word *safineh* (ship, vessel) could describe a scrapbook, or it may be the title of a collection of hagiographic lore about Shaykh Ahmad. A few other hagiographical works go by this title, such as the

Bu Bakr 'Ali of Sahâqar said:

One day I went to see the Shaykh al-Islam, who said, "Just now [I had a vision that] two sheep [265] were brought before me. I do not know what it means."

I said, "Let's go set a trap." This was during the time that Shaykh al-Islam did not eat any lamb. I went and set traps. Soon I caught two sheep and brought them to set before the Shaykh al-Islam.

He said, "This was it exactly—[the thing I saw]!"[101]

302. A Woman Seeks Advice From the Shaykh

He further relates:

One day Amir Mohammad-e Jamâli came on behalf of the sister of Amir Rashid, who had just arrived from Nayshabur, saying, "She would like to see you."

The Shaykh al-Islam went to see her. That veiled one asked certain questions and received answers to them. One of the questions was as follows: "Is it advisable for me to go on to the city of Herat?"

The Shaykh al-Islam responded to that with, "No, someone is coming to see you and they have just left that city."

She said, "Very well." Rashid's mother asked, "Will they arrrive here tonight?"

The Shaykh answered, "They are just now leaving the city."

The fifth day after that they arrived. I asked them, "When did you leave from Herat?" They said, "On such-and-such day." We figured out that it was exactly the same time that the Shaykh had indicated.

Safinat al-owliâ, a work about the Sufi saints by Dârâ Shokuh, and the *Safineh-ye nafiseh-ye Mevleviân* (Cairo: Wahbiyya, 1283/1866), a work by Sâkıb Dede (d. 1735) about the history of the Mevlevi Order, based upon the oral lore current among the Mevlevis in the early 18th century.

[101] Cf. Story 257.

303. The Shaykh Knows the Whereabouts of a Lost Donkey

He furthermore relates:
The Shaykh al-Islam was in my home when an Indian servant from that same village came in. He said, "A donkey belonging to me has been lost. I am a poor man and I can find no trace of it. For the sake of God, show me where it is."
The Shaykh al-Islam said, "What village lies on this side of the mountain over in that direction?" "Oshtu," I said.
"What village lies on the mountain in the other direction?," he asked. "Tu'i [*T-v-i*]," I said.
He said, "On the outskirts of that village there is an orchard. A donkey and a colt are there grazing in that orchard."
We sent that servant hurrying off in that direction. He arrived there the following day. They were grazing in the orchard which the Shaykh had indicated. He found them and brought back both the donkey and the colt. [266]

304. The Shaykh Knows What He Cannot See

There was also the time when a messenger of the Sultan of Ghazna came from Iraq [i.e., central Persia]. He alighted at the village of Sanjân and summoned Khvâjeh Imam 'Ali Haysam.
At the night prayer the Shaykh al-Islam was sitting in the village of Amghân. He informed us where the messenger was sitting and what they were talking about and where the lamp was placed.
We asked them the next day and everything had been exactly as he described.

305. A Soldier Possessed of Vision

The son of the Shaykh, Khvâjeh Imam Borhân al-Din Hojjat al-Islam Nasr, God have mercy upon him, related what the learned Abu al-Hasan Sarsarbeshi [?], who is an esteemed man, said:
One day I was on the way from Nayshabur to Jâm. I had a great big turban. Along the way, soldiers took it from me. I wound a tiny old turban around my head. When I reached the barracks [*mohâreb-sarây*], I saw a military man, one of the caravan

travelers, sleeping on the bank of a stream....I went near him and he called out to me. I went closer.

He asked me about the nobles of Nayshabur. Every time I started to mention one of them, he would cut me off and proceed with a description of them that was better than mine. He even described my mother and father. He then asked, "What kind of a man is Shaykh Ahmad?" I lauded and praised him. He laughed. I asked, "Why are you laughing?" He said, "On account of his awareness, for at this very moment he hears what we are saying about him."

When I got to Sâghu, the Shaykh al-Islam was there. When his eyes lit upon me, he said, "Did they steal your turban that you should have this old turban?" I said, "Indeed." He said, "Along the way you were talking about me and this and that happened."

He recounted the entire adventure.

306. Healing Just because the Shaykh Asks

He further said:

There was a reddish inflamation[102] on my foot and I was in great pain. One day, in the presence of the Shaykh al-Islam [267] I had [...][103] I said, "I am unable to come see you. Rub some medicine on my foot."

He said, "Do you suppose they'll untie the donkey from the donkey-mill simply because I request it?"[104] Then he added, "But then, why shouldn't they?" He spit on that sore with his own saliva and rubbed it with his hand. After two days the sore turned to a scab and fell off.

Later I got the sores all over my body and they turned to blisters. I was in extreme pain. I remained ill for nearly ten years, but the spot where his saliva had touched me remained healthy and was never affected.

---

[102] *Bâdozh-fâm*, spelled in many different forms in the dictionaries, which indicate this is the same as *bâd-e sorkh*, or erysipelas in modern medical terminology (see *Borhân-e qâte'*, ed. Mo'in, and *Farhang-e Nafisi*). It is described as a reddish-black inflammation of the skin that was commonly believed to indicate the onset of leprosy.

[103] There is apparently a lacuna in the manuscript here.

[104] Meaning, do you suppose I can just work miracles by the asking?

307. The Shaykh Looks to the Outcome

He furthermore said:
There was a muezzin in our neighborhood who talked too much. One day the Shaykh al-Islam was in that fellow's mosque. I said, "Reprimand that muezzin and don't let him talk so much."

When the muezzin came in, he began speaking and talked a lot. We asked the Shaykh al-Islam, "Why did you keep quiet and let him talk?" He said, "You are only looking at the present, but I am looking to the outcome. His end will be good."

Much later he was disputing a doctrine with someone, arguing on the basis of the Sunna and orthodoxy. His opponent was drunk and ran in the house, got a knife, and killed him. He became a martyr. [268]

308. The Shaykh is a Great Guy

He further related from the Learned Jâme·, who was a noble old man, prominent and respected. Jâme' said:
Once I was coming down the mountain slopes around Nayshabur. There was a hermit in the congregational mosque who knew the secrets of the Lord Almighty and of His Messenger. People would ask all manner of questions from him, and he would give them a true answer.

He asked me, "Where have you been? It has been a long while since I have seen you."

"I was on the mountain slope," I said, "where three people have appeared who are claiming to be spiritual guides [*piri*]."

"Who are they?," he asked.

I said, "One of them is Ahmad-e Kharâvi. Another is 'Ali Hâji-ye Husbi, and the third is Shaykh Ahmad Abu al-Hasan."

The hermit said, "God have mercy on them, for the Lord Almighty says: 'Little Ahmad Kharâvi used to have a certain quality, but now his well is dry.' And concerning 'Ali Hâji, He said: 'He is a brick still in the mold.'[105] And as for Shaykh

---

[105] Meaning perhaps that his powers are not yet fully-formed or that

Ahmad Abu al-Hasan, he said: 'He is a great trail-blazer on Our path.'"

309. Mohammad-e Mansur of Sarakhs and the Shaykh[106]

Khvâjeh 'Omar 'Ali-ak was a reliable man. He related the following:

One day the Shaykh al-Islam went to the lecture of Khvâjeh Imam Mohammad-e Mansur in the city of Sarakhs in the new school that had recently been built there. The people laid out a brick [*khesht-i*] for the Shaykh al-Islam to sit on. Khvâjeh Imam had a disease which had paralyzed the right half of his body and he required someone's help to get on the lectern.

After the Shaykh al-Islam sat and the people quieted down, the Imam began speaking. "We have present in this assembly some men through whose blessings the Almighty Lord works wonders. O Lord, [269] upon the honor of those men, cure this affliction." As he was saying this, the Shaykh al-Islam was engrossed in thought, working some wonder.

All of the sudden the Imam lifted up his right leg and crossed it over his left leg. The people let out a great cry and began shouting. Some of the people were looking at the Shaykh al-Islam. When the Imam noticed this, his pride was wounded and he said, "O People, do not think that the teachings of that other sect[107] are certainly true, and that whatever they say is of benefit. Beware not to set your heart on them!"

When he had spoken these words, the Shaykh al-Islam became enraged, and said, "Cross your legs now, if you are a man!" The next moment his leg stopped functioning and fell paralyzed, and

---

he has a limited capacity.

[106] See Story 15, which is a more detailed version of this simple report about Mohammad-e Mansur and the Shaykh al-Islam.

[107] The manuscript reads *fariqayn-e mazhab-e digar*, which would mean "the two sects of the other creed." "Two sects" does not, however, seem to make particular sense in this context, and instead we may understand this phrase as a scribal error for *bar yaqin mazhab-e digar*, "for certain the other sect." In any case, it evidently refers to the Sufi teachings adhered to by the Shaykh al-Islam Ahmad.

he lapsed back into his paralysis.

310. Curing a Sick Girl

He also said:
There was to be a feast at the home of Mayor Khvâjeh Mohammad-e 'Aziz, who told the Shaykh al-Islam, "I have a bedridden daughter who is on the verge of death. Your blessed step should cross our threshold, in hopes the Almighty Lord might cure her."

The Shaykh al-Islam went to the home of Khvâjeh Abu al-Qâsem Zarrâb,[108] where they fetched a jug of water. The Shaykh recited something over it. When that water wet her throat, she said, "Help me sit up." They sat her up. Signs of health began to return to her and within a week she was on her feet in perfect health.

311. The Shaykh Knows the Hearts of Others

Khvâjeh Imam Shams al-Din related that he heard the following from Sadr al-Islam 'Ali-ye Haysam, God sanctify his soul:
Once the Shaykh al-Islam, his spirit be sanctified, was in Asfarghâbad. They were telling me, "You have lost control in Jâm because you have spoken of him with extremely exaggerated praises." I had been beating his drum quite loudly, though I had not yet seen him perform anything. These people [270] would say such things to me and I kept quiet.

[The Shaykh al-Islam] had told the learned Mohammad-e Mas'ud in Asfarghâbad, "They are mocking me in front of the learned Imam (Shams al-Din) and he ['Ali] keeps his silence." When I arrived in Asfarghâbad, Mohammad-e Mas'ud related this to me.

The following day, I mounted the lectern and the thought twice crossed my mind, should I talk about the Shaykh or not? In the end, I did. When I came down from the lectern, the Shaykh told

---

[108] The manuscript has *Sarrâb* (with *sâd*), but it seems likely a dot is missing and this should be read with *zâd*, Zarrâb.

me, "Twice it crossed your mind whether to speak of me or not. In the end you did not cave in, and spoke your mind."

312. How the Shaykh Measures Up to Others

He also related:

My son, Abu Bakr, was in Nayshabur and I was in Jâm. He had wondered to himself whether Shaykh Ahmad or the learned 'Ali-ye Panjgerdi was the greater. When he came to Jâm, the Shaykh al-Islam said to him, "You put me in the scale and weighed me."

313. Determining the Sex of a Child Before its Birth

He also said:

I was standing by the gate of the khâneqâh in Buzjân with the Shaykh al-Islam. I said, "We are expecting a child. What do you think, is it a boy or a girl?"

He said, "I am seeing a little girl, tiny thing." And it came about just as he said.

314. Predicting the Birth of a Son

Further:

I told the Shaykh al-Islam in the house of Ahmad the Black in the village of Bizd, "My son, Mas'ud, is expecting a child. Will it be a daughter or a son?"

He said, "Write to them in the village that a son will be born to you, [271] and you should name him Haysam." My letter arrived there on the day of his birth.

315. Predicting the Birth of a Son

The Shaykh was likewise in the village when I wrote him a letter, saying, "We are expecting a child. Do you see a boy or a girl?"

He said, "I will not say on the basis of what I see; let us make a divination to see what will be....Mohammad-e Haysam will be born."

A boy was born. I named him Mohammad.

316. The Shaykh is Aware of Others Conversations

He also recounted this:

We were in Ma'd-âbâd in the home of a certain man.[109] They had served grapes one evening, and we told stories about the Shaykh al-Islam as we ate them.

[The Shaykh] was in the neighborhood of Sarpas. The next day his followers said that the Shaykh al-Islam had said, "The scholar is eating grapes and talking about me."

317. Curing a Sore Foot

He further related:

I was in Nayshabur. It was the beginning of winter and I had had a sore on the bottom of my foot. I said, "It's winter and I have this sore and it will be very difficult to observe ritual purity. Usually when I get such a sore, it lasts for at least two months and causes me pain. Do something for me and give me a medicine for it."

The Shaykh al-Islam rubbed his finger over his teeth and then rubbed it on my sore. The sore immediately formed a scab and the pain stopped.

318. Curing a Toothache

He further related:

I was in the village of Bizd and my tooth was hurting. I said to the Shaykh al-Islam, [272] "My tooth hurts something awful."

I took his finger and put it on the tooth that hurt. Right away the pain subsided. He said, "If you had wished for all the teeth you have lost to grow back, they would have grown back."

319. Curing a Diseased Leg

He also relates that he heard the learned Esma'il of Oshtu say:

---

[109] The name of a person is given in the text, *'-Q-N-Y*, but it is not a familiar morphology for a name, and we are unable to suggest a convincing reading for it.

One day a girl was brought before the Shaykh al-Islam with a sore leg which was completely unable to walk. He placed his hands on that girl's leg and right away she got up and began walking on it.

320. A Dream of the Shaykh's Station

He also related:
I heard the following from the mother of Ostâd Abu Moti':
"One night I had a dream that a marvelous gentleman came in and took the hand of the Shaykh al-Islam. He said, 'This is one of those about whom it is said—*by his efforts calamity and contention on earth are averted.*'"
She was a learned and chaste woman who had been in doubt about the Shaykh al-Islam.

321. The Angel Gabriel Heralds the Arrival of the Shaykh

He has also related:
The year when the Shaykh al-Islam was off on his pilgrimage there was an epidemic. I was very worried about it, wondering what would happen. One night I dreamt that 'Abd Allâh-e 'Abbâs[110] told me, "The Shaykh is in good health." Still my heart was restless. Another night I dreamt Gabriel was marching and announcing, "He will arrive anon and is in good health."
I thought, "He is a great man to have Gabriel as his herald!"

322. The Shaykh Foretells the Death of a Man in Nayshabur

The learned Yusof of Ma'd-âbâd related that:
One day the Shaykh al-Islam was sitting, head bowed in meditation, in the khâneqâh of Ma'd-âbâd, [273] when all at once he said, "Verily we are from God and to Him do we return."[111]
"What has happened?," I asked.
He said, "Khvâjeh 'Abd al-Rahmân-e 'Âbedi has been called to

---

[110] Probably a reference to 'Abd Allâh ibn 'Abbâs (c. 620-c. 688), the cousin of the Prophet Mohammad.
[111] This is a pious phrase that Muslims say when someone dies.

God." He was in Nayshabur.

The news of this spread in Buzjân. Some said it was true and others called it a lie. Then someone came from Nayshabur and the news proved true. The very day and hour that the Shaykh al-Islam had said this, he had been called to God.

323. Father and Son

He also related this:

At the village of Kharjerd I asked permission to go visit my father in the area of Bâkharz. The Shaykh said, "It's not yet time."

I said, "I have a duty toward my father" [*saleh-ye rahem ast*].

He said, "I have said what I thought. If you still want to go, that is your decision."

I left. When I reached my father, I greeted him. He did not respond but made several insulting remarks. He went so far as to pick up a stick and hit me as hard as he could.

When I returned, the Shaykh al-Islam was in the village of Bizd. I was still some distance away when he called out to me, "Didn't I tell you it was not time to go? You did not listen. So, what would you have me do about him now?"

I said, "Nothing, long live the Shaykh al-Islam! After all, he is my father."

When I entered the house, he said, "I was watching when he picked up the stick and was hitting you, but did not intervene, thinking I should see you first. Since you do not have the heart to do anything about it, I forgive him on your account."

324. Jars of Gold Hidden in the Wall

He also related as follows:

One day the Shaykh al-Islam Abu al-Qâsem of Hamadân, God have mercy on him, was sitting next to the Shaykh al-Islam in Nayshabur. They were talking about the nature of the world and its defects. The Shaykh al-Islam said, "Yes, indeed, those ten jars which you have stashed away in such-and-such place and all the gold in them—[274] you will keep all of that hidden."

He said, "Where is that?"

The Shaykh al-Islam described where it was and which wall it was hidden in, and how much there was.

Abu al-Qâsem said, "Here you are and you see and know all this? For God's sake, leave this city, for no one knows of all this."

So we asked him, "Is this true, what the Shaykh al-Islam said, there are ten jars and so much gold?"

"Yes," he replied.

325. Revealing the Location of a Lost Boy

Once Khvâjeh Imam 'Ali-ye Haysam, God have mercy upon him, came looking for his son, Imam Nasr al-Din Abu Bakr. Some people said he was in the region of Dâvar[112] and others said he was in Ghazna, but no one really knew where he was.

The Shaykh al-Islam said, "I see a town near a river and in the middle of the town is a hill." He gave a description of the whereabouts of Khvâjeh Imam Abu Bakr and his companions.

Later it was discovered that there is a town in the province of Kerman called Ganjeh,[113] situated on the bank of the river, just as he had described.

326. The Shaykh Sees Inside the Homes of Others

Khvâjeh 'Ali-ye Yahyâbâdi recounts that Nâseh said:

One day I asked the Shaykh al-Islam, "Will it ever come to pass that you pay a visit to my house?" I was living in Hasan-âbâd. He told me, "When you enter your house there is a room to the right-hand side. You are using that room to keep your valuables [275]. Over the door of that room there is a plaster decoration of a hand [*panjeh*] on the wall."

---

[112] This is a wide valley through which the River Hirmand/Helmund flows on its way from the Hindu Kush mountains to Bost. The Arab geographers refer to this entire area as (Zamin-)Dâvar. See Le Strange, *Lands of the Eastern Caliphate*, 345.

[113] There is no mention in the standard geographies of any place named "Ganjeh" in the province of Kerman. However, there are several places in Kerman with similar-sounding names (Ganj, Ganjân, Ganâju), to one of which the word in our text most probably refers.

I, myself, being the owner of the house had not noticed this detail. He, sitting in Buzjân, described it thus, and when I later looked at it, it was just as he had said.

327. The Shaykh Accepts Only Licit Gifts

This same Nâseh related:
One day I went before the Shaykh al-Islam. I had a sheep that was black and white. I thought I should take it for him, but then remembered that I had not yet paid for it. I took a different sheep with me. When I came near him, he said, "You did good not to bring that black and white sheep, for I would not have accepted it."

328. The Shaykh Knows What People Say at Home

Another:
I went to the khâneqâh of Jamâl in Bizd. Khvâjeh Imam 'Ali-ye Haysam, God have mercy on him, was there. He took me home and kept me there that night. We discussed all manner of subjects, such as faith, disbelief and the Shaykh al-Islam. The following day when my sermon was over....[114] I went to see the Shaykh al-Islam. He recounted everything that had happened, from beginning to end.

329. Balm for the Eye

The Chief [*Mehtar*] Sattâr recounted this:
I would get an eye ache every year. I would have to stay at home in the basement for nearly forty days. Then I once went to see the Shaykh al-Islam. He rubbed his saliva on my eye and it was cured. I never had pain again.

---

[114] There seems to be a lacuna in the text here. The Persian gives an incomplete sentence–*dar javâb âmad* (it/he came in reply; it appeared in the answer), which does not make sense in this context.

330. An Invitation to the Shaykh Brings Blessings

He also related:
I would harvest twenty donkey-loads of wheat at the end of every autumn. [276] I had to pay ten donkey-loads in taxes. The year when the Shaykh al-Islam came to our village, I invited him to a feast in his honor. That year I had only four donkey-loads of wheat. For one full year we lived on that and were only obliged to pay fifteen maunds.[115]

331. A Mother Bears a Son and Dies

He also related:
I had no children. My wife [*qowm*] asked the Shaykh al-Islam for a child. He said, "You will have a child; do not worry." Nine months from the day he said this, a daughter was born to her.
Some time later she asked him for a son. The Shaykh al-Islam said, "One will come, but it will go badly for her." Later a son was born to her, but twelve days later the mother died and never enjoyed the baby.

332. The Shaykh Blesses an Almond Tree

Brother Mohammad-e Hamzeh, God have mercy on him, said:
Once the Shaykh al-Islam had pains in his chest. He said, "Almond oil would be good for me." I went home and fetched what almonds we had.
The village had a thousand almond trees, and I had ten more in my orchard. The following year, not a single tree had any almonds, except the one from which I took the almonds for the Shaykh al-Islam, which produced twenty-seven maunds of almonds.

---

[115] A donkey-load (*kharvâr*) was a specific measurement, of various value, depending on the place and the period of history. In the present century it was officially fixed by the Iranian government at 300 kilograms. Likewise, there are approximately 100 maunds in each donkey-load.

333. An Amulet for an Aching Leg

He also related:
One of the members of my household had an aching leg and was in great pain. One day I went before the Shaykh al-Islam and got an amulet from him. From the very moment I stepped out of the house, that pain subsided. I tied the amulet to her and she was better immediately.

They kept it in the clothes chest [jâmeh-dân]. When we looked for it later, it was lost. It was lost for around seven years, until [277] the pain reappeared again one day. The cupper came to let her blood. We looked for a tourniquet [rag-band] and discovered the amulet in the clothes chest. She tied it to her leg and was immediately cured and never sensed the pain again.

334. A Feud Between the People of Ma'd-âbâd and Kâriz

Ahmad the Hacker [So'âl] related the following:
A long-standing feud had developed between the people of Ma'd-âbâd and the people of Kâriz over blood that had been shed in Ma'd-âbâd. The Shaykh al-Islam mediated between them. He tried very hard to convince the Kârizis it would be better to collect [be-stânid] two hundred dinârs[116] or they would lose seven thousand gold dinârs in the end. The Kârizis thought this suggestion was in jest.

Seven days later a youth came with a demand for payment of [ten][117] thousand gold dinârs. The people came and fell at the feet of the Shaykh al-Islam and he intervened. They collected 7,500 dinârs and the remainder was forgiven on account of the Shaykh.

335. A Medicine for Leprosy

He also related:

---

[116] As blood-money payment.

[117] This word is not in the original Persian text. Some number equal to or greater than 7,500 must have been originally demanded by the Ma'd-âbâdis, but was accidentally omitted by the scribe.

My son was five years old. He developed leprosy in his mouth such that entire pieces of flesh would fall from his mouth and he could no longer sleep or rest. I took him to Buzjân. The Shaykh al-Islam blew and then spit in his mouth. He soon fell asleep in my arms, though he had had no sleep or comfort for twenty days. His mouth no longer smelled bad and the disease was cured.

336. Healing a Slipped Disc

Khvâjeh 'Ali Bu Nasr, the Mayor [*Za'im*] of Nowdeh related the following:

Once the disc in my neck [278] had begun to ache[118] and I was in extreme pain. For nearly twenty days I had been unable to sleep at all. One day I went to see the Shaykh al-Islam. He placed his hand on it and the pain left in such wise that I could not remember which side it had been on.

337. An Amulet Helps to Escape the Flood

He also related:

He once wrote an amulet for me. He said, "Treat this with the proper respect and you can go either into water or into fire."

One night it so happened I was coming back from Bizd. I had the amulet with me. I came to the river which had rushed over its banks. I went into the water, which carried me away. I was heedless of the amulet and the people were running along the river bank and shouting. In the midst of this, I remembered the amulet. I touched it with my hand and repented, promising never to take it for granted again. I invoked its help.

A smaller stream had branched off from the floodwater. It lifted me up as high as a hill and cast me up on the bank, on the side of the river where my house was. From there I went on with no trouble until I arrived home.

338. A Thousand-fold Reward

He also related:

---

[118] *Dard-i dar mohreh-ye gardan-e man âmadeh bud.*

In Sarakhs they bought a camel litter for the Shaykh al-Islam for one dinâr. It was I who paid that dinâr. The Shaykh al-Islam said, "In return for this one dinâr of yours, I will reward you with a thousand."

Once Amir 'Omar arrested me and the Mayor Khvâjeh As'ad dealt with me in an exceedingly harsh manner and demanded a thousand dinârs. The Shaykh al-Islam ransomed me and freed me from their clutches. No one could take a single farthing from me after that.

339. Escaping From a Turkish Jail

Mohammad-e Bu Nasr-e Kârizi said:

Once ten Turkish soliders [gholâm] entered my home. They detained and arrested me. My Hindu servant went to the Shaykh al-Islam and reported my situation. [279] The Shaykh al-Islam said, "Do not worry, for they cannot keep your master; he will say the morning prayers in our company."

At the night prayer, I felt I should go see the Shaykh al-Islam. I let out a great roar and was inspired to jump in the air. I ran and jumped over the wall, in such wise that none of the guards dared to ask where I was going.

I performed the morning prayer with the Shaykh al-Islam. When the prayer was completed, he said, "How did you escape?" I told what I had experienced.

340. The Shaykh Blesses the Oil of a Lamp

Nasru of Kâriz was a reliable and abstemious man. He said:

One night I invited the Shaykh al-Islam for a meal. I was holding a little lamp. It burned all night until I wanted to go to bed. Before going to sleep, I looked and it was full. After sleeping a while I got up and looked again. It was still full.

Finally I asked the children, "Have they put any oil in the lamp?" They said no. It kept burning all the way till morning. When I got up in the morning, it was still full!

341. Sustenance from the Other World

He also related:
Once we were destitute. A crowd of guests arrived to see the
Shaykh al-Islam. They asked me, "Is there any bread?" I said,
"No."[....][119]
He was delighted. He returned home dancing all the way.

When the guests had settled down, someone came knocking at
the door. He brought a basket of bread and a basket of grapes. I
took them. Someone else came with a basket of flour. I took that,
too. We reckoned there were nearly fifty people there and all of
them ate their fill.

342. The Seed of a Son in a Quince

Khvâjeh Imam Mahmud, the son of the Shaykh al-Islam, said:
I had a son who was gathered to God. One day they brought a
little boy from a village before the Shaykh al-Islam. From his lips
came the sentence, "Nothing will happen."[120] [280]

I felt in my heart the wish that my son were still alive. Right
away the Shaykh al-Islam said, "Take this," and gave me a quince.
He said, "I have placed the seed of a son within this fruit."

I took it and brought it home. Nine months from that day, a son
was born.

343. Punishment for a Man who Would Not Give His Land to the Shaykh

Shaykh 'Ali Hâji said:
The Shaykh al-Islam sent me and Nasruy to see Khvâjeh
Mohammad-e Asir, who was the Lord of Sanjân. The Shaykh
requested a piece of land from him that was adjacent to the

---

[119] It appears that there is a lacuna in the manuscript at this point.
There may also be something missing from the last sentence of this
story.
[120] The meaning of *chizi na-khvâhad âmad*, literally "nothing will
come/happen," is not quite clear. Perhaps the Shaykh means to say that
nothing will come of the boy.

hospice of Sanjân, so that he could build a retreat [*sowme'eh*] there and grow something for the Dervishes. Mohammad at first said, "I will give it to him." He gave me his hand.[121]

Later on they talked him out of it and he said, "It would not be right. He is an important man and all manner of people fall in with him.[122] I must not let this village slip from my hands on his account."

The Shaykh said, "Since the matter now stands like this, let him try and keep Sanjân." Shortly thereafter word arrived that the Sultan had seized the village from him, for it [belonged] to the Sultan.

344. The Shaykh Predicts the Collapse of a House

Khvâjeh Mahmud Mohammad, the son of the Shaykh al-Islam, reported:

I entered a house in a village with a group of companions. They made a place for them to sleep in that house and they stayed the night there. The next day the Shaykh al-Islam told his followers, "Let them get up and clear out of that house."

We came out and the house immediately collapsed. [281]

345. Famine and Inflation [in the words of the Shaykh]

[The Shaykh al-Islam] said:

Once I had closed my eyes and I had a vision that several people were lying dead in every house in the village of Nâmaq. I opened my eyes and I understood that a famine was to come in which most of the people would perish. I had a disciple who was a sincere man. He was called the Learned Pâydâr.[123] I told him, "Go

---

[121] *Dast dâd-am.* This gesture, as in modern Europe, seals an oath or pledge of fealty, and is attested in other medieval Persian sources.

[122] He apparently is worried that sectarian conflict may develop and cause trouble for him.

[123] See Story 164 for this same Learned Pâydâr.

and buy some grain." He said, "I have twelve gold dinârs, but at 150 maunds per dinâr it is too expensive, so I did not buy any."

The Shaykh said, "Go and buy it." As Pâydâr narrates:
I went back and the price had gone up to 130 maunds per dinâr. I did not buy any. In the morning the price in our village had been 100 maunds per dinâr. I went back and it had gone up to 100 maunds per dinâr. Eventually it got to the point that no more could be found and a famine ensued."
The Shaykh narrates:

He paid his twelve dinârs and bought sixty maunds of millet with it. A voice in my heart warned me that if I buy even one maund of it, I would be an infidel.[124] Eventually I saw with my own eyes that ten people had died in one house and there were places where around twenty people had perished. But of my own people, not one had died; all escaped unharmed. The whole village was in need of me and I had no occasion to seek out help from anyone else, by the grace and blessings of God, the Almighty.

346. The Shaykh Discovers Stolen Goods Among the Gypsies[125]

Khvâjeh Khatib-e Bezdi said:
He had three disciples in the village of Sâghu [...],[126] called Mohammad Hayyati [? *H-y-t-i*]. A thief had stolen something of his and nearly a month had gone by. A sum of forty dinârs was brought to the Shaykh in the village of Bizd.
The Shaykh al-Islam showed them how to get to the village, and they went off. They went there and found bracelets which belonged to them in the possession of the elder of the village. This

---

[124] Meaning that it would reflect doubt that God would provide for him and his family.

[125] This story is rather confused and the text seems to be deficient.

[126] There is a lacuna in the text here.

resulted in fighting and ill-feelings. Then they recovered all of the goods from the gypsies, just as the Shaykh al-Islam had indicated. [282]

347. The Shaykh Encourages a New Preacher

Khvâjeh Khatib of Bizd also related:
When the congregational mosque of Bizd was completed, the Army Commander, Shojâ' al-Molk, held a celebration and had all the religious leaders, judges and Sufi shaykhs of the region come. For the first Friday meeting, my father asked me to give the sermon, but I had not memorized any of the conventional salutations. It was on a Thursday and I, with great effort, memorized one such salutation, but I could not recite it smoothly from memory. I kept my notes with me so that I could look at them if I got stuck.

When I ascended the pulpit and stood up to deliver my sermon, I was paralyzed with fear, to the extent that two or three times I almost vomited. Try as I might, I could remember nothing. Twice I said, "God be praised," but, of course, I could read nothing further.

The Shaykh al-Islam gazed on me and said, "You feeble fellow, pull yourself together and act like a man!" Once again I said "God be praised," and my courage returned. I recited the entire sermon without stumbling over a single letter. Everyone was amazed, for no one had ever delivered his first sermon so bravely.

348. The Blessed Presence of the Shaykh

Shaykh 'Ali-ye Amghâni told the following:
Once I invited the Shaykh al-Islam to dinner. A crowd of followers arrived. I took sixty maunds of flour from the vat and made bread, along with eighteen maunds of meat. That night a hundred people sat down to eat, and the neighbors had also asked to borrow thirty maunds of bread, which I gave them. There were so many loaves of bread left over that I filled up two jars with them and we continued to eat them for some time.

For eight months after that, we continued to use the flour from that vat and the amount had not decreased a bit.

349. The Blessing of a Lock of the Shaykh's Hair

He also said:
Once we went to visit a Turkoman. We arrived at a dilapidated [283] run-down house. I said, "Alas, had there only been enough water for the mounts to drink, it would have been good."

Khvâjeh Abu al-Fath, the son of the Shaykh al-Islam,[127] had (a lock of the Shaykh's hair with him).[128] He dropped a few strands of that hair down that well. I said, "O Lord, by virtue of the majesty of his hair, I ask that you make water flow forth!"

Three days later, we reached that place [again] and it had filled with water.

350. Curing The Sore on a Thigh

The son of the [Shaykh's] servant in Sâghu had developed a sore on his thigh. He waited for a while until the Shaykh al-Islam came there. He spit on it and muttered something over it. The sore was cured and no trace of it remained.

351. Restoring a Broken Clay Pot

He also said:
That night[129] we washed the bowls and put them away. A

---

[127] See the note in Story 162.

[128] The parenthetic text is missing from the manuscript, but is supplied by *Rowzat al-rayâhin* (63), which tells a more concise version of the story, as follows:

Shaykh 'Ali Amghâni relates that: Once we were going somewhere. We saw a well that had no water. Khvâjeh Abu al-Fath had a lock of the Shaykh al-Islam's hair with him. He cast a few strands in the well and said, "O Thou God! By the majesty of this hair, may the water rise in this well." We returned there three days later and it had filled with a great deal of water.

[129] Perhaps referring to the gathering described in Story 348.

sieve[130] fell off the wall and broke one of the smaller bowls. I was upset about that, because it did not belong to us. My mother suggested that I replace it with one of our own small bowls, and return them to the owner. There were ten little bowls we had borrowed; one had broken and nine were left. So we left them there to return them to the owner the following day.

We went to sleep and when we got up in the morning, we saw a stack of ten little bowls, all in tact, and not a single potsherd. That bowl had been fixed!

352. The Shaykh's Store of Grain Never Diminishes

Once the Shaykh al-Islam had accumulated 1250 maunds of grain in Zâhed-âbâd. He gave 140 maunds as a tithe, but did not inform the mother of Imam Borhân al-Din Nasr,[131] at home. [284] She also gave a tithe of 130 maunds. In due time they weighed their wheat, and still had a full 1250 maunds, not one maund less.

353. Buying an Ass on the Way to Pilgrimage

Khvâjeh Imam Abu al-Fath[132] related:

While the Shaykh al-Islam was on the way to pilgrimage and we arrived at the village of Panjgerd,[133] he said, "We should buy a

---

[130] The word *ghelbâr* does not appear in Persian dictionaries, but appears to be a variation of *gherbâl*. Such metathesis of the liquids "l" and "r" is not uncommon in regional dialects, for example, *qolf* for *qofl* and *khalvâr* in place of *kharvâr* (e.g., in Hamadan).

[131] A polite circumlocution to avoid saying the word "wife" in reference to the Shaykh's own spouse, and mother of his son, Borhân al-Din Nasr.

[132] The son of the Shaykh al-Islam; see the note in Story 162.

[133] This village near Nayshabur is attested in Arabized form in Yâqût's *Mu'jam al-udabâ* as Fanj-kird (see Margoliouth's edition, 5:103, under the entry for 'Alî ibn Ahmad al-Fanjkirdî). Story 312 in the present text also mentions a "learned 'Ali-ye Panjgerdi," evidently from this same village. The *Rowzat al-rayâhin* gives this toponym once as Panj-mard (62), and once (34) without any pointing over the initial letters [---*kerd*, which could be construed a variety of ways, as

donkey here."

I did not have more than four drams [*dâng*] and two grains [*jow*]. I said, "With this much gold, we can't afford one."

He said, "You go on ahead and I will make up the difference of whatever amount is required."

I entered the village with two other followers, and was offered a good donkey for three dinârs and four drams. We weighed our gold and there was exactly three dinârs and four drams.[134]

354. The Shaykh as Chamberlain at the Court of God's Majesty

Ebrâhim, the son of 'Ali-ye Sa'id, related on the authority of Kvâjeh 'Osmân-e Jowrmadi:[135]

In the beginning of the Shaykh al-Islam's ministry, when he came to the region of Jâm, I was in the village Jormad [sic]. I had not yet seen any miracle from the Shaykh al-Islam.

One night I sat thinking about him and saw a vision of a meadow. I saw erected there something big as a mountain; a spacious, towering pavilion, around which a crowd had gathered. I asked, "What place is this?" They said, "It is the pavilion of God's Majesty."

I went closer and saw the Shaykh al-Islam, standing at the door in the garb of a chamberlain, holding the [285] cord of the curtain in his hand. I was told, "Anyone whom Shaykh Ahmad allows to pass is permitted, and those whom he does not allow have no

---

Panjkerd, Sehkerd, Bankhkerd, Tanakhkerd, etc.], perhaps indicating that the name of the village had changed or was unfamiliar by the the 16th century, when Darvish 'Ali Buzjâni compiled his book on Shaykh Ahmad. As a suffix *–kerd* or *–gerd* means "town" and appears in many Iranian place names.

[134] This story is related twice, with minor differences, in the *Rowzat al-rayâhin*, 34 and 62, using not the usual word for donkey [*khar*], but rather "long ears" [*derâz gush*]. *Rowzat al-rayâhin* both times relates the anecdote on the authority of Khvâjeh Abu al-Fath, but apparently takes the stories from different sources, once from the *Spiritual Feats* of Ghaznavi (62-"It is mentioned in the *Maqâmât* of the Shaykh al-Islam that..."), and the other time without specifying the source (34).

[135] See Story 186 for this toponym.

permission."

355. The Shaykh and the Ismaili Highway Men

Khvâjeh Abu al-Fath said:

We were on our way to the Hijâz for pilgrimage. When we reached Jâjarm,[136] the Sufi leaders and religious scholars gathered and asked all kinds of questions, both concerning religious law and the Sufi path, which the Shaykh al-Islam answered. They were much impressed.

When we were about to leave, they said, "From the gate of... 'Ali Hâmed, the Ismailis have blocked the road you are taking. They will be expecting you. We will not let you and your thirteen men go this way any further." They pleaded again and again, but the Shaykh al-Islam would not remain.

The Ismailis had a spy there, who went on ahead of them. When we alighted at the next stage, another Ismaili spy appeared, pretending to hunt. From there it was three farsangs to the territory of the Ismailis.

We were greatly afraid and the Shaykh al-Islam would reassure us, saying, "God is the Protector, do not fear." Proceeding further, we reached a desolate village where the Ismailis were camped around fires, waiting in ambush. When we saw this, we were terrified.

When the Shaykh al-Islam saw how scared we were, he prayed and encouraged us. "Prepare to join battle and have no fear." He was sitting on his mount, holding a double-axe and shield. He struck the shield with that double-axe and it made a loud sound. Hearing this noise, we felt a great power come over us. The more this power surged over us, the more severe became the punishment of the Ismailis.

There were nearly two hundred of them engaged in battle. All of them fled and we saw them flee with our own eyes. We thought they were drawing us into an ambush. There was a mausoleum [*gur-khâneh*] nearby, into which a large number of them fled. Our

---

[136] A town some two hundred kilometers to the northwest of Nayshabur and 100 kilometers to the southwest of Bojnurd.

path led past that mausoleum. We went through a passage that was so narrow the packs [286] on our camels rubbed against the walls, but not one of those Ismailis had the courage to make even the slightest sound.

After we had passed that place, we alighted at H-y and M-gh-r [?]. The people there were astonished and asked, "How did you manage to get here? They had the road blocked!" The Shaykh al-Islam said, "By the grace of the Almighty God."

On our return, we found out that the Amir of Ba'nân had sent an army to catch those robbers and had killed all the Ismailis.

356. Finding a Stolen Cow

Hosayn Abu al-Qâsem of Sanjar related:

Two men once came to see the Shaykh al-Islam with a letter from Khvâjeh Mohammad-e Zarashki. A pair of his cows had been lost and he couldn't find any trace of them.

The Shaykh al-Islam said, "The description you give brings Bâkharz to mind, specifically a village there called Amyâd. If he wants to go there, he must first go to the village Arzaneh. There is a watchman to look over the crops [*dashtvân*] there called Mohammad, who repented to me once. If he has broken his vow of repentance, it is he who took the cows."

These two men went searching. When they arrived there, they found that that Mohammad had broken his vows. They went to the village of [A]myâd and found both cows there. That Mohammad had stolen them and sold them there, but they brought them back.

357. Sustenance for the Shaykh's Followers

Ahmad of Ghazarâbâd related the following:[137]

Once they were planting saplings [? *chub mi-zadand*] in the

---

[137] Or perhaps 'Azar-âbâd; the vocalisation of this unknown toponym is uncertain, but in *Kholâsat al-maqâmât* it is identified as the place where the Shaykh's son, Fakhr al-Din Abu al-Hasan, is buried, while the *Rowzat al-rayâhin* (66) gives his resting place as Qâder-âbâd. Perhaps the form *ghazar*, over time, has permutated to the more familiar *qâder*.

garden of [287] Ma'd-âbâd. When they finished, it was time for the noon-prayer. After performing their prayers, the Shaykh al-Islam asked, "Have you nothing for these friends to eat?"

They said, "We do not." 'Omar Asfarghâbadi said, "I will go home to see what I can find."

The Shaykh al-Islam said, "Wait and see what turns up." An hour passed and someone came from Ghazarâbâd with a donkey-load of sweetbread and halvâ.

358. Why Didn't You Speak Up Last Night?

Khvâjeh Khatib-e Tarjerdi[138] said:

In the mosque of Asfarghâbad the Shaykh al-Islam asked me, "Why didn't you speak up last night?"

"I don't know that I have ever failed to speak up on your behalf," I said.

The Shaykh al-Islam said, "There were such-and-such number of you last night. One of them was asking you, 'Why did you come before the Shaykh al-Islam Ahmad?' You said, 'Just to see him.' Someone else said, 'Many fools are attracted to him.'"

I said, "That is true, we were sitting last night and that is word-for-word what was said."

359. The Blessings of the Shaykh's Presence

Khvâjeh 'Ali-ye Yahyâbâdi said:

I have a vineyard in Fasâvarz which always used to yield five hundred maunds of syrup. Since the Shaykh al-Islam paid a visit to that vineyard, it yields a thousand maunds of syrup, nor have I added to the size of the plot.

360. I Grant You a Son

The same [Brother Mohammad the Turner][139] said:

---

[138] Perhaps a manuscript corruption of Farjerdi, Farjerd being a toponym mentioned in the *Hodud al-'âlam*, s.p. 164, 3.

[139] He appears in Stories 140 and 158. The current story, which

I went to see the Shaykh al-Islam, who asked me, "How many children do you have?"

I said, "I have two hags."[140]

He said, "I grant you a son."

I came home and asked if we were expecting any children. I was told, "No." Later a son was born to me. I named him Abu Bakr. [288]

361. The Repentance of a Womanizing Qur'ân Reciter

Once a Qur'ân reciter from Qâ'en came to Buzjân. I was sitting with the Shaykh al-Islam one day, who explained, "Anyone who commits such a sin, such will be his recompense."

The Qur'ân reciter said, "Would the pious commit such a sin?"

The Shaykh al-Islam said, "Yes, from time to time it happens that they seize upon a woman in the Motarrez mosque,[141] fancy her and make a secret rendezvous with her."

The Qur'ân-reciter said, "Ohhh, this is true! That happened to me." He repented and turned back (from his sin).

---

begins with "he also relates" (*hamu goft*) is evidently out-of-place in the Chester Beatty Library manuscript. The phrase would seem to indicate that this story, and others in the Chester Beatty ms. which begin with it, originally belonged to the text of Mohammad-e Ghaznavi's *Maqâmât*, which uses this introduction frequently, and were not added later.

[140] The word '*ajuzeh* is usually reserved for an ugly old woman, but sometimes occurs, as it does here, certainly in a derogatory sense, for daughter (see *Farhang-e Mo'in*).

[141] The name of a mosque in Nayshabur destroyed in 1153-4 / 548 A.H. According to Râvandi (*Râhat al-sodur*, 180) it was a large mosque, accomodating 2000 worshippers, located on the edge of the Bazaar of Nayshâbur. It had a tall dome, inlaid with oiled wood, and the pillars were also inlaid with oiled wood. The Ghuzz set fire to it and the flames rose so high that the whole city was illuminated. The Ghuzz plundered the city by its light and took many captives.

362. The Shaykh's Prayers are Effective

Brother 'Ali Bu al-Hasan Holvi told this story:
I took a wife. She was eighteen years old. I had no children. One day I told the Shaykh al-Islam, "Give me a child."

He said, "When the feeling comes over me, I will pray that you have a child."

Then one day in the village of Zarashk the Shaykh al-Islam was in a state of joy. I reminded him and he said a prayer. Then he said, "It is taken care of."

Later a daughter was born to me and I named her Fâtemeh.

363. One of the Shaykh's Premonitions

Shaykh Abu al-Hasan-e Pârsi[142] said:
In the beginning of the Shaykh al-Islam's ministry, the Chief Constable of the region decided to come to Nâmaq. The people were afraid and said, "We must resist." They sat in the mosque and consulted about the matter.

The Shaykh al-Islam took the Learned Bu Nasr[143] by the hand to the mosque and said, "Tell them that someone has had a dream and saw that eighteen people from this village were slain and the vultures were coming down to perch on the roof of the [289] congregational mosque. You must put aside all thought of resistance, that you fall not into error and have many people perish."

The learned Bu Nasr apprised them of this. Barâdar Hakim was the chief of the village, a respected man. He said, "Enough of your dreams! We no longer wish to follow your advice." He yelled at Bu Nasr and offended him.

The Shaykh al-Islam said, "The man has your best interests at heart; you need not yell at him!"

Barâdar Hakim, in turn, began talking like an ignoramus. The Shaykh al-Islam said, "The first arrow will pierce your throat, or I

---

[142] See Story 75, in which this Abu al-Hasan-e Pârsi has a role, and which appears to be connected to the events mentioned here.

[143] One of the sons of the Shaykh al-Islam.

am a liar and you are telling the truth!"

It then came to pass that the Chief Constable arrived and they fought against him. The first arrow hit this Khvâjeh in the throat and killed him. Altogether eighteen people were killed.

364. "Get Down to Business, for I have Granted You a Son"

Khvâjeh Imam Mohammad-e Mansur, who was one of the leading men of his age,[144] related the following:

Khvâjeh 'Ali Bu Ghânem had three daughters, but no son. He asked the Shaykh al-Islam for a son. The Shaykh al-Islam said, "Is there an empty room in your house right now?"

"There is," he said.

The Shaykh said, "Go home and get down to business, for I have granted you a son."

Exactly nine months later a son was born to him.

365. The Shaykh Beats His Host

He has also related the following:

Once Khvâjeh Ra'is Mas'ud-e Bu Shojâ' invited the Shaykh al-Islam to a feast. The Shaykh al-Islam said, "I do not come alone."

He said, "Bring your followers with you," though he was opposed to the Dervishes. He went and made preparations and took the Shaykh al-Islam there. He set bread, leeks and yoghurt curd before them[145] [290] and explained, "I haven't cooked anything."

The Shaykh al-Islam said, "You cooked some stew, which is simmering in the kitchen. Go and get it."

He had, indeed, cooked that, but had changed his mind about serving it. The Shaykh al-Islam gave him such a slap on the back of his neck that his turban fell off. The Shaykh himself got up, went to the kitchen and brought the stew.

---

[144] See Stories 15 and 309 for Mohammad-e Mansur of Sarakhs.

[145] *Shiráz* was a dish of chopped dill with yoghurt and some milk, left in a bag for days to produce a thick sour curd (see *Borhân-e qâte'* under "Shiráz" and Mo'in's footnote to the entry).

366. Opening the Door Without a Key

Khvâjeh Zaki Mohammad-Hâmed-e Sarakhsi is a righteous and trustworthy man, one of the in-laws of the Shaykh al-Islam. In the beginning he was opposed to the Shaykh. He related the following:

When the Shaykh al-Islam married this woman [qowm] of Sarakhs, he brought her to my house. It was cold, so I prepared a warm room for them. At the night prayer the Shaykh al-Islam used to go to the mosque. My mother was worried that he might return home late, and since his wife was but a child, she might fall asleep and someone might enter the room and steal some of the cloth.

At night I locked the door of the house and sat down with a rosary to pray. After a while I fell asleep. I woke with a start and saw the Shaykh al-Islam undressing. I thought to myself, "Didn't I lock the door?" Satan planted a doubt in my mind. The following night, I carefully locked the door, and both of us fell asleep. The Shaykh returned and took hold of the door handle, and it opened. He came in and went to sleep.

Khvâjeh Zaki further explained:

The following night I went and secured the door with two strong chains. That great one returned from prayers. We were all awake, waiting to see what would happen. When he touched the door handle, the chains fell off and made a clatter. We were astounded and said, "Shaykh, the door was locked, how did you get in?" He said, "True, it has been like this for a few nights."

367. The Shaykh Wills a Torrential Rain

He also related this:

Once I was with the Shaykh al-Islam in Ma'd-âbâd. I said, "Will you give me leave to go to Amghân?" My family [kudakân] was there. He asked me, "Shall I send someone with you?"

All of a sudden 'Ali Hâji of Sanjân came in, sobbing. He said, "Long live the Shaykh al-Islam! [291] I have a vineyard which is drying up for lack of water. Write a letter to the headman of Amghân so that he will give me some water."

The Shaykh al-Islam said, "I will write a letter. Go and take

378   *The Colossal Elephant and His Spiritual Feats*

Khvâjeh Mohammad-e Sarakhsi to Amghân. There is no need to ask a favor from the headman and constable; God, the Almighty, will grant you enough water to fill up you and all of the dervishes."

He sat me on a donkey and we went to Amghân. There was a flood and the vineyard of 'Ali Hâji, all of Sanjân and the entire district were filled with water, and that in summertime.

368. The False Coin and its Owner

He also related that Abu Mansur-e Nazzâm said:

In the beginning of the Shaykh al-Islam's ministry, I was going to see Shaykh Bu Tâher. When I arrived there, he said, "It is not proper to pray when you have a knife and such gold on your person."

I told him how much the gold weighed.[146] He said, "This gold is illicit [*qalb*]. It is a dinâr and a half from the village of Bar-âbâd and it belongs to Mohammad-e Sani'i."

We discovered it was true and returned it to its owner.

369. The Village of Bars is Plundered

He also related:

One day we were with the Shaykh al-Islam in the vicinity of Nâmaq. He was heard to say, "The village of Bars was plundered yesterday."

The next day we learned that the Ismaili heretics had plundered it. Nâmaq was five farsangs away from the village of Bars. It was true, just as he said.

---

[146] Probably he means that the small amount of gold he has would not invalidate his prayers according to Islamic law.

PART TWO

THE POSTHUMOUS MIRACLES OF THE SHAYKH

THE POSTHUMOUS MIRACLES OF THE SHAYKH

The *Kholâsat al-maqâmât* (ed. Ivanow, 19) and the *Rowzat al-rayâhin* (ed. Moayyad, 25) indicate that a certain Ahmad-e Tarkhestâni had:

> compiled stories about the miracles and spiritual states of the Shaykh al-Islam Ahmad. He wrote what he witnessed of the Shaykh's miracles and spiritual stations and added to it everything that happened after the Shaykh's death.

As described in the Introduction ("Ahmad-e Tarkhestâni and the Posthumous Miracles of Shaykh Ahmad"), Tarkhestâni's work was written after the death of Shaykh Ahmad-e Jâm, probably at about the same time as Ghaznavi compiled his *Spiritual Feats*. No separate work known as the "Posthumous Miracles of the Shaykh" has survived in the name of Ahmad-e Tarkhestâni. Though the manuscripts from which the current text is derived do not identify Tarkhestâni as the author, the following stories may very well be excerpted from his presumably now lost work. Mohammad-e Ghaznavi perhaps incorporated these stories into his *Spiritual Feats of Shaykh Ahmad*, but more likely they were added as an appendix to some manuscripts of his *Spiritual Feats* at a later date.

The Nâfiz Pâshâ manuscript includes the first eleven of the following stories after it presents the *Epistle to the Samarqandians*.[1] It is not entirely clear whether this chapter on the Posthumous Miracles and the phrase that introduces it were added to the text by Ghaznavi himself, or by a later scribe. That introductory phrase goes as follows:

> We will further add to this book the miracles which have occurred and continue even now to appear, since the death of the Shaykh al-Islam Ahmad, may God sanctify his precious soul.

---

[1] From line 4 of folio 145b.

Stories 381 through 386 are found only in the Chester Beatty manuscript, and occur in the section on miracles after the death of the Shaykh.

As for the dating of these "Posthumous Miracles," Story 373 was apparently composed "several years after the death of the Shaykh." A date of composition in the 1140s or 1150s would be consistent with either the *Spiritual Feats* of Ghaznavi or the work of Tarkhestâni, but since the following stories are not presented as part and parcel of Ghaznavi's *Spiritual Feats*, we may tentatively assume that it represents part of Tarkhestâni's otherwise lost text. However, Story 381 dates to some time after the year 1252, over a century after the death of Shaykh Ahmad, and cannot have been compiled by either Tarkhestâni or Ghaznavi.

It would seem, therefore, that the descendants or disciples of Shaykh Ahmad continued to record the posthumous miracles manifested in the name of Shaykh Ahmad or his shrine. The caretakers of the shrine of Shaykh Ahmad, who were the descendants of the Shaykh, would of course want to keep a record of all the instances where someone had been healed at the shrine of the Shaykh. This would enhance the prestige of the family and the reputation of the shrine as a place of pilgrimage. We may therefore assume that this chapter incorporates part or all of Tarkhestâni's posthumous miracles, to which his descendants added some additional stories over the centuries.

The Posthumous Miracles of the Shaykh
By Ahmad-e Tarkhestâni (?)

[295] We will further add to this book the miracles which have occurred and continue even now to appear, since the death of the Shaykh al-Islam Ahmad, may God sanctify his precious soul. Anyone in need or desirous of obtaining some aim who turns his face toward that sanctified and blessed resting place with pure heart, absolute belief and sincere intent will find fulfillment. Should his hopes go unfulfilled, it is on account of his weak faith and infirm belief. This is clear, evident and certain, and there is no room for doubt about these miracles, for they have been repeatedly experienced.[2]

370. One of the Disciples Dreams of the Shaykh's Resting Place

Shaykh Abu al-Hasan-e Salâh, God have mercy upon him, was a man of the path, a favored disciple of the Shaykh al-Islam Ahmad, God sanctify his precious soul. One night he dreamed that a tent had been pitched by the gate of Ma'd-âbâd on the same spot where today the Shaykh al-Islam, God have mercy upon him, lies buried. [296] He describes as follows: "It seemed to me the ropes of that tent extended to all the horizons of the earth."

It happened that the Shaykh al-Islam was one day on his way to Sâghu, accompanied by this Shaykh Abu al-Hasan-e Salâh. Along the way Abu al-Hasan said to Shaykh Ahmad, "I had this dream last night."

The Shaykh al-Islam said nothing in reply until they arrived in the vicinity of Ma'd-âbâd, where he said, "Abu al-Hasan, do you have any idea where that tent and its poles were pitched?"

He said, "I do." The Shaykh al-Islam told him to go on ahead.

---

[2] The numbering in the edition of the Persian text begins here anew from one, but we have numbered all 386 stories about the Shaykh consecutively in the translation. It should be remembered, however, that the "Posthumous Miracles" of the Shaykh were not necessarily part of Mohammad-e Ghaznavi's original work, as explained in the introductory comments at the beginning of this chapter.

He went on and the Shaykh al-Islam followed behind him until they came to the spot that today marks his grave. Prior to this no graves had been erected there.

The Shaykh al-Islam asked Abu al-Hasan, "Where was this tent and its ropes, can you describe them?"

"It was right here," he said, "and its central pole was dug in this spot here."

The Shaykh al-Islam prayed at the spot and prostrated himself for a while. He said, "This spot will become a fountain of prayer and its influence will be felt throughout the world," and he placed a few stones in the shape of a mosque on that spot.

Soon afterwards, death overtook him and he took the final journey to join the grace of God, the Almighty. His grave was erected in that spot and the dream was fulfilled, and the fountain of prayers was unleashed.

So that you know.

371. A Collection of Prophetic Traditions

The first miracle which occurred at the grave of the Shaykh al-Islam Ahmad, God sanctify his precious soul, after his death was the following:

Three days after his passing, the Qâzi 'Alâ al-Din of Marv, God have mercy upon him, came to Ma'd-âbâd and a huge crowd gathered to mourn the Shaykh al-Islam. The Qâzi was deeply grieved and wept. "I had come in the hope of studying Hadith with the Shaykh al-Islam, as I had heard that he was able to distinguish the true from the false Hadith. Alas that I have not attained his presence and my hopes are shattered."

Among the sons of the Shaykh al-Islam, Shaykh al-Islam [297] Borhân al-Din Nasr was his successor, and he comforted Qâzi 'Alâ al-Din. Qâzi 'Alâ al-Din would come to the holy grave of the Shaykh al-Islam twice a day, weeping and grieving.

One day he sat by the grave and fell asleep. The Shaykh al-Islam Borhân al-Din Nasr immediately appointed two servants to keep all others away from the grave. The Qâzi remained asleep for three days and nights. When he awoke, he saw in front of him the book of Hadith authorities[3] which belonged to the library of Borhân al-Din Nasr.

Weeping and sobbing, he came to the khâneqâh to recount his dream for Borhân al-Din Nasr. Borhân al-Din asked him, "O master, what need is there to explain?"

Qâzi 'Alâ al-Din answered that, "neither the dream nor the miracle are such that they should remain hidden." Thus, in the presence of a crowd of scholars and nobles and common folk, alike, he described:

I was sitting by the grave of the Shaykh al-Islam, grieving and weeping, thinking to myself, "Would that I had attained his presence and had heard some hadith from him. Now, alas, I must return with my hopes unfulfilled." I was engrossed in this thought when sleep overtook me. Falling asleep, I saw the Shaykh al-Islam sitting on a throne in an exalted place. I went forward and greeted him. He did me honor and told me, "Sit, for your hopes will not go unfulfilled."

At this moment, Imam [sic] Borhân al-Din Nasr appeared and was instructed, "O Nasr, go and fetch the books of Qâzi al-Din and my Hadith authorities." After he brought them, the Shaykh said, "Now you must read."

I started and read aloud a few thousand hadith, crossing out those that he indicated to be false. When it was done, I asked the Shaykh al-Islam, "By what criteria do we know which of them are false?"

He said, "While I listened, so too did Mohammad, the Messenger of God, listen. I watched the spot between his two blessed eyebrows, God's blessing upon him, and whatever he indicated to be false, I told you, and you crossed it out. This is the way it must be done."

Then I said, "O Shaykh al-Islam, if you would have Borhân al-Din Nasr honor me with your copy of the Hadith authorities, it

---

[3] *Ketâb-e asânid*, literally "Book of chains of transmission." Each Hadith is prefaced by its chain of transmitters, indicating that so-and-so heard it from so-and-so, who heard it from his father, that so-and-so heard the Prophet Mohammad say....It appears that *Ketâb-e asânid* is a description of the contents of the book, rather than a title, per se. Perhaps it is a notebook that the Shaykh himself or his students had prepared.

would be an immense favor to me." [298] The Shaykh al-Islam signalled for Nasr to give the book of Hadith authorities to Qâzi 'Alâ al-Din, "that he might have a memento of me and pray on my behalf."

At this point I woke up and found the book of Hadith authorities in my hand and the collections of Hadith which I had heard was in front of me, with the false ones crossed out.

Then Qâzi 'Alâ al-Din added:

This was a most wondrous and mighty miracle which appeared after the death of the Shaykh al-Islam at his grave. It must not be forgotten and left untold; it must be written down, so that all may see and read about it and know the extent of this Shaykh's power, spiritual state, miracles, station and his proximity to the presence of the Divine Majesty. I never expected that his powers would be so great. If someone else had told me this story, I would not have believed it, but since I experienced it myself, what can I say? I can only submit to it, for, as it is said, "the eye is honest and the ear a liar."

372. A Sick Man is Cured by a Vision of the Shaykh

Another of the well-known miracles which occurred after his death is the following, which happened to the Qâzi 'Emâd al-Din Vâseti, God have mercy upon him. This Qâzi 'Emâd al-Din was one of the great practitioners of asceticism and miracles. In the beginning of the Shaykh al-Islam's ministry, he was in 'Omar-âbâd near Jâm with 'Omar-e Dâyeh. He served the Shaykh for a while and acted as his patron.

The majestic Khwârazmshâh, may God make his proof resplendent, went to Marv to do battle with Sultan Sanjar. They fought there and Marv was plundered.[4] This 'Emâd al-Din was in

---

[4] This certainly refers to the famous battle between the Khwârazmshah 'Alâ al-Din Atsez and Sultan Sanjar in 1141-2 / 536 A.H., which resulted in the defeat of Sanjar and the sacking of Marv, wherein many perished (see Ibn Athîr under the year 536 and Abbâs Eqbâl, *Vezârat dar 'ahd-e salâtin-e Saljuqi*, 257). However the Shaykh probably died just a matter of months before this battle, not a full two years as indicated at the end of

a certain college at the time and was wounded [299] so badly that he had no hope of survival. The legal scholars of that college had all fled and he was left alone in a room with no one to take care of him. His wounds became infected, but there was no one to treat him and look after him. A few other scholars had also, like him, been abandoned, and they would occasionally look after him. He grew weak in the extreme.

He relates:

One night I saw a light appear in my house. I did not know what it was. Someone came and laid a hand upon my head. The touch of this hand comforted me. I said, "Who are you, for I do not know you?"

"I am Shaykh Ahmad of Jâm."

When I heard this I cried out, "O Shaykh al-Islam! See what has become of me, how wretched I am, with no one to look after me! Save me."

"Do not worry, that is why I have come here." All of a sudden he placed his hand upon my wounds and everywhere his hand touched me got better. Eventually he laid hands on all my wounds until, in the end, there was only one wound the size of a fingertip left. He said, "I have left this much as a memento for you." Then, he got up and left.

When I came to my senses I looked down and saw that of all the wounds that had been upon my person none was left. There had been nearly fifty wounds upon my limbs and members, but none of them were left, they were all were healed. I got up and went into the middle of the college and began to shout until I was overcome by a spiritual state.

The scholars woke up and came running from every direction to see what had happened. I recounted for them what took place, that I had had a spiritual master in Jâm, so-and-so, and that he had passed away from this world nearly two years prior, but that tonight he has produced this effect on me. They observed my wounds and all professed themselves disciples and wrote down the whole incident, which is one of the great wonders. As for the one wound which he left as a memento, it was there for a while until it got better.

---

this story.

373. The Shaykh Cures Yet Another Disease

There was also the similar case of Khvâjeh Musâ of Khalid-âbâd, as follows: [300]

My brother, 'Emâd al-Din,[5] God have mercy upon him, went to the village of Estâd near Zur-âbâd several years after the death of the Shaykh al-Islam. There they looked after him and treated him with respect on account of his devotion to the Shaykh and because of his family ties. A maternal aunt of 'Emâd al-Din was in Khalid-âbâd. Her husband, Khvâjeh 'Osmân-e Âl-e Kaleh [*K-l-h*], would invite 'Emâd al-Din and take him to their village. The grandfather of 'Emâd al-Din urged him to go and see Khvâjeh Musâ whenever he was in Khalid-âbâd, for, "Khvâjeh Musâ is an old friend, even though there is a feud between him and the Âl-e Kalehs. They will not let you look him up, but make sure not to follow their advice. Instead, follow my instructions, for Khvâjeh Musâ is a relative of long-standing."

'Emâd al-Din related as follows:

When I arrived there I waited for days, but this Khvâjeh Musâ did not ask after me, on account of the fact that I was staying in the home of Khvâjeh 'Osmân. Whereas if I had tried to ask after Khvâjeh Musâ, they would have told me, "What do you want with him, he is opposed to you. Don't you feel loathe to look him up?" One day I said, "My grandfather has instructed me to do this and not to follow your advice. I must comply with his instructions."

And so, I set out one day for his house. Someone informed him that I was on my way to see him. He rushed barefoot into the street to welcome me and displayed great humility, falling to the ground in front of me. I later told Khvâjeh 'Osmân, "This 'opponent' behaves in such manner, while you 'supporters' never behave in the least like this."

When Khvâjeh Musâ took me into his house, he said, "I know they must have told you that I am an opponent. I will tell you of an incident and you judge if it is possible or not for me to be your opponent. This is the story: Once I was afflicted with the

---

[5] The identity of the narrator of this passage, 'Emâd al-Din's brother, is unclear.

dropsy—may God spare you from it. It took such violent hold of me that I looked from head to foot like an inflated leather bag and had despaired of recovery. I had taken several treatments, all in vain.

"Finally I grew sick of life and others were sick of me, and I had no hopes of survival. My relatives and children stayed by my side until well into the night and finally all of them got up to go to their own place. [301] They were telling each other, 'He will certainly not make it through the night; we must not neglect him.'

"My mind was alert and I could hear all of this. A while after they had gone and closed the door a light appeared within my room. I thought they were bringing a lamp to set beside me, but it was not so. Someone came and placed his hand upon my forehead. It comforted me. I asked, 'Who are you?'

"He said, 'I am Shaykh Ahmad, I have come to heal you.' He placed his hand upon my head and said, 'Look here, at the treatment.' He ran his hand down my head and the pain and swelling disappeared with the movement of his hand. When he reached the ends of my toes, he said, 'Stand up straight.'

"I looked and saw that there was no trace of swelling in any of my limbs and my suffering was completely dispelled. I left the room in search of my children. They awoke and began shouting, 'Thief, thief!' I said, 'It is no thief, it is me, Musâ.' They said, 'Musâ is in the other world.' They took hold of me and brought the lamp and held it before my face, yet they still could not believe it until they looked in the room and could not find me there. I told them what happened."

"After that, there is no way I could be opposed to you. Judge for yourself and see how what they say is untrue."

374. Khvâjeh Tâher and Khvâjeh As'ad

Here is another event that happened after the Shaykh's death. Khvâjeh Tâher-e Marvi was the chief of Amghân. The mayor of the district of Jâm, Khvâjeh As'ad-e Sâlâri, had a falling out with him over the control of Amghân and was continually making accusations against him and offending him. Then a rumor started that Khvâjeh As'ad was getting an order for the arrest of Khvâjeh

Tâher and the expropriation of his property, and that an official had been designated by the Sultan's ministry for this purpose.

Khvâjeh Tâher fled from Amghân to Ma'd-âbâd and remained in there in hiding to see what would occur. His whereabouts were unknown to his children. [302] Several days went by and he had no news about the situation in the village and was very anxious. One day during the afternoon prayer he thought to himself, "Let me go to Amghân after dark and have a look around to see what has happened and what is going on."

He left Ma'd-âbâd and stopped to visit the grave of the Shaykh al-Islam. He did not, however, show proper respect, but rather kept his footwear on, as was their custom. Having left, it occurred to him that he had not performed his visit with proper decorum, and on this account he was ill at ease. He went to the well and performed the ritual of purification and, holding his footwear in hand, he returned barefoot to visit the grave. He complained to the Shaykh al-Islam about Khvâjeh As'ad. This time he was satisfied with his visitation and knew that it would be well-received.

He went on and arrived in Amghân at night. He went up to the door of his own house and, trembling with fear, lifted the knocker. The womenfolk did not answer, as they feared it might be someone who had come after them. When they realized it was Khvâjeh Tâher, they opened the door. They asked him, "Why have you come? Someone may have been watching you. They have appointed watchmen; take care not to let them capture you."

"I am exhausted now," he said, "let me rest for a while and then I'll go."

At the end of the night someone came and knocked at the door. The women were even more frightened than before and said, "They must be coming after Khvâjeh Tâher; perhaps they have been informed."

They ran to the door to find out. The person said, "Do not fear, I am Khadijeh Mosammari. I come from the next neighborhood over."

"Is there good news?" they asked.

"Yes there is," she said, "I have a message for Khvâjeh Tâher."

"God alone knows where Khvâjeh Tâher is," they said.

She said, "The one who has sent me would not tell a lie."

"Who is that?," they asked.

"The Shaykh al-Islam Ahmad," she said.

Hearing this, Tâher said, "Open the door." She came in, conveyed the greetings of the Shaykh al-Islam and said, "The Shaykh al-Islam Ahmad says: 'O you who came once yesterday to visit my grave and did so without paying proper respect, [303] and then performed a ritual purification and came from the well barefoot and paid a second visit, complaining of As'ad, know that within one week you will be rid of him.'"

When she conveyed the message and all the signs given therein were true, Khvâjeh Tâher was relieved and did not hide anymore. The next week Kvâjeh As'ad received the summons for the next world and Khvâjeh Tâher then felt safe.

375. A Tyrant is Disposed Of

Shaykh 'Omar the Kilnmaker [*Dâshgar*] was one of the sincere disciples and had attained the power to perform miracles, and could even put his hand in the fire without getting burned. One day he was sitting at the foot of the Shaykh al-Islam's grave, his head bowed down. A crowd from the district of Esfandâr-sanj[6] in the province of Herât arrived there and stood in ranks at the head of the grave of the Shaykh al-Islam, God sanctify his soul, their minds occupied with a grave matter.

Shaykh 'Omar lifted his head and saw them. He addressed them, "Brave men!," and asked them, "Where have you come from and do you have a complaint against anyone?"

"How do you know this?," they asked.

He said, "Just now I saw the Shaykh al-Islam drawing an arrow in his bow, which he fired in the direction of Herat. There was a bald man, chubby and of ruddy complexion. He was struck in the head by the arrow, fell down and gave up the ghost."

The men all broke out shouting and rent their clothes, saying, "These signs are all true! What you say—there is a person just as

---

[6] Yâqût calls it "Esfidhâsanj" and indicates it was a village in the region of Herat. It is mentioned both in classical geographical works in both forms, Esfidhâ- and Esfandâr-sanj.

you describe, an official of the governor in that district, and we are greatly oppressed by him. We have tried again and again and spent a sum of money to get rid of him. We even went to the Royal Court but were unable to get him off our back. We thought we should go to the presence of the Master, that he might get rid of this man. It is for this that we have come."

When they returned, that fellow was sitting in the middle of the bazaar, pushing forward his affairs and exchanges to his advantage. Suddenly he fell down and gave up the ghost and the people [304] were delivered from his clutches [*sharr*].

376. Capture of a Thief and Retrieval of Stolen Property

There was also the case of 'Osmân the Coppersmith:

There was a man in the village of Sâghu near Jâm who was called 'Osmân the Master Coppersmith. He was a trustworthy man, true to his word, one of the sincere disciples of the Shaykh al-Islam Ahmad, God sanctify his precious soul. He had a daughter who had been given away in marriage[7] after being provided with clothing [*qomâsheh*]. Then a burglar got over their wall and broke into their house. He took all the clothes they had, whether silk or canvas and no one knew who had taken them.

'Osmân would go around looking for the thief, but found no trace of him. He gave up the search and went to the shrine of the Shaykh al-Islam Ahmad, God sanctify his precious soul, placed his face to the threshold of that sanctuary and wept. He said, "O Shaykh al-Islam, it has been fifty years that I have bowed my head to this threshold in complete sincerity and armed my soul with devotion to you, serving your sons and disciples. Why must a whole donkey-load of my wretched daughter's [*'ajuzeh*] clothes be stolen? For some time I have searched, but found no trace of them. I believe you have the power and grace to discover them and restore them to us. Now I turn the matter over to your Eminence and am returning home. I will not look any further for them, nor

---

[7] Literally, who had joined her "enemy" [*khasm*]! This brings to mind the Cockney rhyming slang for wife (i.e., trouble and strife) except that the man was clearly presumed to have an upper hand over his wife in medieval Iran. See the note to Story 28.

will I expect anyone but your Eminence to find them. However, if you fail to find my goods and restore them to me, I will drink wine, return to my old ways and break my vow of repentance!" This he said out of insolence in the heat of the moment and returned to the village of Sâghu and busied himself with his profession.

There was another person in this village called 'Osmân-e 'Affân. This man grew reeds [*nây-kâr*], and it was he who had taken the clothes and then laid low. Once [305] the wrath of the victims died down somewhat, he gave the clothes to a relative of his called Mohammad-e 'Affân, to take to Herat and sell. When he arrived in the city of Herat and was making the rounds and inquiring [after a potential buyer], it so happened that that same week some thieves had been arrested. Every day they would bring two or three of these people to a certain place for punishment. Some they would hang, others would have their hands and feet cut off and some were beaten with clubs.

Mohammad-e 'Affân grew fearful and his heart was filled with terror, for, as it is said, "the traitor lives in terror." He did not unpack his wares, but turned back and set out for home. By the time of the afternoon prayer, he had reached Ma'd-âbâd, but was afraid to enter the village. He came to the grave of the Shaykh al-Islam Ahmad, God sanctify his precious soul, and set the bundle down near the door of the khâneqâh and waited for nightfall to set off toward Sâghu. After it grew dark, he fell asleep and did not wake up.

There was a member of the weaker sex ['*owrat*] in this khâneqâh called Mâmân Hâji, who was old and could not see. She had served at the holy shrine for some time and had experienced many good rewards. After a part of the night had passed, she saw the Shaykh al-Islam in a dream, telling her, "Some of the clothes of 'Osmân the Master Coppersmith have been brought to the door of the khâneqâh. Look out for them and let him know."

Mâmân Hâji got up, came out of the khâneqâh, and approached the holy shrine. She paid her respects and came over to the door of the khâneqâh in search of the clothes. Suddenly her hand felt a sack. She said, "Here are the clothes of Master 'Osmân."

Mâmân Hâji came back into the khâneqâh. She had a son called

'Osmân-e Loqmân. She woke him up and told him about it.
Together they brought the sack inside the khâneqâh and she right
away despatched the son in the direction of Sâghu to find Master
'Osmân.

Meanwhile Mohammad-e 'Affân did not wake up until morning.
At dawn Master 'Osmân arrived and opened the sacks. All of his
clothes were there and he got them back without any expense or
damage. All this through the blessings of the grace of the Shaykh
al-Islam, God sanctify his precious soul. [306]

377. Punishing an Evildoer

There was also the case of 'Ali-ye Sâqi, as follows:
Amir Tâj al-Din Moqaddam-e Ghuri was the ruler of the village
of Ma'd-âbâd. He had a brother-in-law [self] called 'Ali-ye Sâqi.
'Ali was a corrupt and evil man, always engaged in sin and
creating mischief. Amir Tâj al-Din Moqaddam had entrusted
Ma'd-âbâd to him, and people used to tell the Amir, "You are
aware that 'Ali-ye Sâqi is a man of weak faith and a sinner. This is
a delicate situation and risky; what if he were to do something and
get you entangled in the matter."

He said, "I have given him a warning; if he doesn't comply, he
knows what will be happen. Let him suffer the consequences."
There was a home in the village of Ma'd-âbâd where the Shaykh
al-Islam Ahmad, God sanctify his precious soul, used to live in the
beginning. When 'Ali-ye Sâqi took up residence in this home, he
turned to corruption and pursued sin and vice beyond all limits.
Then one night someone in the village had a dream of the Shaykh
al-Islam, who was coming toward the village with a whip in hand.
He was asked, "Where are you going, your Eminence?" He said,
"I'm going to tell Tâj al-Din Moqaddam to chastise 'Ali-ye Sâqi,
or else I will chastise the both of them."

The next day they came to tell 'Ali that two or three trustworthy
citizens had had such a dream. "Don't do this! Repent, lest some
incident or event befall you and cause your ruin." Though they
insisted, he would not listen.

Tâj al-Din Moqaddam was the Amir of Sarakhs and was

stationed in the city of Sarakhs. That same week, 'Ali-ye Sâqi set out for Sarakhs. When he reached the village of Shurâb,[8] Ekhtiâr al-Din, the son of Tâj al-Din Moqaddam-e Ghuri, met up with him and immediately ordered that his beard and moustache be plucked [307] and that he be clubbed by a Daghmaji[9] mace. His bones and members were all crushed. When he perished, Ekhtiâr al-Din rode off to Ma'd-âbâd and without stopping went straight to the grave of the Shaykh al-Islam Ahmad. With head uncovered he wept and asked forgiveness.

When he entered the village they asked him, "What was the reason for killing 'Ali-ye Sâqi, for you killed him on the road without any investigation?"

He said, "Early in the week, my father, Amir Tâj al-Din, saw the Shaykh al-Islam Ahmad in a dream, complaining of 'Ali-ye Sâqi. He threatened my father, saying, 'You have appointed Sâqi and left him in power to the point that he has transgressed all bounds of decency. If you fail to punish him, I will punish you.' My father was greatly frightened and afraid on this account. He sent me with instructions to go towards Jâm and to kill 'Ali-ye Sâqi without delay wherever I came across him, for, he said, 'I love myself better than I love him.' This was the reason for killing 'Ali-ye Sâqi; more than this we know not."

378. Prince Ziâ al-Din Asks for the Hand of the Daughter of the Ghurid Sultan Ghiâs al-Din

Another case is that of Ziâ al-Din of Ghur, as follows:

There was in Ghur a prince called Ziâ al-Din, who was a relative of the Ghurid Sultan Ghiâs al-Din,[10] may God make his proof resplendent. He wanted to marry the daughter of the Sultan, but they would not consent.

---

[8] In the vicinity of Nayshabur and Torbat-e Jâm there are several villages with the name Shurâb.

[9] The Persian word, *D-gh-m-j-i*, which we have vocalized Daghmaji, is not given in any of the standard dictionaries.

[10] Ghiâs al-Din Mohammad ebn-e Sâm of Ghur in Afghanistan, died in 1203 / 599 A.H.

When this girl was betrothed to Prince Toghânshâh,[11] who was the son of Prince Moayyad of Nayshabur, Prince Ziâ al-Din, in his despair, set out on a pilgrimage to Mecca. After completing the pilgrimage, he passed through the district of Jâm on his return. because of the devotion he had for the Shaykh al-Islam Ahmad, God sanctify his precious soul. He paid a visit to the blessed shrine of the Shaykh and stayed in the khâneqâh. At [308] nightfall, he wrote down on paper his feelings and his suit for the hand of the Sultan's daughter. This paper he gave to a confidant of his called Hâji Bachcheh,[12] whom he trusted completely with his affairs, and told him to go to the shrine of the Shaykh al-Islam Ahmad. "Find a stone near the grave and put this paper underneath it. Then sit at some distance to see what happens. Then come back."

Hâji Bachcheh went and did as he was instructed. After waiting a while, he went up to the immaculate and holy grave and saw that the paper which he had put underneath the stone was now on top of the stone. He picked it up, took it to the Prince and laid the paper in his hands, explaining what had happened. When the Prince looked at it, he found that a clear answer had been written on it. He rose up and performed a ritual purification and went to the holy shrine of the Shaykh al-Islam. He remained awake there until daylight.

The following day he set out in the direction of Ghur. When he arrived at the city of Firuzkuh, Sultan Ghiâs al-Din gave the order to go and welcome him, and he was led in complete honor into the city of Herat. He annulled the contract betrothing his daughter to Toghânshâh and betrothed her to Ziâ al-Din, bestowing the title Prince 'Alâ-Din on him.

All this was from the grace and blessings of the holy spirit of the Shaykh al-Islam Ahmad, may God sanctify his precious soul. Such

---

[11] Toghânshâh ebn al-Mo'ayyad Ây Âbeh conquered Khorasan after the death of Sanjar and ruled in Nayshabur from 1173-1185 / 569-581 A.H. He was not a member of the Seljuk clan (see *Habib al-sayer*, 1:422 and *Lobâb al-albâb*, 1:228, 278, 329 and 361). There is no mention of the present story in any of the historical sources.

[12] The letter "ch" is undotted in the manuscript, but this seems a likely reading.

things have appeared since the passing of the Shaykh at his grave site, at his request and supplication. There are many such things, and it is well known, so that you know.

379. The Truthful Dervish and the Ruler of Herat

Then there was the case of Qâzi 'Ali of Herat, as follows:

Sultan Mo'ezz al-Din of Ghazna,[13] who would later be a few dervishes. When the Sultan's retinue arrived and the dervishes had retreated into the khâneqâh, Qâzi 'Ali blocked the Sultan's path and adjured him as follows: "Hold your reins a moment and listen to what I have to say."

Nâser al-Din Alb Ghâzi was riding side-by-side with the Sultan. He asked, "Dervish, what do you have to say? Speak and do not be afraid."

Qâzi 'Ali said, "There is no king in the whole of Islam who is greater or more just than you. Would you permit this city of Muslims to be turned over to the clutches of this tyrant?"

The Sultan said, "Alb, do you hear what this Dervish is saying? If you tyrannize the people, I will chop off your head."

When the Sultan set off for Ghazna, Alb Ghâzi returned to the city and summoned Qâzi 'Ali. He said, "Dervish, do you know what you were saying in front of the Sultan?! You called me a tyrant. Now tell me what I should do with you."

---

[13] Sultan Shehâb al-Din Abu al-Mozaffar ebn-e Sâm ebn-e Hosayn, the brother of Sultan Ghiâs al-Din. He assumed the throne in 1203 / 599 A.H., at the death of Ghiâs al-Din and took the title Mo'ezz al-Din. During his brother's lifetime he had been the governor of Ghazna and repeatedly campaigned in India, capturing the cities of that country, including Dehli. In 1205 / 602 A.H. while returning from a battle, he was assassinated by the blade of an Ismaili. There is a quatrain in the *Habib al-sayer* (2:607) about him, as follows:

The king of land and sea, Mo'ezz al-Din,
martyr whose like the world has never seen:
He fell near Ghazna in Damanak quarter
the third of Sha'bân, the year six-hundred two.

'Ali asked, "How should one respond to the truth? Whatever it may be, do what you like, but do not tyrannize the people, if you don't want to be called a tyrant."

Fear took hold of the heart of Alb Ghâzi at these words and he said, "Dervish, I forgive you. What reward would you have of me?"

He said, "I want nothing [310] from you, only that you do not tyrannize the people."

Alb Ghâzi said, "You must, of course, ask for something, before I release you."

Qâzi 'Ali said, "If I am required to request something, give me a few ounces[14] of lawful thread to sew into my cloak."

Alb Ghâzi said, "Dervish, where am I going to get these few ounces of lawful thread?"

Qâzi 'Ali said, "What can I ask of a man who does not have access to even a few ounces of lawful thread? I want nothing more from you than that you act justly with God's creatures."

Alb Ghâzi said to his attendants, "Go to the treasury and get that sword which was brought to me from India—there can be no doubt about its lawfulness." They fetched the sword, which was a fine and precious one, very ornate, with a gold-plated hilt. He said, "I give this to you, you leave me be."

Qâzi 'Ali said, "I have no need of the sword. If you do not tyrannize the people, I will leave you be."

Alb Ghâzi said, "You absolutely must accept the sword."

Qâzi 'Ali said, "You have relinquished the sword and made it a gift to me. Whatever I want to do with it, whoever I wish to give or sell it to, you will not renege?"

He said, "I will not. Go ahead."

Thus Qâzi 'Ali took the sword and left. He went to a cook's shop and said, "Take this sword; I will sell it to you for two hundred maunds of bread and one hundred maunds of meat."

The cook said, "They will not allow this sword to remain in my possession." Qâzi 'Ali said, "They will allow it. Now how about

---

[14] That is *dah sir*, ten *sir*. Forty *sir* make one maund, which is, depending on the locale and the time-period, about three kilos or six kilos. The point is that this is a small amount of cloth or thread.

the price, the bread and meat?" The cook said, "Give it here."[15]
Qâzi 'Ali gave the sword, took his bread and meat and invited the
dervishes to a feast.

A few days passed. Alb Ghâzi was informed what Qâzi 'Ali had
done with the sword. "Go and pay him an amount of bread and
meat equal to the sword and bring it back here," he ordered. They
did as they were told.

Qâzi 'Ali found out and went to see Alb Ghâzi. "Didn't I tell
you that you could not bring yourself to let go of this sword? Is it
right to make a gift of the sword and then renege and never stop
tyrannizing the people? Is this how the great have acted?"

Alb Ghâzi grew angry. "Cut out his tongue," he ordered, "for it
offends me greatly." They brought him to the place of punishment
and cut out [311] his tongue.

Qâzi 'Ali proceeded to the holy shrine of the Shaykh al-Islam
Ahmad, God sanctify his precious soul, and hid there. A few days
later, he saw the Shaykh al-Islam telling him in a dream, "Qâzi
'Ali, that tyrant has treated you cruelly and cut out your tongue.
But the cutting off of your tongue will become the cause of his
repentance. Do not worry, just say, 'In the name of God.'" He did
so. The Shaykh told him, "Turn and go back to Herat." When he
arrived, he could talk.

Alb Ghâzi was informed that Qâzi 'Ali had returned and that he
was talking. Alb Ghâzi asked, "Have you indeed cut out his
tongue?" They said, "We did cut it out." He said, "Bring him here
so I can see this."

Qâzi 'Ali was produced. Alb Ghâzi asked, "Have they cut out
your tongue?"

"They have," he said.

"Let me see it," said Alb Ghâzi. He stuck out his tongue, and
Alb Ghâzi saw it had been cut off. He was amazed and said, "How
have you managed to speak?"

"I have a spiritual Master called Shaykh al-Islam Ahmad of Jâm,
God sanctify his precious soul. When my tongue was cut out, I
went to his holy shrine to live. I saw him one night in a dream,
telling me, 'That tyrant cut out your tongue, but the cutting out of

---

[15] Reading *biâr* for *be-bâr* in the text.

your tongue will be the cause of his repentance. Do not worry any
more, but say, *In the name of God.':*"

He could not, however, pronounce the letter "R," so Alb Ghâzi
said, "The miracles of the Almighty God's saints are true, but
miracles do not admit of defect and imperfection. If what you say
is true, why can't you pronounce your "R"s? If you were to say
"R" it would become clear to me that what you say is true and I
will repent of my tyranny, and spread justice such that even the
animals will benefit from it."

Qâzi 'Ali got up and set out for Jâm. He came to the holy shrine
of the Shaykh al-Islam and said, "O Shaykh al-Islam, did you not
tell me that the cutting off of my tongue would be the cause of his
repentance? Now it is conditioned upon my saying the letter 'R.'
The rest is up to you." Having said this, after a while he fell
asleep.

Qâzi 'Ali relates: I saw the Shaykh al-Islam [312] in a dream,
telling me, "Say, 'In the name of God, the Merciful, the Ruthful.'"
Immediately I was able to say it correctly, just as you hear me
pronounce it now. He then commanded me to return and tell Alb
Ghâzi to be true to his word, or else a calamity he would not
survive would befall him.

When he returned and went before Alb Ghâzi, he said, "In the
name of God, the Merciful, the Ruthful," correctly and conveyed
the message of the Shaykh al-Islam. Alb Ghâzi immediately
repented and wept and made profuse apologies to Qâzi 'Ali, and
spread justice throughout the province of Herat, such that cannot
be described.

This was from the grace and blessings of the holy spirit of the
Shaykh al-Islam Ahmad, God sanctify his precious soul, and in
this incident is more than one miracle, as we have set
down.assassinated, [309] may God make his proof resplendent,
recalled him, as he had given the city of Herat to Prince Nâser al-
Din Alb Ghâzi.[16] He was an impossibly oppressive man, corrupt
and evil, and for this reason the people of Herat were upset and

---

[16] Nâser al-Din Alb Ghâzi was the nephew of Sultan Mo'ezz al-Din.
Mo'ezz al-Din, upon his ascension to the throne in 1203/599 A.H., chose
him to be governor of Herat.

troubled in the extreme.

Dervish Qâzi 'Ali was one of the followers of the Shaykh al-Islam Zahir al-Din 'Isâ, the son of the Shaykh al-Islam Ahmad. He was a wise man, a close friend of the Shaykh's family who had served Zahir al-Din and enjoyed his company. He was brave and fearless, spoke well and spoke the truth. One day the Sultan of Ghazna was returning from a visit to the shrine, when he passed by a place called Sarsangân.

Qâzi 'Ali was sitting in this place at the door of a khâneqâh with

380. How the Shaykh Removed Ziâ al-Molk, An Enemy of the Family

Then there was the case of Ziâ al-Molk of Samarqand, as follows:

On the 24th of Sha'bân in the year 650 [30 October 1252], Ziâ al-Molk came to the village of Ma'd-âbâd and paid a visit to the holy sanctuary of Ahmad, the King of Saints, may God perpetuate his blessings, and attained the presence of the Shaykh al-Islam Qotb al-Din,[17] the chosen successor of that King of Religion, who was living at that immaculate shrine. He said, "I have done my utmost so that I could break my fast during Ramadan at your table and perform the supererogatory prayers [*tarâvih*] behind you."[18]

---

[17] The grandson of the Shaykh Ahmad, called Abu al-Fath Qotb al-Din Mohammad ebn-e Shams al-Din Motahhar, born in 1162 / 557 A.H. and died some time after 1252 / 650 A.H. (at which time he would have have been 93 lunar years). According to the *Mojmal-e Fasihi*, he died in 1268 / 667 A.H. He was the author of a Sufi manual called *Hadiqat al-haqiqat* (not to be confused with the famous poem of this name by Sanâ'i), written in 1244 / 642 A.H. Manuscripts of this work have survived; Mohammad-'Ali Movahhed prepared a critical edition of the text, published in 1964 (Tehran: Bongâh-e Tarjomeh va Nashr-e Ketâb, 1343). For more information on Abu al-Fath Qotb al-Din, see also *Rowzat al-rayâhin*, 85-97, and the accompanying endnotes, 138-9.

[18] This prayer of 22 prostrations is often performed during the night in the month of Ramadan. Every four prostrations are followed by a period of rest, which is why the prayer is called "relaxations," *tarâvih*, the plural of *tarvihah*. Worshippers perform their prayers standing behind and in

The Shaykh al-Islam Qotb al-Din said, "You are most welcome!" and ordered that a place be prepared for him in the village, into which he settled.

At night a group of evil people sat with him spreading calumnies and misrepresentations [313] about the Shaykh al-Islam Qotb al-Din, and thereby changed his opinion. The following day he sent someone with the message, "You have tyrannized the people of the village and enjoyed unlawful benefits [loqmeh]."

The Shaykh al-Islam Qotb al-Din sent back this answer: "You cannot fathom the nature of our benefits, and you do not know lawful from unlawful, but concerning the benefits you have enjoyed, we shall send someone to the Royal Court and have an observer come to look into the matter and distinguish tyranny from justice. If I have committed tyranny, I will pay for it."

Ziâ al-Molk said, "Am I not the governor?"

The Shaykh al-Islam Qotb al-Din replied, "No, what right do you have to govern over the district or the village?"

The next day Ziâ al-Molk got up and went to Bizd near Jâm to stay. The people who had been spreading misrepentations kept going to visit him and he would soothe them. Finally, on the morning of the day of 'Arafeh [!][19] someone came on behalf of Ziâ al-Molk and the folks who had acted disrespectfully to punish [the Shaykh al-Islam Qotb al-Din].[20]

---

unison with a figure of religious authority or piety, who is therefore called Imâm, literally, one who stands in front.

[19] See the note on 'Arafeh in Story 203. 'Arafeh is the day prior to the 'Id-e Qorbân in the month of the pilgrimage to Mecca, Dhi al-Hijjah. This 'Id, or festival, is known as the Greater Festival of Islam. However, from the context of this story, it seems clear that the 'Id, or festival, intended here is not 'Id-e Qorbân, but the so-called Lesser Festival, or 'Id-e Fetr, a feast day which occurs on the first of Shavvâl, after Ramadan, the month of fasting, ends. This confusion is likely due either to a mistake by the compiler of the stories or the scribe who copied out the manuscript. In the much-abbreviated version of this conflict between Qotb al-Din and 'Aziz al-Din narrated in the Rowzat al-rayâhin (92), no mention of the time of year is made, perhaps in part because the author of that book, writing 300 years later, could not make sense of this discrepancy.

[20] The text has a lacuna here and the words in brackets are assumed to

The Shaykh al-Islam Qotb al-Din grew concerned and said, "If I keep silent about this, he will go beyond the limit, and if I do not, I will have to debate with him. I desire neither the former nor the latter." He was occupied with such thoughts until the noon-prayer. When he performed this, Ziâ al-Molk had not yet arrived.

Suddenly someone came announcing the arrival of Khvâjeh 'Aziz al-Din Owhad,[21] may God honor him in both worlds, who was a pillar of state at the court of the King of that time. The Shaykh al-Islam Qotb al-Din said, "A miracle of the Shaykh al-Islam Ahmad, God sanctify his precious soul, who sends him here at this point in time! His arrival has brought comfort to my distracted heart!"

Just then he arrived and visited the holy shrine, asking, "What has happened? The moment I heard that your eminence's mind was worried, I mounted and left everything behind, galloping uncontrollably on."

The Shaykh al-Islam [314] Qotb al-Din said, "The sacred spirit of this King of Religion has brought you here; now that you have come, welcome!"

At the afternoon prayer Ziâ al-Molk arrived from Bizd, as well, and, on the morning of the Festival[22] he came to see the Shaykh al-Islam Qotb al-Din. After the ceremonial prayers and consumption of food, the Shaykh al-Islam Qotb al-Din told Ziâ al-Molk, "You came before Ramadan and said you were in a hurry to break the fast with me and pray behind me. What was the reason, what came to your attention, that you accused me the following day of tyranny and unlawful behavior? Did you dream it all up?"

"Well," he said, "let's forget about all that."

The Shaykh al-Islam asked, "How can one forget about it?! Rather one should note the miracle by which the Shaykh al-Islam Ahmad, God sanctify his precious soul, one hundred and fourteen

---

be the gist of the missing text.

[21] The first time he is mentioned, the text calls him 'Ezz al-Din, but subsequently he is called 'Aziz al-Din. The *Rowzat al-rayâhin* (92) refers to him as 'Ezz al-Din in a very abbreviated and variant version of this story.

[22] See the note above about 'Arafeh.

years after his death, has led such a person here under such circumstances."[23] He told Khvâjeh 'Aziz al-Din, "You ought to get up and look into this matter. I will not remain present in this gathering, so that no one will say that they were unable to speak freely in my presence." They all got up and went to another room [vesâq] and said all that needed to be said.

God cleared up the matter and Qotb al-Din was proved correct. The traitors withdrew their accusations and Khvâjeh 'Aziz al-Din (may God make him true to his name in both worlds!) boxed the ears of Ziâ al-Molk, and threatened him, upbraiding him severely. He also punished the folks who were making accusations and ordered someone to enchain Ziâ al-Molk. Then Ziâ al-Molk sent a messenger to tell Shaykh al-Islam Qotb al-Din, "God, the Exalted and Almighty, releases demons from their chains on this Festival Day. Will, then, the Shaykh al-Islam Qotb al-Din, have Muslims chained up?"

Shaykh Qotb al-Din ordered, "Tell him that any demon which escapes its chains during Ramadan will be locked up on this day. It is you who stirred up this trouble; let us see, then, how you will free yourself!"

Ziâ al-Molk said, "I will come to Ma'd-âbâd with a horde of Mongols and do what should be done, or else I am not the son of my father!" [315] And he left.

After dark, Master Qotb al-Din [went] to the shrine of his grandfather, the King of Saints, Shaykh al-Islam Ahmad, God sanctify his precious soul and said, "O Shaykh al-Islam, I reside here on your account. Otherwise, how could I withstand a horde of drunken Mongols? Give me leave to go or else reveal to me, either in a dream or a vision, some sign that this threat will be repelled, that my heart may be assured."

For seven days after the Festival of the Feast [Id-e Fetr] he waited, at which time a member of the weaker sex ['owrat] belonging to Master Qotb al-Din woke up at dawn, all upset and in tears, terrified and in fear. Master Qotb al-Din asked her, "What

---

[23] These are 114 lunar years. According to the Islamic calendar, Shaykh Ahmad died in 536 (1141 A.D.). The incident mentioned took place in the year 650 (1252 A.D.), 114 years later according to the Islamic lunar calendar, but only 111 solar years later.

has happened to you?"

"I had a terrible dream," she said.

"What was your dream?," he asked her.

"In the middle of our yard a huge black serpent, all coiled up with its head poised, was looking at you in awe, but intending to strike. You were gazing on it and I was terribly afraid. All of a sudden a dog came along, grabbed it by the neck, dragged it all around the yard of the house, chewed off its head and ran off with it. The fright it gave me woke me up."

Master Qotb al-Din said, "Do not be afraid. This is the sign which I had asked for from the pristine and sanctified spirit of the Shaykh al-Islam Ahmad, God sanctify his precious soul, and he has revealed it to you."

Then, on the 16th day of Shavvâl 651 [9 December 1253], Ziâ al-Molk was put to death in the city of Herat and the order was given to skin his head. They did so with the intention of filling the skin with straw and sending it to the district of Ghur. When they went looking for straw after skinning his head, a dog came and carried it off. They looked everywhere but could find neither the dog nor the skin of Ziâ al-Molk's head. This story of his execution is famous and well-known throughout Khorasan and Transoxania.

This is one of the miracles performed by the spirit of the King of Saints, Shaykh Ahmad, God sanctify his precious soul, for what had been revealed in a dream came to pass a short while later, and all the various sections of this district are aware of it. Many similar examples have been witnessed and [316] observed. And God is the Guide, His blessings be upon Mohammad and his entire family, all the righteous and the pure.

Six Further Posthumous Miracles of the Shaykh[24]

381. A Woman is Cured in Her Sleep by the Shaykh

The Imam and Shaykh of Shaykhs in all the World, Zahir al-Din 'Isâ, Exemplar to the saints, source of pride, the son of Shaykh al-Islam Ahmad, God have mercy on them both, related:

Two years after the death of the Shaykh al-Islam, I went to serve Borhân al-Din Nasr, God have mercy upon him, the successor of the Shaykh, in the region of Pir.[25] The mother of Khvâjeh Bu Sâleh had been bedridden for more than two years and was sorely afflicted by palpitations. She sat propped up by three pillows, for she could in no wise move. I saw her myself in this condition. During the week I was there, this member of the weaker sex saw the Shaykh al-Islam in a dream, walking along the bank of a river.

She related to us:

I cried out to the Shaykh, saying, "For God's sake, help me, for I am a follower of yours and was born to one of your followers, and here I am afflicted with this disease." When I said this, the Shaykh al-Islam told me, "Hold the hem of your skirt." I held the hem of my skirt and he scooped up a handful of water from the stream and threw it in my direction. The water turned to rock candy in the air and fell into my lap. I picked up a bit of it and ate it. I felt an improvement in my being. The joy of it woke me up. I rolled over and got to my feet and let out a yell in the middle of the night. The entire household jumped up and came to me to see what had happened. I asked for the ewer and performed a ritual ablution and said my prayers.

The news of this [317] spread throughout the village. The next morning we went to greet her and saw that she was healthy and on

---

[24] These six stories come from the Chester Beatty Manuscript of Ghaznavi's *Spiritual Feats* under the rubric of posthumous miracles of the Shaykh, but are not attributed to Ahmad-e Tarkhestâni as author or compiler in that manuscript. See "Manuscripts of the Spiritual Feats" in the Introduction.

[25] *Dar sar-hadd-e pir*; no such place is recorded in the region of Jâm. It may perhaps reflect a corruption of the manuscript. With the addition of a final -*i* to this phrase, one could read "at a very advanced age."

her feet, walking around. All this, through the blessings of God, Mighty and Exalted be He.

382. Stolen Iron Is Returned Through The Shaykh

One of the Sufi followers of the Shaykh al-Islam 'Abd Allâh Ansâri, God have mercy upon him, relates as follows:

Thirty-two years after the death of the Shaykh al-Islam Ahmad, we were going on our way to Nayshabur. We arrived at his grave and spent the night there. One of our packs of iron was stolen that night.

I bowed my head for a while and heard a voice saying, "Get up, the pack has been recovered." Instantly the caravan leader[26] came to say, "We have found the pack; it was cast off in such and such place." We loaded it up and went on our way.

383. The Fate of Imam Fasih-e Valvâleji

During the lifetime of the Shaykh al-Islam, Khvâjeh Imam Fasih-e Valvâleji[27] had written a letter to him containing many reflections on poverty as well as questions for the Shaykh. The Shaykh al-Islam answered it,[28] but the Imam was offended by the reply because it [undermined] his scholarly reputation. After the death of the Shaykh al-Islam, he came to Buzjân, intending to visit the Shaykh's grave.

When he reached Ma'd-âbâd he said, "The Master draws me here from a great distance." He removed his turban and placed it at the foot of the grave. After a while he said, "This turban ought to pay for a feast."

"What is the matter?," he was asked.

---

[26] *Khar-bandeh*, the owner of the pack animals hired to make the journey.

[27] Valvâlej is a town in the district of Badakhshân, beyond Balkh and Takhârestân (see Yâqût). This Imam Fasih appears as the recipient of a letter from the Shaykh al-Islam in the latter's *Epistle to the Samarqandians* (see below).

[28] This letter is extant; see the *Epistle to the Samarqandians* in Part Four.

"I saw the Master standing on the grave and reminding me that I had once written him a letter which failed to observe proper decorum.[29] I offered that turban [318] as penance for that."

They took the turban and held a feast at which much food was consumed. The Imam left in the direction of Sarakhs and was killed on the road.

384. The Healing Power of One of the Shaykh's Letters[30]

Thirty years after the death of the Shaykh al-Islam, one of his letters was found in the library of his son, Borhân al-Din, God have mercy upon him. The Shaykh al-Islam had written this letter to his sons Borhân al-Din and Qotb al-Din when they had gone to Sarakhs as tutors. They would give this letter to all afflicted people, most of whom would say, "I am cured."

But one night my own member began to hurt in such wise that I could no longer stand it, though I was ashamed to mention it. I performed the night prayer and picked up that letter to intercede on my behalf with God, asking for release from that pain.

Even as I was in that position, a feeling of tranquility came over me through the blessings of that letter. And that incident was a miracle.

385. A Flood In the Middle of Summer

Khvâjeh Imam Serâj al-Din related the story of the year 577 A.H. [1181 A.D.] in Shâfelân,[31] as follows:

---

[29] Reading *tark-hâ*, probably meaning *tark-e adab-hâ*, i.e., failure to observe all the expected niceties of expression. It is also possible to read *tork(i)-hâ*, which would mean rude or gruff language or behavior, by association with the Turkish tribesmen who invaded Iran (see Ânandrâj).

[30] Here the narrator is Imam Fasih-e Valvâleji, but in *Rowzat al-rayâhin* (59), the narrator is ʿAli-ye Buzjâni, who ascribes the incident to Imam Razi al-Din Jamâl al-Islam Tâybâdi and gives slightly different details, the most important of which is that Khvâjeh Borhân al-Din was going to Sarakhs to study, not to teach.

[31] This place is not mentioned in most of the geographical dictionaries, but the *Târikh-nâmeh-ye Harât* (319) does describe the "plain [*sahrâ*] of

I had planted a field of cotton and there was no water, in Shâfelân. [319] One day I went to my cotton field and saw a third (of it)[32] dry and wilted. Disappointed, I went home and could not sleep that night. I picked up the ewer, did my ablutions and performed two prostrations of prayer. I laid my head on the ground and I beseeched God, the Exalted and Almighty, in the name of the Shaykh al-Islam Ahmad, to send water down to us.

At dawn in the middle of the summer, heavy flood waters overtook us from a direction I would never have hoped or expected. God knows where it came from. For a period of two months it filled the field, and none knew where the water had come from.

This happened forty-three years after the death of the Shaykh,[33] and everyone in the region of Shâfelân is aware of how hope replaced such despair, so that all may know.

386. The Battle of Toghânshâh and Soltanshâh[34]

The Shaykh al-Islam 'Emâd al-Din 'Abd al-Rahim[35] stayed in Ma'd-âbâd forty-five years after the death of Shaykh Ahmad. During the reign of Prince Mo'ayyad he would stay for a while in Nayshabur each time he went there. Prince Mo'ayyad and the

---

Shâfelân," and in the *Rowzât al-jannât fi owsâf-e madinat-e Harât*, Shâqelân [incorrectly reading "q" for "f"] is described in the section about the city of Herat (1:104-5) as "a very wide and broad plain, fruitful and prosperous, in the mountainous region beyond the Harirud river."

[32] *S-Y-M*, the meaning of which is not entirely clear. It might mean "one-third" [*seyyom*] of the field, though it is likely that in drought conditions much more of the cotton crop would be lost than this. There is an obscure word of Arabic origin, *senem* (and the letters in the manuscript might be construed this way), meaning "tall blossoming plant," but one would not expect to find this word in the current text.

[33] Since the Shaykh died in the year 536 A.H. (1141 A.D.), either the text should read 41 years (lunar years–every 33 lunar years being approximately equal to 32 solar years), or the date at the beginning of the story should read 579 A.H.

[34] Compare the version of this story as given in *Rowzat al-rayâhin*, 70.

[35] The ninth son of the Shaykh al-Islam Ahmad.

pillars of his administration were firm believers in the family of the Shaykh al-Islam, especially in 'Emâd al-Din.

When Prince Mo'ayyad returned to the mercy of God, his son, Prince Toghânshâh, who had complete faith in the Shaykh al-Islam, set out for Marv Rud to do battle with Soltanshâh, the son of the Khwârazmshâh. 'Emâd al-Din had a dream in which the Shaykh al-Islam gave a robe of honor to Soltanshâh. [Thereupon] he went to warn Prince Toghânshâh, "Do not go to fight with Soltanshâh, for victory will be his and you will be disgraced."

"Why do you say this?," he asked.

'Emâd al-Din said, "I saw father in a dream, [320] giving Soltanshâh a robe of honor."

Toghânshâh cancelled his expedition. Some people, not believing in the Shakyh, looked on this with a critical eye and urged him to go to war. He did go to war with his army fully-equipped and was put to rout by Soltanshâh. Quite a number of Toghânshâh's soldiers were killed, but he, by a thousand strategems, was able to save his own life. Toghânshâh's dominion lost all its splendor after that and Soltanshâh captured the greater part of Khorasan. ·

PART THREE

On the Greatness of Shaykh Ahmad-e Jâm

By Shehâb al-Din Esma'il

SHEHÂB AL-DIN ESMA'IL
AND HIS FATHER'S FOLLOWING

The following short treatise on the life of Shaykh Ahmad is credited to Shehâb al-Din Esma'il, the fourteenth and youngest son of the Shaykh. It attempts to establish the greatness of Shaykh Ahmad using logical proofs for the benefit of those readers who do not believe in the miracles attributed to him. It would appear that the majority of Shaykh Ahmad's followers were simple folks who readily believed in miracles, but throughout his career, he had a number of antagonists among the legal scholars and learned classes who either opposed the principles and practices of Sufism, and/or did not credit the miraculous claims Shaykh Ahmad's followers made on his behalf. It is to the objections of this more learned and skeptical audience that Shehâb al-Din Esma'il addressed this treatise.

Instead of the focus on miracles of transmutation, clairvoyance or other supernatural powers which we find in *The Spiritual Feats*, Shehâb al-Din chooses to adduce miracles of a different order as proof of the Shaykh's sainthood. Shehâb al-Din mentions three:

1) That his father, Shaykh Ahmad, was able to convert enormous numbers of people to Islam.

2) Shaykh Ahmad had never been formally schooled and was, in fact, illiterate when he began his spiritual hermitage on the mountain, but was able to read and write and was conversant with the arguments of scholars of religion upon his return;[1]

3) He raised sons who were all Imams and leading authorities in the field of religion in their own day.

Shehâb al-Din Esma'il's treatise was obviously composed in the twelfth century, probably about the same time as *The Spiritual Feats* of Ghaznavi. It appears to have circulated from an early date with Ghaznavi's work, and to have been considered part and parcel of *The Spiritual Feats*, at the very latest by the early 15th century, since it

---

[1] This was one of the miracles traditionally attributed to the Prophet Mohammad, though not necessarily a miracle confined to the prophets, per se.

occurs in the Nâfiz Pâshâ manuscript of Ghaznavi's *Spiritual Feats*, copied out in 1422. Buzjâni, writing in the early 16th century, quotes in his *Rowzat al-rayâhin* (49) from the list of sons of Shaykh Ahmad as given in Shehâb al-Din Esmaîl's treatise, which Buzjâni indicates he has taken from the "old Spiritual Feats" (*Maqâmât-e qadimeh*). 'Abd al-Rahmân Jâmi also had access to this treatise of Shehâb al-Din Esmaîl in composing his *Nafahât al-ons* in the 1470s.[2]

---

[2] See Meier's comparative table in his article, "Zur Biographie Ahmad-i Gàm's," *ZDMG* 97:1 (1943).

*TREATISE ON THE GREATNESS OF HIS FATHER,
SHAYKH AHMAD*

by Shehâb al-Din Esma 'il, a son of Shaykh Ahmad-e Jâm

[323] Written in the hand of our master and leader, the foremost and greatest Imam, the authoritative scholar, the Shaykh al-Islam, the Star [Shehâb] of Truth and Religion, the Pillar of Islam and the Muslims, the Mufti of the East and Imam of both Sanctuaries, Abu al-Mo'ayyad Esmâ'il,[3] the son of the Shaykh al-Islam Abu Nasr Ahmad, exemplar of the saints, beloved of all nations, he who calls the people to God, who strives in the path of God, the just ruler in the Realms of God, the son of Abu al-Hasan ebn-e Ahmad, ebn-e Mohammad, ebn-e Jarir, ebn-e 'Abd Allâh, ebn-e Lays al-Bajali of Nâmaq, known as Jâmi, God sanctify their souls, illuminate their shrine and make fragrant their graves.

The Shaykh al-Islam Shehâb al-Din Abu al-Mo'ayyad Esmâ'il, the son of the Shaykh al-Islam Abu Nasr Ahmad ebn-e Abu al-Hasan of Nâmaq and latterly of Jâm, God sanctify their souls, says:

Once I was in Shâdyâkh.[4] My brother, the Shaykh al-Islam 'Emâd al-Din 'Abd al-Rahim, used to go see Khvâjeh Mo'affeq al-Din, God have mercy upon him, more frequently than I did. Khvâjeh Mo'affeq al-Din was the vizier and ruler of Shâdyâkh and a learned man. 'Emâd al-Din had told him of several of the miracles of my father, such as, when the khâneqâh of Ma'd-âbâd was completed, a wondrous state overcame the Shaykh al-Islam, in which everything his gaze fell upon in that khâneqâh turned to pure gold—the walls, doors, ceiling, etc. It was such that all

---

[3] Here the name is spelled as Esmâ'il, where elsewhere it appears in the less common form of Esma'il.

[4] Originally a town neighboring Nayshabur, after the destruction of Nayshabur by the Ghuzz in 1153 (548 A.H.), Nayshabur was rebuilt on the site of Shâdyâkh. It was destroyed again by the invasion of the Mongols led by Changhiz Khan in 1220 (617 A.H.), after which the city was rebuilt again on the original site.

those present there witnessed it. A great clamor arose from all sides and all were overcome with excitement. A few of the people who had seen this were present in that gathering with my brother, 'Emâd al-Din, and confirmed this and testified to its truth. Still, Khvâjeh Mo'affeq al-Din [324] would not accept it and was inclined to deny it.

Later that same day I went to see Mo'affeq al-Din and he told me, "Your brother 'Emâd al-Din was here today, and he related unto me something of the miracles of your father, the Shaykh al-Islam. Every time he comes, he relates something of your father's miracles, but you do not speak of them at all. Why is that?" Before deciding to go see him, his refusal to believe had become apparent, so I went to reason with him.

I told him, "I will tell you miracles of my father that you can in no wise deny and must of necessity admit to their truth. If you deny them and do not become convinced, you will be in conflict with reason, for these miracles are based on the truth itself."

"You must tell me," he said, "for this is a strange claim, that a thing would not admit of refutation and denial."

I said, "First of all, as you know, people love gold and consider it dear to their hearts and it is very precious. The kind of miracles people talk about—that gold turned to dust in the hands of my father, the Shaykh al-Islam Ahmad, God sanctify his precious soul;[5] that pebbles and stones have turned to gold;[6] that sugar and dates have turned to gold;[7] that having rubbed the sweat on his brow, it turned to gold;[8] that reeds and straw turned to gold; that he twisted the threads of a prayer carpet, which then turned to gold;[9] that a rowan berry, at his demand, has turned to ruby;[10] that three pearls have melted under his gaze and one of them was made solid again;[11] that the khâneqâh turned to gold under his gaze; that whatever he wanted, God, the Almighty,

---

[5] See Story 248.
[6] See Stories 40-41.
[7] See Stories 36-38.
[8] See Story 141.
[9] See Story 84.
[10] See Story 133.
[11] See Story 29.

through His grace, beneficence, bounty and blessing, brought it about on account of my father—miracles such as these, true as they are, are retold and wondered at by the people because their hearts incline towards gold and jewels and hold them dear. But my father, the Shaykh al-Islam, God sanctify his precious soul, has performed miracles much greater and more wondrous than this that the people don't talk about and don't consider miracles."

Khvâjeh Mo'affeq al-Din said, "And what are those? Let me hear about them."

I answered, "One of them is the following. Changing the color of things or altering their appearance [325] is a trick that humans can perform. All dyers and pigmenters and magicians dye things and alter their appearance. Doing this or things like it is neither amazing or unusual. But changing the color of people's hearts and altering their nature and condition can be done only by God, glorified be His name, who transforms the hearts of men. Even the chosen Mohammad, God's blessings upon him, who was the essence of all beings, the goal of creation and guide of all creatures, though he desired to give the heart of his uncle—Abu Tâleb, the Qurayshite—the hue of faith and remove the stain of infidelity, was unable to do so, no matter how much he tried. The call came from above:

O Mohammad, this is not within your hands: 'Thou guidest not whom thou likest, but God guides whom He wills.'[12]

And in another verse we read:

Hadst thou expended all that is in the earth, thou couldst not have brought their hearts together; but God brought their hearts together.[13]

The greatest of my father, the Shaykh al-Islam's, miracles, God sanctify his precious soul, in the eyes of the people of

---

[12] Qur'an 28:56.
[13] Qur'ân 8:63.

insight, those possessed of spiritual understanding and the
followers of truth, is this: He, God sanctify his precious soul,
has written in his book, *Serâj al-sâ'erin* (A Lamp for Travelers):

> I was twenty-two when God, the Mighty and Exalted,
> granted me repentance through His grace and bounty. And I
> was forty when I was sent among the people and now that I
> am preparing this book by His order, I am sixty-two, and to
> this day one hundred and eighty thousand men have
> repented on my account.

My father lived for 21 more years after that,[14] during which
time a great many more repented. My brother, the Shaykh al-
Islam Zahir al-Din 'Isâ, son of the Shaykh al-Islam Ahmad,
[326] God sanctify their precious souls, wrote in his book *Romuz
al-haqâ'eq* (The Mysteries of Truth) that, by the end of the life
of my father, the Shaykh al-Islam, God sanctify his precious
soul, there were six hundred thousand persons who attained
repentance and turned away from sin to the path of piety. These
six hundred thousand corroded hearts, wandering and lost in the
valley of sin and corruption, waylaid by lust and the material
world, more base and wretched than the dust and thistles, were
imbued with the hue of repentance and remorse through the
Arabian, alchemical, spiritual zeal and the magnetism of the
blessed mind of that one succored by divine grace and chosen by
His exalted blessings, namely the Shaykh al-Islam Ahmad of
Jâm, God sanctify his precious soul.

The dross of abasement was, by His polishing grace, burnished
from the mirrors of their dusty hearts and some of them even
attained the stations of Love, Sainthood, Miracles and Spiritual

---

[14] According to all biographies of Shaykh Ahmad, he was born in 1048
(440 A.H.) and died in 1141 (536 A.H.), which means he lived to be
about 95 or 96 according to the lunar calendar (93 solar years), whereas
acording to the above statement, he would have lived only eighty-three
years. The *Kholâsat al-maqâmât* indicates (14) that *Sarâj al-sâ'erin* was
written in 1118 (512 A.H.), when the Shaykh would have been 72 lunar
years old. Perhaps a mistake upon the part of the author or scribe of the
manuscript accounts for this discrepancy.

Insight. These miracles are, in the eyes of the people of spiritual understanding and the possessors of knowledge, intellect and wisdom, and the followers of the Truth, greater and more powerful than turning dust and rock to gold, rowan berries to rubies or pearls to water.

When I recited these miracles to Khvâjeh Mo'affeq al-Din, he said, "These are more wondrous. There is nothing amazing about transmuting matter or defying the laws of nature."

Another miracle and bounty which God, exalted be His station, granted to my father, the Shaykh al-Islam Ahmad, God sanctify his blessed soul, was this: My father was ignorant[15] when he repented and went up onto the mountain. Eighteen years later when he was sent back among the people, the doors of divine knowledge and the secret of wisdom had been opened unto him, such that, in the end, the scholars, wise men, and thinkers of his age were astounded and amazed by his knowledge and actions and his miracles and wondrous deeds. He, God sanctify his precious soul, composed over 600 pages[16] concerning the unity of God, human knowledge of God and His mysteries, wisdom, the Sufi path and the hidden realities, to which no scholar or wise man ever objected or could object. The scholars and wise men who have seen these books, all of which are substantiated with verses of the Qur'ân and the reports about the Messenger, God's blessings upon him, have praised them. This bounty and miracle is more significant than turning dust to gold or rowan berries to rubies [327] or melting and re-solidifying pearls. Peace upon you.

---

[15] *Ommi*, a word used in reference to the Prophet Mohammad, is popularly understood to mean illiterate. In the case of Mohammad, it probably meant that he was a gentile, unschooled in the Bible or other religious knowledge. In the case of Shaykh Ahmad, it seems to mean, likewise, that he had never studied the Islamic religious sciences in a seminary or under any teacher.

[16] *Si-sad tâ-ye kâghaz*. According to dictionaries, *tâ-ye kâghadh* means a large sheet of paper. Evidently, this would have been folded into folios or quires, as the number of pages written by the Shaykh does exceed 600. A list of these works is given below by Shehâb al-Din, but they are discussed more fully in the introduction.

Another of God, the Almighty and Exalted's, acts of grace and bounty toward my father, the Shaykh al-Islam, God sanctify his precious soul is this: The Blessed and Almighty Lord granted him forty-two children—thirty-nine sons and three daughters. Fourteen of the boys and all three girls survived him, God sanctify his precious soul. These fourteen sons were all scholars, observant and distinguished [*kâmel*], authors of books and miracles, possessing authority and leadership, guides to the masses; and the least among them in terms of age, knowledge and piety is the author and narrator of the present chapter, your Esmâ'il. What miracle could be greater and more obvious? But the people who worship outward forms and appearances are senseless of these miracles and ignorant of these bounties.

When this subject had been explained in this manner to Khvâjeh Imam Mo'affeq al-Din, God have mercy upon him, he wept copiously and said, "There is nothing greater than the miracles you have described, and no denying these spiritual powers. One can only admit and submit to such bounties." And it is God who best knows the truth.

As for the writings of the Shaykh al-Islam, God sanctify his precious soul, they are as follows: *Serâj al-sâ'erin* [A Lamp for Travelers] in three volumes, *Anis al-tâ'ebin* [Companion to the Repentant] in one volume,[17] *Konuz al-hekmah* [Treasures of Wisdom] in one volume, *Fotuh al-qolub* [Revelations to the Heart] in one volume, *Fotuh al-ruh* [Revelations to the Spirit] in one volume, *Behâr al-haqiqah* [Seas of Truth] in one volume, *Rowzat al-moznebin* [The Sinners' Garden] in one volume,[18] *Meftâh al-najât* [The Key to Salvation] in one volume,[19] the *Resâleh-ye Samarqandiyeh* [The Epistle to the Samarqandians]

---

[17] In the manuscript, this title is given as *Anis al-tâ'ebin*, but the published work has appeared as *Ons al-tâ'ebin*, edited 'Ali Fâzel (Tehran: Enteshârât-e Bonyâd-e Farhang, 1350/1971). See the Introduction to the present work for more details on this work.

[18] edited 'Ali Fâzel (Tehran: Enteshârât-e Bonyâd-e Farhang, 1355/1976).

[19] edited 'Ali Fâzel (Tehran: Enteshârât-e Bonyâd-e Farhang, 1347/1968).

in one volume,[20] *Ketâb-e tazkirât* [The Book of Admonitions] in one volume, a book of poems in one volume, and *Ketâb-e zohdiyât* [On Asceticism] in one volume.

As for the names of the sons of the Shaykh al-Islam, God sanctify his precious soul, who survived him after his death, they are as follows, God sanctify their precious souls: [328]

1) The Shaykh al-Islam Rashid al-Din 'Abd al-Rashid
2) The Shaykh al-Islam Safiy al-Din Mahmud
3) The Shaykh al-Islam Jamâl al-Din Abu al-Fath
4) The Shaykh al-Islam Qotb al-Din Mohammad
5) The Shaykh al-Islam Fakhr al-Din Abu al-Hasan
6) The Shaykh al-Islam Najm al-Din Abu Bakr
7) The Shaykh al-Islam Borhân al-Din Nasr
8) The Shaykh al-Islam Ziâ al-Din Yusof
9) The Shaykh al-Islam 'Emâd al-Din 'Abd al-Rahim
10) The Shaykh al-Islam Shams al-Din Motahhar
11) The Shaykh al-Islam Badr al-Din Sâ'ed
12) The Shaykh al-Islam Hamid al-Din 'Abd Allâh
13) The Shaykh al-Islam Zahir al-Din 'Isâ
14) The Shaykh al-Islam Shehâb al-Din Esmâ'il

As for the spiritual guide and companion of the Shaykh al-Islam, God sanctify his precious soul, it was Shaykh Bu Tâher the Kurd, whose own spiritual guide was Shaykh Abu Sa'id-e Abu al-Khayr,[21] whose spiritual guide, in turn, was Abu al-Fazl Shaykh Hasan-e Sarrâj, who was called "The Peacock of the Poor" (*Tâvus al-Foqarâ*).[22] He was a disciple of Abu Mohammad ebn-e 'Abd Allâh, who was a disciple of the Shaykh

---

[20] A translation of a portion of this treatise is included below, in Part Four.

[21] The famous mystic Abu Sa'id (967-1049 / 357-440 A.H.) whose exploits the *Asrâr al-towhid*, or *The Secrets of God's Mystical Oneness*, relates.

[22] That is, the famous Shaykh Bu Nasr-e Sarrâj of Tus [d. 988], a disciple of Ebn-e Khafif and author of the Sufi manual, *Kitâb al-luma' fi al-tasawwuf*, ed. R.A. Nicholson (London and Leiden, 1914). The manuscript of the present text gives his name incorrectly.

al-Islam Jonayd[23] and Jonayd was the disiciple of Sari-ye Saqati, who was the disciple of Ma'ruf-e Karkhi, who was the disciple of Dâvud-e Tâ'i, who was the disciple of Habib-e 'Ajami, who was the disciple of Hasan-e Basri, who was the disciple of the Commander of the Faithful, 'Ali, may God be pleased with him. The Commander of the Faithful, 'Ali, was the disciple of the lord of creation, Mohammad the Chosen, God's peace and blessings upon him and his family.

---

[23] This is the famous Sufi, Jonayd (d. 910 / 298 A.H.) and all the subsequent figures mentioned are historical and/or legendary figures of Sufism, and this *selseleh*, or chain of spiritual teachers, is frequently claimed by Sufis. Refer to *Muslim Saints and Mystics*, tr. A. J. Arberry, for further details.

PART FOUR

An Epistle by Shaykh Ahmad-e Jâm

A Chapter from an Epistle by Shaykh Ahmad

The following treatise consists of letters which Shaykh Ahmad wrote in reply to questions received from various places, in particular, from Samarqand. The Nâfiz Pâshâ manuscript of Ghaznavi's *Spiritual Feats* begins with this *Epistle to the Samarqandians* (folios 14 to 38), but a number of pages have been lost from the manuscript and as a result both the beginning, as well as a part of the end of the treatise, are missing. Before the *Epistle to the Samarqandians* comes to a natural close in the Nâfiz Pâshâ manuscript, The Spiritual Feats of Ghaznavi begins.

Oddly, a second copy of a portion of the Epistle to the Samarqandians appears, bound up with this manuscript, following the completion of Ghaznavi's *Spiritual Feats*, repeating the text with which the manuscript opens. Perhaps one of these two quires or albums was meant to be distributed to someone else, but has been sewn into the binding of this copy. In any case, these two redundant portions of the text of the Epistle have been compared with one another to help establish the text.

EPISTLE TO THE SAMARQANDIANS
(Resâleh-ye Samarqandiyeh)

by Shaykh Ahmad-e Jâm

Question about the Hadith
"On the Day of Resurrection All Blood Relations and Family Affiliations Will Be Severed, Except for Relation and Affiliation to Me,"
and the Answer of the Shaykh

Concerning the saying of the Prophet, the peace and blessing of God upon him, "*All blood relations and family affiliations will be severed, except for relation and affiliation to me*," the Shaykh al-Islam, the king of the Sufi path, the proof of Truth, the Spiritual Axis of the World, the Proof of God to mankind, He who calls the people to God and exerts himself in the path of God, Abu Nasr Ahmad ebn-e Abu al-Hasan of Nâmaq and latterly of Jâm, God sanctify his precious soul, was asked, "Clarify for us what blood relation and affiliation with him are."[1]

The Answer (and all confirmation comes from God):

The Prophet, the peace and blessing of God upon him, means that affiliation to him is a matter of affiliation to his heart and relationship to him is a matter of relationship to his body. Know, however, that all the prophets, peace be upon them, had altogether 117 spiritual traits. All these spiritual traits were summoned to join together in the person of the lord of creation, Mohammad. At that point, every spiritual trait, moral characteristic and deed that existed in the heavens and on the earth joined together in his person, as well as everything the angels in the heavens [332] possessed by way of exaltation, sanctification, praise, glorification, laudation and magnification. When the turn of the

---

[1] These explanatory paragraphs are almost certainly added by a later scribe; it is quite unlikely that Shaykh Ahmad would have described himself with these titles.

Prophet came, God's blessing upon him, all those noble spiritual traits appeared gathered together in him. And then the cry arose, "All of those on heaven and on earth who seek spiritual traits and dealings with God, neither seek nor search anywhere but at the threshold of the Prophet, God's blessings upon him, for he is the Way unto all." As the Almighty has said, "Say: If you love God, follow me and God will love you."[2] Eighteen thousand worlds, including one hundred twenty-odd thousand founts [*noqteh*] of prophethood, were no more than a drop in the ocean of the magnificent finality of Mohammad's prophethood. In the heavenly kingdom there is but one lord, and it is he; Adam was but the deputy of his stock.

But as to the essence of the matter, in the world of reality, the true deputy throughout all the realms of God, was none other than the Prophet, God's peace and blessings upon him. The Prophet, Gods blessings upon him, says, "Adam and everyone else are under my banner"[3] and "Verily thou art exalted in spiritual traits."[4] Since the interpretation of the significance of this hadith has shown that none like him has ever been singled out in spiritual traits, it then properly follows that none in the heavenly realms has ever been so completely faithful as this perfect youth. He is the one source of wealth from whom all the denizens of the world may become wealthy, for his treasuries are inexhaustible. His primacy is without beginning, and his suzerainty and greatness are endless. When you consider his essence, the perfection of his spiritual traits are manifested in his deeds. He achieved all this because he never fell into error [*ghalat*] concerning his own self, and when he attained the Divine court, he uttered these words: "O Lord, bring me to life as a meek one and make me die meek, and number me on the Day of Resurrection among the ranks of the

---

[2] Qur'ân 3:31.

[3] A fuller version of this hadith goes as follows: "It is no boast to say I am the lord of the sons of Adam, and it is no boast to say that Adam and everyone else will stand under my banner on the Day of Resurrection" (*Mesbâh al-hedâyah*, 43; see also *Kanz al-'ommâl*, 6:1555 for a different version).

[4] Qur'ân 68:4.

meek."[5] God says it was you who fulfilled the command to stand firm,[6] [333] and yet you call out, "Lord, increase my knowledge."[7]

O great sea of finality [khâtami]! The messengers have received their knowledge of messengership from the sea of your finality, and the prophets have received their knowledge of prophethood from your sea of finality, and the saints received their knowledge of sainthood from your sea of finality, and the righteous received their knowledge of righteousness from your sea of finality, and the traditionists received their knowledge of Hadith from your sea of finality, and the mystics received their knowledge of mysticism from your sea of finality, and the unitarians [movahhedân] received their knowledge of God's oneness [towhid] from your sea of finality, and the seekers and ascetics and those who fear God, and those who yearn for and love God, and the lovers ['âsheqân, i.e. the Sufis] and the disciples, all received their knowledge from your sea of finality. Why then did you need to say "Increase my knowledge," for the heavens and the earth were filled with your knowledge?

The Prophet, God's peace and blessings upon him, has said, "Your knowledge and the knowledge of all people is as nothing compared to my knowledge, and my knowledge is as nothing compared to God's knowledge." Consider, then, this comparison that you may see the light of "There is no God but God" and understand the glory of the Messenger of God.

O Muslims! Know that God, the Mighty and Exalted, has so manifestly revealed to my heart the greatness and majesty of this lord, that whenever I think on him, every hair from head to toe on my body stands on end. All of this may be, yet no matter how I try

---

[5] This hadith is related in the *Sunan* of Ibn-e Mâjah (Egypt, 1953), #4126 in the edition of Muhammad Fu'âd 'Abd al-Bâqi under the rubric "asceticism". See also Abu Nasr-e Sarrâj, *al-Luma' fî al-tasawwuf*, ed. Nicholson, 97; and Shaykh 'Alâ al-Din 'Ali al-Mutaqqi's *Kanz al-'ummâl fî sunan al-aqwâl wa al-af'âl* (Hyderabad, 1312-1314/1894-96), vol. 3, #4719 and 4865.

[6] Probably a reference to Qur'ân 11:112 and 42:15.

[7] A version of this hadith is given in Wensinck's Concordance (Leiden, 1936), *al-Mo'jam al-mofahras*, "s" (p. 373), as related by Abu Dâvûd and Ibn Mâjah.

to explain his attributes and utter praises to him, I can in no wise reach the least of Mohammad's majesty and greatness. Know for a certainty that whatever felicity a person may obtain, he obtains from Mohammad's court. The most splendid diadem of the brilliant tradition was placed upon his head, because to follow him is so significant. He who turns toward Mohammad's greatness will soon be admitted to the Divine court and he who forgets Mohammad's honor will risk being cast out from that threshold. Now the heart must needs be filled with the might of "There is no God but God" and the honor of "Mohammad is the Messenger of God," that it might recognize the greatness of this noble one.

When a novice sets out on the path, in the beginning he has no awareness of the spiritual dominion of [334] that great one. Therefore, when novices set out on the path, [the majesty of the phrase] "There is no God but God" so overwhelms them that they cannot move beyond to [the phrase] "Mohammad is His Messenger." In the realm of "There is no God but God" the novice realizes that this is the threshold of pre-eternity, and the existence of all created beings and the absence of all non-created beings ['adam-e ma'dumât] emanates from this threshold. Seek the permanence of the permanent and the annihilation of the annihilated from this threshold.

When such inspirations take uninterrupted hold of his heart, the novice will imagine that he is special. Not until twenty more years go by and one of the windows of the court of Prophecy are opened to him and one of its breezes wafts over him and fire overtakes him and burns to the ground his harvest of vain imaginings, will he escape from these passions and melancholy. Once his harvest of vain imaginings is completely scorched, he will say, "Oh, that I had not done what I did in the beginning! But now that I have done it, God be praised that it has caught fire and burned so that I am free of all these imaginings!"

O Muslims! Our God is independent and mighty. He is self-sufficient yet succors the needy. Even should all the pious ones of the world turn into sinners, all are as naught before His court. But the point is that God forgives thousands upon thousands of [sins against Him], but not one sin committed against those who are honored at His court.[8] Do you know why what befell Iblis[9] befell him? Because he waxed proud and vainly imagined himself to be the honored one of His court. As a consequence, he received such a blow that his wound will never heal. Who in this or in the next world, other than Him, can crush anyone or anything that has been magnified by him? Peace.

A Discourse on the Meaning of God's Bounty and Unity

On another day the following words fell from the blessed lips of the Shaykh al-Islam Ahmad, the king of the Sufi path, the proof of Truth, God [335] sanctify his precious soul, concerning the attributes of the Prophet, God's blessings upon him: "When the Prophet renounced his own essence, God's bounty entered in its place, and when he renounced his own attributes, God's holiness entered in their place." The Shaykh then continued:[10]

By "God's bounty" and "God's holiness" is meant not that the Pre-eternal Godhead becomes contingent so that created beings may attain to God. Anyone who believes so is a heretic [elhâd] and atheist [zendeqeh]. Rather, by "God's bounty" is meant the effects of the divine bounties which flow from him, not the bounty itself. For whatsoever is an attribute of God is pre-eternal and subsists in His essence, the Mighty and Exalted, whereas that which descends to His servant is but the effects of that attribute. Likewise, if anyone were to suppose that incarnation takes place, it would be blasphemy, just as, when it is said in the physical world, "The Sultan of the day has bestowed a bounty on so-and-so," the meaning is that he gave him a robe of honor, some special attention or paid him some stipend, gave him some gift or estate. That which is an attribute of the Sultan subsists in the essence of the Sultan, and that which the subject receives is but the effects of the bounty and generosity of the Sultan. Likewise, if anyone were

---

[8] See the almost identical language attributed to the Shaykh in his letter to Sanjar given in Story 17, above.

[9] Lucifer, the angel who fell from grace for pride.

[10] Again, the preceding introductory paragraph was obviously added by an editor, perhaps one of the sons of Shaykh Ahmad.

to say that the Sultan has punished and vanquished so-and-so, that means that the Sultan demonstrates the effect of his wrath, not that he gives a portion of it to him. For that attribute subsists in his essence. Know that it is the same case with the Creator, may He be glorified; whatever descends upon creation is but the effects of His bounty, generosity and grace.

From his holiness, the Prophet, comes the command: "Think upon the creation and not upon the Creator."[11] About Him reflection and deliberation is impossible and impermissible, for reflection and deliberation and meditation should be directed to His creation and action, and knowledge of Him must be gathered by means of His creation and action. [336]

The [confession of] God's unity consists in leaving behind yourself and the world and recognizing in all quarters and divisions of the world the decrees of He Who decrees and the plans of He Who plans and recognizing in them the fleetingness of things and the permanence of He Who is permanent. That which, in their seclusion, the disciples say concerning Him and His magnanimity and bounty and generosity, though it is true and is a [confession of] God's unity, yet it is a child's concept of God's unity. It is as if, in this world, he who carts off the town's sewage [*sergin-kesh*] and shovels rubbish into the furnace of the baths [*golkhani*], were to say at the door of the furnace, "This world belongs entirely to the Sultan—Khorasan, Iraq, Damascus and Syria, Rome, Sindh, India and Transoxania, and so on—and the creatures are all servants, retainers and subjects of his. All that exists belongs to him." Likewise, a disciple is one who regards whatever he or another, or Satan or the angels, possess as nothing, for unless he passes beyond all this, that which is God's will not become apparent.

What the disciples say is a weak and childish confession of God's unity. One who attends the bath furnace must busy himself with carting off sewage and firing the bath furnace, since the rulers of the state and the inner circle of the Sultan and his court

---

[11] This hadith appears with minor variations in Jalâl al-Din Suyûtî's *Jâmi'-i saghîr* (Egypt, 1352/1933), 1:131, *Kunûz al-haqâ'iq*, 52; Tha'alabi's *Qisas al-anbiyâ*, (Egyptian edition), 10; as cited in Foruzanfar, *Ahâdis-e Masnavi*, 142.

attendants all know how to manage the affairs of state and the Sultan's treasury; where it is; what and how much is in it; to what extent the Vizier complies with his orders; who the commanders, companions, chamberlains and elite of the Sultan are; the extent of each one's standing and his place; what wages they receive and what lands they own. The rank of the man who knows all this is, in the sight of God, glorified be He, like one who has traveled far and wide and returned once again, leaving absolutely everything behind. Such a one looks with open eyes [337] and sees the inner realities of things and the wisdom of heavenly blessings, because the world contains innumerable secrets and mysteries. Do you not see how Adam, the blessings of God upon him, was brought forth from clay? And yet he rose above all to become king and lord over both the denizens of the Fire and the denizens of the Light!

There is no end or limit to what God has ordained. One sees the act of ordination in what is ordained, and one sees the power in the act of ordination, and the All-Powerful in the power; for what is ordained in this world comes about through the act of ordination, and the act of ordination comes about through power, and power comes from the All-Powerful. "Therein lies the sovereignty of God, the True."[12] This is why it is said, "He who knows his own self has known his Lord,"[13] and one ought to correctly understand the unity of the physical world.

Know, however, that the lover never merges with the beloved, nor the beloved with the lover. Each retains his own attributes; the lover has the fire of love in his heart and the image of the beloved's form in his breast and is happy with this image in his breast. Do you not see how, when the image is veiled by negligence, love disappears and the lover finds peace and will eat and drink and work and associate with others, but when the image reappears and returns to him, the lover becomes sad and

---

[12] Qur'ân 18:44.

[13] The saying is attributed to 'Ali (Nahj al-balâgha, 4:547), and is given in Kunuz al-haqâ'iq (9), but in al-Lu'lu' al-marsû' of Sayyed Mohammad Abu al-Mahâsen al-Qâvoqchi, on the authority of Ibn Taymiyyah, it is discredited as a false hadith (az mowzu'ât, 86). Rumi alludes to it in the fifth book of his Masnavi (Nicholson, ed., 5:135, line 2114). Cited in Foruzânfar, Ahâdis-e Masnavi, 167.

disconsolate? He can neither work nor speak, nor eat nor sleep. Peace.

Sultan Sanjar's Question About the Characteristics of the Friends of God and the Answer of the Shaykh

The Sultan of Sultans, Sanjar ebn-e Malekshâh asked the Shaykh al-Islam Ahmad, God sanctify his precious soul, about the signs and characteristics of the friends of God [i.e., the Saints], the Mighty and Exalted.

The answer (and confirmation comes from God).

The Shaykh al-Islam, God sanctify his precious soul, replied:

Know that [338] the signs and characteristics of the friends of God, the All-Glorified, are five in number:

First, they take pleasure and comfort in obedience and worship and service to the Lord, not in lust and worldly pleasure.

Second, their joy and companionship reside in the laudation, glorification and exaltation of the Lord, not in the praising or eulogizing of mortals and service to them.

Third, their wealth and riches reside in the unveiling and witnessing of the Lord, not in the goods and treasures of the world.

Fourth, the days of their lives are spent in solitude and separation from people, not in keeping company and mingling with them.

Fifth, eating and drinking and the wearing of garments, which are a necessity for human beings, are to them a trial and tribulation.

All their joy and felicity, the light of their eyes and their yearning lies in the mention, praise and glorification of the Lord. Their food comes from the heavenly table and their wine from the chalice of God, their clothing and garments come from the treasury of the Lord. Their knowledge comes from the teachings of the Lord. Their mystical wisdom comes from the instruction of the Lord. The light of their hearts and souls comes from the bounties of the Lord. The zeal and delight of their obedience comes from the generosity and glory of the Lord. Their gardens and rose bowers lie in perceiving the gifts and graces of the Lord. The world is a bridge across which they are passing. The heavens and the earth ['arsh va farsh] are their two halting places. Such a people as this flee from the company of mortals; they take no delight in their companionship, find no rest in their presence nor any tranquility in any creature.

As for those who seek out the people of the world and mingle with the heedless, it is love and desire of the world that compels them to do so, though they may conceal it from the masses. But those who live amongst the tents and camps of the women who follow the army [zanân-e lashkari], testify to their own alienation from the court of Majesty. The friends of the Almighty God shy away even from the company of the divine angels; how could they descend and mingle in the camps of oppression and the tents of lust? The Lord of Creation knows that these words are but words of kindly counsel, not of censure. Not every tailor is capable of sewing the cloak of the Sultan of the day; an experienced tailor, [339] a complete master is needed. Not every cupper is worthy of bleeding the Sultan of the day; a master cupper, one with experience, is needed. Not every physician can treat the Sultan of the age; a skilled physician, one with much experience and a full knowledge of constitutions. Not every preacher or admonisher can preach to the king of the age; a preacher knowledgeable about mystical states and the requirements of religious law, is needed, one with insight into the Sufi path, aware of the frailties of the material world, informed of the excellences and virtues of creation and human nature.

He was at age forty a novice in the knowledge of all this; and at age fifty-two, at the mid-point of it; and at the age of sixty-three, he had a perfect knowledge of all this. Such was the mettle of the Prophet, God's peace and blessings upon him, when he departed from this world (aged sixty-two years).[14] All the Messengers were

---

[14] The phrase in parentheses is attested in the Berlin and Nâfiz Pâshâ manuscripts, but not in the Chester Beatty manuscript. The Prophet, Muhammad (?570-632), is traditionally believed to have received his first revelation at the age of 40, migrated to Medina at the age of 52 and died, according to most Muslim historians, at the age of 63, as per the lunar calendar.

called at the age of forty and all the saints achieved sainthood at the age of forty. Whoever is under the age of forty and lays claim to sainthood, his claim is meaningless, by my life! There may be something to it, but he is not yet mature.

May the Sultan of the day and the leader of the age—God confirm him with perfect assistance—not receive these words with a hostile and judgmental ear, but rather consider them a kindly counsel. Just as he would look for perfection in a tailor, a cupper and a physician, let him look to perfection in the way of religion and if he should see one who is perfect, let that one be chosen. If he chooses to forget the present author, no harm will come to me, for my object is that he should attain to God, the Almighty, through this perfect guidance. This author is saying that he has no enmity or quarrel with anyone, but there is no neglecting [the duty to give] correct advice. Capturing military fortifications is not a sign of friendship [*sohbat*] and the claim of uncovering a treasure is a baseless claim, for all people conceal their treasure from the Sultan, fearing that he will take it away. Therefore, making claims is nothing but hypocrisy and deceit.[15]

O Lord, protect us from hypocrisy and deceit and array the Sultan of the age with bounty and justice, through Your bestowals and bounties! Praised be to God as befits Him, and blessings upon the Prophet, Mohammad, and his family. [340]

On Alchemy

Imam Ilâqi, God have mercy upon him, wrote a letter to the Shaykh al-Islam, God sanctify his precious soul, with the following question: "They say you have the knowledge of alchemy. You should inform us about it and give us guidance about the substances needed."

The Shaykh al-Islam, God sanctify his precious soul, wrote back to him as follows:

I believe that alchemy consists of the following: The first

---

[15] The intent of this last passage remains somewhat obscure; perhaps it alludes to one of the incidents between the Shaykh and Sanjar referred to in the anecdotes, or some other discussion that had transpired between them.

substance is to be derived from *"We have portioned out,"*[16] and the next from *"Say, O God, Lord of Dominion, Thou givest dominion to whom Thou pleasest and takest dominion away from whom Thou pleasest."*[17] And the third substance is, *"And he who puts his trust in God, God will be sufficient unto him."*[18] The fourth ingredient is, *"And he who fears God, God will show him a way out and provide for him from sources he could not have imagined."*[19] The fifth substance is: *"Hold fast unto God; He is your protector, the best of protectors and the best of helpers."*[20]

One should take these five substances and mix them in the bowl of *"Those who strive in Our cause, surely We will guide them in Our ways."*[21] Let him mix it with the water of contentment and pour it into the oil of need with the ladle of *"I commit my affairs to God."*[22] Then let him immerse it in the sea of disinterest and submit it to the gaze of the Source of All Bounties. Then let him drop it in the crucible of patience and fill it with the *verse "We appointed for Moses thirty nights and completed the period with ten more."*[23] Let him melt it with the fire of love in the inmost corners of his heart, retrieve it through the guidance of mystic knowledge, and place it on the anvil of love, and pound it with the hammer of *"and he restrained his soul from passion."*[24] Let him add the dye of sincerity and stamp it with the seal of divine unity in the mint [341] and place it in the purse of piety and fear of God, and then tie it with the string of "He who remains silent is saved."[25]

Once this has been accomplished, it will become the philosopher's stone and anything within range of its smell will

---

[16] Qur'ân 43:32.
[17] Qur'ân 3:26.
[18] Qur'ân 65:3.
[19] Qur'ân 65:2-3.
[20] Qur'ân 22:78.
[21] Qur'ân 29:69.
[22] Qur'ân 40:44.
[23] Qur'ân 7:142.
[24] Qur'ân 79:40.
[25] Hadith #8819 as quoted in Suyûtî, *al-Jâmi' al-saghîr*.

take on its color.[26] When a man reaches this station, he will sit king-like upon the throne of good fortune and in this earthly realm of loss will become an example unto the world, as it will transform the entire world for him—stone, clay, plants, fruits—into pure gold. At last it will reach the point that when he takes it to the marketplace, he will win with every penny of it a pious man and every glance of his will leave its mark.

It is in the above sense that this friend of yours has been able to transmute the elements; "And God doth not charge any soul with more than its capacity."[27] God willing the aim will be achieved, for it is well proved as effective. If it should fail, that is due to a lack of certitude, so that you may know. Peace.

Commentary on the Verse "And Thy Lord Revealed Unto the Bees...."

In response to the letter of Imam Fasih al-Din Valvâleji,[28] God have mercy upon him, [the Shaykh wrote the following]:

In the Name of God, the Merciful, the Compassionate.

The noble letter [ketâb] and speech of Khvâjeh Imam Fasih al-Din Mohammad Ebn-e Shahid-e Saʿid of Valvâlej, God have mercy upon him,[29] has been received, containing what he had written concerning various matters. Let me refer to some of them,

---

[26] A similar alchemical prescription had been previously attributed to Buzorjmehr, the Vizier of the Sasanian king Nushiravân. See *Târikh-e Bayhaqi*, ed. Fayyâz (Tehran, 1324/1945), 336.

[27] Qurʾân 2:286.

[28] Concerning Imam Fasih, see also Story 383, above.

[29] The occurence of the phrase "God have mercy upon him" [*rahmat Allâh ʿalayhi*] indicates that the person mentioned is deceased. Imam Fasih was obviously still alive at the time the Shaykh al-Islam wrote this response to him (see the last paragraph, wherein Shaykh Ahmad wishes a long life for Khvâjeh Imam), but the compiler of this manuscript, or a later copyist, knowing that Imam Fasih had since passed away, must have added this pious formula after his name. The word "*Saʿid*", meaning auspicious, is not part of this man's name, but appears as a rhyming adjective for *shahid* "martyr." The formulaic expression *shahid-e saʿid* remains common to the present day

according to the capacity of my own clouded intellect.[30] God, the Almighty, willing, the matter will become clear.

First, you had mentioned that the verse of God, the Almighty and Exalted, "*And thy Lord revealed unto the bees, saying: 'Take unto yourselves, of the mountains, houses, and of the trees, and of what they are building'*"[31] is a confirmation of the Sufi path. In these very words are contained the complete answer to what you wrote, and this verse completely [342] suffices. Considering that the multi-colored peacock and the sharp-clawed eagle and high-climbing hawk, the majestic kingly falcon, the long-lived vulture, the silk-garbed and crowned Hoopoe, the heart-captivating partridge and pheasant, and the melodious song-bird of a thousand tunes had all been created and were present, why were the tiny bees inspired with Revelation and favored with this honor for no reason?

Because the honor bestowed by the All-Wise is not bound by meri, "*God leads unto His light whom He will.*"[32] What you have recounted concerning the goodness of God, the Almighty and Exalted, to the Bee, is a source of consolation, as the poet says:

> Thou who art hidden in manifestation
> and invisible yet manifest,
> How can the sun be seen with the naked eye?

Should the bee wish to express something of what has been revealed to it, it could not do so, yet its own nature [*hâlat*], which restores people to health, is a sign of God's Revelation. What it produces is a sign of its essence, though its buzzing cannot put this into words. When we consider its wholesome, invigorating, spirit-lifting honey, we know that there is something in the bee that cannot be found anywhere else. As the poet says:

> A thing lies in it that other beauties lack

---

[30] *Khâter-e ghobâr-âlud-e mâ.* This reference to the weakness of his intellect is a traditional self-deprecating gesture of humility and is not intended to be taken literally.

[31] Qur'ân 16:68.

[32] Qur'ân 24:35.

When this quality was invested in the bee, all those others were left clutching the air. Any sick person in search of a cure must neeeds eat that which it produces. People are disgusted by the excretions [*afzuni*] of all animals and avoid them and guard their clothes and nose from them; yet from the bee's, they make the most delectable and nutritious foods. Why is that? Because there is something invested in the bee. O my friend and brother, what is invested in the bee is efficacious, as the poet says:

The day they stamped the heavens with its seal
the lovers' gold they coined in other mold;
How this mold was made, your mind cannot conceive,
this gold was stamped beyond the mint of intellect [343]

The Signs of Poverty and Being Poor

To ask about the signs of poverty is the question of a child. A mature man would not ask this, because he is reasonable. A man whose heart has embraced poverty would not need to explain nor to search after it, and a spiritual wayfarer is also beyond such a need. If the Chosen One, God's blessings upon him, had ascended of his own to the heavens, he would not have ascended, but because he was borne up, he attained the place he did and saw what he saw. But all of that is another story. The sign of poverty is that it lacks any outward sign; however, in such a state of mind, things will happen to a man and become visible which point to his inner endeavor.

Brackish soil will never yield fresh water. Poverty is an alchemy that imbues everything it touches with its own quality. When poverty takes root in a person it appears as a change in his character and nature. Anyone whose constitution is altered from what it was, his character will change as well. The basic characteristics of devil and beast and man—and the base qualities, such as desire, greed, stinginess, anger, jealousy, envy, pride, idle fancy, and so on—will depart from his composite nature and the ensign of his good fortune will be raised in the realm of Divine Unity. When a man becomes a true believer of Divine Unity, this verse will properly apply to him: "Count not those who were slain in the path of God as dead; rather they are living and are sustained by God; and they rejoice."[33]

Listen to what experience has taught me. Any task that you begin and learn well you will become expert in, but as far as poverty is concerned, whoever enters through the door of imitation will exit through the door of heresy. The Chosen One, the blessings of God upon him, was asked:

"What is poverty?" He said, "One of the riches of God." He was then asked a second time, "What is poverty?" He said, "One of the treasures of God." He was then asked a third time, "What is poverty?" He said, "It is something God gives only to a major prophet or a righteous man or a believer generous with God."[34]

[344] When the Prophet raised this call among the people and said, "God is the All-sufficient, it is you who are the poor,"[35] he also meant to include himself. Just as God is always Self-Sufficient, so too the poor man is always needy.

You had mentioned the question of tears [âb-e hasrat],[36] saying one should shed tears. A poor person should never be dry-eyed. The presence of tears is itself bemusement, their absence is regret, to quest for them is bemusement, to speak of them is bemusement, to welcome[37] them is bemusement; their roots, branches, leaves and blossoms are bemusement. An afflicted one should not be taught how to lament; witnessing his own state is his lamentation and his pain is his testimony. One in pain cries out in various ways; his crying out is the testimonial of his pain.

The sayings which you mentioned concerning divine knowledge

---

[33] Qur'ân 3:169. The manuscript includes the first word of the next verse, *fa-rihîna*, meaning "they rejoice," but this is likely a scribal error as the appropriation of this verb with verse 169 would render verse 170 grammatically incomplete.

[34] We have not located a source for this hadith.

[35] Qur'ân 47:38.

[36] Meaning the hadith which has just been quoted, "What is Poverty....etc."

[37] Reading *pasandid*, but the first letter is not marked in the manuscript.

and the question of the other world and the matter of Hosayn ebn-e Mansur [Hallâj] and one's vision and knowledge and the path one follows—all of these are implicit in the feeling of poverty. As for the saying of the *Qur'ân "And Thy Lord revealed unto the bees,"* the shining sun, from where it rises in the east to the place it sets in the west remains unchanging, yet in some of its positions its heat feels less and in some greater, though the sun itself knows neither decrease nor increase. If a puff of cloud were to pass before the eye of an on-looker and veil his gaze, the fault is in his eye, not in the sun, which remains true to its essence. As the Chosen One, God's blessings upon him, says in a hadith: "My satan has submitted [to God]."[38] This saying is true and none can contend with it. In another saying, the poor will also read this statement (and in yet another place, *"Verily, thou shalt have no authority over my servants"*),[39] which indicates: *"And they followed him [Satan], except for a group of the believers."*[40]

These people[41] are not belligerent or quarrelsome men; when the Pen recorded their destiny, this call was raised in heaven: *"...the Foremost ones! And the Foremost are they who are nigh unto God."*[42] Allusion is made in another place to *"...for them are glad-tidings in this life and in the next. [345] No change is there in the words of God. This is, indeed, the supreme felicity."*[43] They are a people whose sins are recorded as acts of piety; the verse *"for God will change the evil of such persons into good,"*[44] is a description of them. The Chosen One, God's blessings upon him, gloried in this people, saying, "O Lord, bring me to life as a meek one and make me die meek and number me on the Day of

---

[38] We have not discovered the source of this hadith, but it was evidently in circulation amongst Iranian Sufis and is attested in the *Ma'âref* of Bahâ al-Din Valad, the father of Mowlânâ Jalâl al-Din Rumi (ed. Foruzânfar, Tehran: Châpkhâneh-ye Majles, 1333/1954, 1:81).

[39] Qur'ân 15:42.

[40] Qur'ân 34:20. Both this and the preceding passage are taken from Qur'ânic pericopes about the rebellion of the archangel Iblis (Satan).

[41] That is the Poor, i.e., the Sufis.

[42] Qur'ân 56:10-11.

[43] Qur'ân 10:64.

[44] Qur'ân 25:70.

Resurrection among the ranks of the meek."[45] And he has declared, "Poverty is my pride."[46]

It is good that an allusion to the question of vision and meeting was made in your letter; but how could one seek vision from one who has no sight? The truth of the matter is this: to harbor a desire in the heart for a vision [of God], whether physical or spiritual, comes from attachment to idols [*tâghut*]. *"He who disbelieves in idols and believes in God."*[47] Until you become a disbeliever in idols, your faith in God is not complete. "Spiritual poverty is virtually a kind of disbelief,"[48] and unless those who claim to have faith all mark you down as a disbeliever, poverty will not unveil itself to the poor man and reveal its beauty to him. A man who believes himself to be poor hampers Poverty, and to believe that one knows he is poor completely hampers Poverty. Poverty is like a ball; a ball does not enter into the arena on its own, nor does it roll of its own desire, nor does it desire the polo stick to hit it, nor does it know when or by whom or for how long or why it will be hit. They just hit it right and left, back and forth. Everyone keeps their eye on it, each thinking, "Let me hit it." All are eager to and rejoice in striking it, while the ball, in the midst of it all, lies innocent and without fault. All strut and take pride in striking it and the Sultans and Shahs run and scurry after it, everyone charging forward to hit it first and hit it the hardest. He who builds

---

[45] This hadith is quoted earlier, in the first section of the Shaykh's Epistle to the Samarqandians (See note 5 in Part Four).

[46] This hadith is related in Shaykh 'Abbâs ebn-e Mohammad-Rezâ Qommi's *Safînat al-bihâr* (published in Najaf, 2:378) among the Prophetic Hadith, but Sayyed Mohammad Abu al-Mahâsen al-Qâvoqchi in his *al-Lu'lu' al-marsû'* (55) accounts it, on the authority of Ibn Taymiyya, among the forged hadith. Cited in Foruzânfar, *Ahâdis-e Masnavi*, 23.

[47] Qur'ân 2:256.

[48] This hadith figures frequently in Sufi texts, which are divided over the virtue of poverty. It can also be found in *Kanz al-'ummâl*, v. 3, nr. 4879. See also 'Abd al-Ra'ûf ibn Tâj al-'ârifîn al-Munâwî, *Fayz al-qadîr* (Cairo, 1938), nr. 6199; al-Ghazzâli's *Ihyâ 'ulûm al-dîn* (Cairo, 1334 A.H.), 3:163, 4:167; Qushayrî's *al-Risâla fî al-tasawwuf* (Cairo, 1330 A.H.), 125; Jalâl al-Din Rumi's *Masnavi*, ed. R. Nicholson, 2:157; and the discussion in Ritter, *Das Meer der Seele*, op. cit. 225.

his life on such a foundation is incomplete. That which was ordained to be comes about, [346] the rest is simply talk. It is the Prime Mover who runs affairs and there is nothing left to be said about it—any discussion of the matter is but idle fancy.

You had written concerning "He."[49] Since God, the Mighty and Exalted, has enjoined the human tongue not to utter the word "He," we, likewise, have restrained the pen from writing about it. Anyone who would permit himself to utter the word "He" has not grasped its reality, and the beauty and inner meaning of "He" has not revealed itself to him, inasmuch as the word "He" arises from the core and depths of the heart and the inner breast. This should suffice. A single "He" suffices the entirety of created beings. To mention the word "He" sixty times in one piece of writing, to constantly debate about "He," to demonstrate one's eloquence and reveal his immaturity? God forbid! I turn to God in repentance!

As for the verse "*But draw not nigh unto this tree*,"[50] the outward allusion is to wheat and its tree [*derakht*], but in truth it signifies greed and covetousness, as well as the quest for immortality and superiority [*afzuni*]. If Adam, God's blessings upon him, had not been selfish and covetous of eternality, Satan would not have scattered seeds in the trap he set for Adam. Satan pronounced "I" but once, and a myriad worlds of knowledge and worship were cast to the winds of damnation. What blessing and salvation does it bring, then, repeating "I" again and again in the head of a letter? "He who has known God, his tongue falls silent."[51] Beware, O brother, beware, lest you cast to the winds of

---

[49] *Hu*, the Arabic word He, a term used by the Sufis to indicate God in His aspect of absolute Being.

[50] Qur'ân 2:35.

[51] A version of this hadith is quoted in *al-Jâmi' al-saghîr* (2:158) and in *Kunûz al-haqâ'iq*, 122. The same hadith is alluded to in Rumi's *Masnavi*, ed. Nicholson, 2: 3013:

Words always fail their meaning to convey;
hence the Prophet said, "...the tongue falls silent."

See Khvâjeh Ayyub's commentary on the *Masnavi*, *Asrâr al-ghoyub* (w. 1120/1708) and Shaykh Yûsuf ibn Ahmad al-Mawlawî's, *al-Manhaj al-qawî li al-tullâb al-Mathnawî* (Cairo, 1289 A.H./1872), 2:580; cited in Foruzânfar, *Ahâdis-e Masnavi*, 67.

conjecture whatever may be on your plate! Do not circle around the fire; lamps which are lit next to a fire appear dim. As it is said, "The moth goes in search of light and falls [347] into the fire."

The characteristic of poverty and being poor is that whatever desire and longing and passion and hope and so forth that is on your plate will disappear. If you do not remove it and cross it out, and efface both negation and affirmation, these truths will not take hold in your being. Poverty cannot be recounted. Any account given is shop-keeping, not poverty. And God is the All-knowing.

If in this epistle I have said things which do not meet with the good-pleasure of Khvâjeh Imam—God lengthen his life—that, too, is a sign of poverty, for "spiritual poverty is virtually a kind of disbelief." You should continue in your efforts until you reach your goal. Forgive my bluntness, for I have tried to restrain myself. Peace upon you; sufficient unto us is God, the best of helpers.

APPENDICES

The Persian text of the *Spiritual Feats of the Colossal Elephants* contains a number of detailed indices, including the names of persons, places, sects and books mentioned. In addition it provides a table of quotations from the Qur'ân and Hadith, as well as a list of unusual Persian words, expressions, and grammatical formations. Specialists interested in further research on such matters will want to consult the indices to the Persian text, but most readers of the translation will not need such detailed information.

Instead, we have prepared the following appendices to help those interested in querying the text for information on the archetypes of Islamic sainthood and the construction of hagiography. The numbers given in these tables refer to the number of the story (1 through 386) as given in Parts One and Two of *The Colossal Elephant and His Spiritual Feats*. These lists can therefore be used both with the English translation, as well as by those consulting the Persian text.

APPENDIX A..444
Motif Index of the Miracles of Shaykh Ahmad
This groups the miracle stories told about Shaykh Ahmad into general categories and further describes in summary form each miracle attributed to the Shaykh, followed by the number of the story in which it is to be found

APPENDIX B..450
Table of Transmitters of the Reports About Shaykh Ahmad
This table lists alphabetically the names of individuals reporting anecdotes about the Shaykh and the specific stories they have related. It is hoped this table, in conjunction with the Table of Place Names, will assist those wishing to compare the kinds of people who reported information about the Shaykh and the types of story each reporter was most interested in.

APPENDIX C..454
Table of Place Names Where the Anecdotes Occur
This table gives a clearer idea of the theater of operation of Shaykh Ahmad, listing alphabetically the places associated with the various stories about the Shaykh. It will also be useful for those trying to track down information about specific locales in Khorasan.

APPENDIX D..458
Historical, Political and Mythical Personages and Sects Mentioned
Though legendary in character, the anecdotes related here often contain a kernel of historical truth. They also provide the names of local army commanders and other officials which the larger historical chronicles may ignore; these names are listed here alphabetically.

APPPENDIX A

MOTIF INDEX
OF THE MIRACLES OF SHAYKH AHMAD

Acts of Asceticism
 general: 172
 physical hardship: 3
 fasting: 5, 206
 continence: 8
 eating without voiding: 20
 self-mutilation: 182
 stirring a boiling pot with barehands: 33

Affliction of Enemies and Confounding the Disobedient
 via dreams: 205
 via tarantulas: 135
 with dumbness: 15, 54, 107, 201, 222
 with blindness: 60, 61, 158
 with broken bones and eye ailments: 35
 with paralysis: 62, 99, 110, 309
 with tumors: 106
 with disfigurement: 107, 269
 with severe illness: 98
 with death: 23, 55, 63, 105, 106, 110, 282, 363, 374-375
 with death of a son: 290
 with loss of knowledge: 15
 with loss of position: 291, 300, 343
 with fines or financial loss: 97, 207, 247, 258, 300
 with a beating: 365
 of non-Muslims: 184
 of followers of the Cheshti Order: 27
 making enemies to flee: 27, 355
 unspecified afflictions: 289
 regret for afflicting others: 55

APPPENDIX A (Motif Index of miracles, Continued)

Assistance to Friends and Disciples
Intercession with people in power: 17, 123-25, 177-78, 334, 338
deposing or appointing officials: 49, 259, 280, [343], 377, 380
recalling emissaries from a distance: 73
stopping an attack: 75
freeing captives: 339
warning of impending trouble: 293
saving from a dragon: 136
saving girl from rubble: 179
saving from locusts: 204, 267-268
saving from hail: 276
with money, goods or property: 28, 162, 237, 330, 332, 338, 376
to speak eloquently: 18, 199, 243, 347
to experience spiritual states: 202, 355
with sexual performance: 25, 198, 364
with marrying the girl of his choice: 378
with troublesome husband: 270
overlooking boorish behavior for a good cause: 307

Clairvoyance
of future events: 6, 17, 27, 47, 72, 90, 94-95, 101-102, 116-19,
    129, 176, 179, 189-92, 223, 237, 301, 322, 331, 344-345
of physical features: 128, 166, 292
of birth of a boy or girl: 210, 220, 290, 313-315, 342, 362, 364
of visitors from another city: 302
of illicit food or goods: 5, 47, 48, 104, 277, 327, 368
of a shortage of food: 94
of location of hidden gold: 65, 108-109, 324
of locusts: 71, 268
of the deposing or appointing of officials: 88-89, 92-93, 241
of machinations: 92

APPPENDIX A (Motif Index of miracles, Continued)

APPPENDIX A (Motif index of miracles, Continued)

APPPENDIX A (Motif index of miracles, Continued)

Telekinesis (continued)
  moving a boulder: 173
  lengthening beams: 10
  hands or objects in the fire do not burn: 65-68, 226
  opening doors: 51, 171, 261-262, 366
  averting locusts: 70
  control over a snake: 74
  blades cause no injury: 131-132
  unbreakable glass: 173
  self-repairing bowls: 351
  automatic writing on paper: 378

Telepathy
  Communicating with animals: 167
    horses: 2
    goats: 3, 257
    dragons: 3, 81, 136
    birds: 126
  Communicating with others: 5
    the dead: 297
  Knowing how to answer: 21
  Knowing what others have seen in a dream: 142
  Reading minds: 25, 69, 110, 122, 128, 130, 145, 164, [181],
    [183], 188, 195-197, 199, 203, 205, 218, 230, 232, 246, 248,
    260, 266, 273-274, 296, 311-312, 361, 364
  Seeing the Shaykh in a dream: 143, 175 , 177, 179

Transmutation
  Wine to honey: 1
  to dust: 11, 248
  dust or clay to gold: 16, 19, 28, 40, 57
  pearls to liquid: 29
  boulders to gold: 41
  sugar to gold: 36-38
  thread to gold: 84, 120
  thread to silver: 140

APPPENDIX A (Motif index of miracles, Continued)

APPENDIX B

TABLE OF TRANSMITTERS
OF THE REPORTS ABOUT SHAYKH AHMAD

The stories in the text often occur in clusters, grouping together either similar miracles, similar locations, accounts from a given source (whether written source or oral transmitter), and/or accounts pertaining to specific locations (some of the sources may have been small albums of the recollections of miracles collected in various villages where the Shaykh spent some time). It has not been possible in every case to determine who the authority for a given story is.

Shaykh Ahmad: 1-6, 8-9, 13, 82, 83, 163, 167, 171, 242, 345

Mohamad-e Ghaznavi: 10-12, 14-17, 19-37, 40-43, 47-52, 54-62, 65, 70-83, 87-100, 102, 107, 109-114, 116-121, [122-125], 126-136, 154-155, 159, 164-166, 176, 179-180

It is not absolutely clear that Mohammad-e Ghaznavi was the author or compiler of Stories 185-369, which come only from the Chester Beatty Manuscript, but we have assumed for the purposes of this list that Ghaznavi is the author, as follows: 185, 187, 189-192, 200-201, 204-205, 228 230, 241-243, [244], 245-246, 251, [257-270], [275], [281] [283], [296], 314-315, 328, 352, 361, [384]

Compiler of the Berlin Manuscript: 181-184

A

'Abd al-Samad, Dâneshmand: 68-69, 226-227
Abu Bakr the Tailor of Oshtu (Darzi-ye Oshtavi): 231-232
Abu Bakr-e Kusavi, Khvâjeh: 84, 193
Abu Bakr-e Lâlaki/Lâzaki: 104, 218-219
Abu Bakr-e Moghanni (The Singer): 150-152
Abu Bakr, Khvâjeh (son of Shaykh Ahmad): 194
Abu al-Fath, Khvâjeh Imam (a son of Shaykh Ahmad): 353, 355
Abu al-Hasan-e Pârsi: 363
Abu al-Hasan-e Salâh: 44-46, 53, 63-64

APPENDIX B (Transmitters, Continued)

A (continued)

B

D

APPENDIX B (Transmitters, Continued)

APPENDIX B (Transmitters, Continued)

APPENDIX C

TABLE OF PLACE NAMES
WHERE THE ANECDOTES OCCUR

A

Amghân: 19, 57, 71, 99, 138, 164, 202, [203], 204, 212, 225, 230, 270, 280, 300, 304, 367, 374
Amyâd, village near Bâkharz: 356
Arzaneh, village near Bâkharz: 234, 356
Asfarghâbâd: 296, 311, 358

B

Baghdad: 284, 288
Bâkharz, district and town: 109, 159, 252, 323
Balkh: 90
Ban'ân, on road to Kâriz-e 'Omar: 157, 217
Barinân or Barniân, mountain and village owned by Âgah: 68-69, 189-190
Bars, in Rokh district, in the district of Torbat-e Heydarieh, five farsangs from Nâmaq: 164, 369
Bazâvandaqân, mountain near Mehneh[?]: 184
Bizd: 41, 53, 98-99, 141, 147, 195, 199, 201, 205, 216, 232, 250, 253, 265, 300, 314, 318, 323, 337, 346, 347, 380
Buzjân: 31, 33, 35-36, 42-43, 63, 68, 91, 104, 107, 115, 118, 135, 142, 207-209, 221, 223, 225-226, 229, 245, 247, 250, 254, 258, 269, 286, 313, 322, 326, 335, 360

D

Dahaneh-ye Shir, near Sabzevâr: 91
Dâvar: 325
Delshin: 239

E

'Erâq-e 'ajam (Western Iran): 6, 73
Esfandâr-sanj, near Herat: 375
Estâd, near Zur-âbâd (a village and mountain): 16, 62, 114, 276, 373

APPENDIX C (Place names, Continued)

F

Farâmad-âbâd (near Sabzevâr ?): 109-110
Fashkân, village near Herat: 27
Fesâvarz: 57, 261, 359
Firuzkuh: 378

G

Ganjeh in Kerman Province: 325
Ghazarâbâd: 357
Ghazna: 35, 117, 122-125, 178, 260
Golzhin, near Amghân: 204
Gorgân: 118-119

H

Hamadan: 116
Hasanâbâd: 284, 326
Hayânân: 101
Hell: 103, 169
Herat:24-27, 29, 302, 376, 378-379

I

India: 178

J

Jâm: 17-18, 35, 70-71, 90, 130, 305, 312, 379
Ja'far-âbâd, village near Nayshabur: 267
Jâhenân River, outside Kâriz: 28
Jerusalem: 121
Jowrmad/Jormad/Jowrbad: 186, 354

K

Kâheh, village in Bâkharz district: 252
Kâriz-e 'Omar: 214, 217
Kâriz-e Ma'd-âbâd: 235
Kâriz-e Sâ'ed: 28, 113, 247
Kâriz, village of: 28, 97, 155, [235], 236, 334
Khalid-âbâd: 373
Kharjerd: 323
Kukuriân, Mountain in Qohestân: 65
Kusu (also Kuseh): 113, 242

APPENDIX C (Place names, Continued)

APPENDIX C (Place names, Continued)

APPENDIX D

HISTORICAL, POLITICAL AND MYTHICAL
PERSONAGES AND SECTS MENTIONED IN THE TEXT

APPENDIX D (personages and sects, Continued)